The Origins of Worker Mobilisation

T0300096

This is a book on how and why workers come together. Almost coincident with its inception, worker organisation is a central and enduring element of capitalism. In the 19th and 20th centuries' mobilisation by workers played a substantial role in reshaping critical elements of these societies in Europe, North America, Australasia and elsewhere including the introduction of minimum labour standards (living wage rates, maximum hours etc.), workplace safety and compensation laws and the rise of welfare state more generally.

Notwithstanding setbacks in recent decades, worker organisation represents a pivotal countervailing force to moderate the excesses of capitalism and is likely to become even more influential as the social consequences of rising global inequality become more manifest. Indeed, instability and periodic shifts in the respective influence of capital and labour are endemic to capitalism.

As formal institutions have declined in some countries or unions outlawed and severely repressed in others, there has been growing recognition of informal strike activity by workers and wider alliances between unions and community organisations in others. While such developments are seen as new, they aren't. Indeed, understanding of worker organisation is often ahistorical and even those understandings informed by historical research are, this book will argue, in need of revision.

This book provides a new perspective on and new insights into how and why workers organise, and what shapes this organisation. The Origins of Worker Mobilisation will be key reading for scholars, academics and policy makers the fields of industrial relations, HRM, labour economics, labour history and related disciplines.

Michael Quinlan is professor of industrial relations in the School of Management at the University of New South Wales, Australia. He is also an adjunct professor in the School of History and Classics at the University of Tasmania and a visiting professor at the Business School, Middlesex University in London. Born in Sydney he divides his time between this city and Launceston, Tasmania where much of this book was written.

Routledge Studies in Employment and Work Relations in Context

Edited by Tony Elger and Peter Fairbrother

For a full list of titles in this series, please visit www.routledge.com

The aim of the *Employment and Work Relations in Context Series* is to address questions relating to the evolving patterns and politics of work, employment, management and industrial relations. There is a concern to trace out the ways in which wider policy making, especially by national governments and transnational corporations, impinges upon specific workplaces, occupations, labour markets, localities and regions. This invites attention to developments at an international level, marking out patterns of globalisation, state policy and practices in the context of globalisation and the impact of these processes on labour. A particular feature of the series is the consideration of forms of worker and citizen organisation and mobilisation. The studies address major analytical and policy issues through case study and comparative research.

8 Privatization of Public Services: Impacts for Employment, Working Conditions, and Service Quality in Europe
Edited by Christoph Hermann and Jörg Flecker

9 Rediscovering Collective Bargaining
Australia's Fair Work Act in International Perspective
Edited by Breen Creighton and Anthony Forsyth

10 Transnational Trade Unionism
Building Union Power
Peter Fairbrother, Marc-Antonin Hennebert, and Christian Lévesque

11 Temporary Work, Agencies and Unfree Labour
Insecurity in the New World of Work
Edited by Judy Fudge and Kendra Strauss

12 Human Resource Management in Emerging Economies
Piotr Zientara

13 The Origins of Worker Mobilisation
Australia 1788–1850
Michael Quinlan

The Origins of Worker Mobilisation
Australia 1788–1850

Michael Quinlan

Routledge
Taylor & Francis Group

LONDON AND NEW YORK

First published 2018
by Routledge

2 Park Square, Milton Park, Abingdon, Oxfordshire OX14 4RN
52 Vanderbilt Avenue, New York, NY 10017

Routledge is an imprint of the Taylor & Francis Group, an informa business

First issued in paperback 2019

Library of Congress Cataloging-in-Publication Data
A catalog record for this book has been requested

ISBN: 978-1-138-08408-7 (hbk)
ISBN: 978-0-367-89046-9 (ebk)

Typeset in Sabon
by Apex CoVantage, LLC

By no other means than by making the ruling few uneasy, can those they oppress obtain redress (Jeremy Bentham to the Lords cited in the *Sydney Monitor* 17 September 1831)

In defence they all commenced . . . expatiating upon their respective merits;-better servants never lived—they were quite the thing—always did as ordered, couldn't think how it occurred (assigned-convict servants Kate Hoy, Maria Hely, and Ellen Gorman parody their Sydney trial, 1836)

You speak of working men as degraded beings and willingly enter the list on behalf of employers. The reason why, I suppose, is because you belong to their class (bootmaker unionist George Wells to Adelaide newspaper editor, 1846)

Contents

List of Tables, Figures, and Illustrations   ix
Abbreviations/Acronyms   xiii
Acknowledgements   xv
Introduction   xvii

1 Reconsidering the Collective Impulse and the
   Colonial Context   1

2 Law, the Courts and Inequality at Work   35

3 Overview of Worker Organisation, 1788–1850   75

4 Analysing the Components of Organisation   111

5 Organisation in Transport and Maritime Activities   147

6 Organisation in the Rural and Extractives Sectors   167

7 Organisation in Construction and Building Materials   201

8 Organisation in Manufacturing and Related Trades   217

9 Organisation in Government and Community Services   235

10 Organisation in Commercial, Personal Services and Retailing 251

11 Peak and Political Organisation   267

12 Re-Evaluating Worker Mobilisation   293

Index   301

Tables, Figures, and Illustrations

Tables

2.1   Employment-Related General Orders and Regulations,
NSW and VDL 1790–1827   36

2.2   Employment-Related Regulations and Laws: Australian
Colonies 1828–50   38

3.1   Formal Worker Organisation by Occupation and
Duration in Australia 1825–50   77

3.2   Number of Workers Involved in Organisation
by Period, Australia 1788–1850   82

3.3   Worker Organisation by Industry, Australia 1788–1850   88

3.4   Worker Organisation by Occupation, Australia
1788–1850   89

3.5   Worker Organisation by Objectives/Issues Pursued,
Australia 1788–1850   92

3.6   Worker Organisation by Methods Used, Australia
1788–1850   94

4.1   Strikes and Non-Strike Collective Action (NSCA) by
Colony in Australia 1788–1850   113

4.2   Summary of Collective Action in Australia 1788–1850   115

4.3   Number of Workers Involved in Strikes and NSCA
by Period, Australia 1788–1850   118

4.4   Strikes and NSCA by Period and Number of Workplaces
Involved, 1788–1850   120

4.5   Strikes and NSCA by Average, Median and Total
Duration 1788–1850   123

4.6   Strikes and NSCA by Industry and Period in Australia
1788–1850   126

4.7   Strikes by Occupation and Period in Australia
1788–1850   128

4.8   Non-strike Collective Action by Occupation
and Period in Australia 1788–1850   131

4.9   Strikes and NSCA by Issues and Period in Australia
1788–1850   134

4.10   Strikes and NSCA by Period and Outcome, Australia
         1788–1850   136
4.11   Court Actions by Issue/Charge and Period, Australia
         1788–1850   139
4.12   Court Penalties Imposed on Workers Taking Collective
         Action by Decade   141
5.1   Summary: Organisation/Activity in Maritime/Whaling
         and Road Transport 1788–1850   150
5.2   Strikes and Non-Strike Collective Action by Issue
         in the Maritime/Whaling Industries 1788–1850   152
6.1   Summary: Organisation/Activity in the Rural Industry
         1788–1850   170
6.2   Strikes and Non-Strike Disputes by Issue in the Rural
         Industry 1788–1850   172
6.3   Summary: Organisation/Activity in the Mining Industry
         1788–1850   190
6.4   Strikes and NSCA by Issue in the Mining Industry
         1788–1850   191
7.1   Summary: Organisation/Activity in Construction
         and Building Materials 1788–1850   202
7.2   Strikes and NSCA by Issue in Construction and Building
         Materials 1788–1850   204
8.1   Summary of Organisation and Activity in Manufacturing
         1788–1850   219
8.2   Strikes and NSCA by Issue in Manufacturing 1788–1850   220
9.1   Summary of Organisation and Activity in Government
         Services 1788–1850   236
9.2   Strikes and Non-Strike Disputes by Issue in Government
         1788–1850   237
10.1   Summary of Organisation and Activity in Services
         and Retailing 1788–1850   252
10.2   Strikes and NSCA by Issue in Services and Retailing
         1788–1850   253

Figures

3.1   Instances of Worker Organisation by Capital/
         Non-Capital Location   83
3.2   Instances of Convict and Free Worker Organisation
         Australia 1801–1900   83
3.3   Instances of Formal and Informal Worker Organisation
         in Australia 1801–1900   84
4.1   Strikes and Non-Strike Collective Action (NSCA)
         Australia 1801–1900   112
4.2   Court Appearances Involving Collective Action
         by Convict and Free-Labour, 1801–1900   138

Illustrations

4.1	Rules and Regulations, Parramatta Female Factory	143
5.1	Lower Murray St Cab-Drivers 1848	161
8.1	Launceston Printers Rules Title Page	230
9.1	Convict Chain Gang	239
10.1	Title Page Hobart Mercantile Assist Rules	262

Abbreviations/Acronyms

AA Company	Australian Agricultural Company
AOSA	Archives of South Australia
AOUNSW	Archives of New South Wales (NSW Records Office)
AOWA	Archives of Western Australia
APA	Australian Patriotic Association
CPM	Chief Police Magistrate
CSO	Colonial Secretary's Office
GGO	Government/Governor's Orders, Notices and Proclamations
GO	Governor's Despatches Outbound
HRNSW	Historical Records of New South Wales
HTTU	Hobart Town Trades Union
JP	Justice of the Peace
LC	Lower Court Bench Book Tasmania
MPA	Mutual Protection Association (NSW)
NSCA	Non-strike collective action
NSW	New South Wales
NSWGG	New South Wales Government Gazette
OHS	occupational health and safety
SA	South Australia
SAWMA	South Australian Working Men's Association
TAHO	Tasmanian Archives and Heritage Office
UK	United Kingdom
USA	United States of America
VDL	Van Diemen's Land (Tasmania)
WA	Western Australia

Acknowledgements

In a gestation spanning over three decades this book has benefited from the assistance and encouragement of many colleagues, including my then Ph.D. supervisor Malcolm Rimmer who encouraged me to explore global labour history. I received generous assistance searching colonial government records from Ian Pearce, then chief of the Tasmanian State Archives and his counterparts in other states as well as librarians in Hobart, Sydney (Mitchell Library), Melbourne, Adelaide, Perth and Griffith University (thanks Colette Smith-Strong). The Trove collection of the National Library of Australia proved an invaluable addition to an earlier search of colonial newspapers. Geoffrey Stillwell alerted me to the wealth of ships logbooks held in Tasmania while Vicki Pearce and Trudy Cowley provided important leads on the role of women. The Register of Friendly Societies of NSW provided index records to early unions registered as friendly societies. (Unfortunately the actual records hadn't survived along with other records like the rule book of an early South Australian builders' trade union and a manuscript on early worker organisation by Meredith Atkinson). Historians Barrie Dyster, Deborah Oxley, Hamish Maxwell-Stewart, Terry Irving, Michael Roe, Bill Robbins, Nick Clements, Tom Dunning and others provided important leads, support or critical commentary as did industrial relations scholars Greg Patmore, John Shields, Wayne Lewchuk and Richard Croucher. The work of Maxwell-Stewart, Oxley, Dyster and Robbins, especially the gentle probing of Deborah Oxley, eventually persuaded me to include collective action by convicts (sorry Deb I was too dumb). Thanks to Hamish I was able to access important sources on collective convict dissent which will be expanded for a follow-up to this book. Also of great assistance were legal historians Adrian Merritt, Mary Banton, Doug Hay and Paul Craven. Mary's control/resistance approach to slaves aligned with my own work, while Paul and Doug's path-breaking book on master and servant law emphasised the centrality of the state/regulation and both free and unfree-labour to the emergence of capitalist societies.

In the 1980s Margaret Gardner (then a collaborator and now Vice Chancellor of Monash University) and I received important funding support from the Australian Research Grants Scheme (thanks Don Aitken and the panel) and from the Commerce Faculty at Griffith University (thank you, Christine Smith). Kim Pearce and Robyn Hollander proved excellent research assistants. At the suggestion of Margaret, we asked Griffith University's Commerce Faculty IT expert Peter Akers to develop a relational database which went through 19 iterations becoming both more complex but user-friendly. Without Peter the project would have barely left the ground and at UNSW Liang Li ensured the package would run as each round of computer replacements and software upgrades occurred. Andy Thompkins was indispensable in preparing of several charts.

Finally, critical aspects of this book were shaped by discussions with Laura Bennett, whose incisive knowledge and observations about capitalism, workers and the law lifted my own blundering efforts to any worthwhile heights they subsequently attained.

Introduction

This book examines why and how workers combine—an issue as relevant today as it was a century or more ago. The book builds on a body of previous scholarship but uses a novel combination of sources, methods and approach to provide new insights on the spread, scale and origins of worker organisation. Until the 1980s, accounts of worker organisation (both general and industry/occupation group accounts) predominantly focused on the rise of formal institutions (mainly unions but also political bodies) in the 19th and 20th centuries—especially those that prospered or survived lengthy periods. The three decades from the 1960s witnessed a refashioning of labour historiography. In two especially influential books, *The Making of the English Working Class* and *Customs in Common*, Edward Thompson argued for the importance of ideas and worker agency, including the need to consider informal alliances, 'failed' movements and the role of customary modes of behaviour—some centuries old, some more recent—in shaping worker actions. Work by Rudé, Hobsbawm, Montgomery and others also emphasised the importance of informal social mobilisations. This in turn helped to spawn studies by Way, Rediker and others of groups of workers who engaged in widespread collective action but mostly on an informal basis including navvies/canal builders and seamen. Charles Tilly pioneered the analysis of long-term trends in strikes. Other researchers began to address the neglect of female workers. Paralleling this was research into the historical importance to capitalism of various categories of unfree-labour, including slaves in the Americas, convicts in Australia and the Americas and indentured workers in Africa, Mauritius and the Pacific. A number of studies, most notably the edited work of Craven and Hay, pointed to the critical role of regulatory apparatus in subordinating labour and resistance to this. Finally, other researchers pointed to the deeper historical roots of worker organisation, both formal and informal.

However, as far as I am aware, no attempt has been made to integrate these disparate themes together and try to map the relationship between informal and formal organisation, between unfree and free-labour, between white men and others in a country (including different patterns across industries). This book attempts to do this, drawing on Australian evidence, arguing that collective action was more widespread than is generally depicted, was shaped by the political economy of the colonies and their chief industries, and that much of this can only be understood in the context of a fierce regulatory struggle over the conditions of work (amounting to hundreds of thousands of trials in colonies that only reached a European population of 400,000 in 1850) and customs and experiences of the predominantly immigrant (forced and voluntary) workforce. Founded in the late 18th century as a penal colony to act as a safety valve for the distress and disorder accompanying the industrial revolution, the Australian colonies quickly transformed into vibrant capitalist societies.

But why bother with such a small appendage of imperialism? There are two reasons. First, Australia was small in terms of population but not unimportant. By the 1830s the colonies had become important parts of global capitalism, exporting wool for Britain's expanding textile mills, a major hub of the Pacific whaling industry (then at its height globally) and were setting the foundations of other export industries that became increasingly important after 1850 (coal, minerals, wheat and meat), a strong trajectory of growth (though subject to periodic sharp falls) that saw Australia achieve the highest per capita income in the world in 1900 and today ranks as the 13th largest economy on the planet—roughly the same size as Russia—with around 0.3% of world population. Economic developments were coincident on social progress, including pioneering the 8-hour day (1855), much of the Chartist platform (1856), pioneering social protection laws (minimum wage laws began in 1896 in Victoria and spread federally in a decade) and universal adult suffrage (1901). Second, the widespread use of unfree-labour (predominantly convicts) provides an opportunity to systematically compare collective action by free and unfree-labour, especially as the treatment of convicts was minutely documented by government, and the use of court, newspaper and other records affords opportunities to uncover collective action of the most informal and small scale.

The Purpose and Structure of the Book

This is a book about how workers come together to address fundamental inequalities at work—inequalities that in great measure are still to be found today (worse in some countries than others). The book examines how and why this occurred, drawing on evidence from Australia, 1788–1850. It charts the origins of the collective impulse and the forms it took, what is more fashionably known today as worker or social mobilisation. This struggle began many centuries before Europeans invaded/settled Australia and this book tries to place Australian experience in this wider context, including the influence of earlier organisation and customary modes of protest.

This book examines collective action—formal and informal—and the relationship between them. The 1850 cut-off was partly determined on logistical grounds. The database already contains over 4000 instances of organisation covering the period 1851–1900. This data has been used to better situate the earlier period but to finalise data collection would have added years to an already lengthy gestation. The 1850 cut off doesn't mark a watershed although convict labour had become far less important by this time. Some early unions continued after 1850 (the Sydney shipwrights until 1980) and short-lived unions remained the dominant pattern of union formation in Australia until the 1880s, notwithstanding growing numbers that survived. Most strikes were informal (didn't involve a union) and this pattern also continued well into the 1860s. Worker organisation did undergo change but there was no sharp divide around the gold rushes of the early 1850s. Nonetheless, focusing on the period to 1850 enables a detailed examination of the origin of worker organisation, including the relationship between unfree and free-labour, informal and formal organisation, early political mobilisations by workers and how the political economy of the colonies influenced worker organisation. It is also runs parallels with and hopefully contributes to a global reassessment of the origins of worker organisation.

The book is structured as follows. Chapter 1 reviews previous research on collective action and worker organisation, as well as the economic, political and labour market structures of the Australian colonies prior to 1851. Chapter 2 provides further context for understanding collective action by examining regulation that sought to subordinate labour and how the resulting struggle over the terms and conditions of employment played out in the courts. Chapters 3 and 4 provide an overview of worker organisation, sources of solidarity and patterns of collective action. Chapters 5 to 10 examine worker organisation in some important industries—transport; rural/agriculture and mining; construction; manufacturing; government and community services; and retailing and personal services. Chapter 11 examines attempts at peak organisation and political mobilisations by workers. Chapter 12 concludes with a re-evaluation of worker mobilisation including avenues for further research.

Some Conventions and Definitions

Today Australia is composed of six states and two territories, the states being colonies that federated in 1901. Prior to 1851 only four colonies—New South Wales (NSW), Van Diemen's Land (VDL)/Tasmania, Western Australia and South Australia) existed as separate entities. Located in the southeast corner of the continent, the colony of Victoria separated from New South Wales in 1851 while Queensland in the north-east became an independent colony in 1859. For several reasons, including making inter-colonial comparisons relevant with later periods, worker organisation in districts that became Victoria and Queensland are categorised as occurring in these future colonies, not New South Wales.

For this book's purpose a strike is defined as a refusal to work or temporary withdrawal of labour involving two or more workers and the same threshold is applied to absconding/desertion or other forms of collective action. Whereas strikes constitute a temporary withdrawal of labour from an employer, absconding/desertion constitutes a permanent withdrawal with workers seeking to rehire elsewhere under better terms which included as 'free workers' in the case of unfree or indentured labour. On ships, road-gangs and remote farms, absconding commonly required a degree of planning to escape detection. Even where two workers were prosecuted for refusing work or neglect, this doesn't mean only two were involved. Employers commonly charged ringleaders, hoping their punishment would serve as warning to others (*pour encouragez les autres*) and also because gaoling the entire crew of a ship or a group of workers engaged in harvest/ shearing, for instance would impose significant costs on the employer. It is central to this book's purpose that the smallest actions were included and their relationship to larger organisation examined. Adopting this approach uncovers important stages or markers of the mobilisation process.

1 Reconsidering the Collective Impulse and the Colonial Context

Introduction

This book examines how and why workers organise, drawing on Australian evidence. It charts the origins of the collective impulse and the forms it took. To do this, it is essential to examine what is known about early worker mobilisation, including its roots. Mobilisation began in Australia at the end of the 18th century but has far deeper roots in Europe and even North America. The first workers to organise in Australia were transported convicts and free immigrants from the British Isles who brought customs and methods of organisation, some stretching back many centuries. The first three sections of this chapter assess pre-existing research on the emergence of worker organisation, identifying several problems and gaps that are a focus of this book. The fourth section describes the sources and research methods used. The last two sections describe aspects of the colonies in terms of their political economy which provide an important context for understanding patterns of worker organisation, like the prominence of the state and initial dependence on convict labour.

Unions and the History of Worker Mobilisation

Institutional Accounts of the Rise of Organised Labour

The first writers to examine worker organisation in a systematic fashion, like Sidney and Beatrice Webb in the UK and John R Commons in the United States, were primarily interested in trade unions.[1] Nevertheless, as reforming activists they were also concerned with the political off-shoots or allies of unions. The Webbs defined trade unions as 'a continuous association of wage earners for the purpose of maintaining or improving the conditions of employment.'[2] This definition—using employment conditions in its widest sense to include those affecting living conditions—has been widely accepted ever since. Using a card system, the Webbs collected and examined a prodigious amount of material drawn from union documents and interviews, government reports and other sources (principally in England) to produce two tomes, *History of Trade Unions* (1894) and the more analytical *Industrial Democracy* (1897). Several decades later, John R Commons produced a multi-volume history of organised labour in the United States followed by often more modest contributions on other countries like Australia.

While the Webbs identified worker organisations (like London watermen and journeymen like tailors) stretching back to the 14th century, they viewed the industrial revolution from the late 18th century as transformative.[3] Identified as pivotal was the development of 'new-model' craft unions with solid governing structures/rules and reliant on the combination of mutual insurance/friendly benefits and unilateral regulation after 1850 and then from the 1880s the emergence of relatively effectively organised union of unskilled workers like the London Dockers, more enamoured of striking and political agitation. Notwithstanding more radical contributions from contemporaries like GDH Cole and Carter L Goodrich, the Webbs' emphasis on institutional permanency and measures they identified like the common rule (setting a uniform wage level across the industry or trade) and collective bargaining (which they viewed as industrial democracy) remained received wisdom until the 1970s.[4] This included Australia, where histories of worker organisation usually focused on unions and the period after 1850,[5] notwithstanding evidence of earlier organisation.[6]

The Webbs and Commons made reference to legislative attempts to suppress unions, notably combination laws enacted in the 18th century. Writing over 60 years later, Alan Fox gave greater prominence to the role of the state but largely ignored the wider regulatory net of labour subordination, including laws governing free and indentured servants, merchant seamen, convicts and slaves.[7] In contrast, this book will argue that far greater attention to the role of the state is pivotal to understanding worker mobilisation, not just on effects on the capacity to combine but on the everyday lived experience of workers.

The Webbs' timelines, typologies and preoccupations didn't go unchallenged within still predominantly institutionalist accounts of worker organisation. Union histories increasingly highlighted the role of economic and social factors, including community influences. A few books revisited the origins of worker organisation. In *Masters and Journeymen: A Pre-History of Industrial Relations* Dobson sought to recover 18th century industrial conflict involving craft workers in Britain, arguing this period entailed well-developed patterns of collective action.[8] More ambitiously R A Leeson published *Travelling Brothers: The six centuries road from craft fellowship to trade unionism* which argued trade unionism arose from a far longer and more continuous pattern of development than generally accepted.[9] Leeson focused on the tramping system and House-of-Call (a pub which acted as the 'office' of early unions) where journeymen could move from town to town in search of work, stopping at a House-of-Call where they would receive temporary accommodation. The process enabled early journeymen's associations to promote employment/mitigate unemployment. The tramping regime also facilitated information distribution ('networking' in today's parlance) about wages, working conditions and the local demand for labour. It was but a short step from journeymen carrying such messages to craft unions using letters and newspaper advertisements to warn of unfavourable labour conditions. While the tramping system wasn't adopted in the Australian colonies, the House-of-Call was.

In 1994 Catherine Lis, Jan Lucassen and Hugo Soly edited a supplement to the *International Review of Social History* entitled 'Before the Unions: Wage Earners and Collective Action in Europe, 1300–1850.'[10] Notwithstanding the somewhat misleading title, the collection drew on extensive evidence to counterbalance the preoccupation with mobilisation after 1850, pointing to a far longer heritage of organised struggle. This included examinations of journeymen's associations in Western European countries during and after the Middle Ages, as well as collective action amongst iron and calico production workers, merchant seamen, seasonal labourers, mercenaries and miners. This and other studies demonstrated that the division of labour associated with the emergence of capitalism wrought an almost coincidental collective impulse amongst workers dependent on wages or analogous forms of remuneration.[11] The industrial revolution accelerated and reshaped worker organisation, but it didn't initiate mobilisation.

The contributions made a number of other salient points. First, articles on journeymen traced the medieval origins of organisational structures—like the printers' chapel as a form of workplace organisation—that remained important into the 20th century. Early journeymen societies' methods included control of apprenticeship/skill recognition; the tramping system/ House-of-Call; the closed shop/compulsory unionism; mutual insurance; wage bargaining and unilateral regulation. In every meaningful sense these bodies were trade unions using devices identical to those of the 1800s. Many had formal rules and survived well over a decade—the longevity/permanency test. They were also politically active. Indeed, cutting deals with local government authorities was essential to survival in autocratic societies with no freedom to associate.

Second, the Lis et al. collection demonstrated that early worker organisation extended to a wide array of other occupations, including miners and seamen who regularly engaged in collective action and repeatedly attempted more wide-reaching organisation. Conceding their review was by no means exhaustive, Lis et al. pointed to collective action amongst groups viewed as late arrivals to unionism like soldiers and agricultural workers. The study of labourers highlighted how seasonal changes in labour market conditions affected patterns of organisation/bargaining and modes of collective action including mass absconding.[12] This book will provide further evidence on all these points.

While offering important insights for revising understandings of worker mobilisation, the contributions just described had little resonance. Interest in union history declined, initially supplanted by the radical new labour history (see following section). Mirroring the global decline in union density, this in turn gave way to a wider social history perspective and more recently identity analysis influenced by post-modernism and the rise of neoliberalism and the individualised discourse it promotes.[13]

Radical Critiques and Class Analysis

From the 1960s institutionalist accounts of worker organisation were increasingly displaced by a group of predominantly Marxist historians, including Edward Thompson, Eric Hobsbawm, Christopher Hill, George Rudė, Charles Tilly, David Montgomery, David Brody and Robin Gollan. For the purpose of this book only the most pertinent aspects of this vast body of work will be described. Hobsbawm dealt with the rise of industrial capitalism in the 19th century, its increasing global reach and how this shaped both union development and widespread informal resistance epitomised by the Captain Swing movement.[14] Examining two different periods, Hill and Thompson pointed to the pre-industrial revolution roots of resistance by the poor and dispossessed using ideas and sometimes invented 'customs.'[15] Focusing on the 18th century, Thompson drew on a wide range of sources to reconstruct plebeian culture including customary or common rights and modes of resistance. Thompson extended Rudė's[16] argument, contending that riots like mob or crowd behaviour were not isolated or spasmodic responses to a bad harvest, food shortages or a harsh master, but part of a wider struggle by men and women 'defending traditional rights or customs' with wide community support.[17] *The Making of the English Working Class* and *Customs in Common* didn't ignore formal organisation.[18] Thompson strengthened the case that unions were well established by the early 18th century but placed this within a broader context of social mobilisation by those at bottom.[19] He included groups of workers (like field labourers and stockingers) and movements/organisation underplayed/ignored in conventional union histories. Thompson pointed to the importance of ideas—those of the free-born Englishman, Owenite socialism and Chartism—and those carrying them, not just formal institutions. He advocated the need to recognise those whose ideas/struggles had failed, been discredited or abandoned. Thompson tried to capture the life experiences of workers, the communities they formed and how this shaped ideas and organisation. For industrial relations historians this meant considering a wide array of workers, forms of organisation and modes of action like strikes, petitions, riots, sabotage and threatening letters—a point this book will reinforce.[20] Thompson and others also showed it was possible, through diligent and innovative use of historical sources, to provide a history from below.

In the United States, David Montgomery, David Brody and others provided new perspectives on worker mobilisation, including consideration of the era prior to formal unions, addressing the neglect of Black Americans, immigrants and women, pointing to wider social movements and giving greater recognition to the role of the State.[21] Another important contribution was Shorter and Tilly's *History of Strikes in France, 1830–1968* which demonstrated that a detailed examination of strikes over time could shed new light on worker organisation.[22] Their book traced how strikes had changed in size (number of workers, establishments and duration), form and objectives over time as well as pointing to industry/occupational and regional differences, including the impact of urbanisation. The book identified a number of strike waves (one in 1840, corresponds to one identified in this book) and considered both union and non-union strikes, highlighting the role of unions in coordinating larger multi-workplace strikes—something this book also finds.[23] Relating strikes to wider economic/industrial and social developments, including State intervention, Shorter and Tilly highlight their ritual character compared to earlier forms of protest like riots. While accepting strikes have become ritualised, the current book argues refusals to work began as reflexive informal responses by workers—a direct way of refuting the employer's power to direct. More importantly perhaps, Shorter and Tilly's focus on strikes, while illuminating in many respects, is delimiting because strikes need to be considered alongside other forms of collective action.[24]

Highlighting the last point from the 1980s, other historians refashioned labour history, placing less emphasis on institutional developments and winners and retrieving previously neglected groups and movements, including women, ethnic and racial minorities and more ephemeral organisation amongst workers like canal builders, navvies, whalers and seamen. Marcus Rediker, Judith Fingard and others analysed the intersection of working and living conditions for seamen and the different modes of collective protest employed, including piracy and absconding.[25] Researchers like Dublin began to address the neglect of female workers.[26] Much of this research was qualitative, but there was also growing use of quantitative analysis drawing information from a range of sources and exploiting computers' capacity to 'crunch' large amounts of historical data. Cooper-Busch used whaleship logbooks to explore dissent amongst whalers.[27] Peter Way's book on canal builders in North America 1780–1860 included detailed analysis of the workforce, working and living conditions and collective action amongst workers, both riots and strikes. Like others, Way demonstrated that workers who didn't form unions engaged in collective action on a regular basis often involving more workers than contemporary strikes by unionised journeymen.[28] Way, Rediker and others pointed to the diverse modes of collective action, including riots and mass absconding and how this continued in some industries far longer than others. Other historians combined qualitative and quantitative methods to examine working and living conditions (including diet, disease and health), exemplified by Jane Humphries's study of child labour using surviving diaries.[29]

Resistance by Slaves, Convict and Other Unfree-Labour

Another group of researchers turned their attention to recovering groups of unfree workers, including slaves, bonded labour/indentured workers and convict workers as important elements in global capitalism (not just the Americas) from the 16th to early 20th centuries. Examining slaves in this light wasn't new, most notably perhaps the pioneering work of Oliver Cromwell Cox,[30] but a growing body of research provided insights into the economics of slavery, complex relations between slaves and other categories of workers (like indentured labour and convicts), and depicting an often fractured transition to peonage, indentured and free-labour.[31] Mary Banton employed a nuanced control/resistance model in elucidating slave struggles in the Americas. Former slaves in Jamaica, Trinidad and other Caribbean islands responded to their emancipation following abolition of slavery in the British Empire with widespread refusals to work and revolts but soon found waged employment entailed substantial subordination.[32]

As a number of reviews indicate, slave societies and production regimes differed considerably. This included variations between locations and over time due to requirements of different products (for example sugar and tobacco), the intensity of labour management regimes (including giving space, opportunities to work for themselves and other incentives), punishments for dissent and the use of corporal punishment.[33] These factors also influenced the likelihood of violent revolts, though caution is required in attributing too much calculated rationality to management—a point the current book will reinforce in regard to convicts.[34] Absconding, neglect, temporary absence/work refusals, feigning illness, insolence and revenge/sabotage were more endemic forms of slave resistance.[35] Absconding (sometimes termed marronage or petit marronage for temporary absence) was often collective and perhaps the most costly, with slave-owners trying to curb it by posting notices offering significant rewards to encourage recapture[36]—analogous to efforts to combat convict absconding in Australia. Research suggests the level of absconding was influenced by gender, climate/season, opportunities to abscond (for example, harder on remote islands), surveillance costs, alternative food sources and work opportunities and other factors.[37]

Slave studies frequently refer to revolts/conspiracies and the larger ones have often been the subject of detailed research.[38] However, with notable exceptions like Banton, there has been little systematic assessment of collective action more generally. Research difficulties, like employers' ability to punish slaves without recourse to the courts for minor infractions—unlike convicts or indentured workers—only partly explains this. Slave owner records, court records, absconding notices, company and government records (including correspondence from employers or to imperial authorities) have seemingly been rarely used to identify/chart collective action or attest to its absence. Similarly, although informal/unorganised work organisation has received increased attention with the partial exception of the

United States, there have been few attempts to locate collective action by slaves within a broader context of worker organisation—both informal and formal—in these societies.[39]

Another important category of unfree-labour was convicts. Use of convict labour can be traced back to the Middle Ages, but it became especially important with the growth of European imperial expansion into the Americas and Asia/Pacific from the 16th century. In Britain in particular the social dislocation associated with the industrial revolution and the related expansion of capital property offences led to a burgeoning prison population.[40] As with slavery, research has demonstrated that convict transportation was used by Britain, France, Portugal and other countries as a mechanism of enforced labour migration to meet imperial economic interests.[41] With regard to Australia for example, convicts were drawn overwhelmingly from the urban and rural proletariat. Only a minority were transported for political/industrial agitation or were career criminals. Convicts were selected by British authorities and many assigned to private employers with a view to their economic value in building infrastructure (like roads, bridges and land clearing) and key industries (food and wool production).[42]

In some locations transported convicts preceded slaves, in North America and parts of the Caribbean both were used between the 17th to 19th centuries (though like Brazil slaves were by far the more significant in the United States) and others, most notably Australia, used transported convicts but not slaves in the 18th and 19th centuries.[43] Britain sent about 50,000 convicts to its American colonies from the 17th century.[44] After the American Revolution, about 150,000 British/Irish convicts were transported to Australia and small numbers to the Caribbean while Indian convicts were sent to Mauritius.[45]

Paralleling research into slavery, studies of convict workers have examined the management of convict workers and forms of resistance. In North America studies using employer notices and other sources pointed to widespread absconding by convicts in the 18th century.[46] Morgan's study of Maryland found that absconding was pronounced amongst those with marketable skills; absconders often took their tools, food and extra clothing; and that 29% of absconding was collective. On occasion convicts absconded with slaves although this could increase risk of recapture, as did having tattoos or physical disfigurement (like pox marks) associated with imprisonment.[47]

In Australia Atkinson's pioneering study identified four types of convict resistance; verbal and physical attacks, appeals to authority (petitions and making complaints of ill-treatment before magistrates), withdrawal labour (temporary absences as well as outright refusals to work and disobedience), and retributory actions (like sabotage including incendiarism).[48] Subsequent research by Nichol, Duffield, Oxley, Reid, Maxwell-Stewart and others tapped into extensive convict records to document their treatment, including modes of resistance.[49] Nichol and others pointed to widespread go-slow/effort-bargaining.[50] For women in particular, the use of 'flash' language was another mode of protest especially in a legal regime bent on zipping workers' tongues. Oxley argued that unlike 'Britain's labour force, Australia's workers faced a legal system which permitted incarceration for the worker who had a quick tongue, sharp wit and a tendency to drink or who was rude with a proclivity to affront a 'superior".[51] Paralleling US research, Maxwell-Stewart pointed to widespread absconding by convicts, the use of distinguishing physical features like tattoos to aid identification/apprehension, and its links to bushranging.[52] While research has made increasing reference to convict strike, mutinies, revolts and riots in Female Factories, there has been no systematic assessment of collective action.[53]

Another category of, at best semi-free labour, is indentured workers, especially non-European indentured labour. The roots of indenturing date back to the Middle Ages with apprenticeship to various trades, but it extended to other occupational groups and by the 17th century was being used to bond rural labourers and other workers sent to the New World.[54] From the 18th to mid-20th centuries, it was widely used to provide both European and non-European labour—although generally to different jobs or locations—including Indians for the sugar plantations in Fiji and Pacific Islanders and later Italian workers to Australian sugar plantations. It is worth noting in passing that work arrangement analogous to indenturing flourishes today, including the provision of third-world crews by crewing agencies to the shipping industry and the exploitative use of foreign guestworkers and seasonal workers in rich/middle income countries who are bound by a combination of agency/employment agreements, debts and residency/visa requirements. Even more oppressive controls and fear of detection are to be found with regard to undocumented immigrants.[55]

With regard to European indentured workers, the North American experience in the 17th and 18th centuries is perhaps best researched. It was an important source of labour for the American colonies and critical to capitalist work relations until the late 18th century.[56] While those with in-demand skill sets exercised some bargaining power, workers were subject to a punitive regime entailing harsh penalties (gaol, the stocks, flogging) and a degree of master-initiated violence. Evidence indicates absconding was widespread.[57] Both male and female indentured workers also regularly petitioned courts for unpaid wages or over other terms of their engagement as well as to complain of ill-treatment.[58]

The indenturing of non-European labour has received more attention in the past quarter century, especially its use in Africa and the Asia-Pacific Region. As with slaves, convicts and European indentured labour absconding was a prevalent form of dissent, notwithstanding an elaborate surveillance/apprehension and punishment regime that sometimes included arrest of suspected runaways without warrant.[59] Studies also refer to passive resistance (go-slows) and resort to the courts, and higher suicide rates amongst some groups like the Chinese.[60] Notwithstanding its value in pursuing other issues the growing literature on indentured non-European work (mainly those working on plantations) has made limited reference to dissent let alone collective action by these workers.[61] There are exceptions. Saunders's study of Pacific Islanders in Queensland identified a range of individual and collective dissent including go-slows, absconding, strikes, complaints to the courts and absconding, and Gupta's overview of plantation workers in India also refers to a range of dissent, including strikes.[62] Few explore the relationship between non-European and European workers in ways that give recognition to how labour markets and regulation were deliberately structured in ways to weaken unions and pit groups of workers against each other.[63]

The foregoing discussion pointed to parallels between slavery, convict labour and indentured labour notwithstanding important differences.[64] Slaves, convicts and indentured workers were all subject to subordinating regimes, and there were parallels both in their lived experiences and preferred forms of resistance.[65] Linebaugh and Rediker pointed to similarities and associations between sailors and slaves in the Atlantic world of the 18th century while Christopher contrasted dissent amongst sailors and convicts in the early Australian colonies.[66] McCoy identified the role of working people, including absconding servants and sailors, in the Philadelphia election riots of 1742.[67]

The foregoing research also reinforces a wider observation that the emergence of free-labour was a slow, fragmented and fitful process not only entailing the co-existence of various categories of unfree, semi-free and free workers and that even the latter group was subject to considerable regulatory subordination until the early 20th century if not longer.[68] It is also worth noting in passing that unfree-labour (including slavery and bonded labour in South Asia and Africa) continues to play a significant role in global capitalism.[69] Of more immediate concerns to this book is that focusing on particular categories of labour can obscure the pivotal role of the State in facilitating capitalism by subordinating all categories of labour— even if some categories were more ruthlessly exploited. This was central to enshrining inequality at work, legitimating and indeed extending the power of employers.

The State's Role in Shaping and Enforcing Work Arrangements

In tracing the history of worker mobilisation it is critical to recognise the centrality of regulation. Efforts to regulate labour can be traced to the very beginnings of capitalism, which itself long preceded the industrial revolution.[70] In England (the *Ordinance of Labourers*, 1349 and *Statute of Labourers*, 1350) and elsewhere in Europe laws were introduced to require compulsory service, combat worker absconding, wage demands and strikes.[71] The immediate impetus was severe labour shortages and social dislocation arising from the Black Death that killed over a third of Europe's population. This in turn accelerated the emergence of capitalism by undermining feudal agriculture and a shift to less labour-reliant sheep/cattle raising, thereby encouraging the expulsion of agricultural labour from estates who drifted to towns (precursor to the enclosure movement), and forcing changes to property/inheritance laws—some benefiting women.[72]

These developments make peasant revolts, like that led by radical cleric John Ball and Wat Tyler affecting large parts of England in mid-1381, more comprehensible. The rebel's key demands included abolition of unfree-labour (serfdom), a reduction in tax and changes to the courts. This and some other peasant revolts in Europe were not simply evidence of oppressive rulers (including the Church) but the breakdown of feudalism, social dislocation and collective dissent amongst the labouring poor associated with the rise of capitalism.[73] Organisation amongst journeymen became more prevalent after the Black Death. Laws proscribing combinations enacted from the early 15th century were indicative of the emergence of early unions.

But this was only one aspect of the State's efforts to shape work arrangements and subordinate labour. Further laws passed in the 14th century (including the *Statute of Cambridge* 1388) provided the foundations for master and servant law and the gentry-based magistracy that administered it. Hay and Craven argue critical elements of this

> early legislation (compulsory service, apprenticeship, penalties for leaving work, attempts to tie workers to particular status and employers) were recapitulated in the forty eight sections of the Statute of Artificers (1562), whose categories dominated the law until the nineteenth century.[74]

Master and servant law developed alongside and borrowed from laws regulating seamen and codes/laws governing slavery, indentured workers and transported convicts.[75]

The shift to free-labour was complicated, with distinctive regulatory regimes for different categories of workers like apprentices and seamen. Further, master and servant and related laws like those covering indentured workers aimed at subordinating labour were disseminated throughout the British Empire as part of the imperial project, with parallel developments elsewhere in Europe and its colonial appendages. Nevertheless, there were historically contingent differences in the form and administration of these laws between England, Ireland, Canada, the United States, Australia and British colonies in the Caribbean, Africa and Asia. The evidence of *Masters, Servants and Magistrates* is that prosecution rates were higher in colonies where labour control was more problematic,[76] and they were also used against collective action—observations this book will reinforce. Combination Acts were used against larger and more threatening strikes, like that of London journeyman tailors in 1721, where prosecuting thousands under master and servant law simply wasn't feasible. The critical point is that collective action occurred as part of wider contestation of the legal form, terms and conditions of work that began long before the first industrial revolution and was played out in North America, Australasia and elsewhere.[77]

To only examine explicit efforts to suppress collective dissent, affords a misleading view of the regulatory shaping of work and the degree of contestation that occurred with regard to it. It was a terrain where wages, the right to leave a job, workloads, employers' authority, discipline and other 'bread and butter' industrial relations issues were fought out on a daily basis. The scale of the struggle, especially prior the 18th century, is under-researched but there is enough evidence to indicate it was extensive and grew in intensity, probably peaking (at least in Britain, North America and Australia) in the second quarter of the 19th century both in terms of legislative enactment and the number of workers prosecuted under these laws.[78] The struggle provides an important lens on inequality at work (see Chapter 2).

The regulatory context also raises important questions about confining consideration of worker organisation to wage earners. The involvement of economically dependent groups of self-employed workers at particular periods like the revolts of home-based weavers in early 19th century England have been seen as a passing phase in the emergence of a wage earning class. Alliances of small producers and wage earners like the New England Association of Farmers, Mechanics and Other Working Men (1832) have been viewed in the same way.[79] The re-emergence of home-based production and self-employed subcontractors (like Uber drivers), exploitive supply chains and the so-called 'Gig Economy' demonstrate the paucity of seeing such arrangements and wider social alliances as transitional. Or indeed seeing the 'Gig Economy' and producer/worker/community alliances like Fairwear as entirely new—as specious as claims about the so-called new social movements in the late 1960s.[80] Capitalism involves a continuous search for unorganised workers with minimal if any regulatory protection who can be most readily exploited, whether they be in a factory in Thailand at the end of contractual chain producing toys or electronic goods for Europe, working on short-term contracts/temporary agency arrangements, franchisee home-services providers, or self-employed workers in App-enabled subcontracting arrangements like Uber drivers.[81]

Any meaningful analysis of the origins of worker mobilisation must examine collective action by all workers, as well as the influence of the state and particularities in that country's capitalist development. The next section deals with the last point.

The Colonies in Context: Population, Political Economy and Labour Market

Australia began as a penal settlement after the American Revolution. As with causes of the American Revolution itself, reasons for settlement were complex including using convict transportation as a social safety valve and pre-empting French claims. The French had sent a series of scientific expeditions to the continent, one being present when the first fleet arrived in January 1788. Almost starving in its first years, settlers/invaders slowly learned to farm a land of climatic extremes and fragile soils. Critical land clearing and infrastructure (like roads, bridges and ports) building was undertaken by convict labour. French expeditions continued to arrive periodically, interested outsiders who noted its rapid development, particularly under Governor Macquarie (1809–21). In 1819 Jacques Arago—artist on Freycinet's ship—waxed lyrically about Sydney's buildings, mansions, fine sculptures, furniture and fashionably dressed residents—'a fine European city 4000 leagues from Europe.'[82] His superlatives ignored the equally visible dark side of convict chain-gangs but favourable accounts of NSW and VDL were not uncommon, nor confined to French visitors.

The total European population grew from a tiny 2,542 in 1790 to 12,099 by 1810 and then more strongly over succeeding decades from the combination of convict transportation, free emigrants and natural increase. By 1820 the combined population of NSW and VDL reached 31,045, more than doubling in each of the next two decades and totalling 334,373 in 1850.[83] The European population of all Australian colonies, including South Australia (founded 1836) and Western Australia (founded 1830) was 190,408 in 1840 and reached 405,356 by December 1850. Initially the population was dominated by convicts. Around 123,308 men and 24,960 women were transported from Britain/Ireland to Australia between 1788 and 1868— most arriving before 1840. The vast majority went to New South Wales (1788–1840) and Van Diemen's Land (1803–53), with a small number going to Western Australia, which opted for convicts between 1852 and 1868.

Unlike slaves, convicts became free after serving their sentence, though to anti-slavery campaigner William Wilberforce the commonalities with slavery were striking. The vast majority remained in the colonies. Absolute pardons were rare, travel costs high, family ties were established, and colonial living conditions generally more favourable. Some families joined convicts but a more typical case was Fairford carpenter Richard Bishop who left a wife and three children when transported in 1837, served his time, remarried and became a bridge builder in Western NSW. By 1800 ex-convict numbers exceeded those still serving sentences but escalating transportation after 1820 reversed this situation. Serving convict numbers peaked at 56,178 in 1840 (with an estimated 27,785 ex-convicts) before dropping to 46,792 in 1845 and 23,801 in 1850. By 1845 ex-convict numbers matched (46,976) those still serving sentences and by 1850 was (at 72,590) over three times those still under sentence as transportation wound down.[84]

Gender imbalances in convict transportation and (to a lesser extent) immigration created a male-dominated workforce and population. In 1790 working age males constituted 77.7% of the population. The proportion didn't fall below 60% until the late 1830s, dropping to 45% in 1850. The female convict/ex-convict population rose from 1048 in 1800 to 13,293 in

1840. In 1790 females (convict, free emigrants and native born) constituted 19.6% of the population and 40 years later it had only reached 22.9%. Increased female emigration and colonial births helped to offset the gender imbalance. The number of female emigrants increased from 3,395 in 1830 to 26,242 in 1840 and 58,617 in 1850. Numbers of colonially born females grew from 5,862 in 1830 to 21,118 in 1840 and 57,236 in 1850. The female proportion of total population increased to 32.4% in 1840 and 39.9% in 1850.[85]

The initially tiny free population grew progressively due to convicts completing their sentences, natural population growth and increased immigration. Initially free emigrants mostly consisted of government officials, the military and a few wealthy settlers. After 1830 working-class emigrants began arriving and this increased in succeeding decades. British and local governments promoted migration, driven by a confluence of interests including colonial labour demand, providing impoverished females to mitigate the gender imbalance, and Whitehall's desire to address population/poverty/social pressures associated with the industrial revolution. Australia's remoteness meant travel costs were beyond the means of working families and passage assistance was essential.[86] Between 1837 and 1842 60,243 emigrated from the UK to NSW alone, just over 80% receiving passage assistance. In the period 1837–50 45,683 emigrants arrived in NSW under one scheme—the Bounty Scheme whereby emigrants were bound for a term to employers who had sponsored their passage.[87] Typical was Annie Stinson, young and single, who arrived from County Antrim, Ireland in 1839, marrying in 1840 John Smith Glover, an ex-London now Sydney waterman who migrated in 1833. Immigration grew over time although there were large annual fluctuations, partly in response to shifts in colonial labour demand. Lags, economic volatility and UK government push factors led to mismatches as occurred in 1841–42 when 30,224 emigrants arrived (nearly 84% assisted) as NSW was experiencing a severe depression.[88] Similar patterns can be identified in other Australian colonies. Some employers introduced indentured workers from Asia and the Pacific but numbers were small.

Political Economy and Industry

Several factors shaped the colonial economy, including heavy initial reliance on convict labour and the prominence of the State in economic activities. Until the 1830s—even longer in VDL—convicts constituted the bulk of the labour force. Imperial government funds administering this prison beyond the seas, was a critical initiating source of capital inflow. In a vast, sparsely populated and remotely located continent State-deployed convict labour built critical economic infrastructure, established or facilitated local manufacturing (soap-making, foundries, brickworks and timberyards and cloth-making in female factories) and assisted in land clearing and harvests.[89] Building an extensive road network in NSW and VDL especially from the mid-1820s, often dealing with rugged terrain and harsh climatic conditions (heat/cold, wind, rain and sometimes snow) was critical to expansion of the pastoral economy. Demonstrating the complex, nuanced and even contradictory aspects of using unfree-labour, Darling's (NSW Governor 1825–31) expansive use of road-gangs combined with harsh working conditions to induce widespread disorder and absconding but archaeological evidence attests to the quality of construction.[90]

The Commissariat (government store) in NSW and VDL was an important impetus for capitalist development by providing meat, flour and other products for convicts purchased from local settlers.[91] The administrative apparatus of the convict regime—officials, clerks and constables, surveyors, engineers and others—also pumped funds into the economy. Macquarie's (NSW Governor 1809–21) ambitious public works program further stimulated manufacturing both through government operations and from private ventures. Individuals involved in private ventures formed a small but influential group of merchant capitalists who invested heavily in import/export of goods, pastoral and maritime activities (including sealing/whaling) like Simeon Lord, Robert Campbell, John Blaxland, Richard Jones and Samuel Terry in Sydney and Edward Lord and Peter Degraves in Hobart.[92]

Reliance on imperial government funds initially limited capital formation and borrowing. However, from 1817 growth of a banking sector and efforts to stabilise currency arrangements (including reversion to Sterling) aided domestic capital formation, financing maritime, commercial and pastoral ventures. From the 1820s private British investment became increasingly important but even here government played an influential role. In NSW the Australian Agricultural Company (AA Company) was granted large parcels of land and a monopoly on coal production in the Hunter Valley. Similarly, the London-based Van Diemen's Land Company was granted extensive landholdings in the island's north-west, building its own port at Circular Head/Stanley.

The colonies required export industries to attract UK investment. Given their remoteness, many rural/agricultural exports were not an option prior to improvements in shipping and refrigeration. With a few exceptions—like coal in the Hunter Valley and copper at Burra—the continent's vast mineral resources remained undiscovered until after 1850. The southern coast of the continent contained large seal populations. The east coast was a seasonal migratory route for whales (notably the Southern Right Whale) and Australia was close to the deep sea whaling grounds of the Great Southern Ocean. Beginning in the late 18th century seal pelts, whale oil and associated products generated significant export income. Sealing was predominantly a local venture while whaling included local and overseas (British, US and French) operators using ports like Sydney, Hobart and Fremantle as reprovisioning/repair bases. Seal populations were rapidly decimated but whale products remained the colonies' single most important commodity export until the early 1830s.[93] Hobart and Sydney had their own whaling fleets while ports like Launceston, Fremantle and Point Rosetta were smaller bases for whaling ventures.[94] Whaling generated support activities like shipbuilding/repair, cask-making (coopering) and provisioning.

The other major commodity export derived from pastoral activities, primarily fine wool, grew more slowly (in 1810 most sheep were bred for mutton) as the Spanish merino breed suited to the climate were refined and won acceptance in the British market. After the duty on colonial wool was cut, wool exports grew more than fivefold between 1822 and 1830, becoming the colonies' primary export in 1834 and within a decade supplanting Bavaria as the major wool supplier to expanding British textile manufacturers.[95] As with sealing/whaling, this had flow-on effects to colonial manufacturing and commerce. The expansion of Australian wool production (actually a range of products suited to different industrial processes) coincided with a substantial increase in global demand for textiles. The type and quality of wool (and sheep breeding including the infusion of new breeds) and its marketing underwent significant change throughout the 19th century.[96]

From the 1830s other commodity exports developed, including timber products (like shingles), hides and leather, horses to India, tallow (boiling down animals was especially important during the 1840s depression), copper and wheat. The VDL economy was also boosted by grain exports to feed NSW and later food and stock exports to the Port Philip District (Victoria) and South Australia but by the early 1840s increased competition from mainland colonies had a depressing effect on the island.[97]

Land was essential to the pastoral economy. While early ex-navy governors (like Arthur Phillip, Philip King and William Bligh) made small land grants (30 acres) to emancipated convicts to promote food production/social control, land grant policies increasingly favoured emigrants possessing capital and UK investors. The NSW Corps was there to suppress any uprisings by convicts but officers like John Macarthur focused more on commercial opportunities through a monopoly on critical items, (notably rum which was a de facto currency in the early colony) and land grants to pursue agricultural (principally grain but also wine and other produce) and pastoral pursuits (beef, sheep and especially wool). King and Bligh sought to control their activities, the more abrasive Bligh of *Bounty*-mutiny fame being deposed in Australia's first coup. Effectively controlling the colony for several years after the coup (1807–09) the so-called Rum Corps cabal engineered large land grants for themselves and others, making reversal of these decisions difficult.[98] Larger land grants favouring the rich continued even if moderated somewhat under ex-army Governor Lachlan Macquarie (1809–21).

The ending of the Napoleonic wars and the Bigge Report (1822–23) both had profound effects. Amidst economic depression in Britain, large numbers of retrenched naval and army officers sought opportunities in the colonies, becoming large landholders and a significant component of the magistracy. Growing numbers of middle-class settlers also took up land, most planning a triumphant return after making their fortune. Some like Maitland landholder Naval Captain Robert Lethbridge and Braidwood District landholder Major William Elrington returned to the UK though far more chose to stay. Growing social unrest and petty crime associated with the post-Napoleonic war depression also increased numbers of transported convicts. John Thomas Bigge, former chief justice in the slave colony of Trinidad, produced three influential reports on NSW and VDL, their judiciary and agriculture/trade. Bigge's instructions were to cut transportation costs including convicts used in Macquarie's ambitious public works program. He was also swayed by evidence from large landholders, who advocated more private assignment to themselves. Their self-serving claims that small landholdings of ex-convicts were ill-managed/wasteful matched Bigge's own predilections.[99] Bigge proposed more unequal land-grant and convict-assignment practices, arguing large and 'respectable' landholders would inculcate more diligent and obedient attitudes amongst those who served them.

Bigge's recommendations altered purchasing by the Commissariat, setting minimum tender sizes that excluded small farmers, curtailing growth of the latter. More activities were to be undertaken by private employers using assigned-convicts rather than government. Aside from advantaging the rich, the cost-cutting pressures and tendering processes encouraged disorganisation/inefficiency with adverse effects on the quality and quantity of public works like the Sydney Courthouse.[100] Privatisation of the government lumberyards like similar measures today didn't deliver an 'efficiency dividend.'[101] The combination of Bigge's reports and Macquarie's departure signalled a sea-change in the colony's political economy and industrial relations.[102] For the vast majority of convicts completing their sentence meant a shift to waged labour not economic independence and the same applied to successive waves of working-class emigrants after 1830.

Even before Bigge's Report was tabled in the House of Commons, changes it foreshadowed were under way.[103] Existing settlers with capital and new arrivals with £500 or more received large land grants to establish pastoral holdings in the 1820s and NSW/VDL governors continued the practice into the 1830s notwithstanding British efforts to restrict this. Rich farm/pastoral regions like northern VDL saw the building of manor-estates with grand Georgian residences and a surrounding 'village' of convict-quarters still evident today. More generally it reinforced a shift to capital-intensive pastoralism dependent on wool until the arrival of refrigeration in the 1870s.

Exploration promoted by NSW Governors Darling and Bourke provided information on lands then rapidly taken up by predominantly large squatters who illegally occupied crown land. Many were existing landholders who used political influence to acquire leasehold title to these lands under 'favourable terms.'[104] The pastoral expansion spread to ever more distant parts of NSW including areas that later became Victoria and Queensland. In VDL most good land had been acquired by the mid-1830s, leaving the poor with few opportunities apart from subsistence farming/hunting in marginal areas. Launceston residents—including Batman, Faulkner and the Hentys—sailed across Bass Strait to found the Port Philip settlement (Melbourne) exploiting vast and less mountainous surrounding lands well-suited to sheep-raising. There were no land grants in this district dominated by middling to large squatters who favoured transportation like their counterparts elsewhere.[105]

Restricting access to land was also a founding principle for the free colony of South Australia (1836), drawing on lessons from Western Australia and Gibbon Wakefield's idea of a planned relationship between capital, land and labour, where land was priced to exclude poorer emigrants and the revenue used to fund emigration of labour.[106] Marx labelled it a policy perfectly formulated to create a capitalist mode of production.[107] Wakefield proposed an agricultural economy model, but the South Australian settlement soon abandoned this in favour of the pastoral capitalism model that had succeeded elsewhere. The outcome was unequivocal. Access to land in Australia was largely confined to those with substantial capital. Population also limited the demand for small-scale agriculture and dairying though this began to change from the 1850s. Capital-intensive land use limited rural populations and by 1850 Australia was already becoming a highly urbanised society.[108]

Government also shaped the types of labour that would be available. Unlike the Americas, settlement occurred when the British slave lobby was in retreat and, importantly, much of Australia was climatically unsuited for labour-intensive plantation crops. Australia's European inhabitants, including emancipated convicts, enjoyed the civil rights of UK citizens. Aboriginal people were used, including assigning native prisoners to settlers in Western Australia in 1849, and some were used to track escaped convicts, but didn't constitute more than a fraction of labour requirements.[109] Unlike slaves in North America, from which terms like servitude and emancipation were readily borrowed, convicts became free citizens once they had served their sentence and in practice they exercised property and other rights prior to this.[110]

Convict labour was used across a wide range of activities. Many were directly employed by government in constructing/maintaining roads, bridges, wharves, buildings and other public works, as well as lumberyards, sawyers' pits and workshops. Increasingly, newly arrived convicts and those in places of secondary punishment were housed in barracks/prison-buildings reducing their mobility. Special buildings for the incarceration of female convicts, known as Female Factories, were built in towns like Parramatta, Bathurst, Hobart, Launceston and Ross. Their inmates were engaged in laundry, sewing/dressmaking and picking oakum. Additionally, large numbers of convicts were assigned to private employers on farms, sheep-stations, in workshops, factories, shops, and as domestic servants. From 1839 assignment was replaced by a more graduated and formalised probation passholder system—the upper level receiving wages (below market rates) and having some say in choosing their employer.

After serving part of their sentence (depending on conduct), convicts were granted a ticket-of-leave enabling them to hire themselves to employers. They were restricted to a specific district and had to attend regular 'musters' until completing their sentence or receiving a conditional pardon. Introduced to reduce the financial burden of feeding/clothing convicts and to reward meritorious service, convicts soon viewed it as an entitlement enabling them to serve less than half their sentence before being conditionally released into the community.[111] Transitioning to ticket-of-leave and then a pardon was influenced by the convict's skill-set, conduct and their employer's attitude. Rural employers desperate to retain labour sometimes refused to support a ticket-of-leave application and in September 1823 a group of NSW magistrates proposed an annual bench sitting to review contested applications.[112] Tickets-of-leave could be suspended for misbehaviour.

There were five distinct categories of convict workers. Ticket-of-leave holders were at the pinnacle just below free workers. Below them were convicts assigned to private employers or government-engaged convicts employed in civil construction and other activities. Both groups had to be fed, clothed and housed at levels specified by the state. The next step down were convicts employed on road-gangs as a result of misconduct. More serious recidivists like the repeatedly contumacious were sentenced to chain/iron-gangs to work while heavily manacled. Road- (ironed and unironed) and bridge-building gangs ranged in size from 30 to over 100 with 50–60 being typical. At times multiple gangs engaged in major road construction meant many hundreds could be located at a particular spot like the No.2 Stockade at Cox's River in the early 1830s. The bottom rung of convict status were remote feared points of secondary punishment (which changed over time) like Newcastle, Port Macquarie and Moreton Bay on the eastern mainland; Norfolk Island; and Macquarie Harbour, Maria Island and Port Arthur in VDL.

The convict system was administered in bureaucratic detail. Each convict's trial records, appearance (hair and eye colour, height, skin complexion, disease-marks like smallpox, tattoos and scars), arrival date, ship, occupation, subsequent behaviour/offences, assignment history, issuing of ticket-of-leave or conditional pardons were recorded in multiple cross-referenced sources including convict indents, conduct and court records and absconding notices. Governor Philip began assigning convicts to private employers, both to increase food production and accommodate resistance from military officers to being involved in supervising convicts aside from those being used for their own direct benefit.[113] The practice soon encompassed a wide range of employers/activities, including pastoralists, tradesmen and domestic service.

Early governors set hours of work and the scale and type of rations to be provided to convicts, including assigned-convicts. Encountering problems in the effort/reward bargain, overseers turned to task-work, specifying a certain amount of work—like land cleared or bricks made—to be done each day. While informal, task-work became the norm even on government farms defended by convicts themselves because it enabled them to undertake additional work for reward in their own time.[114] Wages were also paid at harvest time to reapers and others. By 1816 the system of convicts working in their own time was so entrenched that in shifting from local currency (dollar dumps) to Sterling, Governor Macquarie called a meeting of magistrates. This set a £10 per-annum wage rate for 'convicts who regularly devoted their own time (that is after 3pm) to his master's service.'[115] Originally conceived as a reward, convicts treated it as an entitlement and standard rate.

Dyster persuasively argues paying convicts for their labour was one of a combination of factors that transformed the colony into a thriving capitalist economy rather than remaining a southern Siberia. Assignment boosted production and consumption in the private sector, with payment in cash/ kind to serving-convicts further increasing domestic consumption beyond that arising from ticket-of-leave holders and emancipists. This increased demand for imports which, in turn, created additional pressure for exports to pay for this.[116] The arrival of free immigrants boosted rather initiated a vibrant domestic market.[117]

Ex-slave colony administrator Bigge opposed paying serving convicts and NSW Governor Brisbane (1821–25) revoked it. Many employers continued paying wages notwithstanding the prohibition. Convicts saw additional rations/wages as entitlements and masters failing to provide them risked go-slows or other forms of dissent (see Chapters 2 and 6). The scale, content and quality of rations (like substituting maize for wheat) and additional rations for meritorious tasks or during harvests were recurrent sources of disputation. On large pastoral runs killing sheep to supplement rations occurred (with some masters averting their eyes) along with profit-sharing rewards for shepherds maximising lambing/flock numbers and curbing scabby or fly-blown sheep.[118] Informal practices left ample scope for arbitrary justice/punitive retribution if convicts fell out with their master as well as revengeful sabotage by aggrieved convicts (Chapter 2). Female convicts— predominantly employed as domestics—also demanded indulgences, including time to visit friends.[119]

Rules regarding assignment were systematised and the 1824 *Transportation Act* entrenched the 'propertied' status of assigned-convicts. Nonetheless, governors continued to exercise their power 'to recall assigned-servants or pardon them before the termination of their sentence without compensation.'[120] Some landholders obtained additional workers on temporary 'loan' for particular tasks like land clearing or during harvests. Regulations stipulated employers allowing their assigned-servant to work for another employer would forfeit their services. Giving evidence to a British parliamentary committee, Colonel George Arthur—superintendent in the slave colony of Honduras (1814–22) and Lieutenant Governor of Van Diemen's Land (1824–36)—stated the only difference between assigned-convicts and slaves was that the master couldn't inflict corporal punishment directly on convicts (offences had to go before a court) and had 'property in him only for a limited period'.[121]

There were, however, other important differences. Convicts were supplied to employers without charge apart from the need to support them and could be returned to government service if they proved unsuitable/sickly, recalcitrant, became pregnant in the case of women or were no longer required.[122] Reinforcing arguments about the economics of convict workers, VDL Bench Book records show it was common for convicts to be returned as no longer being 'required', as 'useless' or 'unfit for farm labour' apparently without fear this would affect prospects of obtaining labour in the future. Large returns also coincided with the end of harvesting/shearing. In early March 1844 several Oatlands District employers returned no fewer than 37 convicts to government service.[123] On the other hand, assigned-convicts could be withdrawn due to mistreatment or if the master was deemed too lax in allowing their servants to absent themselves. In October 1821 farmer Robert Jillett had three servants returned to government after they were apprehended in the town of New Norfolk without a pass—that two became involved in a fight probably sparked this action.[124] In most instances masters were simply warned.

There were other differences between slaves and convicts arising from modes of production. Plantation slaves could be closely supervised and their availability as cheap labour inhibited technological innovation whereas pastoral activities in Australia were capital intensive, with shepherds and others working in comparative isolation subject to, at best, episodic supervision.[125] At harvest and shearing time, bargaining by convicts was common and the comparatively high cost of labour encouraged labour-saving technologies (scythes rather than sickles, reaping machines and ultimately mechanical shears).

As transportation wound down, governments continued to shape the labour market, establishing Immigration Committees with the explicit aim of remedying perceived labour shortages and keeping wages down. One settler (T Walker Esq) told the Immigration Committee of the NSW Legislative Council in 1845 that the 'only object of pursuit here is the accumulation of wealth' and others like VDL Lt Governor George Arthur attested to the prevalence of this viewpoint.[126]

Two important subcategories of free-labour were immigrants who had signed indentures with employers in return for their passage costs being paid. These workers were commonly bound for longer periods (3–5 years) than colonial engagements (typically one year at most) and at wages significantly below colonial rates. There was no subtlety. In 1835 a VDL committee was established to import agricultural and other labour under contract to work at half prevailing colonial wages.[127] Unsurprisingly, these disparities became a source of friction.[128]

Indentured workers can be further subdivided into those engaged in Europe (predominantly Britain/Ireland) and elsewhere (predominantly

India, China and Pacific Islanders). As today, employers were ever looking for cheaper labour options and the introduction of 'coolies' was subject to considerable public debate in the 1830s and 1840s.[129] This option offered lower transport and labour costs. Attempts to import non-Europeans under indentures increased from the 1830s. Typifying the racist sentiment under-pinning this in 1846 Moreton Bay settler J Friell published a pamphlet on the advantages of Indian labour and how they should be managed.[130] Unlike Europeans, indentured non-Europeans were viewed as temporary (guest-workers) not migrants, though some employers failed to provide for their return upon completing their indenture. For several reasons, including UK and Indian government opposition, numbers of non-European indentured workers remained small.[131]

Another subcategory of free workers was apprentices serving an inden-ture while they learned a trade regulated under local apprentice or master and servant laws. Masters assumed parental authority and could use physi-cal chastisement. Ill-treatment and failure to teach the trade were common sources of complaint, with the apprentice's parents not uncommonly getting involved.[132]

Seamen and whalers (bay and pelagic/deep sea) constituted another important category of free-labour, although the ranks of sealers and whal-ers included ticket-of-leave holders. They signed articles—essentially fixed-term contracts not unlike indentures. Like many convicts they worked and live in close confinement and depended on the rations provided by their employer. Maritime labour laws bestowed shipmasters with greater disci-plinary powers than those applying to other free workers—not dissimilar to the military. Unlike other free workers, they could be placed in irons for particular offences at sea.

The economic and labour market policies just described were as much an outcome of colonial politics as imperial oversight. The state apparatus in the colonies was dominated by a small and closely connected group of large landholders, merchant capitalists, lawyers and civil/military officers. Employers/landholders dominated the part-time magistracy. Early gover-nors ruled autocratically, drawing on advice from senior government officers (the colonial secretary, superintendent of convicts, chief legal officers) and prominent settlers. The first legislatures in NSW and VDL were comprised of landholders, merchants, lawyers and senior government officials. Even after partly-elected legislatures (1843 in NSW) were established, property qualifications restricted the franchise prior to 1851, with only more affluent workers like tradesmen having a vote.[133]

Colonial economies expanded rapidly, especially after 1820, but were vol-atile, subject to business cycles in Britain affecting exports/capital flows and local factors. Currency shortages and bad harvests in VDL in the mid-1820s exacerbated the effects of a depression in the UK. Australia's recurring pat-tern of extreme climatic shifts was another influence, affecting key exports, especially wool. A severe drought from 1828 helped precipitate a downturn in NSW though assisting VDL through grain exports. Another drought contributed to the severe depression of the early 1840s.[134] This depression in the Eastern colonies affected Western Australia (which missed the 1830s boom) along with a recurring shortage of currency and capital investment.[135] Economic volatility accentuated the concentration of wealth because more capital-endowed individuals were likelier to survive downturns.[136] Samuel Terry became one of NSW's wealthiest merchant/ industrialists and landholders by 1840 by resuming the property and lands of speculators and farmers indebted to him after falling on hard times.[137] Terry was among a handful of ex-convicts to become rich—all early arrivals as this window of opportunity quickly closed. Most who built commercial empires like Robert Campbell arrived free and with a bankroll of capital to begin their ventures.[138]

In sum, colonial economies were dependent on a small array of exports (wool, whale-oil, minerals) tied into a volatile global economy, as well as substantial private and public sector capital funds from the UK, and a labour force composed of forced and voluntary migrants.

Sources and Methods Used

The foregoing sections argued it is time to re-visit some 'big picture' issues about the history and nature of worker organisation, systematically comparing different categories of worker, different modes of organisation and collective action, including the influence of regulatory and political economy factors. To do this an array of sources was examined.

Archival and Documentary Sources

A search was made for early union documents and other information on collective action held by public and university archives and libraries in Australia. The search revealed few union records (most held by Mitchell library) but a set of early ship logbooks, containing evidence of collective action (Tasmanian State Library/TAHO). State archives contained correspondence, governor's despatches, petitions and reports relating to worker organisation as well as lobbying from employers, correspondence from magistrates, copies of laws, draft bills, prosecution records and legal opinions on labour laws. This included regulation applying to convicts, free-labour, merchant seamen and whalers. Records held by Friendly Societies Register were also perused (especially NSW) along with early colonial documents collated in the Historical Records of NSW and Victoria.

Government Gazettes

Each colony published a gazette of official notices including new laws, government appointments, court proceedings, insolvencies, reward notices, impounding of animals, land grants, desertion by members of the armed forces, tickets-of-leave granted or cancelled. Similar to absconding slave notices, the NSW and VDL gazettes included detailed lists of convicts absconding from government and private employment to assist in their apprehension as well as lists of those apprehended. They provided voluminous evidence of collective absconding, although they cannot be treated as exhaustive especially in relation to absconding from rural estates.[139] The NSW and Port Phillip (from 1843) gazettes were searched from the early 1800s to 1850 (gazettes prior to 1832 were published in newspapers) identifying over 3000 instances of collective absconding by convicts (and a few involving soldiers). Maxwell-Stewart has collected absconding data for VDL which also reveals widespread collective absconding but is not included in this book.

Court Records

Notwithstanding significant (missing) gaps, lower/magistrates court records contain vast evidence on the disciplining of both convict and free workers for absconding, refusing work, neglect and insolence as well as complaints they brought before magistrates. The court records for NSW 1788–1820, VDL 1806–50 and some records for areas (Victoria) were searched. These records were the initiating source (multiple sources existed for some organisations) for about 1700 instances of collective action, many—especially in rural districts—not reported by the colonial press. Early court records, or those pertaining to more significant cases, contained more detailed accounts of the issues involved than found in newspapers. However, the two sources were complementary because not all court records survive and newspaper accounts were written by reporters at the trial who sometimes added information not in the court record. Thus, for example in May 1842 it is from the newspaper reports not the court records that we know the crew of the *Isabella* moored in Hobart were striking over poor rations.[140] On the other hand the court records indicate that an additional three seamen were charged with refusing to work after the initial strike by 13—something not reported in the press.

Colonial Newspapers

Another major source was colonial newspapers. The first newspaper (the *Sydney Gazette*) commenced publication in 1803 followed by the short-lived *Derwent Star* in VDL (1810–12) and the *Hobart Town Gazette* in 1816. Additional newspapers followed in the 1820s. By 1839 all principal towns (Sydney, Hobart, Launceston, Adelaide, Melbourne and Perth) had multiple newspapers, and by the mid-1840s Brisbane and regional towns like Bathurst, Geelong, Maitland, Parramatta and Portland had newspapers. Unlike court records, copies of almost all colonial newspapers survive and their advertisements, obituaries, news reports and editorials contain a wider array of information on worker organisation including meetings, activities (not just those subject to litigation) and even summaries of union rules and elections as well as political mobilisations. Two complementary methods were used to search newspapers. First, in 1982–94 most colonial newspapers were manually read sequentially to identify and copy relevant material which was then organised chronologically and by occupation, yielding just over 500 instances of organisation. Second, between 2011–16 the National Library's Trove of extensive digital copy of newspapers was searched using an array of search terms like 'strike/struck work', 'insubordination', 'refused work' and 'they absconded' along with others to identify unions like 'operative society' or reference to specific occupations like 'seamen', 'miners' and 'journeymen printers'. This search, aided by information collected in the earlier search, was the initiating source for identifying around another 600 instances of organisation.

Publications, Theses, Diaries and Other Unpublished Material

Other sources used included diaries/books by early settlers/officers like David Collins, Peter Cunningham and G F Moore that were especially valuable in identifying collective action not reported elsewhere.[141] Unpublished theses provided another valuable source, including those dealing with pre-gold rush trade unions, Crowley's Ph.D. on working-class conditions in Australia, Adrian Merritt's Ph.D. on master and servant law in NSW, Bill Robbins's Ph.D. on convicts and labour process, and Nick Clements's thesis/book on the 'Black War' in Tasmania. Published research of local/family and professional historians was valuable especially for the early period or information in sources I hadn't examined.[142] Published research by Oxley, Maxwell-Stewart, Irving and others provided significant insights and contextual material.[143]

Sources Requiring Further Investigation

As indicated, court records for Victoria, NSW (1821–50), South Australia, Queensland and Western Australia and government gazette absconding notices for VDL remain to be searched. While I tried to be thorough regarding CSO records in all colonies, new material was continually coming to light and undoubtedly this will continue. Convict conduct records survive for VDL (not NSW) and preliminary research by Hamish Maxwell-Stewart indicate they include a significant number of references (perhaps hundreds) to collective action where court records no longer survive. Investigation of these additional records will extend information on collective dissent.

Methods

This book uses both a big data approach and qualitative methods to do this. Big data refers to the analysis of large historical data-sets, often enabled digitally, which is yielding significant advances in historical/social sciences analysis.[144] A relational database was constructed which contains a file for every organisation no matter how small or ephemeral. Each file contains sub-files for activities like strikes and court actions which can be analysed independently, as well as recording other activities like membership, meetings/marches and use of bans. The database also enabled significant amounts of qualitative material to be entered, including verbatim reports of meetings, strikes, court proceedings and the like.[145] Entering data was time consuming and required expert judgements regarding the type of organisation and action taken. I did almost all the data entry, securing a degree of consistency. Collecting, reading and entering information has the advantage of bringing the researcher closer to the material and to see the subject in its wider social context, on occasion revealing new or unsuspected connections. Computer-generated databases afford opportunities not available to earlier generations of scholars. It is not simply fact grubbing but enables testing of hypotheses, previous findings. It may even suggest new insights or lines of inquiry. Worker organisation can be examined, as far as the records allow, in a holistic fashion where every small collective act has an imprint and where activity by a wider array of workers is considered not just those who formed permanent institutions.

Such methods need to be extended by qualitative analysis providing depth, meaning and context as well as insights into the motives of workers, employers, government officials and others. The book tries to synthesise these two complementary methods of inquiry. Using written documents requires caution and wherever possible multiple sources were examined. To avoid repetition of the term 'database' statistics on organisation and collective action derives from the database described in this book unless otherwise stated. Based on sources already interrogated and others known to exist (see above), the 6426 instances of worker organisation in the database represents on my best estimate around 60–70% of the total of worker organisation for which evidence survives. This caveat needs to be borne in mind throughout the book.

Conclusion

Worker organisation long predated the industrial revolution, although the latter exerted a significant influence. Tracing the evolution of research on worker organisation and related fields like the history of slavery, this chapter pointed to the importance of considering this longer history and all categories of workers. This includes the roots of organisational methods, both formal and informal organisation, the diverse modes of collective action used by different categories of workers, and the interrelationships between them systematically. The critical role played by the state in shaping work arrangements and different categories of labour, the importance of unfree labour to capitalism amidst a slow and fitful shift to free labour—itself still heavily subordinated—was also emphasised as forming an essential context for any examination of worker mobilisation. Later chapters will expand on all these points.

The chapter also examined characteristics of the colonies' political economy that shaped worker organisation. The Australian colonies are an exemplar of how critical the state was in building a capitalist society. Convict transportation simultaneously mitigated social pressures and dislocation associated with industrialisation in the UK and aided the capital accumulation process; it provided a cheap workforce to build infrastructure and form the 'sweat and toil' backbone for initiating industries serving broader imperial interests. Free-labour was critical to maritime-related activities (merchant shipping and whaling) and from the 1830s free immigrants—most receiving state-sponsored passage assistance—transitioned the workforce, progressively replacing convict labour in the older colonies (NSW and VDL) and building free colonies (Western Australia, South Australia and what was to become Victoria and Queensland). These newer free colonies benefited from the infrastructure and trading links created by convict-built NSW and VDL, a point perhaps reinforced by the struggling free colony of Western Australia though other factors like its more extreme climate played a part in its travails. Government land distribution policies (not just the Wakefield scheme) were also critical in shaping the capitalist mode of production, distribution of wealth and labour market in the colonies.

Australia was by the dictates of location, climate, soils, the transplanting of existing socio-economic hierarchies, dependent on links to Britain, and with local power elites ensuring pastoral/farming activities were large and relatively capital intensive. It was a society shaped by big capital. Small settler-farmers, like Edwin and Anne Parrish who left the Midlands (paying their own fare) to begin farming at Foxground south of Sydney in 1849, played a relatively inconspicuous role compared to North America and New Zealand. The number of settler-farmers increased in the 1850s typified by John and Betsy Shephard who left Huntingdonshire for the Coffs Harbour District. Nonetheless, the trajectory of capital-intensive development applied to most export industries that developed after 1850. Gold exports in the early to mid-1850s were sufficient for Britain to pay off its foreign debt, indicative of the growing economic importance of the Australian colonies globally. The next chapter examines the regulatory struggle that provides an important if neglected context for understanding worker mobilisation.

Notes

1 Commons, J R and associates (1918) *History of Labour in the United States*, Vol. 1, McMillan, New York.
2 Webb, S. and Webb, B. (1907) *The History of Trade Unionism*, Longman Green & Co, London, 1.
3 Webb, S. and Webb, B. (1907) *The History of Trade Unionism*, 3–11.

4 Most clearly explicated in Webb, S. and Webb, B. (1914) *Industrial Democracy*, Longman Green & Co, London; Cole, GDH (1920) *Self-Government in Industry*, G. Bell & Sons, London; and Goodrich, C. (1920) *The Frontier of Control: A Study in British Workplace Politics*, Harcourt, Brace & Howe, New York. See for example, Pelling, H. (1979 3rd ed) *A History of British Trade Unionism*, Penguin, Harmondsworth.

5 Sutcliffe, J. (1967 reprint) *A History of Trade Unionism in Australia*, Macmillan, Melbourne. For a former activist account see Murphy, W.E. (1896) *History of the Eight Hours Movement*, Spectator Publishing, Melbourne.

6 Thomas, L. (1919) *The Development of the Labour Movement in the Sydney District of New South Wales 1788–1848*, M.A. Thesis, University of Sydney; Terry, D. (1951) *The Development of the Labour Movement in New South Wales 1833–1846*, M.A. Thesis, University of Sydney; Hume, L. (1950) *The Labour Movement in New South Wales and Victoria: 1830–1860*, M.Ec. Thesis, University of Sydney; Crowley, F. (1949) *Working Class Conditions in Australia, 1788–1851*, Ph.D. Thesis, University of Melbourne; Hartwell, R.M. (1954) *The Economic Development of Van Diemen's Land 1820–1850*, Melbourne University Press, Melbourne.

7 Fox, A. (1985) *History and Heritage: The Social Origins of the British Industrial Relations System*, Allen & Unwin, London.

8 Dobson, C .R. (1980) *Masters and Journeymen: A Pre History of Industrial Relations*, Croom Helm, London.

9 Leeson, R. A. (1980) *Travelling Brothers: The Six Centuries Road from Craft Fellowship to Trade Unionism*, Granada, London.

10 Lis, C., Lucassen, J. and Soly, H. eds. (1994) Before the Unions: Wage Earners and Collective Action in Europe, 1300–1850, *International Review of Social History*, 39(Supplement):1–194.

11 See for example Dekker, R. (1990) Labour Conflicts and Working Class Culture in Early Modern Holland, *International Review of Social History*, 35:377–420; Rosenbland, L. (1999) Social Capital in the Early Industrial Revolution, *The Journal of Interdisciplinary History*, 29(3):435–457; Ferguson, D. (2000) The Body, the Corporate Idiom, and the Police of the Unincorporated Worker in Early Modern Lyons, *French Historical Studies*, 23(4):545–575.

12 Lucassen, J. (1994) The Other Proletarians: Seasonal Labourers, Mercenaries and Miners, *International Review of Social History*, 39(Supplement):171–194.

13 Kocka, J. (2001) How Can One Make Labour History Interesting Again? *European Review*, 9(2):201–212.

14 Hobsbawm, E. and Rudè, G. (1972) *Captain Swing*, Penguin, Harmondsworth.

15 See for example, Hill, C. (1991) *Change and Continuity in Seventeenth Century England*, Yale University Press, New Haven.

16 Rudè, G. (1964) *The Crowd in History: A Study of Popular Disturbances in France and England 1730–1848*, John Wiley & Sons, New York.

17 Thompson, E. (1991) *Customs in Common*, Merlin Press, London, 187–188.

18 Thompson, E. (1968) *The Making of the English Working Class*, Penguin, Harmondsworth.

19 Thompson, E. (1991) *Customs in Common*.

20 See also Thompson, E. (1977) The Crime of Anonymity, in Hay, D., Linebaugh, P., Rule, J., Thompson, E. and Winslow, C. eds. *Albion's Fatal Tree: Crime and Society in Eighteenth Century England*, Penguin, Harmondsworth, 255–308.

21 See for example Brody, D. (1960) *Steelworkers in America: The Nonunion Era*, Harvard University Press, New York; Montgomery, D. (1995) Wage Labor, Bondage, and Citizenship in Nineteenth-Century America, *International Labor and Working-Class History*, 48:6–27; Montgomery, D. (2004) *Black Workers Struggle for Equality in Birmingham*, University of Illinois Press, Champaign.

28   Reconsidering the Collective Impulse and the Colonial Context

22 Shorter, E. and Tilly, C. (1974) *Strikes in France 1830–1968*, Cambridge University Press, London.
23 Shorter, E. and Tilly, C. (1974) *Strikes in France 1830–1968*, 174–193.
24 Reichard, R. (1991) *From the Petition to the Strike: A History of Strikes Germany, 1869–1914*, Peter Lang, New York.
25 See for example, Rediker, M. (1987) *Between the Devil and the Deep Blue Sea: Merchant Seamen, Pirates and the Anglo-American World, 1700–1750*, Cambridge University Press, Cambridge and Fingard, J. (1982) *Jack in Port*, University of Toronto Press, Toronto.
26 Dublin, T. (1981) *Women at Work: The Transformation of Work and Community in Lowell Massachusetts 1826–1860*, Columbian University Press, New York.
27 Cooper-Busch, B. (1994) *Whaling Will Never Do for Me: The American Whaleman in the Nineteenth Century*, University Press of Kentucky, Lexington.
28 Way, P. (1993) *Common Labour: Workers and the Digging of North American Canals 1780–1860*, Cambridge University Press, Cambridge.
29 Humphries, J. (2010) *Childhood and Child Labour in the British Industrial Revolution*, Cambridge University Press, Cambridge.
30 Cox, O. (1948) *Race, Caste and Class*, Monthly Review Press, New York.
31 See for example Schweninger, D. (1991) The Underside of Slavery: The Internal Economy, Self-hire, and Quasi-freedom in Virginia, 1780–1865, *Slavery & Abolition*, 12(2):1–22; Chinea, J. (1996) Race, Colonial Exploitation and West Indian Immigration in Nineteenth-Century Puerto Rico, 1800–1850, *The Americas*, 52(4):495–519; Vink, M. (2003) "The World's Oldest Trade": Dutch Slavery and Slave Trade in the Indian Ocean in the Seventeenth Century, *Journal of World History*, 14(2):131–177; Proctor, F. (2003) Afro-Mexican Slave Labor in the Obrajes de Panos of New Spain, Seventeenth and Eighteenth Centuries, *The Americas*, 60(1):33–58; Harris, L. (2004) Slavery, Emancipation and Class Formation in Colonial and Early National New York City, *Journal of Urban History*, 30(3):339–359; Carter, M. (2006) Slavery and Unfree-labour in the Indian Ocean, *History Compass*, 4(5):800–813; Roberts, J. (2013) *Slavery and the Enlightenment in the British Atlantic, 1750–1807*, Cambridge University Press, New York; Allen, R. (2014) Slaves, Convicts, Abolitionism and the Global Origins of the Post-Emancipation Indentured Labor System, *Slavery & Abolition*, 35(2):328–348.
32 Banton, M. (2004) The British Caribbean, 1823–1838: The Transition from Slave to Free Legal Status, in Hay, D. and Craven, P. eds. *Masters, Servants and Magistrates*, University of North Carolina Press, Chapel Hill, 303–322.
33 Campbell, G. and Alpers, E. (2004) Introduction: Slavery, Forced Labour and Resistance in Indian Ocean Africa and Asia, *Slavery & Abolition*, 25(2):IX-XXVII.
34 Kay, M. and Cary, L. (1976) "The Planters Suffer Little or Nothing": North Carolina Compensations for Executed Slaves, 1748–1772, *Source: Science & Society*, 40(3):288–306.
35 Lack, P. (1982) An Urban Slave Community: Little Rock, 1831–1862, *The Arkansas Historical Quarterly*, 41(3):258–287; Bush, B. (1984) Towards Emancipation: Slave Women and Resistance to Coercive Labour Regimes in the British West Indian Colonies, 1790–1838, *Slavery & Abolition*, 5(3):222–243; Beckles, H. (1985) From Land to Sea: Runaway Barbados Slaves and Servants, 1630–1700, *Slavery & Abolition*, 6(3):79–94; Handler, J. (1997) Escaping Slavery in a Caribbean Plantation Society: Marronage in Barbardos, 1650s-1830s, *New West Indian Guide*, 71(3):183–225; Kyles, P. (2008) Resistance and Collaboration: Political Strategies Within the Afro-Carolinian Slave Community, 1700–1750, *The Journal of African American History*, 93(4):497–508.

36 Morris, R. (1948) Labor Controls in Maryland in the Nineteenth Century, *The Journal of Southern History*, 14(3):385–400; Bly, A. (2012) A Prince Among Pretending Free Men: Runaway Slaves in Colonial New England Revisited, *Massachusetts Historical Review*, 14:87–118.
37 Wood, B. (1987) Some Aspects of Female Resistance to Chattel Slavery in Low County Georgia 1763–1815, *The Historical Journal*, 30(3):603–622: Rashid, I. (1998) "Do Dady Nor Lef Me Make Dem Carry Me": Slave Resistance and Emancipation in Sierra Leone, 1894–1928, *Slavery & Abolition*, 19(2):208–231; Nash, G. (1998) Reverberations of Haiti in the American North: Black Saint Dominguans in Philadelphia, *A Journal of Mid-Atlantic Studies*, 65:44–73.
38 Levy, C. (1970) Slavery and the Emancipation Movement in Barbados 1650–1833, *The Journal of Negro History*, 55(1):1–14; Gaspar, D. (1978) The Antigua Slave Conspiracy of 1736: A Case Study of the Origins of Collective Resistance, *The William and Mary Quarterly*, 35(2):308–323.
39 Mandel, B. (1953) Slavery and the Southern Workers, *The Negro History Bulletin*, 17(3):57–62; Montgomery, D. (1979) *Workers' Control in America: Studies in the History of Work, Technology, and Labor Struggles*, Cambridge University Press, New York; S. Foner, P. and Lewis, R. eds., (1980) *The Black Worker: A Documentary History from Colonial Times to the Present*, Temple University Press, Philadelphia; Trotter Jr., J. (1994) African-American Workers: New Directions in U.S. Labor Historiography, *Labor History*, 35(4):495–523: Grivno, M. (2007) *"There Slavery Cannot Dwell": Agriculture and Labor in Northern Maryland, 1790–1860*, Ph.D. Thesis, University of Maryland.
40 Hay, D. (1977) Property, Authority and the Criminal Law, in Hay, D., Linebaugh, P., Rule, J., Thompson, E. and Winslow, C. eds. *Albion's Fatal Tree: Crime and Society in Eighteenth Century England*, 17–63.
41 Maxwell-Stewart, H. (2010) Convict Transportation from Britain and Ireland 1615–1870, *History Compass*, 8(11):1221–1242.
42 Nicholas, S. ed. (1988) *Convict Workers: Reinterpreting Australia's Past*, Cambridge University Press, Cambridge.
43 Usner, D. (1979) African Captivity to American Slavery: The Introduction of Black Laborers to Colonial Louisiana, *Louisiana History*, 20(1):25–48.
44 Prison labour didn't disappear; see McLennan, R. (2009) *The Crisis of Imprisonment: Protest, Politics, and the Making of the American Penal State, 1776–1941*, Cambridge University Press, Cambridge.
45 Nicholas, S. and Shergold, P. (1988) "Transportation as Global Migration" and "Convicts as Migrants", in Nicholas, S. ed. *Convict Workers: Reinterpreting Australia's Past*, 28–61; and Anderson, C. (1997) The Genealogy of the Modern Subject: Indian Convicts in Mauritius 1814–1853, in Duffield, I. and Bradley, J. eds. *Representing Convicts: New Perspectives on Convict Forced Labour Migration*, 164–182.
46 Morgan, G. and Rushton, P. (2003) Running Away and Returning Home: The Fate of English Convicts in the American Colonies, *Crime, Histoire & Sociétés*, 7(2):61–80.
47 Morgan, K. (1989) Convict Runaways in Maryland, 1745–1775, *Journal of American Studies*, 23(2):253–268.
48 Atkinson, A. (1979) Four Patterns of Convict Protest, *Labour History*, 37:28–51.
49 See Oxley, D. (1996) *Convict Maids: The Forced Migration of Women to Australia*, Cambridge University Press, Cambridge; and Duffield, I. and Bradley, J. eds.(1998) *Representing Convicts: New Perspectives on Convict Forced Labour Migration*, Leicester University Press, London.
50 See Nichol, W. (1984) Malingering and Convict Protest, *Labour History*, 47:18–27; Walsh, B. (2007) *Heartbreak and Hope, Deference and Defiance on the Yimmang: Tocal's Convicts 1822–1840*, Ph.D. thesis, University of Newcastle, 237.

51 Oxley, D. (1997) Representing Convict Women, in Duffield, I. and Bradley, J. eds. *Representing Convicts: New Perspectives on Convict Forced Labour Migration*, 89.

52 Maxwell-Stewart, H. (1990) *The Bushrangers and the Convict System of Van Diemen's Land, 1803–1846*, Ph.D. Thesis, University of Edinburgh.

53 McQueen, H. (1968) Convicts and Rebels, *Labour History*, 15:3–30; Dunning, T. and Maxwell-Stewart, H. (2002) Mutiny at Deloraine: Ganging and Convict Resistance in 1840's Van Diemen's Land, *Labour History*, 82:35–47.

54 Hay, D. and Craven, P. eds. (2004) *Masters, Servants, and Magistrates in Britain and the Empire, 1562–1955*, University of North Carolina Press, Chapel Hill.

55 ILO (2016) *Non-standard Employment Around the World: Understanding Challenges, Shaping Prospects*, International Labour Office, Geneva.

56 Salinger, S. (1981) Colonial Labor in Transition: The Decline of Indentured Servitude in Late Eighteenth-Century Philadelphia, *Labor History*, 22(2):165–191; Salinger, S. (1983) Artisans, Journeymen, and the Transformation of Labor in Late Eighteenth-Century Philadelphia, *The William and Mary Quarterly*, 40(1):62–84.

57 Prude, J. (1991) To Look upon the "Lower Sort": Runaway Ads and the Appearance of Unfree Laborers in America, 1750–1800, *The Journal of American History*, 78(1):124–159; Haygood, T. (2014) *Slavery White: A Study of Runaway Servants in Eighteenth-Century Virginia*, M.A. Thesis, Appalachia State University, Boone NC.

58 Righi, B. (2010) *The Right of Petition: Cases of Indentured Servants and Society in Colonial Virginia, 1698–1746*, M.A. Thesis, College of William and Mary, Virginia.

59 Behal, R. and Mohapatra, P. (1992) "Tea and Money versus Human Life": The Rise and Fall of the Indenture System in the Assam Tea Plantations 1840–1908, *The Journal of Peasant Studies*, 19(3–4):142–172.

60 Dorsey, J. (2004) Identity, Rebellion, and Social Justice Among Chinese Contract Workers in Nineteenth-Century Cuba, *Latin American Perspectives*, 31(3):18–47; Stanziani, A. (2013) Beyond Colonialism: Servants, Wage Earners and Indentured Migrants in Rural France and on Reunion Island (c. 1750–1900), *Labor History*, 54(1):64–87.

61 See for example Baak, P. (1999) About Enslaved Ex-Slaves, Uncaptured Contract Coolies and Unfreed Freedmen: Some Notes about "Free" and "Unfree" Labour in the Context of Plantation Development in Southwest India, Early Sixteenth Century-Mid 1990s, *Modern Asian Studies*, 33(1):121–157; Gordon, A. (2001) Contract Labour in Rubber Plantations: Impact of Smallholders in Colonial Southeast Asia, *Economic and Political Weekly*, 36(10):847–860; Banivanua-Mar, T. (2007) *Violence and Colonial Dialogue: The Australian-Pacific Indentured Labour Trade*, University of Hawaii Press, Honolulu; Anderson, C. (2009) Convicts and Coolies: Rethinking Indentured Labour in the Nineteenth Century, *Slavery & Abolition*, 30(1):93–109; Speedy, K. (2009) Who Were the Reunion "Coolies" of 19th-Century New Caledonia?, *The Journal of Pacific History*, 44(2):123–140.

62 Saunders, K. (1979) Troublesome Servants, *The Journal of Pacific History*, 14(3):168–183; Gupta, R. (1992) Plantation Labour in Colonial India, *The Journal of Peasant Studies*, 19(3–4):173–198.

63 For exceptions, see Graves, A. (1993) *Cane and Labour: The Political Economy of the Queensland Sugar Industry 1862–1905*, Edinburgh University Press, Edinburgh; Kaur, A. (2004) *Wage Labour in Southeast Asia Since 1840*, Palgrave McMillan, Basingstoke.

64 Not least being issues of race though not all convicts were European. See for example Yang, A. (2003) Indian Convict Workers in Southeast Asia in the

Late Eighteenth and Early Nineteenth Centuries, *Journal of World History*, 14(2):179–208.

65 A point made by others like Eltis, D. (1993) Labour and Coercion in the English Atlantic World from the Seventeenth to the Early Twentieth Century, *Slavery & Abolition*, 14(1):207–226.

66 Linebaugh, P. and Rediker, M. (1990) The Many-Headed Hydra: Sailors, Slaves, and the Atlantic Working Class in the Eighteenth Century, *Journal of Historical Sociology*, 3(3):225–252; Christopher, E. (2004) "Ten Thousand Times Worse Than the Convicts": Rebellious Sailors, Convict Transportation and the Struggle for Freedom, 1787–1800, *Journal of Australian Colonial History*, 5:30–46. For a similar argument regarding sailors in African slave trade and soldiers see Christopher, E. (2004) Another Head of the Hydra? *Atlantic Studies*, 1:2, 145–157.

67 McCoy, M. (2007) Absconding Servants, Anxious Germans and Angry Sailors: Working People and the Making of the Philadelphia Election Riot of 1742, *Pennsylvania History*, 74(4):427–451.

68 Steinfeld, S. (1991) *The Invention of Free-labour: The Employment Relation in English and American Law and Culture, 1350–1870*, University of North Carolina Press, Chapel Hill; Tomlins, C. (1993) *Law, Labor and Ideology in the Early American Republic*, Cambridge University Press, Cambridge; and Hay, D. and Craven, P. eds. (2004) *Masters, Servants, and Magistrates in Britain and the Empire*.

69 See for example Phillips, N. (2013): Unfree-labour and Adverse Incorporation in the Global Economy: Comparative Perspectives on Brazil and India, *Economy and Society*, 42(2):171–196; Gilmore, K. (2000) Slavery and Prison-Understanding the Connections, *Social Justice*, 27(3):195–205.

70 As did the environmental degradation it wrought. See Moore, J. (2003) Nature and the Transition from Feudalism to Capitalism, *Review*, 26(2):97–172.

71 Bennett, J. (2010) Compulsory Service in Late Medieval England, *Past & Present*, 209:7–51.

72 Hilton, R.H. (1974) *The English Peasantry in the Late Middle Ages*, Clarendon, Oxford; Cohn, S. (2007) After the Black Death: Labour Legislation and Attitudes Towards Labour in Late-Medieval Western Europe, *Economic History Review*, 60(3):457–485. Hilton, R.H. (1974) *The English Peasantry in the Late Middle Ages*, Clarendon, Oxford.

73 Vallance, E. (2009) *A Radical History of Britain*, Little, Brown Book Group, London, 47–99.

74 Hay, D. and Craven, P. (2004) Introduction, in Hay and Craven eds. *Masters, Servants and Magistrates*, 6.

75 Stanziani, A. (2013) Local Bondage in Global Economies: Servants, Wage Earners, and Indentured Migrants in Nineteenth-Century France, Great Britain, and the Mascarene Islands, *Modern Asian Studies*, 47(4):1218–1251; Rugemer, E. (2013) The Development of Mastery and Race in the Comprehensive Slave Codes of the Greater Caribbean During the Seventeenth Century, *The William and Mary Quarterly*, 70(3):429–458; Croucher, R. and Didier, M. (2014) "Legal at the Time?": Companies, Governments and Reparations for Mauritian Slavery, *Journal of African Law*, 58(1):89–108.

76 See Hay and Craven eds. (2004) *Masters, Servants and Magistrates*.

77 See chapters by Hay, Tomlins, Craven and Quinlan in particular in Hay and Craven (2004) *Masters, Servants and Magistrates*.

78 Hay and Craven (2004) *Masters, Servants and Magistrates*.

79 Kornblith, G. (1990) The Artisanal Response to Capitalist Transformation, *Journal of the Early Republic*, 10(3):315–321.

80 Calhoun, C. (1993) "New Social Movements" of the Early Nineteenth Century, *Social Science History*, 17(3):385–427.

81 Johnstone, R., McCrystal, S., Nossar, I., Quinlan, M., Rawling, M. and Riley, J. (2012) *Beyond Employment: The Legal Regulation of Work Relationships*, Federation Press, Sydney.

82 Dyer, C. (2009) *The French Explorers and Sydney*, University of Queensland Press, St Lucia, 39–40.

83 Butlin, N. (1994) *Forming a Colonial Economy: Australia 1810–1850*, Cambridge University Press, Cambridge, 34.

84 Butlin, N. (1994) *Forming a Colonial Economy: Australia 1810–1850*, 38.

85 Butlin, N. (1994) *Forming a Colonial Economy: Australia 1810–1850*, 38–39.

86 Morrissey, S. (1970) The Pastoral Economy 1821–1850, in Griffin, J. ed. *Essays in Economic History of Australia*, Jacaranda Press, Milton Qld, 84.

87 Duffield, I. and Bradley, J. (1997) Introduction: Representing Convicts?, in Duffield, I. and Bradley, J. eds. *Representing Convicts: New Perspectives on Convict Forced Labour Migration*, 3.

88 Colonial Land and Emigration Commissioners' report reproduced in *The Australian*, 17 February 1844.

89 Cloth-making was occurring at the Parramatta Female Factory by 1810. *HRNSW 1809–11*, 27 October 1810, 437. For detailed studies of several activities see Robbins, W. (2001) *The Management of Convict Labour Employed by New South Wales Government, 1788–1830*, Ph.D. Thesis, University of NSW and Rosen, S. (2006) "That Den of Infamy, the No. 2 Stockade Cox's River", *An Historical Investigation into the Construction, in the 1830s, of the Western Road from Mt Victoria to Bathurst by a Convict Workforce*, Ph.D. Thesis, University of Western Sydney.

90 Karskens, G. (1986) Defiance, Deference and Diligence: Three Views of Convicts in New South Wales Road-gangs, *Australian Historical Archaeology*, 4:17–28.

91 Morrissey, S. (1970) The Pastoral Economy 1821–1850, 63.

92 Phillips, D. (1970) Development Under Macquarie, in Griffin, J. ed. *Essays in Economic History of Australia*, Jacaranda Press, Milton Qld, 33–37.

93 Morrissey, S. (1970) The Pastoral Economy 1821–1850, 55.

94 Mills, J. (2016) *The Contribution of The Whaling Industry to the Economic Development of the Australian Colonies: 1770–1850*, Ph.D. Thesis, University of Queensland, St Lucia; Dyster, B. (1979) John Griffiths, Speculator, *Tasmanian Historical Research Association Papers and Proceedings*, 27(1):20–29.

95 Morrissey, S. (1970 2nd ed) The Pastoral Economy 1821–1850, 55–60.

96 Barnard, A. (1958) *The Australian Wool Market 1840–1900*, Melbourne University Press, Melbourne.

97 Morrissey, S. (1970 2nd ed) The Pastoral Economy 1821–1850, 90.

98 Maxwell-Stewart, H. (2008) *Closing Hell's Gate*, Allen & Unwin, Sydney, 144–149.

99 Ritchie, J. ed. (1971) *The Evidence to the Bigge Reports: New South Wales Under Governor Macquarie, Volume 2: The Written Evidence*, Heinemann, Melbourne.

100 Dyster, B. (2007) Bungling a Courthouse, *Journal of the Royal Australian Historical Society*, 93(1):1–21.

101 Dyster, B. (1987) A Series of Reversals, Male Convicts in NSW 1821–31, *Push from the Bush*, 25:18–36.

102 Dyster, B. (2007) Bungling a Courthouse, 21.

103 Maxwell-Stewart (2008) *Closing Hell's Gates*, 152.

104 Morrissey, S. (1970 2nd ed) The Pastoral Economy 1821–1850, 52–53.

105 Morrissey, S. (1970 2nd ed) The Pastoral Economy 1821–1850, 76–78.

106 Crowley, F. (1949) Working Class Conditions in Australia 1788–1851, 346–350.

107 Marx, K. (1867) *Das Kapital*, chapter 33 cited in Moss, J. (1985) *Sound of Trumpets: History of the Labour Movement in South Australia*, Wakefield Press, Adelaide, 37.
108 By 1890 one of the world's two most urbanised countries. Weber, A. (1899) *The Growth of Cities in the Nineteenth Century: A Study in Statistics*, Macmillan, New York.
109 *Inquirer* 12 September 1849.
110 Neal, D. (1987) Free Society, Penal Colony, Slave Society, Prison? *Historical Studies*, 22(89):497–518.
111 Hirst, J. (1983) *Convict Society and Its Enemies*, 54, 67.
112 AONSW CSO Reel 6058 4/1769, 129–129a.
113 *HRNSW*, Vol. 1 20 August 1789, 258 and 17 June 1790, 349.
114 Hirst, J. (1983) *Convict Society and Its Enemies*, Allen & Unwin, Sydney, 34–35.
115 Hirst, J. (1983) *Convict Society and Its Enemies*, 45.
116 Dyster, B. (1979) Argentine and Australian Development Compared, *Past and Present*, 84:91–110.
117 Dyster, B. (1996) Why New South Wales Did Not Become Devil's Island (or Siberia), in Dyster, B. ed. *Beyond Convict Workers*, Department of Economic History, University of NSW.
118 Hirst, J. (1983) *Convict Society and Its Enemies*, 30, 51–52.
119 Hirst, J. (1983) *Convict Society and Its Enemies*, 53.
120 Maxwell-Stewart (2008) Closing Hell's Gates, 152–153.
121 Maxwell-Stewart (2008) Closing Hell's Gates, 155.
122 See for example LC83–1–5 Campbell Town 15 March 1841.
123 LC390–1–1Oatlands 1–4 March 1844.
124 LC247–1–1Hobart 6 October 1821.
125 Hirst, J. (1983) *Convict Society and Its Enemies*, 65–66.
126 Crowley, F. (1949) Working Class Conditions in Australia 1788–1851, 452–53.
127 *Trumpeter* 3 November 1835.
128 Crowley, F. (1949) Working Class Conditions in Australia 1788–1851, 336.
129 Cullen, R. (2012) Empire, Indian Indentured Labour and the Colony: The Debate over "Coolie" Labour in New South Wales, 1836–1838, *History Australia*, 9(1):84–109.
130 *Sydney Morning Herald* 3 December 1846.
131 One reason was the imperial government had designated the Australian colonies for European settlement. Quinlan, M. and Levertracy, C. (1990) From Labour Market Exclusion to Industrial Solidarity Australian Trade Union Responses to Asian Workers, 1830–1988, *Cambridge Journal of Economics*, 14(2):159–181 and Crowley, F. (1949) Working Class Conditions in Australia 1788–1851, 417–420.
132 For such a case involving a bootmaker's apprentice see *Adelaide Observer* 30 March 1850.
133 Crowley, F. (1949) Working Class Conditions in Australia 1788–1851, 481–482.
134 Morrissey, S. (1970 2nd ed) The Pastoral Economy 1821–1850, 64–65, 86–89.
135 Morrissey, S. (1970 2nd ed) The Pastoral Economy 1821–1850, 68–70.
136 Morrissey, S. (1970 2nd ed) The Pastoral Economy 1821–1850, 89.
137 Dow, G. (1974) *Samuel Terry: The Botany Bay Rothschild*, Sydney University Press.
138 Steven, M. (1965) *Merchant Campbell 1769–1846*, Cambridge University Press, Melbourne.
139 Walsh, B. (2007) Heartbreak and Hope, Deference and Defiance on the Yimmang, 212, 231.
140 *Hobart Town Courier* 3 June 1842.

141 Collins, D. (1798) *An Account of the English Colony of New South Wales*, Cadel and Davies, London; Cunningham, P. (1827) *Two Years in New South Wales*, Henry Colburn, London; Moore, G.F. (1884) *Diary of Ten Years Eventful Life of an Early Settler in Western Australia*, M. Walbrook, London, 91.
142 See for example, Roberts, A. (2008) *Marine Officer Convict Wife: The Johnston's of Annandale*, Annandale Urban Research Association, Sydney.
143 Irving, T. (2006) *The Southern Tree of Liberty: The Democratic Movement in New South Wales Before 1856*, Federation Press, Sydney.
144 Maxwell-Stewart, H. (2016) Big Data and Australian History, *Australian Historical Studies*, 47(3):359–364 and Maxwell-Stewart, H. (2016) The State, Convicts and Longitudinal Analysis, *Australian Historical Studies*, 47(3):414–429.
145 For details on the database see Quinlan, M. and Gardner, M. (1994) Researching Industrial Relations History: The Development of a Database on Australian Trade Unions 1825–1900, *Labour History*, 66:90–113; Quinlan, M. and Gardner, M. (1995) Strikes, Worker Protest and Union Growth in Canada and Australia 1801–1900, *Labour/Le Travail*, 36:175–208; Quinlan, M., Gardner, M. and Akers, P. (2003) Reconsidering the Collective Impulse: Formal Organisation and Informal Associations Amongst Workers in the Australian Colonies1795–1850, *Labour/Le Travail*, 52:137–180.

2   Law, the Courts and Inequality at Work

Introduction

Previous research on the history of worker organisation has commonly made limited reference to the regulatory framework governing work and labour markets more generally, focusing on laws used against unions and those social-protection laws unions helped to secure like minimum labour-standard/industrial relations, workers compensation, mining and factory laws. This book takes a different approach, arguing collective action by workers can only be understood when the centrality of the state and regulation is recognised. While anti-combination laws were important, master and servant laws, merchant-marine laws and laws regulating bonded labour, slaves and convicts were far more widely used to subordinate labour. These laws enshrined individualised employment arrangements in ways that advantaged capital. Nor were they a passing phase superseded by collective labour laws. The distinction between employment contracts and self-employment continues to be exploited by employers today. These laws were both used and contested. In the 19th century large numbers of workers were brought before the courts, charged and almost invariably convicted for not fully cooperating with their employers—in essence a failure to accept the inequality, indignity and exploitation associated with formal legal subordination. The laws didn't simply represent a tool to secure capitalist work relations; they became a source of struggle in their own right. Played out in the colonies from settlement, it involved both convict and free workers. Describing this struggle is essential to understanding worker mobilisation for several reasons, including that many of the issues and individual actions rapidly translated into collective action as workers tried to redress the power imbalance.

Regulating to Subordinate Workers

From their very founding, labour control was a central concern for the colonies. The UK regulatory framework was transposed to the colonies. Additionally early governors used their wide-ranging powers to introduce regulations, known as Government and General Orders, to fill gaps or better meet local conditions, notwithstanding some ambiguity as to their legal standing.[1] When colonies established legislative bodies, they rapidly enacted their own laws. Tables 2.1 and 2.2 summarise colonial labour regulation, indicating the breadth and frequency of regulatory activity. The Tables would be even 'busier' if lapsed bills were included. For the purposes of this

Table 2.1 Employment-Related General Orders and Regulations, NSW and VDL 1790–1827

*New South Wales**	*Van Diemen's Land (Tasmania)*
1791 Prohibit convicts selling rations or slops; Norfolk Island convict labour	
1795 Convict rations, hours of labour & assigned-convicts reside on farms, reapers wages and men to unload ships	
1796 Men to gather thatch, hours of work, recall of assigned-convicts, convict clothing issue	
1797 Wages determination, application for certificates of freedom, & Incendiarism	
1798 Hours of labour, seamen on shore	
1800 Employment, harbouring and convicts working for themselves; Assignment, masters duties & banning issue of spirits; Wages for reapers, sawyers and clearing ground	
1801 Seamen deserters or onshore after hours; hours of work; convict rations	
1802 Assignment & travel passes; Government stonemasons; Hours of labour	
1803 Status check to employ convicts; Wage rates; Convict absconding & passes	
1804 Free & convict absconding/employment; Wage rates for labour; Convict discipline/assignment; Harbouring ship deserters & penalties	
1805 Absconding on American vessels	
1806 Rations; Tickets-of-leave; Assignment conditions including wages; Crimping & desertion of seamen	
1807 Bans embarkation of Pacific Islanders; Newcastle port regulations	
1809 Hours of labour cut due to reduced rations; Musters	
1810 Hours of labour; Travel passes; Port regulations(desertion); General muster, tickets-of-leave & absconding convicts; Newcastle convicts	

	New South Wales*	Van Diemen's Land (Tasmania)
1811	Convict muster/discipline; Hours of labour; Tickets-of-leave & pardons	
1813	Assignment of females; Hire/discharge of females; Rations; Tickets-of-leave & pardons; Harbouring/employing absconders; Certificates of freedom; General muster; Female Factory	
1814	Assigned-servants & their masters; Evidence of status; Tickets-of-leave, Pardons; Passes & musters; King's birthday holiday	
1815	Assigned-convicts not to be returned except for crime or sick	
1816	Wages paid in Sterling; Harbour/ employing absconders; Winter work hours; Assigned-convict wages; Winter clothing; Muster documents	
1817	Starting time artifacers; Settlers & overseers issuing travel passes; Absence of convicts from masters	
1818	Sunday musters; JPs adjudicate work disputes; Single JP & corporal punishment; Orphan apprentices; Gang hours; Constables pay; Sunday musters	Rations & hours; Extends NSW 1816 Order re: pay in Sterling and harvest wages to VDL
1819	Time for breakfast/dinner; Barracks & absconding; Rations scale female factory; Rations scale EMU plains; Port Regulations; Convict accommodation	
1820	JP instructions assignment/sentences; Road-gang discharge to serve settlers; Convict absconding/piracy; Musters; Voyage ration arrears compensation	Masters need vigilance re: assigned-convicts
1821	Employment of Labourers; Assigning convict mechanics	
1822	Desertion/absconding	Ticket-of-leave harvest wage demands/sets wages; Muster
1823	Regulations re: Bathurst; Newcastle hours & conditions; reiterates 1813 absconding order;	
1824	Employment of mechanics & ploughmen etc; Convicts sent to treadmill; Working hours Moreton Bay; Rewards for apprehending ship deserters	
1825	Employment of convicts; Ban young boys from clearing gangs; Convicts mechanics; Apprehension rewards for runaways	Harbouring absconding convicts; Government officers; Powers to punish convicts; Convict grievance procedures

(Continued)

Table 2.1 (Continued)

New South Wales*	Van Diemen's Land (Tasmania)
1826 Notice re: convict conduct, absence & ill-treatment; Tickets-of-leave	
1827 Tickets-of-leave;	Ticket-of-leave holders harvest wage demands/sets wages

* Covered areas which became Victoria until it separated in 1852 and Queensland which separated in 1859.

Note: Disallowed means law disallowed by British Authorities, generally as seen as repugnant to British notions of justice.

Table 2.2 Employment-Related Regulations and Laws: Australian Colonies 1828–50

	New South Wales*	South Australia	Van Diemen's Land (Tasmania)	Western Australia
1828	Master & servant; apprentices		Order re: harvest labour repeated	
1829	Orphan apprentices			Port regulations
1830	Road-gang rations notice		Absconding order; Convicts working for themselves; Convict discipline/ punishment	Order master & servants;
1831				Order returning absconders
1832	Orphan apprentices; Merchant seamen; Transportation including convict rations, clothing etc			Order returning offenders to master
1833	Magistrates Act			
1834	Orphan apprentices			
1835	Assignment regulations		Whalers	
1836				
1837		Master & servant (disallowed)	Master & servant (disallowed); Orphan apprentices; Merchant seamen	Notice re: resident mag's authority to discharge seamen

	New South Wales*	South Australia	Van Diemen's Land (Tasmania)	Western Australia
1838	Order re: convict Indulgences	Merchant seamen	Orphan apprentices; Whalers; Merchant seamen	
1839	Abolition female transportation			
1840	Master & servant; Merchant seamen (disallowed); Reporting absconding notice; Transportation & absconding Act	Whalers (disallowed)	Master & servant; Orphan apprentices	Master & servant (disallowed); Merchant seamen (disallowed); Whalers
1841	Transportation & JPs; Port regulations; Hard-labour for 2nd offences/ transportation; Tickets-of-leave regs; Female convicts; End assignment notice; Runaway convict rewards notice	Master & servant		Master & servant;
1842	Port regulations; Continued hard-labour	Merchant seamen		Master & servant; Orphan apprentices; Whalers
1843	Merchant seamen; Convicts in Sydney notice; Female Factory earnings	Whalers		
1844	Apprentices			Orphan apprentices
1845	Master & servant			
1846	Foreign/abandoned seamen; Tickets-of-leave; Pardons			Port regulations
1847	Master & servant; Crimping; Transportation	Master & servant	Passholder regulations	Whalers
1848	Merchant seamen; Moreton Bay muster	Apprentices	Crimping	
1849	Merchant seamen	Master & servant		
1850	Orphan apprentices			

book, it is only possible to make a few salient points about this complex and shifting web of regulation.

Convict Workers

The UK government enacted and periodically amended laws on convict transportation that mandated shipboard rations, required surgeons on transport-ships and set rules governing convict sentences. Imperial government also oversaw the system, including initiating inquiries into convict engagement and conditions like the Bigge Report (Chapter 1). Notwithstanding this, colonial Governors exercised considerable discretion regarding the use and treatment of convicts, including those assigned to private employers. The Governors of NSW (including Norfolk Island[2]) and VDL (when it separated from NSW) issued Orders and Notices setting hours of work, rations, payment of wages or 'indulgences' (additional rations of tea, sugar and tobacco) and discipline (see Table 2.1). By 1806 annual wage payments of £10 to assigned-convicts had been semi-formalised. The Governor also specifically rejected calls from some employers to punish their servants at their own 'discretion'—in other words without recourse to courts/magistrates like slaves—as 'equally impolitic as inhuman.'[3] Later Orders reinforced the last point.

Other Orders dealt with the issuing of travel passes, procedures for masters returning convicts, as well as regular musters of assigned-convicts and ticket-of-leave holders. Additional measures to control absence/absconding included large rewards for apprehension and the establishment of a dedicated 30-man police 'squad' in VDL in 1825.[4] Sabotage also attracted attention. In December 1797 Governor Hunter issued an Order against incendiarism after the house and harvest of a Concord settler (Mitcham) was destroyed by three men, two with blacked faces.[5]

In addition to Orders circulars were issued to magistrates to update/remind/advise them regarding regulations like one in 1816 instructing magistrates not to interfere with Government labour-gangs except in the case of criminal acts.[6] As convict labour morphed into free-labour via tickets-of-leave and conditional pardons, additional General Orders and Notices were issued dealing with the determination of wages paid (in Sterling) by settlers and empowering magistrates to adjudicate disagreements involving servants (see Table 2.1).[7] When NSW and VDL secured legislatures, they enacted laws dealing with transported convicts (including additional punishments) but Orders and Notices continued to be issued especially in VDL (Table 2.2).

Free-Labour

Governors issued Orders, Notices and Proclamations on free-labour in both penal and free colonies (South Australia and Western Australia). In 1795

Governor Hunter issued Orders specifying the rates for various categories of labour in an effort to contain wage demands by free-labour especially during harvests. While initiated at the behest of settlers, by 1797 Hunter was issuing additional orders to punish employers evading the limits. Hunter also complained of mutinous conduct amongst free workers and networking facilitated by illegal movements of convicts between districts, indicative of extensive informal worker bargaining over wages.[8] When Hawkesbury District settlers again petitioned for regulatory controls to dampen high wages in 1800, Hunter drily observed how readily employers broke these codes when it suited them.[9]

In the penal colonies some regulations made no clear distinction between convict and free-labour or specifically covered both like the NSW Proclamation of 1818 on settling disputes between masters and employees, convicts and free.[10] Instructions specific to particular regions were also issued, like those on free mechanics wages at Fort Dundas, Melville Island and working hours at the Moreton Bay in 1824.[11] The Western Australian Governor issued a Proclamation requiring indentures of imported agricultural workers to be registered and imposing substantial fines on employers hiring workers already engaged. The Governor also set rations and working hours (eight in summer and nine at other times) in March 1830 as well as establishing a part-time magistracy to adjudicate disputes.[12] All colonies rapidly introduced port regulations including provisions addressing desertion/insubordination amongst seamen. Those introduced by Governor Macquarie in 1810 directed that ship's deserters could, like convicts, be sentenced to public-works gangs and flogged (up to 31 lashes).[13] Flogging was removed when the Judge Advocate revised the regulations in 1819.[14]

From 1828 onwards as colonies established legislatures, laws regulating servants (widely defined), apprentices, seamen and whalers were enacted (see Table 2.2). There was a clustering of legislative activity during periods of labour shortage, notably 1840 and the early-1850s. In 1840 colonies introduced a raft of punitive master and servant and maritime labour laws (Table 2.2). British authorities ultimately disallowed most, deeming them too lopsided and contrary to English legal principles (excessive fines and prison sentences, arrest without warrant, or being tried before single part-time magistrate). Notwithstanding this, colonies enacted master and servant laws that were broader in coverage, using general definitions of workers, not nominated occupations as in English laws, and included some self-employed pieceworkers like sawyers and fencers. Penalties for offence like absconding were commonly heavier and provisions enabling workers to recover unpaid wages weaker.[15] Recalcitrant female servants, including domestics not covered by English law, were a particular target. For most workers financial costs prevented access to appeal provisions such as they existed.[16] These laws were an effort by landholders and employer-dominated legislatures to curb widespread absconding/dissent and secure obedience and deference. Colonial maritime labour laws adopted a similar approach commonly imposing heavier penalties including longer gaol terms than imperial laws—extended as long as six months by imprisoning seamen unable to pay heavy fines. The NSW *Water Police Act* (1840) established a state-inquisitorial enforcement regime, including arrest without warrant (a practice continuing years after the Act was disallowed) which several VDL laws also permitted. Three colonies passed separate laws to regulate whalers.[17]

The laws were not symbolic but implemented on a massive scale. However, the very harshness of these measures to enhance capital accumulation reinforced worker resistance.

Other Laws

A range of other laws regulated labour. Some came into play in the case of repeated offences like the VDL *Police Act*. Laws on assisted-immigration and employment contracts made outside the colonies sought to reinforce subordination of immigrants (Table 2.2). There were also regulations governing the civil service, police force, military and others employed by government like customs and boat crews. Another important body of laws/regulations set rates/charges, licensing and work practices amongst predominantly self-employed workers in transport like watermen, cab-drivers and water carters.[18]

Just as master and servant laws, convict Orders and the like acted to enshrine modes of production/labour subordination, other laws sought to protect property/capital from the actions of workers (like stealing food and incendiarism). In *Whigs and Hunters* and *Albion's Fatal Tree* Thompson and others like Doug Hay described how property-related capital offences grew in the 18th and early 19th century to protect the wealthy from the social dislocating consequences of their appropriations/exploitation.[19] Equally, in penal colonies composed principally of criminals/ex-criminals and where absconding in the harsh bush environment readily led to armed robbery as a means of survival, crimes against the property of the emerging wealthy were dealt with in a savage fashion. This included execution, flogging and being sentenced to grimmer secondary punishment settlements for theft, cattle duffing/sheep stealing. It entailed a new colony-specific capital offence for armed robbery on the road or in remote farms/settlements—bushranging.[20] The often small step between work-related dissent and a capital property offence is important to understanding labour discipline in the early period, along with the high ratio of constables (many ex-convicts) per head of population to detect crime.

The Scale of Regulatory Activity

Noteworthy is the sheer scale of regulatory activity, indicative not only of power imbalances within colonial society but also widespread resistance amongst workers. The enactment/revision of laws only captures part of this struggle. Records of the various Colonial Secretary's Office (the central administrative arm of colonial government) provide ample evidence of concerns about labour control as do colonial newspapers. In 1814 the *Sydney Gazette* lamented regular publication of absconding notices only served to indicate how widespread the problem was and how many managed to evade capture.[21] Litigation provides a further insight. To this attention now turns.

Situating Collective Action Within the Broader Context of Worker Dissent

Thompson observed the poor largely come to notice in historical records when they collide with the law. The pre-goldrush Australian colonies were replete with such collisions, hundreds of thousands of them, documented in convict conduct records, government gazettes, court bench-books and colonial newspapers. They provide a wealth of evidence on struggles over the inequality inherent in capitalist work arrangements.

Evidence on the scale of litigation is fragmentary but consistent and matches my own reading of over 100 bench-books. For VDL (around 75,000 convicts transported), Reid identified 1884 charges laid against 1344 female convicts brought before magistrates' courts between 1820 and 1839, with the vast majority being for work-related offences like absconding, disobedience, refusing work, neglect and insolence.[22] A study sampling 4% of the 73,000 individual convict conduct registers for VDL (1817–60) found that for the period to 1853 male convicts were brought before the courts on average over six times, mostly for work-related offences.[23] Even using the most conservative assumptions, extending these figures to all convicts transported to Australia would give an estimate of at least 200,000 work-related prosecutions.

There is evidence free workers were also prosecuted in large numbers, though aside from seamen, not to the same extent as convicts. Sifting surviving magistrates' bench-books Merritt estimated there were 58,410 master and servant cases in NSW between 1845 and 1860.[24] Australia-wide evidence suggests especially vigorous use of the laws in 1830s and 1840s followed by a gradual decline.[25] Extrapolating Merritt's NSW estimates to the rest of Australia would give a figure of at least 100,000 cases occurring prior to 1851. There are no comparable estimates for seamen and whalers charged under maritime labour laws, though bench-books reveal seamen being tried on a daily basis in larger ports like Hobart. During the NSW *Water Police Act's* short life (October 1840 to September 1843), 7278 cases were tried in the port of Sydney alone (excluding other ports like Newcastle).[26] While probably abnormal, later statistics indicate litigation levels remained high.[27] A conservative estimate would be of least 30,000 maritime labour cases being tried in Australian ports prior to 1851.

Taken together, these figures would suggest at least 330,000 employment-related cases between 1788 (European population 859) and 1850 (population

405,400). While further research is needed, the inescapable conclusion is that litigation over work was pervasive, involving large numbers of workers. Moreover, this only captures part of the struggle because, as press reports, diaries and other sources demonstrate, not all disputes went to court and litigation was less common or exceptional amongst some categories of workers.

Nor was it a struggle lacking calculation. Maxwell-Stewart's study of VDL convicts found evidence of tactics on both sides. Convicts with vocations for which there was little demand (like weavers), where supply exceeded demand (like tailors), who were assigned to unfamiliar physically demanding tasks (like land clearing), or who could easily be replaced were more likely to be prosecuted, receive corporal punishment and in larger doses.[28] Some employers used prosecution to 'turn over' less skilled workers and obtain replacements whilst litigation peaked in rural districts in summer when workers exploited competition for harvest/shearing labour. Harsh working conditions, especially on road/chain-gangs, also shaped patterns of dissent. Even those working in chains were twice as likely to abscond as assigned-servants.[29]

Similarly, Merritt found that free workers from a wide array of occupations were prosecuted but rural and domestic servants were most likely to be tried and this increased over time while prosecutions of journeymen declined. As for convicts, Merritt identified seasonal patterns in court use, with absconding being the most prosecuted offence (40% of cases in 1845–60) followed by refusal to work and absence without leave.[30] About 39% of convicted workers were gaoled with forfeiture of wages being the next most frequent penalty. The most common worker-initiated claim was for unpaid wages followed by ill-treatment of various types. Unlike worker offences, employers found guilty of these offences didn't risk gaol but only restitution and a fine. It was almost unknown even for employers assaulting workers to be gaoled. The imbalance in terms of obligations, offences and punishment was unequivocal, although Merritt found a shift towards worker-initiated claims (mainly unpaid wages) dominated litigation after 1850.[31] The situation of merchant seamen and whalers was, if anything, worse.[32]

Notwithstanding some important nuances, evidence indicates that colonial workers—be they convict or free—were tried in large numbers for neglecting or refusing work, insubordination, being absent, absconding/desertion other offences. As Chapter 4 will show, the vast majority engaging in collective dissent were charged with precisely the same offences rather than illegally combining, mutiny or conspiracy. For their part, workers used courts to complain of ill-treatment or unpaid wages. The remainder of this chapter will flesh out this struggle but has a related purpose. In *The Making of English Working Class* Thompson made considerable reference to the experience of individuals and groups of workers to demonstrate that class is not simply an objective set of conditions but a historical relationship experienced personally by the Luddite or displaced weaver.[33] Examining interactions with the judicial system provides insights into the inequality, injustice and day to day indignity working men, women and children experienced and reacted against. Court appearances capture a tiny fragment of workers' lives and experiences. However, it reveals something of issues and relationships that were the foundation for mobilisation and class identity.

The Courts as a Venue for Struggle

Courts have long played a central role in the subordination of labour, moving contested interests into an individualised regime of adjudication whereby capital is advantaged well before the hardly impartial decision-making processes of magistrates and judges are considered. Even when groups of workers took collective action through the courts or, more typically, were prosecuted, the legal process treated them as a collection of individuals (sometimes adjudicated by a test case) not as a group with shared interests. This aspect of the legal regime affected how rights, obligations and reciprocity were construed, what evidence was pertinent and how competing claims were weighed. As later chapters will demonstrate, testimony by a single employer usually trumped that of a group of workers. As an important aside, it was only the establishment of special industrial tribunals in Australia (for conciliation and arbitration) in the early 20th century that the right of workers to have a collective voice was recognised and even this avenue was severely weakened after 1980.

Courts played a particularly significant role in the period to 1850, affirming the subordination of workers on a daily basis. Examining this is essential to understanding why workers organised and the impediments they faced. Notwithstanding the stilted process, hearings revealed something of the underlying issues in dispute. To illustrate these and other points, a number of cases will be described. Historians have commonly studied either free or unfree-labour. However, like indentured workers and unlike slaves, convicts exercised legal rights and were not passive, even if the society and its legal apparatus were stacked against them. While the distinctions had important implications examined in later chapters, this chapter will point to commonalities—commonalities that enhance our understanding of worker mobilisation.

A Punitive Regime

The most striking feature of the regulatory regime was its one-sided and punitive character, indicative of the critical role of the state in subordinating labour/entrenching inequality at work. This applied to free and unfree-labour, men and women. Imprisonment for dissent was common and for convicts additional punishments included the stocks, solitary confinement on bread and water and flogging. On 26 January 1838 the Bothwell VDL Bench of Magistrates sentenced James Case, a free worker, to one month's gaol and mulcted £10 from his wages. A day later assigned-servant Thomas Gibson was ordered to receive 50 lashes and serve six months' hard-labour for disobedience and insolence.[34] Four days after, the Launceston Bench sentenced William West, seaman on the ship *Industry*, to two months' imprisonment for refusing work.[35] While flogging declined over time, severe prison sentences didn't.[36] In October 1849 probationer Mary Williams received 18 months' hard-labour for insubordination though shorter sentences of one to six months were more typical.[37] Female apprentices also faced the prospect of gaol. Mrs Windeyer's orphan apprentice girl was sentenced to 10 days' solitary confinement in the Parramatta Female Factory for insolence and refusing work—special cells having been recently completed for this purpose.[38]

Imprisonment was also common in the free colonies of South Australia and Western Australia. In June 1845 the Mount Barker bench of magistrates sentenced farm worker John Smallcomb to 42 days in Adelaide Gaol for refusing work and unauthorised absence.[39] The Bench told another rural worker, Thomas Coles, that he was lucky to be imprisoned only one month not three for deserting his service.[40] Coles's wife, who also deserted, escaped being charged. However, until the mid-1840s fractious female servants were frequently gaoled.

Both convicts and free workers could be returned to service after completing their sentence or seamen sent on board a ship ready to sail. Workers refusing to return went back to prison. In January 1848 a probationer-convict was sentenced to another three months gaol (thereafter to be returned to his employer) for refusing work after completing a two-month stint for the same offence.[41] Punishment might have a salutary effect but could as easily aggravate relations.

In terms of charges and punishments, two distinctions between convict and free should be identified. First, convicts were charged with insolence, an offence unknown under master and servant law. This difference shouldn't be exaggerated because masters often included insolence in their complaint against free servants and it could be readily deemed as misconduct or disobedience. Charging Peter Nightingale with neglecting duty, a Pitt Street, Sydney publican (Watkins) told the court Nightingale was 'generally insolent, but on Sunday was more so than usual, and wilfully spoiled the dinner.'[42] As Rediker has observed at sea, any verbal repost by seamen could be deemed mutinous conduct.[43] Language deemed insulting, disrespectful or unacceptable was a one-way street. *Bengal Merchant* seaman William Rayner told the Bench he refused work after being told 'to go the devil' by the chief mate. The presiding magistrate expressed 'surprise at his delicacy, thinking that he must have heard lingo somewhat similar on board whatever ship he had sailed in.'[44]

The dispute wasn't about plain talking but deference. When assigned-convict Sarah Bellium charged that her employer's daughter had called her a 'strumpet' and 'government whore', the charge was rapidly dismissed on the evidence of daughter and father.[45] This helps explain the rarity of such complaints and provides yet another example of the fundamental asymmetry of the legal process. Despite this, workers weren't passive. In March 1844 (Charles Guthrie) complained to the George Town Bench that probation passholder William Fraser had called him a 'bloody rascal and tyrannical bugger.'[46] Pricking the airs and graces of employers, especially important landholders like Edward Archer, usually resulted in a quick repost from the local bench. When Archer refused to accept his memorial, convict James Edwards told him 'you pretend to be gentleman, you're no gentleman'—three months in chains for insolence.[47]

Second, another important distinction between convict and free related to some punishments inflicted on the former, particularly flogging with the notorious cat of nine tails—each cord including a series of stiffened knots. While an especially common punishment for those in gangs and in penal settlements it was regularly applied against rural workers and others.[48] Stripped to the waist and bound to a wooden frame the victim received their punishment over a period of an hour or longer for 50 or more lashes from a specialist flagellator. Weakened offenders received it in instalments or on the 'breach'. Flogging stripped skin and even pieces of flesh—to the bone in some cases—from the back, resulting in weeks of agony and permanent scarring. Like public executions—only abandoned in the 1840s—it wasn't uncommon for flogging to be administered before other convicts to strike fear/secure obedience.[49] Free workers couldn't be flogged but even here there were exceptions. Deserting seamen were flogged prior to 1819. Decades later, the VDL *Police Act* empowered courts to sentence workers to a road-gang for second offences where, as felons, they could be flogged for misbehaviour (see Chapter 4).

The scale and array of punishments changed over time. Use of lash and the number of strokes inflicted slowly declined as did use of the gaol penalty for free workers from the mid-1840s with a corresponding greater use of fines. While important, these changes do not significantly affect central themes being developed in this chapter. The array and severity-range of punishments, together with the willingness of courts to respond to intercessions by employers when sentencing, gave the latter enormous latitude to subordinate workers, to mete out harsher treatment for ringleaders or downgrade punishment to a reprimand for others. These decisions and intercessions clearly demonstrated employers' controlling power.

Food, Clothing, 'Indulgences' and Wages

A recurring cause of complaint amongst convicts, free rural workers and seamen was the quality and amount of rations provided. By the early 1820s complaints over rations and mistreatment on convict gangs were being regularly referred to government authorities.[50] The *Sydney Monitor* observed road and chain-gang absconders 'always state as a reason for their so doing, the shortness of their ration, and the bad usage they receive from their overseers.'[51] Government-stipulated rations could be slow to arrive or be cut by corrupt overseers colluding with contractor-suppliers.[52] Reporting corruption also risked costly retribution as Sergeant Kelly, 23rd Regiment sent to Carters Barracks for insubordination discovered.[53] Scant/inadequate clothing/footwear was another recurring issue.[54] Complaints were not confined to gangs. William Cook asked John Dalby for extra rations stating otherwise he would go out begging—seven days solitary confinement.[55] Aggrieved workers could lodge complaints before magistrates, superior officials in the case of road-gangs or the Superintendent of Convicts. However, these were routinely dismissed, the authority of overseers and masters reaffirmed, and complainants often punished for insolence, neglect, absence or making frivolous claims. This happened to Flora McCoy who received 10 days' solitary confinement in November 1844.[56]

Stealing additional food was not uncommon. In September 1827 Adam Turpin was convicted of stealing and cooking a suckling pig belonging to his master on Friday when his weekly issue of rations was likely expended.[57] Four passholder shepherds of a Freshwater Point VDL farmer (Griffiths) received 18 months' hard-labour in chains for slaughtering one of the sheep in their care.[58] Stealing other goods could also be linked to rations. In 1830 eight men implicated in systematically robbing materials from the Sydney government dockyard claimed bad rations drove their actions.[59]

As well as demanding extra rations, convicts demanded wages even after the 1823 prohibition. On 28 October 1834 Henry Wyatt of Cockle Bay charged his assigned-servant James Bell with insolence and refusing work after his request for increased wages was rejected.[60] Wyatt's intoxication torpedoed the prosecution but more typically charges succeeded. Six days after Wyatt's case, Joseph Ball received 36 lashes from the Hobart Magistrates Court for the same offence.[61] Similarly, William Welch got 50 lashes from the Sydney Bench after telling his mistress he wouldn't work without wages.[62] In February 1828 the *Sydney Monitor* acknowledged widespread payment of wages and extra rations, stating 'settlers cannot help buying tobacco; the Convicts . . . will not work without it. A pipe in our Australian wilderness is to the peasant-convict, the country ale-house.'[63] The situation was no different 12 years later with William Riley receiving three months on a chain-gang for telling his Hobart employer (Nuttal) he would do him no good unless supplied with tobacco.[64] Threats to do their master 'no good' or like phrases were common, and the demands extended to clothing. Youthful Daniel Lambert received seven days' solitary confinement after stopping work for his Surry Hills master baker (Taylor), objecting to salt beef as 'his standing dish and his apparel was of so mean a description that he was ashamed to be met by his acquaintances.'[65]

Assigned-convicts didn't simply continue to demand wages, extra rations and tobacco, they networked. The *Hobart Town Courier* lamented 'some vague notion has gained credit with the prisoner population, to the effect that they are in future to receive wages for their labour.'[66] To many employers the notion was neither vague nor avoidable. In October 1837 the *Courier* complained assigned-servants were demanding tobacco and wages or trying to hire with other employers if their master resolved to dispense with their services. The *Courier* was appalled assigned-convicts acted as if they were free—a complaint echoed in NSW.[67] The reintroduction of specified wage payments under the probation regime in 1839 didn't end demands. In September 1844 Mr Grubb complained his shepherd was demanding 22 shillings in wages (a third more than stipulated), while John McKenna told his Tamar Valley employer Charles Guthrie if paid government wages he would only do 'a government day's work.'[68]

These demands weren't aberrant but reflected widespread effort-bargaining. Many employers found it efficacious to provide wages and other 'indulgences' or time off to secure more than minimalist efforts. A *Cornwall Chronicle* correspondent observed the:

> master who withholds from his servants the usual comforts of life, or restricts them to what is commonly called bare necessaries will be regarded as a blood-stained tyrant . . . as long as they are compelled to give away their labour for nothing, they will never cease viewing themselves as slaves.[69]

Court reports are replete with evidence of effort-bargaining by both convict and free workers prescient of industrial relations literature a century later. Remonstrated for being idle, journeyman tailor James Sheerer told his Hobart master 'not to be too bouncible with him as he would not stand for it' (one week on the treadmill).[70] Both workers and employers networked about prevailing wage rates. In December 1847 brickmaker John Lake told the Launceston Bench he wouldn't have agreed to £10 per-annum with his employer Thomas Walker Esq when 'Mr Twinning and others would give him £16'.[71] There is also evidence of customary practices. On being assigned to a Bathurst employer named Steele, William Fife was sent to Steele's agent in York Street, Sydney (Martin) who 'desired' him to chop wood. Fife told Martin 'I have been twelve years in the Colony, and am not so green as to go to work the day I come out of barracks.'[72] Fife received 50 lashes and was told to hold his tongue by the magistrate when he said he hoped not to be sent to Martin after punishment.

Rural employers provided wages, extra rations of allowances of grog to workers—both convict and free—during the harvest/shearing season. Failure to meet these customary entitlements caused disputes. In December 1826 Stephen Callaghan refused to reap for his Windsor District master because his grog allowance was less than fellow workers. The *Sydney Gazette* stated Callaghan's master was generous with rations and paid his assigned-convicts wages like 'free men' at harvest time. Callaghan escaped punishment ostensibly because he was apologetic but need for his labour probably influenced the decision. The same edition reported six other cases of servants refusing work, including John Skully assigned to another Windsor farmer after boasting about his capacity with the scythe and then denying he could reap (50 lashes).[73]

One action viewed as especially reprehensible was free workers signing agreements then failing to 'appear' after the employer had paid an advance in wages. Officially frowned on, paying advances were commonplace, especially for rural workers needing travel money and seamen/whalers to meet their accumulated debts and buy clothing.[74] In March 1840 George Turner was gaoled for six months for absconding after signing an agreement and receiving £5 to serve on Mr Parker's station.[75] It was not uncommon for whalers to sign more than one agreement, with Robert Fusson signing agreements with three different employers (two months' hard-labour).[76] Even where advances weren't involved, the individual contract regime encouraged shopping around notwithstanding the penalties. In June 1837 William Woodman received six weeks' hard-labour for refusing to go to James Kelly's Whaling Station. The *Hobart Town Courier* urged whaling employers to take exemplary action against every man who 'misconducted himself.' James Kelly was a highly regarded Hobart citizen, but in the very same issue of the *Courier* Edward Harley from the whaleship *Prince of Denmark*, charged him with failing to pay wages. Highlighting the imbalance in employment relations, Kelly's offence was not viewed as fraud, being only required to pay £2 of the £2,15s Harley claimed.[77]

Instances of workers fraudulently taking advances paled into insignificance compared to the level of wage theft. At worst, employers convicted of not paying wages were ordered to make restitution (without interest) plus court costs. Settlements were commonly discounted for alleged bad behaviour or costs to the employer. In December 1841 George Dickens claimed 5 shillings a day from Robert Bell but was only awarded one shilling per diem for the term of the agreement. Similarly, when summonsed by his shepherd (Caton) Robert Coulson explained he had lost 50 ewes so deducted the cost of 20 at seven shillings each. The Brisbane Bench deemed this deduction 'proper' and dismissed the claim.[78] A Bathurst farm labourer (Lynch) gave due notice after completing his agreement but had to wait another month to claim wages because his employer (Nicholson) was in Sydney. Lynch received only £4, the Bench deducting his ration costs while awaiting Nicholson's return.[79] Seamen too faced difficulties recovering wages, normally payable upon return to the home port—often in Britain. Those convicted of offences found it hard to recover wages or their clothes. William Smith released after 60 days on the treadmill for refusing work discovered his ship (*Larne*) had already left Port Jackson for India.[80]

Anyone viewing these injustices as historical anachronisms should note recent evidence on widespread underpayment and that as in the early 19th century, an employee who steals from their employer can be gaoled while employers who deliberately steal their employees' wages face at worst—if detected, charged and convicted—a fine in addition to paying the amount owed. In January 2015 Priscilla Li Peng Lam and David Wing Leong Lam owners of Dave's Noodle Bar Launceston were fined $15,000 each and the company $70,000 for under-paying by $86,118 a Chinese chef nominated to Australia on a s457 guest-worker visa. The chef was paid a flat rate of between $804 and $213 per week (working 60-hour weeks) between 2008 and 2011. This is not an isolated case but indicative of systematic wage theft (often using false records and exploiting foreign workers) involving small firms and large franchises like 7-Eleven—only a fraction of which results in outcomes like that just described.[81]

Absconding, Breaking the Ties That Bound

As with convicts and indented/free-labour in the United States (slaves too) absconding was widespread and there were positive as well as negative drivers. In 1825 the *Hobart Town Gazette* observed the 'long list of runaways will not appear so appalling when it is considered that many of those advertised have, absconded to obtain, in disguise, labour at a more profitable rate than with the master to whom they are assigned—that some have probably escaped out of the Colony.'[82] For disgruntled workers, including apprentices, absconding was an attractive option with reasonable prospects of escaping detection. The *Sydney Monitor* lamented many runaway apprentices escaped conviction due to improper agreements.[83] Indicative of its extent and costs, efforts to counter absconding/desertion included severe penalties, significant rewards for recapturing convicts and stationing police on roads connecting regions/colonies to apprehend 'waifs and strays'.[84] Courts commonly imposed longer gaol terms on absconders than those refusing work. In November 1846 the Melbourne Bench advised the *Alice Maud's* master that if Edward Wilson kept refusing work he should be charged with desertion for which he would be 'dealt with differently'.[85]

Convicts were bound by their sentences but most free workers too were bound by lengthy agreements. This, better wage prospects and incapacity to renegotiate terms during the contract afforded powerful incentives to abscond notwithstanding penalties. Indeed heavier penalties reflected tacit recognition of the relative attractiveness and success of absconding. Free-labour couldn't quit their job before their contract expired. In June 1842 the Hobart Bench sentenced George Clarke to two months' hard-labour and mulcted all his wages for quitting service without leave.[86] Prior termination could occur with a master's agreement—something workers might encourage through complaints and poor effort. Johanna Cater was alleged to have done this until her Portland employer (Reverend Wilson) cancelled the agreement.[87] Similarly, Launceston employer George Moore was happy to lose the services of John Jones (10 days on the Treadmill and agreement cancelled) because his misconduct had cost him £10.[88] While employers too were ostensibly tied by agreements, it was relatively easy to remove unwanted servants through poor treatment or charging them with an offence.

Masters also tried to contract workers for a year, or three to five years in the case of indentured workers. For their part, workers sought shorter contracts so they could obtain better engagements more rapidly and exploit higher wages during shearing/harvests. Employers facing labour shortages or requiring workers with specialised skills often made little effort to ensure those hired weren't absconders notwithstanding official warnings and penalties. Aggrieved employers' efforts to enforce contracts could prove difficult and costly. In August 1835 free mechanic William Arrowsmith signed a 12-month agreement to serve George Rankin in Bathurst from October 1. Almost immediately after signing with Rankin, Arrowsmith entered into a six-month agreement as an engineer/millwright at F Girard's Darling Harbour mills. Rankin located Arrowsmith who agreed to take up his original engagement but was then charged with breach of agreement by Girard. Both employers hired expensive legal counsel. Girard's argued that since Arrowsmith didn't commence his contract with Rankin, it had been abandoned, a point which was referred to the Attorney General for an opinion. While few cases required the intercession of crown law officers, legal technicalities or other complicating issues were common.

Desertion by seamen was endemic. Apart from coastal shipping, articles signed by seamen were commonly for voyages lasting a year or more. Higher colonial wages encouraged desertion. Repeatedly refusing work was another method of securing a discharge. In February 1841 the schooner *Ireland's* master told the Sydney Water Police Court the men were 'being led away by the high wages given in the port, to suffer imprisonment and the Treadmill to obtain their discharge.'[89] On the same day two seamen from the *Betsy and Sarah* escaped a charge of desertion as their articles were found to be informal. Like convicts, seamen lived in close confinement, were often conspicuous (due to their clothes and particular gait), subject to close surveillance requiring passes to go on shore and in some ports liable to arrest without warrant on suspicion of being a deserter.[90] Desertion was often highly organised via crimps including watermen ferrying people to and from ships, publicans and brothel operators. Every major port had crimping networks in its dock area like the Rocks in Sydney. Deserting without help could be dangerous, with *Duchess of Northumberland* seaman David Jones drowning off Dawes Point while trying to swim ashore with a bundle of his clothing.[91] By the late-1830s desertion/insubordination was seen to be at crisis proportions in Sydney.[92] In May 1838 a meeting of mercantile/shipping interests at the *Pulteney Hotel* was told 106 seamen had deserted 14 ships currently in port and seamen were exploiting laws to defeat prosecutions and lodge their own complaints of assault and ill-usage. The meeting petitioned for more stringent legislation, with ongoing agitation leading to the 1840 *Water Police Act* that established a specialist police, inquisitorial tribunal system, compulsory discharge certificates and arrest without warrant.[93] Disallowed in 1843, desertion continued even while the law operated.

Like seamen, absconding was widespread amongst convicts notwithstanding regulatory measures. Like slaves in the United States, they could be arrested without warrant on suspicion of being a runaway and there were significant rewards for constables and others assisting in their recapture. Those apprehended faced severe punishments including extension of their sentence, being sent to a road-gang or place of secondary punishment. Nonetheless, large numbers absconded and more succeeded making their escape even from Macquarie Harbour than colonial authorities cared to admit.[94] They could move to places where they were unknown or receive support from other sympathetic convicts notwithstanding severe penalties of harbouring/assisting escapees. In September 1841 assigned-convict John Holland was sentenced to 12 months in a chain-gang by the Hobart Bench for supplying a group of absconders with tobacco and tinder.[95]

Employer connivance also assisted absconding. Labour hungry landholders in the Port Philip District and South Australia engaged absconding convicts much to the chagrin of Sydney newspapers.[96] It wasn't necessary to travel that far. In 1841 the *Sydney Herald* reported convicts absconding from the estates of absent landholders were working in Sydney.[97] As population grew, prospects of escaping detection increased. In October 1837 one (William Pearce) of two servants of a Kent Street master tailor (Stephens) charged with unauthorised absence, was revealed as an absconder at large for 17 years.[98] Another convict was sentenced to 12 months on an iron-gang after being at large six years.[99] In 1840 a Bill before the NSW Legislative Council proposed that runaway convicts must serve an additional sentence equal to their time at large.[100] Notwithstanding ever more strident measures, many absconders evaded detection.

On the other hand, convicts choosing to serve out their engagement/sentence could encounter difficulties. Charged with disobedience, third-class probationer Isaac Thorpe told the Ross Bench the agreement with his master (Tucker) had expired. The Bench was unmoved sentencing Thorpe to one month on a road-gang and indicating any appeal about being detained by his employer should be lodged with the Comptroller General.[101]

Women Before the Courts

Court records add an important gender dimension to worker dissent. Apart from Female Factories, women were located in activities with limited opportunities for collective action. However, many disputed their working conditions so prosecutions of female servants—convict and free—were numerous. This applied to female apprentices too, with the *Goulburn Herald* complaining growing numbers of female orphan apprentices were 'getting weary of well-doing' and becoming defiant and impertinent to their employers.[102] Reid's examination of VDL female convicts argued their everyday resistance mostly took the form of petty misconduct but calculated resistance was common like refusing to take orders from any household member apart from those to whom they were specifically assigned.[103]

Resistance and punishment inflicted took several forms. The *Sydney Gazette* of 25 June 1835 reported four female assigned-convicts were prosecuted two days earlier for unauthorised absence, insolence/abusive language and refusing work/insubordination.[104] They were incarcerated for periods ranging from six days to two months in the Female Factory. Short confinements on bread and water or being returned to the third class of the Female Factory—the lowest involving most work and fewest privileges—were typical punishments. When it came to 'moral' offences, there was a clear gender imbalance in punishment. When Elizabeth Huddamy and William Johnston were discovered in their master's (E Hogg) garden for an 'improper purpose', Elizabeth received six months in the Launceston Female Factory while Johnston only got six hours in the stocks.[105]

The colonial press often adopted a condescending tone reporting cases well illustrated by the *Sydney Gazette*.

> Mary Morton, whose countenance evidently evinced a degree of saucy independence seldom excelled, was charged by her mistress with most abusive language, and refusal to work. She endeavoured to soften the hearts of the magistrates with a few tears. It could not however mollify their feelings, and she was accordingly sentenced to six days confinement in the gaol.[106]

Free females too were gaoled. In April 1837 Margaret Gleeson, 'a respectable young woman, and decently attired' was tried for refusing to go to the baker, telling her mistress (Mrs Hart) 'bad luck to you, go yourself'. Convinced of Margaret's contrition the presiding magistrate (Charles Windeyer) urged leniency but Hart's husband, a George Street dealer, would have none of it. She was gaoled for seven days—a sentence *The Sydney Gazette* believed would negatively affect her subsequent behaviour.[107] Mary Morton and Margaret Gleeson might have seemed contrite but unapologetic responses were more common. In November 1836 Ellen Millan told the apprehending constable she was on her way to Parramatta for a 'little relaxation.'[108] Ellen Dillon returning from a sentence at the Female Factory promptly refused to work, telling the court the house required so much cleaning she wouldn't stay for a £1 a week. Dillon, described as a 'stout, fat, jolly looking woman' was sent for another two months in the Factory.[109] Like their male counterparts, women used their limited options to influence judgements. Both convict and free workers raised counter-arguments during proceedings. A few, especially those charged with serious offences, had legal counsel to raise technical challenges—with some success. Some convicts gave false name, as Bridget Corrigan did calling herself Bridget Riley, so their past record wouldn't be considered.[110] While mostly hostile, newspapers capture something of workers' voice. Reporters attended court proceedings and could describe background, atmosphere/ incidents and asides not recorded in bench-books. When her master threatened Mary Fearn with being taken before the courts for insolence, she replied if he didn't she would go there herself unless provided with more than two ounces of tea per week.[111]

Both the scale of dissent and limits to punitive discipline were evident. In 1836 the *Sydney Herald* bemoaned that of 523 women in the Female Factory only 44 were available for assignment because 105 were employed nursing children and 310 were serving sentences for misconduct.[112] Three years later there were 892 women (and 197 children) in the Factory, only 274 available for assignment while 395 were undergoing sentences—eight in solitary confinement.[113] There were concerns incarcerating women; far from having a salutary effect, it rendered offenders even more disrespectful of authority.

Indentured Labour

As noted in Chapter 1 colonial employers used both European and non-European indentured labour, contracted at terms below those prevailing in the colony. Western Australia initially depended on indentured British immigrants. The agreement-terms caused considerable friction, including widespread absconding and complaints over failure to provide adequate rations.[114] Similar problems arose in other colonies. As with HRM spin-doctoring today, those signing agreements frequently found they had been misled or the offer didn't match reality. In October 1849 two Welshmen who signed a seven-year agreement to work at the Kooringa copper smelting works were fined for refusing work in protest at the many un-kept promises made to them.[115]

Wages and conditions were considerably worse for non-European indentured workers. In December 1838 Bengalese Raino Sammy, indentured to Captain Chisholm, was sentenced to seven days hard-labour for refusing to work. The Bench rejected Sammy's plea that the specified pay was insufficient with *The Australian* opining:

> these men who are glad to get service at the current rate of wages in India, are tampered with, and persuaded if they are useful men to get away from their ordinal service on the promise of higher wages. A lesson or two of this sort may perhaps, have a beneficial effect, as the Bengalese eschew hard work.[116]

Employers' racist beliefs in subservient non-Europeans were central to their importation. Some didn't even abide with the terms of these exploitative agreements. Bronie Ayah, a Muslim woman from Calcutta was indentured to John Mackie to work for five years at 16 rupees per month. Ayah claimed Mackie refused to pay her return passage if discharged without just cause as stipulated in the agreement, turning her out onto the street without money or food.[117] Mackie claimed Ayah had refused work but magistrates found she had been unable to work due to a cold. The Australian climate was a cause for complaint amongst some Asian servants. Employers found non-European servants weren't as cheap and malleable as expected. In November 1846 William Charles Wentworth's indentured servant (Ramduell) was gaoled for 21 days for repeatedly refusing work. Ramdeull demanded to see a copy of his indenture agreement which Wentworth refused. The experience was similar in Western Australia where small numbers of Chinese were introduced as shepherds but the *Inquirer* lamented they were slow at their work.[118]

Revenge and Payback

Many aggrieved servants had ample opportunity to damage their masters' capital by, for example, driving a horse too furiously or setting fire to haystacks. In November 1839 a ticket-of-leave holder was brought before the Parramatta Bench charged with setting fire to his master's premises causing damage worth £500.[119] The risk of sabotage was such that convicted servants were commonly sent to road-gangs in a district remote from their former employer. Incendiarism was hard to prove unless directly witnessed by someone prepared to testify and the combination of hot weather and naked flames frequently caused accidental fires. In May 1837 Thomas Bennett assigned to Captain Hector was charged with setting fire to a stack of wheat at Booreenyang but was acquitted for lack of evidence. Bennett claimed he was the victim of his overseer's spite.[120] Sabotage was not confined to rural workers. Charles Rogers assigned to Mr Milson (after whom Milson's Point is named) was charged with trying to set fire to his master's house and store with a fire stick and barrel of gunpowder.[121] Similarly, probationer John Floyd was imprisoned for four months with hard-labour for wilfully burning staves used to make barrels at Degraves Cascades brewery near Hobart.[122]

Reinforcing the protection of capital, servants could be held liable for economic losses to their employer arising from alleged negligence or incompetence. In March 1827 Mr Whaling's two assigned-convicts received 50 lashes for being asleep when four of the nine cattle in their care wandered off.[123] For free shepherds the financial penalty for losing sheep or allowing them to mix with scabby sheep could be considerable. In January 1850 Joseph Woodlands was mulcted £4 for allowing two scabby sheep to mix with his flock on Henry Hopkins Esq Geelong District station.[124] Reflecting its economic significance, worker-related losses from pastoral pursuits was the subject of considerable legislative debate as well as enforcement by magistrates. Shepherds/hutkeepers were not the only targets. In 1849 hired farm labourer Amos Eplegrane was fined £2 plus costs (in default one month's gaol) for damaging 20–30 orange trees while ploughing and harrowing his master's (A L McDougall) Parramatta orchard.[125]

While many employers undoubtedly calculated the optimal mix of rewards and punishment, others didn't or miscalculated, resulting in serial court appearances. In December 1837 Henry Collins was returned to government, his employer 'despairing of ever affecting any reform to him.'[126] Similarly, Launceston master tailor William Jordan repeatedly prosecuted his assigned journeymen, the only clear result being more antagonistic relations.[127] Prosecutions against a servant could include multiple offences indicating growing frustration, determination to obtain a severe penalty or strategic use of the courts. In March 1838 Captain Collins charged William Elliott with absenting himself with a horse on Monday, repeatedly neglecting to clean the curricle and harness when ordered, and refusing to work a thrashing machine or train and attend to horses as engaged to (one month in Carters Barracks).[128] Ever seeking combinations of penalties that would secure obedience by the late 1830s, skilled VDL convicts were being sentenced to a period of gaol at night after work each day—a fate that befell several of Jordan's tailors including Levi Watts.[129] In May 1839 David Grant received 10 nights in the cells for repeated insolence, including telling his master, George Hill Anderson, that he was afraid to lose his services and that all Anderson's servants knew he 'was a very bad man'.[130]

Harsh treatment or repeated punishments not only risked sabotage but threats and physical retribution. In September 1827 a Windsor District master returned George Burgan to the Government for this reason, repeated punishments having failed to halt Burgan's insolent and 'saucy' behaviour.[131] Assaults on masters by disgruntled servants weren't common but nor were they especially rare. In December 1834 George Bloomfield and Nathaniel Stringwall assaulted Samuel Onions when, objecting to their drunk and noisy behaviour, he ordered them to go to bed. Bloomfield was sentenced to nine months in an iron-gang while Stringwall received 36 lashes. The same issue of the *Sydney Monitor* reported a servant (Tenterton) had been committed for trial after aiming a pistol at his Stonequarry master (C Harper) and pulling the trigger.[132] In December 1835 the *Sydney Gazette* reported two assaults involving assigned-convicts. One punched his employer John Kindon Cleaves. The other, John Fisher, struck his overseer with a hoe and attempted to incite a collective assault when he realised a constable had been sent to arrest him for refusing work. Fisher received 12 months in an iron-gang and thereafter to be 'assigned at a great distance in the interior.'[133]

Convicts assaulting their overseer/master might be tried for assault with intent to murder—a capital offence. This fate befell Michael McCabe in February 1836 after he assaulted overseer Thomas Reid on 13 December 1835 at Penrith. Having been flogged for refusing work, McCabe struck his overseer (Reid) on the head with a spade when ordered to return to work. Brought before a magistrate McCabe stated he was 'tired of life and wished to kill someone that he might die for it'.[134] Reid was not seriously injured and the military jury opted to find him guilty of a less serious charge. Unhappy with this, Presiding Judge Burton indicated he would consult fellow judges to see if the prisoner's life should be spared. William Brown too was charged with attempted murder and inflicting grievous bodily harm on sub-inspector of roads William Burley Parker after striking him with a shovel when his gang was ordered to work an extra hour. As with McCabe's, the jury opted to convict on the less serious charge. He was transported to Norfolk Island for life.[135] Assaults often seem a spontaneous response to accumulated frustration with harsh supervision or other conditions, particularly on road/iron-gangs and places of secondary punishment. But the complete despair evident in McCabe's case was not aberrant. In October 1827 nine prisoners convicted of murdering Constable George Rex at Macquarie Harbour responded to their death sentence with one word 'amen'.[136]

The link between ill-treatment and absconding, bushranging and other dissent was acknowledged even by the conservative *Sydney Gazette*.[137] Overseers, commonly ex-convicts, were prone to use the lash as their principle mode of labour management. Gangs brutalised prisoners and developed networks of criminality. Negative drivers of dissent weren't confined to gangs, with the *Launceston Advertiser* acknowledging absconding was also rife amongst the 'haughty, lately-become-rich-and-powerful settlers.'[138] Repressive regimes with ineffectual means of addressing grievances were also conducive to sporadic but violent revolts (see Chapters 4, 6 and 10) similar to those in slave societies of the time. Violent slave revolts, like that in Jamaica in June 1824 and one by slave apprentices in Demerara Guyana in 1836, were reported in the colonial press but the parallels with convicts invariably escaped mention.[139]

More typically harsh treatment of convict gangs encouraged mass absconding to the bush, directly fuelling bushranging activities that sometimes aroused outright panic in rural communities.[140] Once absconders embarked on bushranging, they knew a violent end via shooting or hanging was the likely scenario awaiting them. Bushrangers relied on networks of sympathetic convict servants. Mirroring Rediker's[141] observation about pirates it wasn't unusual for bushrangers to ask servants how they were treated on farms they raided and measure their actions regarding the master accordingly. In June 1828 an Illawarra District settler complained of this practice stating wheat and a large boat had been burned at a farm (O'Brien's) shortly after the arrest of a bushranger there with whom farmworkers had been seen conversing prior to the incident.[142]

Violence Against Workers

On occasion servants bore the physical brunt of their master's displeasure, and female domestic servants also faced a significant risk of sexual harassment. Without independent witnesses prepared to testify, the complainant's testimony seldom persuaded a bench, particularly if they were a convict.

Assigned-convict Mary Pearce tried to lodge a complaint of assault against her Sussex Street Sydney master (Cutler). The Bench remanded the case until the next day when Cutler charged her with insolence and disobeying orders. Notwithstanding evidence Mary had sought medical treatment, her complaint was dismissed and she was sentenced to two months in the Female Factory.[143]

Male convicts complaining of assault/ill-treatment often received short shrift. In September 1841 the George Town Bench dismissed Thomas McKell's complaint of ill-treatment at the hands of Henry Foster because McKell had behaved 'most infamously' to his master and the following day he was 'awarded' 36 lashes for giving false evidence.[144] Free servants including apprentices fared little better. Even when masters were convicted of assault, the penalty imposed was usually minimal. In April 1838 an unnamed Sydney master was fined 10 shillings for ordering a journeyman to 'chastise' his apprentice if he neglected work.[145] Six years later the same fine was imposed when a wheelwright (Hancock) hit his apprentice with a piece of sheet iron.[146]

The same outcome was typical when officers' assaulted seamen, with the Hobart Bench fining the *Mariana's* master five shillings for such an assault.[147] At sea insubordinate seamen could be put in irons, confined in close fetid conditions or (less commonly) stapled to the deck with iron rings, struck or flogged. Even more disturbing were instances of systemic violence and abuse of apprentice seamen or ship's boys. In February 1841 the *Marquis of Hastings'* master (Carr) was charged will ill-treating an apprentice boy, Edward Seppings, on the voyage from London to Sydney. The complaint was lodged by Mr Cheuval Esq JP whose family had travelled on the ship. Passengers testified Seppings had been repeatedly struck with a thick rope by the officers and confined in handcuffs on the poop deck for days exposed to the sun by day and with only a blanket at night. One witness described the boy as delirious, imagining his brother was on board and calling for his dog.[148] The Water Police Court remanded Carr to stand trial but the Attorney General stayed proceedings, stating no jury could convict given evidence Seppings was 'a very depraved and ill-conducted boy.'[149] Just two weeks later the barque *Amelia's* master (Henly) was fined 10 shillings plus costs for ropes-ending (beating with a rope knotted at the end) a young steward for not managing his duties. The Bench informed Henly he couldn't chastise the boy even in the 'mild' manner used—a misleading description of ropes-ending—because he wasn't an indentured apprentice. The ship's crew had a different view, striking the same day.[150]

Close Supervision, Hours and Social Space

Convicts like domestics or journeymen lodging in their master's premises found it hard to escape employer oversight and demands.[151] For domestics particularly, demands and criticism could come day and night. Thomas

Watkins was sentenced to the treadmill for telling his mistress Mrs Leigh she shouldn't come into the kitchen and 'bully-rag' him.[152] As in the 1970s Edwardian period television-show 'Upstairs, Downstairs', the kitchen was typically a location for conviviality amongst servants. Some masters/mistresses accepted this, but others did not. William Kelly got 10 days on the treadmill for refusing to leave his master's (Rogan) kitchen when ordered.[153]

The pub/tavern was a safer refuge for relaxation and gossip, including the respective merits of employers. However, visiting these entailed risks of being charged with unauthorised absence. Those holding a ticket-of-leave were not immune. In September 1838 Joseph Worley and Thomas Conder were sent to the Bothwell and Campbell Town Districts respectively after being found in a Hobart public-house after hours.[154] For rural workers access to pubs was an issue except in closely settled districts. Neighbouring houses might serve as a meeting point—but one with risks. On 20 January 1835 Charles Kellow was ordered to receive 60 lashes by Campbell Town (VDL) Bench for absenting himself and 'drinking with his master's neighbour's servants.'[155] Many employers found it easier to condone periodic short absences, though less so when associated with drunkenness. The duration and regularity of absences was a point of tacit bargaining and occasionally sharp differences.

Like convicts, free domestics faced demands at all hours. In England domestics were not covered by master and servant laws in recognition of this, but colonial laws contained no such exclusion. Even the Sabbath offered no relief. In May 1836 a young female emigrant who refused Sunday work for her laundress-mistress (McGuire) was told by the presiding magistrate (Windeyer) that

> persons in the menial capacity of servants could not claim permission to go to church on a Sunday as a *right*, but were bound to give their services to their employers on Sunday as well as on any other day.[156]

Ironically, Convict Regulations bestowed this very right on convicts. Though framed more as an obligation, convict servants frequently used the time for other purposes. In practice the protection afforded was selective. Mrs Timothy Nowlan permitted her female servant to attend church after preparing the Sunday meal, but fellow-servant John Knight received a month's hard-labour for refusing to cook it and telling her 'I'm no Coolie. I am not going to work on Sunday and all week too.'[157]

Working hours and holidays were an issue for both free and convict workers. In November 1835 Adam Howarth, charged with absence, argued he had worked six and half days the week before. The magistrate was unmoved telling Howarth even if he 'worked seven days one week he was still bound to work the next six, and was not even entitled to keep St. Monday.'[158] The Hobart Bench was equally unsympathetic to painter Henry Nichol's refusal to work after 6 pm on the plea he couldn't see.

His employer (Bossward) stated he needed doors primed in a hurry to go to California (goldrush-related demand for prefabricated buildings). Bossward couldn't afford to lose Nichol's services and urged only a reprimand. The Bench duly obliged.[159]

Apprentices fared rather better. Josiah West, Darling Harbour shipwright, charged apprentice Robert Gale with refusing overtime. However, the Bench ruled the boy shouldn't be 'compelled to work after hours unless in case of emergency.'[160] The Sydney Bench also dismissed a charge against apprentice-printer Frederick Hunt, stating that journeymen could be obliged to work on the Sabbath but it wouldn't sanction compelling a young man to neglect religious duties.[161] Other servants sometimes received dispensation for holy days. In April 1846 the Launceston Bench refused to punish Daniel Crown for refusing to work for a pottery-maker (Hayes) on Good Friday because he was a practising Roman Catholic scrupulously observing a strict fast.[162] These exceptions aside, laws enabled land and maritime employers to dictate working hours—something that clearly grated with workers.

Tasks, Workloads, Health and Safety

Work methods, workloads, quality and acceptable/required tasks were also common sources of dispute. Informed his master (Tilley) wasn't much impressed with riveting of a brass knob onto a piece of iron, assigned-mechanic John Hopner told Tilley to 'do it himself' (seven days confinement on bread and water).[163] The same month Mary Wood assigned to Mrs Gould Pitt Street Sydney refused to wash six sheets belonging to Gould's brother.[164] A female servant hired to do washing refused to do ironing.[165] Asked to fetch milk a probationer told Reverend Dr Browne, 'it was not his place to run errands'.[166] In January 1845 a probationer-journeyman of a Paterson St Launceston bootmaker (Langmaid) refused to wash out the kitchen. In this case the Bench agreed the journeyman couldn't be required to do tasks not specified in his agreement—let off with a reprimand.[167] Two years later the *Geelong Advertiser* lamented that 12 to 16 master and servant cases were coming before magistrates every day, most due to poor engagement practices by masters, like hiring a man as a hutkeeper and then ordering him to grub out trees.[168]

Workers had clear ideas of what constituted an acceptable workload. In January 1849 passholder Alexander Terry threw down his axe telling his Muddy Plains VDL employer (Renton) he had 'done enough' wood cutting.[169] Hired shepherd William Houllaghan (sic) stopped working for his Albert River (Queensland) employer Paul Lawless Esq because the flock included 'twenty crawlers' (three month's gaol).[170] Similar issues occurred at sea. In March 1840 Frederick Lyons on the *Earl Grey* refused work after being reduced from ship's cook to common seaman following emigrant complaints about his meals. This time the Sydney Bench dismissed the charge, finding the shipmaster wasn't entitled to turn Lyons out of the galley.[171]

Ill-treatment/assault, poor rations and hours/fatigue were the main cause of occupational health and safety (OHS) disputes. As Rosen has documented for the Western road-gangs, the combination of poor diet and clothing, long hours and inadequate accommodation, corporal punishment and maladministration in hard climatic conditions was conducive to both injuries and poor health/disease.[172] Seafaring and whaling was also hazardous as was much construction work. In January 1842 HL Cole prosecuted stonemason William Holmes for refusing to work on a Fremantle jetty (WA). Long periods immersed in water had caused problems with Holmes's health, especially his fingers. Cole had accommodated several requests from Holmes (changes to his wages and accommodation) but wouldn't change work methods as one witness proposed. The court ordered Holmes to return to his service or be sent to Fremantle gaol for a month.[173] For both convict and free, refusing work on grounds of illness seldom received a sympathetic hearing as the *Joseph Wheeler's* carpenter John Thompson found.[174] An exception was Western Port shepherd Nicholas Fitzsimmons, who refused to move sheep in wet weather, the Bench accepting evidence (medical certificate) of ill-health, cancelling the agreement and awarding all but one shilling of his wages.[175]

The Logistics and Complexities of Litigation

Taking cases to court was not costless for employers, as one lamented to the *Sydney Herald*.[176] In major towns courts often tried cases within a day or two of the offence. However, for rural employers laying charges could entail a day or more travelling to the nearest magistrate. On the other hand, magistrates frequently took employer's views into account when sentencing so proceedings could be used as a deterrent/warning or the penalty matched to their needs. Patrick Henright charged with refusing work by master tailor John McFarlane and Alexander Hunt charged with neglecting work by Hannah Barrett were admonished and discharged on the same day by the Sydney Bench.[177] Publican John Harris accepted the promise of free-hired steward John Toms to do his duty. Mary Kelly assigned to Mr Gannon Pitt Street was also forgiven her insolence and refusing work on promising to amend her conduct.[178] Agreement to drop charges or not impose a penalty occurred in the maritime industry, although shipmasters could also request seamen be imprisoned and returned on-board when the ship was about to depart. Masters also interceded after sentencing. In August 1837 the remainder of John Sullivan's 14-day sentence was remitted following the intercession of *The Majestic*'s master.[179]

Compromises occurred but were not the norm. Some employers were happy to lose a truculent worker. Convicted of insolence in April 1840, Richard Aymer received two months hard-labour on the roads and then to be returned to the government.[180] However, losing labour imposed temporary difficulties even when replacing a worker was the aim. Courts didn't always listen to employer requests. A sawyer who refused work was sentenced to three months on a chain-gang, leaving the Norfolk Plains settler who charged him with half a sawing pair (useless) and other workers consequently unable to complete a building.[181] Even employers who paid wages to assigned-convicts found it difficult to adjust when they received a ticket-of-leave. Elizabeth Lee received her ticket and refused to work for her master (Atkin) on the same terms. Atkin charged Lee with insolence—unsuccessfully.[182]

Extra 'indulgences' or tacit agreements over work could also stymie court proceedings. While prohibited, some masters allowed their assigned-convicts to work on their own account, even collecting a percentage. Thus, when the Hobart Bench learned James Green's employer (Davis) had allowed him to work as a quarryman, it dismissed the charge of refusing work and forthwith deprived Davis of Green's services.[183] Disagreements over verbal deals were also common. In September 1836 a seaman (Mathews) from the Barque *Pegasus* told the court he refused work because the shipmaster (Howlett) failed to abide by an agreement to discharge him upon reaching Sydney. Howlett claimed the agreement was contingent on Mathews accepting reduced wages of 35 shillings per month, but as this breached the 45 shillings rate specified in the articles, the court advised Howlett to discharge Mathews.[184]

Efforts to sanction workers—convict or free—by removing customary entitlements could also backfire. The *Royal George's* master stopped Charles McCarthy's grog allowance for refusing work only to find it made McCarthy's behaviour 'ten times worse' (one month's gaol).[185] Cases where individuals were tried repeatedly for neglect, refusing work or absence indicate that for a significant minority at least, punishment didn't yield the condign conduct for which employers and magistrates hoped. Within days of McCarthy's sentence, another seven *Royal George* crewmembers went on strike, refused the master's offer of 'forgiveness' and were gaoled for two months. The *Colonial Times* suggested that under the *Police Act* further dissent could result in being sent to a road-gang, joining twice-convicted felons.[186] One of the seamen involved, Thomas Berry, was sent to a road-gang and there received 25 lashes when an overseer claimed he had made a noise with his mouth during muster.[187] The flogging of a seamen like a transported felon caused a public uproar even beyond VDL.[188] Harsh discipline or ill-treatment was a common cause of collective dissent on land and sea. Indeed, the mate's ill-treatment of a Spanish seaman on the *Royal George* sparked the referred to strike. When the *Royal George* returned to Hobart in August 1835, the furore over Berry's treatment was in full flight. Nor had conditions on board improved. Ten crewmembers were gaoled for another strike. This case demonstrates the sometimes seamless intersection of individual and collective dissent.

Courts and the Magistracy's Role in Administering the Law

Courts and the magistracy adjudicating work disputes also warrant comment. Prior to 1820 military officers often served on civilian courts, a clear breach of a principal stretching back to the English Civil War.[189] Even after the establishment of Supreme Courts in VDL and NSW (1823), a long battle was waged to secure judicial independence. Convicts, unlike slaves, had legal standing as British subjects. However, under landholder-stacked (many ex-military) tribunals, or later higher courts stacked with juries of their betters, workers had little prospect of success unless a technical flaw in the proceedings was discovered by legal counsel. Aside from serious charges of conspiracy/revolt, dissent involving convict and free workers were predominantly tried in magistrates' courts presided over by part-time magistrates or justices of the peace.[190] From the 1830s full-time 'police' or stipendiary magistrates were appointed in major towns. Part-time magistrates were drawn from the ranks of military officers, major landholders, merchants (not ex-convicts) and notable citizens. Few possessed legal qualifications; all had competing demands on their time; guidance manuals were only produced from 1835 and the extent of their use remains speculative.[191] Almost all magistrates were employers and, particularly in rural districts, associates of those whose prosecutions they adjudicated. Workers lodging complaints, or more typically responding to charges, generally received short shrift.

Magisterial power exacerbated an already lopsided and punitive regime, where distinctions between convicts and free were blurred, and the legal basis of offences like insolence were questionable at best.[192] In rural districts employer-cum-magistrates played musical chairs trying each other's servants. In VDL former Royal Navy officer Captain Robert Hepburn (born on Wilkins Estate St Dorothy Jamaica in 1782) was appointed a JP in 1833. The surviving Fingal District Bench Books of the early 1840s show a regular interchange between Hepburn trying his own servants and then adjudicating cases brought by other employers. Similarly, the Queanbeyan District Bench Book of the 1830s provides a grim record of 25, 50 or 75 lashes being imposed for often trivial offences by landholder/magistrate James Wright. Supported by numerous constables, masters used passes and informers to inhibit the movement of convict workers, and it was alleged, free workers too.[193] Rural workers sometimes tried to lay ill-treatment complaints before town magistrates, but this generally failed even when they claimed judicial-bias. On occasions newspapers were critical because blatant bias undermined the moral legitimacy of these laws.[194] In 1832 NSW Governor Bourke tried to remedy the situation somewhat, introducing the *Summary Jurisdiction Act* in 1832 and failing to reappoint some magistrates. This sparked attacks from affected interest groups bemoaning widespread convict insubordination and overly lenient magistrates.[195]

The loaded-dice judicial regime continued in NSW as it did in VDL where no governor attempted even Bourke's modest reforms. In October 1838 assigned-convict James Rush asked his Clarence Plains master (Nichols) for a pair of boots—an entitlement under government regulations—being barefoot and unable to walk. Nichols charged Rush with insolence and refusing work. Part-time magistrate Samuel Dawson ordered Rush to receive

36 lashes (duly inflicted). Unusually, this decision came to the notice of Hobart's Chief Police Magistrate (CPM) who referred it to the Board of Assignment, returned Rush to the government, and told Dawson that he wouldn't countenance punishing those refusing work because they didn't have proper clothes. An unrepentant Dawson replied 'he would always punish a man for refusing to work; he would take no set-off of that kind; and it was his opinion, that men ought to work, whether they had shoes or not.'[196] Dawson's hard-line approach extended to his own farm near Rokeby where in January 1840 four assigned-servants were charged with refusing work, two receiving 36 lashes and the other two 10 days' solitary confinement on bread and water.[197]

Country magistrates were repeatedly accused of bias and adopting 'expansive' views on legislative provisions. In December 1846 John Beagly hired to CH Lyon as a bullock driver was mulcted six weeks' wages for refusing tasks after 6 pm that didn't relate to his occupation. The presiding Geelong magistrate told Beagly a man hired as a bullock driver was bound to act as general servant and 'bush servants . . . work whatever hours the employer may name.'[198] Even some employers accused magistrates of arbitrary decision-making favouring their friends at the expense of others.[199]

Many workers, especially convicts, viewed lodging a complaint as ineffectual if not dangerous. A Sandy Bay road-gang-member named Isaacs, charged with refusing work and attempting to strike his overseer (Holland), detailed Holland's goading treatment including devouring portions of their scanty rations. Asked why he hadn't lodged a complaint, Isaacs told the Bench it would serve little purpose as there was 'no probability of redress, but a greater chance of severer treatment' (two months in chains).[200] In February 1847 probationers John Feach and Charles McCarthy engaged to JJ Parker Esq lodged a complaint about poor and insufficient rations with supporting evidence. Their overseer countered, claiming they refused work. The Campbell Town Bench duly sentenced them to the treadmill for six and twelve weeks respectively. Even the conservative *Cornwall Chronicle* was appalled, sarcastically stating the magistrates reasoning demonstrated that decisions by judges of England were clearly in error.[201] It made no difference. Benches in major towns were rarely sympathetic but their rulings paled in comparison to rural magistrates who routinely dismissed complaints about poor food on the basis of the employer's assurances as probationer William Colburn found when he fronted the Longford Bench.[202] Seamen's complaints about bad or insufficient rations too seldom received a considered judgement.[203]

Employers and newspapers sometimes accused town magistrates, especially stipendiary magistrates, of stymieing prosecutions through over technical reading of laws and being 'too soothing' in their rulings on convict and free servants.[204] In 1840 landholder James Macarthur used his position on the NSW Legislative Council to propose the abolition of stipendiary magistrates.[205] Nonetheless, rural magistrates were not the only source of oppressive decisions. The *South Australian Register* expressed outrage in January 1850 when the Port Adelaide Bench mulcted farm servant John William's entire wages (£1.4s) plus £1 court costs for refusing to assist carrying two wool bales on a Sunday evening. The double penalty was exceptionally unfair as employer Henry Robinson freely admitted assaulting Williams and pushing him out of the house.[206]

Biased administration of already lopsided laws destroyed whatever moral authority they might have otherwise had. Workers did not meekly submit to them, contesting their adjudication and guardedly using available avenues for complaint and thumbing their noses at the apparatus. James Shields told Edward Archer's overseer William Bright he wouldn't work for 'all the Archers in the country' (four hours in the stocks), while Edward Burke prosecuted for absence on the same day told Archer he didn't care about being brought before the court 'he was used to it' (35 lashes).[207]The sheer level of litigation was indicative of its subordinating role but also its failure to secure the compliance for which legislators and employers hoped.

Other Evidence of Tensions at Work

Evidence of struggles over inequality at work isn't confined to the courts or absconding notices. It can also be found in diaries, books, reports/inquiries and newspapers including letters from workers. Police constables were charged with neglecting work but there is other evidence of dissent. In May 1830 the *Sydney Monitor* criticised Colonel Wilson's practice of making arbitrary deductions for constables pay in cases of misconduct.[208] Complaints about inadequate salary or disadvantageous changes in management decision-making were not uncommon amongst clerks and others employed by colonial governments. A former NSW Commissariat clerk went so far as to memorialise the UK Lords of Treasury, requesting two years' lost salary following his discharge.[209] More typical were complaints about inadequate salaries, including a flurry of articles and letters protesting cuts to clerks' salaries during the 1843 recession.[210] Excessive hours of shop-assistants were another frequent source of complaint in the press. These examples are merely illustrative.

Discussion and Conclusion

This chapter identified common themes and differences in efforts to subordinate different categories of labour. Notable is the sheer amount of state activity manifested in numerous laws, regulations and notices and the extensive police and court infrastructure enforcing them. The administration of convict labour was especially detailed and intrusive. While regulation of free-labour was not as intrusive or violent, it still amounted to a one-sided regime where often corrupted courts routinely imposed severe penalties for the smallest infractions/dissent. Prosecutions were not aberrant or isolated but an everyday occurrence, revealing part of the lived experience of working people. Courts were venues for widespread contestation of work arrangements, amounting to hundreds of thousands of cases in colonies that only reached a population of 405,000 in 1850. The intensity of struggle did not go unrecognised at the time but has attracted limited attention from researchers since.[211]

Widespread if largely informal collective action becomes more comprehensible in this context. Individual refusals to work were common and from this it was only a small step to collective refusal—a strike—articulating shared experience. Abraham Sharatt who refused work in the hearing of James Lord's other servants, was seen as inciting collective action and charged with insubordination.[212] It was not an isolated case and provides further insights into transmission mechanisms from individual dissent to collective action. The same point can be made with regard to go-slows, absconding and a range of other types of action/dissent. Collective action was in part a response by workers to inequalities entrenched in the legal regime as well as other efforts to subordinate them. As a 'working hand' told the *Moreton Bay Courier*, if they wanted to understand why rural workers in the surrounding districts were 'insubordinate', they only had to look to the behaviour of landholders including exploiting remoteness to overcharge for goods and trying them before courts all too conveniently manned (and they were men) by fellow squatters.[213]

Chapter 2 served another purpose, identifying an array of disputed issues that sets a context for examining how collective action drew on and reshaped the struggle. In Australia initial reliance on convicts led to state-regulated labour conditions that flowed onto free-labour and influenced master and servant and maritime labour laws, whilst also encouraging coercive work-based comparisons amongst workers. Ostensibly individual disputes between workers (convict and free) and their masters were grounded in a wider social context of customary practices and tacit bargaining. Atkinson's study found, as Thompson would have predicted, that convicts appealed to supposedly traditional rights.[214] Both convicts and free emigrant brought ideas/customs with them but also responded to colonial work/labour market conditions and opportunities of a transplanted society where traditional foundations of social-order were weakened. Conflicts over acceptable effort levels, recreation and hours (including customary holidays) provide but a few examples of the merging of influences to set workplace norms, and ones which, mirroring the argument made above, readily became the subject of collective action. The overall pattern of worker organisation and the social networks upon which this was built is explored in the next chapter.

Notes

1 According to English law, their role was subordinate to existing legislation. For a discussion of this, the rule of law and early use of the courts; friction between Governors and the Judiciary; and how laws applied to different groups in NSW,

see Neal, D. (1991) *The Rule of Law in a Penal Colony: Law and Power in Early New South Wales*, Cambridge University Press, Cambridge.

2 See for example *HRNSW 1791–1793*, 10 December 1791, 612.

3 *HRNSW 1806–1808*, 12 August 1806, 153.

4 *Colonial Times* 23 December 1825.

5 *HRNSW 1796–1799* 22 December 1797, 334–5.

6 AONSW CSO 19 November 1816 Reel 6045 4/1735, 199–200.

7 State Archives of NSW (AONSW) Colonial Secretary's Office (CSO) Governors and General Order (GGO) 27 November 1795 Reel 6037: ML Safe 1/18b); GGO 14 January 1797 Reel 6037: ML Safe 1/18b; Government Order (GO) 7 December 1816 Reel 6038, SZ759, 287–9 and Reel 6045, 4/1735, 211–4: and Jurisdiction over disputes re wages conferred on magistrates 6047; 4/1741 pp. 107–114.

8 See for example *HRNSW 1796–1799*, 10 March 1797, 196–7, 204, 225–6.

9 A further wages orders was issued in October 1800, although Hunter's successor (King) was less sympathetic to complaints the following year. *HRNSW 1800–1802*, 1 February and 31 October 1800, 31, 252 and 23 June 1801, 411.

10 AONSW CSO 21 November 1818 Reel 6038, SZ1044, 272–275.

11 AONSW CSO 27 August 1824 Reel 6013, 4/424, 256–7 and 8 September 1824, Reel 6039, 4/424, 271–272.

12 For details of this and subsequent queries about what master and servant regulations applied in the colony from magistrates, see AOWA CSO 2/83 24 March 1830; CSO 2/85 25 March 1830; and CSO 2808 10 April 1842 and Crowley, F. (1949) *Working Class Conditions in Australia 1788–1851* PhD Thesis, University of Melbourne, 381–385.

13 Clause 17, *HRNSW 1809–1811*, 1 October 1810, 414–421.

14 Quinlan, M. (1997) Balancing Trade and Labour Control: Imperial/Colonial Tensions in Relation to the Regulation of Seamen in the Australian Colonies 1788–1865, *International Journal of Maritime History*, 9(1):26.

15 Quinlan, M. (2004) Australia 1788–1902: A "Working Man's Paradise?", in Hay, D. and Craven, P. eds. *Masters, Servants, and Magistrates in Britain and the Empire*, 219–250; Quinlan, M. (1992) Making Labour Laws Fit for the Colonies: The Introduction of Laws Regulating Whalers in Three Australian Colonies, 1835–1855, *Labour History*, 62:19–37; Quinlan, M. (1996) Industrial Relations before Unions: Merchant Seamen in NSW 1810–1850, *Journal of Industrial Relations*, 38(2):269–293; Quinlan, M. (1997) Balancing Trade and Labour Control, 19–56; and Quinlan, M. (1998), Regulating Labour in a Colonial Context: Maritime Labour Legislation in the Australian Colonies 1788–1850, *Australian Historical Studies* No.111:303–24.

16 Crowley, F. (1949) Working Class Conditions in Australia 1788–1851, 302–3.

17 Quinlan, M. (1997) Balancing Trade and Labour Control, 19–56.

18 See for example AONSW CSO 9 December 1820 Scale of rates for services plying within the harbour of Port Jackson, Reel 6050, 4/1746, 117–9.

19 Thompson, E.P. (1977) *Whigs and Hunters: The Origin of the Black Act*, Penguin, Harmondsworth and Hay, D., Linebaugh, P., Rule, J., Thompson, E.P. and Winslow, C. (1977) *Albion's Fatal Tree: Crime and Society in Eighteenth Century England*.

20 Byrne, P. (1993) *Criminal Law and the Colonial Subject, New South Wales, 1810–1830*, Cambridge University Press, Cambridge, 129–154.

21 *Sydney Gazette* 8 October 1814.

22 Reid, K. (1997) Contumacious, Ungovernable and Incorrigible: Convict Women and Workplace Resistance, Van Diemen's Land 1820–1839, in Duffield, I. and Bradley, J. eds. *Representing Convicts: New Perspectives on Convict Forced Migration*, 109.

23 Maxwell-Stewart, H. (2015) Convict Labour Extraction and Transportation from Britain and Ireland 1615–1870, in de Vito, C. and Lichtenstein, A. eds. *Convict Labour: A Global Regime*, Brill, Leiden, 186–187.
24 Merritt, A. (1981) *The Development and Application of Masters and Servants Legislation in New South Wales-1845 to 1930*, Ph.D. Thesis, Australian National University, IV and 191.
25 A Victorian parliamentary return indicated that 1,253 workers received custodial sentences under the legislation between 1859 and 1870 while 118 absconding apprentices were arrested between 1846 and 1870. Quinlan (2004) Australia 1788–1902, 239–240.
26 Quinlan, M. (1996) Industrial Relations Before Unions, 284.
27 Quinlan, M. (1997) Balancing Trade and Labour Control, 45–46.
28 Maxwell-Stewart, H. (2008) *Closing Hell's Gates*, 156–162.
29 Maxwell-Stewart, H. (2008) *Closing Hell's Gates*, 262.
30 Other research indicates this applied to earlier periods. Walsh, B. (2007) Heartbreak and Hope, Deference and Defiance on the Yimmang, 210–211.
31 Merritt (1981) The Development and Application of Masters and Servants Law in NSW, 208–239.
32 Quinlan, M. (1996) Industrial Relations Before Unions, 289.
33 Thompson, E.P. (1963) *The Making of the English Working Class*.
34 *Hobart Town Courier* 9 February 1838.
35 *Hobart Town Courier* 16 February 1838.
36 Edmonds, P. and Maxwell-Stewart, H. (2016) "The Whip Is a Very Contagious Kind of Thing": Flogging and Humanitarian Reform in Penal Australia, *Journal of Colonialism and Colonial History*, 17(1). DOI: 10.1353/cch.2016.0006
37 LC83–1–9 Campbell Town 15 October 1849.
38 *Sydney Gazette* 27 November 1838.
39 *Adelaide Observer* 14 June 1845.
40 *South Australian* 26 October 1847.
41 *Launceston Examiner* 19 January 1848.
42 *Sydney Monitor* 21 March 1838.
43 Rediker, M. (1987) *Between the Devil and the Deep Blue Sea*.
44 *Sydney Monitor* 8 August 1838.
45 LC362–1–3 Longford 29 October 1836.
46 LC156–1–2 George Town 20 March 1844 and *Cornwall Chronicle* 24 February 1849.
47 LC362–1–3 Longford 2 May 1836.
48 In its short life Macquarie Harbour (1822–1834) a total of 1268 floggings were administered and in one week in July 1823 15 convicts received a total of 1700 lashes. Maxwell-Stewart (2008) *Closing Hell's Gates*, 79, 95. See also Walsh, B. (2007) Heartbreak and Hope, Deference and Defiance on the Yimmang, 212.
49 Maxwell-Stewart (2008) *Closing Hell's Gates*, 109.
50 See for example, AONSW CSO Complaint re: supervision and behaviour of overseers of road parties in Liverpool 2 October 1821 Reel 6051; 4/1749, 46–48 and Re rations for road parties 28 March 1822 Reel 6009; 4/7014, 89–91.
51 *Sydney Monitor* 15 August 1829.
52 Karskens, G. (1986) Defiance, Deference and Diligence, 17–28.
53 *Sydney Gazette* 17 November 1838.
54 MacFie, P. (1988) Dobbers and Cobbers: Informers and Mateship After Convicts, Officials and Settlers on the Grass Tree Hill Road-gang, Tasmania 1830–1850, *Tasmanian Historical Research Association Papers and Proceedings*, 35(3):112–127.
55 LC362–1–4 2 Longford September 1839.

56 LC362–1–6 28 Longford November 1844. See also Rosen, S. (2006) That Den of Infamy, the No. 2 Stockade Cox's River, 242–243.
57 *Sydney Monitor* 8 October 1827.
58 *Cornwall Chronicle* 4 November 1848.
59 *The Australian* 26 November 1830.
60 *Sydney Monitor* 1 November 1834.
61 *Colonial Times* 11 November 1834.
62 *Sydney Monitor* 20 December 1834.
63 *Sydney Monitor* 4 February 1828.
64 *Colonial Times* 29 November 1836.
65 *Sydney Monitor* 25 February 1839.
66 *Hobart Town Courier* 26 May 1837, 2.
67 *Hobart Town Courier* 13 October 1837 and *Sydney Herald* 30 November 1837.
68 *Cornwall Chronicle* 11 September 1844 and LC156–1–2 George Town 25 April 1844.
69 *Cornwall Chronicle* 26 January 1839.
70 *Colonial Times* 29 November 1836.
71 *Cornwall Chronicle* 25 December 1847.
72 *Sydney Herald* 21 July 1836.
73 *Sydney Gazette* 9 December 1826.
74 *Adelaide Observer* 17 April 1847.
75 *Sydney Monitor* 4 March 1840.
76 *Colonial Times* 26 April 1842.
77 *Hobart Town Courier* 16 June 1837.
78 *Moreton Bay Courier* 5 September 1846.
79 *Bathurst Advocate* 1 September 1849.
80 *Sydney Gazette* 1 January 1842.
81 *Australian Government Fair Work Ombudsmen*, Press Release 9 January 2015.
82 *Hobart Town Gazette* 26 November 1825.
83 *Sydney Monitor* 17 October 1840.
84 See for example *Melbourne Argus* 9 October 1846.
85 *Melbourne Argus* 1 December 1846.
86 *Hobart Town Courier* 3 June 1842.
87 *Portland Guardian* 22 April 1843.
88 *Cornwall Chronicle* 11 September 1844.
89 *Sydney Monitor* 19 February 1841.
90 Quinlan, M. (1996) Industrial Relations Before Unions, 269–293; Quinlan, M. (1997) Balancing Trade and Labour Control, 19–56; and Quinlan, M. (1998) Regulating Labour in a Colonial Context, 303–324.
91 *Sydney Gazette* 8 November 1836.
92 See for example *Sydney Herald* 11 November 1836.
93 *Sydney Monitor* 11 May 1838 and Quinlan, M. (1997) Balancing Trade and Labour Control, 19–56.
94 Maxwell-Stewart, H. (2008) *Closing Hell's Gates*.
95 LC247–1–8 Hobart 2 September 1841.
96 *Sydney Herald* 24 January 1840.
97 *Sydney Herald* 13 December 1841.
98 *Sydney Monitor* 4 October 1837.
99 *Sydney Monitor* 7 January 1839.
100 *Australasian Chronicle* 27 June 1840.
101 *Cornwall Chronicle* 13 March 1847.
102 *Goulburn Herald* 6 October 1849.
103 Reid, K. (1997) Contumacious, Ungovernable and Incorrigible, 108.
104 *Sydney Gazette* 25 June 1835.

105 LC83–1–6 Campbell Town 23 December 1841.
106 *Sydney Gazette* 25 June 1835.
107 *Sydney Gazette* 18 April 1837.
108 *Sydney Gazette* 8 November 1836.
109 *Sydney Herald* 1 May 1837.
110 *Sydney Herald* 17 February 1834.
111 LC362–1–3 Longford 25 October 1836.
112 *Sydney Herald* 10 November 1836.
113 *The Colonist* 15 June 1839.
114 Crowley, F.K. (1949) Working Class Conditions in Australia, 1788–1851, 386–397.
115 *Adelaide Observer* 13 October 1849.
116 *The Australian* 29 December 1838.
117 *Sydney Gazette* 29 September 1836.
118 *Inquirer* 21 June 1848.
119 *Commercial Journal* 6 November 1839.
120 *Sydney Herald* 11 May 1837.
121 *Sydney Gazette* 22 June 1837.
122 LC247–1–15 Hobart 26 August 1847.
123 *Sydney Gazette* 22 March 1827.
124 *Geelong Advertiser* 5 January 1850.
125 *Sydney Morning Herald* 2 October 1849.
126 *Cornwall Chronicle* 23 December 1837.
127 Jordan's workshop/home in George St named Dumpledale after his Pembrokeshire home still stands. *Cornwall Chronicle* 25 November 1837 and 2, 16 and 23 December 1837.
128 *Sydney Gazette* 31 March 1838.
129 *Cornwall Chronicle* 16 December 1837.
130 LC247–1–7 Hobart 23 May 1839.
131 *Sydney Gazette* 5 October 1827.
132 *Sydney Monitor* 20 December 1834.
133 *Sydney Gazette* 17 December 1835.
134 *Sydney Gazette* 6 February 1836.
135 *The Australian* 6 November 1838.
136 Maxwell-Stewart (2008), *Closing Hell's Gates*, 214.
137 *Sydney Gazette* 11 November 1824.
138 *Launceston Advertiser* 17 May 1830.
139 *Sydney Gazette* 20 January 1825; 23 June 1836 and *Sydney Herald* 4 July 1836.
140 Maxwell-Stewart, H. (1990) *The Bushrangers and the Convict System of Van Diemen's Land, 1803–1846*, Ph.D. Thesis, University of Edinburgh.
141 Rediker, M. (1987) *Between the Devil and the Deep Blue Sea*.
142 *Sydney Monitor* 7 July 1828.
143 *Sydney Monitor* 4 April 1838.
144 LC156–1–1 George Town 8 September 1841.
145 *Sydney Monitor* 23 April 1838 page 2.
146 *Sydney Morning Herald* 11 January 1843.
147 *Colonial Times* 24 July 1838.
148 *Sydney Monitor* 15 February 1841.
149 *Sydney Herald* 20 September 1841 and *Australasian Chronicle* 4 March 1841.
150 *Sydney Monitor* 1 March 1841.
151 The same could apply to free-labour in rural districts; see Atkinson, A. (1988) *Camden: Farm and Village Life in Early New South Wales*, Oxford University Press, Oxford, 59–60.
152 *Colonial Times* 22 September 1835.

153 *Colonial Times* 28 August 1838.
154 *Colonial Times* 2 October 1838.
155 LC83–1–1 Campbell Town 29 September 1838.
156 *Sydney Monitor* 28 May 1836.
157 LC362–1–3 Longford 24 October 1836.
158 *Sydney Gazette*, 28 November 1835.
159 *Hobarton Guardian* 24 November 1849.
160 *Sydney Monitor* 31 July 1837.
161 *The Australian* 14 November 1839.
162 *Cornwall Chronicle* 15 April 1846.
163 *Colonial Times* 4 June 1839.
164 *Sydney Monitor* 10 June 1839.
165 *Sydney Morning Herald* 24 February 1849.
166 *Cornwall Chronicle* 11 September 1844.
167 *Cornwall Chronicle* 22 January 1845.
168 *Geelong Advertiser* 21 December 1847.
169 *Cornwall Chronicle* 27 January 1849.
170 *Moreton Bay Courier* 11 September 1846.
171 *Sydney Monitor* 16 March 1840.
172 Rosen, S. (2006) That Den of Infamy, the No. 2 Stockade Cox's River, 278–282.
173 *Perth Gazette* 29 January 1842.
174 *Sydney Morning Herald* 25 June 1845.
175 *Melbourne Argus* 22 December 1848.
176 *Sydney Herald* 19 February 1835.
177 *Sydney Gazette* 21 December 1837.
178 *Sydney Monitor* 16 March 1840 and *Australasian Chronicle* 24 March 1840.
179 *Hobart Town Courier*, 4 August 1837.
180 *Colonial Times* 14 April 1840.
181 *Cornwall Chronicle* 16 May 1835.
182 *Cornwall Chronicle* 28 April 1838.
183 *Colonial Times* 7 April 1835.
184 *Sydney Herald* 12 September 1836.
185 *Colonial Times* 24 March 1835.
186 *Colonial Times* 7 April 1835.
187 See *Hobart Town Courier*. See *Colonial Times* 16 June 1835 and *Hobart Town Courier* 21 August 1835.
188 It was widely reported in other colonies. See for example, *The Australian* 29 September 1835.
189 Neal, D. (1991) *The Rule of Law in a Penal Colony: Law and Power in Early New South Wales*, 93.
190 They enjoyed the same powers and privileges of the English equivalents, a position that dated back to the 14th century. Neal, D. (1991) *The Rule of Law in a Penal Colony*, 117–118.
191 Neal, D. (1991) *The Rule of Law in a Penal Colony*, 118.
192 Neal, D. (1991) *The Rule of Law in a Penal Colony*, 133–136.
193 Neal, D. (1991) *The Rule of Law in a Penal Colony*, 161; Walsh, B. (2007) Heartbreak and Hope, Deference and Defiance on the Yimmang, 200.
194 See for example *Australian* 3 April 1827.
195 See for example *Sydney Monitor* 18 August 1832.
196 Dawson responded to this report, writing a letter that attempted to justify his stance. *Colonial Times* 2 and 9 October 1838.
197 *Hobart Town Courier* 31 January 1840.
198 *Geelong Advertiser* 30 December 1846.
199 See for example report published in *Cornwall Chronicle* 30 May 1840.

200 *Colonial Times* 23 March 1841.
201 *Cornwall Chronicle* 3 March 1847.
202 *Cornwall Chronicle* 9 October 1847.
203 Quinlan, M. (2012) The Low Rumble of Informal Dissent: Shipboard Protests over Health and Safety in Australian Waters 1790–1900, *Labour History*, 102:131–155.
204 *Sydney Herald* 30 November 1840.
205 *Australasian Chronicle* 1 December 1840.
206 *South Australia Register* 31 January 1850.
207 LC362–1–3 Longford 30 March 1836.
208 *Sydney Monitor* 10 May 1839.
209 *The Colonist* 6 July 1839.
210 See for example *Australasian Chronicle* 4 October 1843 and *Sydney Morning Herald* 23 November 1843.
211 See Merritt, A. (1981) The Development and Application of Masters and Servants Legislation in New South Wales—1845–1930; McQueen, R. (1992) Master and Servant as Social Control: The Role of Law in Labour Relations on the Darling Downs, 1860–1870, *Law in Context*, 10:123–139; Davidson, A. (1975) *An Analytical and Comparative History of Master and Servant Legislation in Tasmania*, L.L.M. Thesis, University of Tasmania; Quinlan, M. (2004) Australia 1788–1902: A "Working Man's Paradise?"; Quinlan, M. (1992) Making Labour Laws Fit for the Colonies; Quinlan, M. (1996) Industrial Relations before Unions, 269–293; Quinlan, M. (1997) Balancing Trade and Labour Control, 19–56; and Quinlan, M. (1998), Regulating Labour in a Colonial Context, 303–324.
212 LC83–1–10 Campbell Town 19 June 1850.
213 *Moreton Bay Courier* 28 August 1847 and 4 September 1847.
214 Atkinson, A. (1979) Four Patterns of Convict Protest.

3   Overview of Worker Organisation, 1788–1850

As in Europe and North America, early organisation by workers in Australia took a wide array of forms. This chapter examines organisation by whether it was formal or informal, involved convicts or free workers, by gender, industry, occupation and the issues/objectives involved. It also examines the origins of organisation in customary practices, labour market conditions and social networks. Informal organisation is defined by action rather than institutional arrangements. Patterns of collective action have changed over time. While mass abandoning from work is now rare, in the 18th and 19th century it was common and even preferred amongst workers tied to their employer for long periods and incapable of renegotiating their conditions. In November 1848 crewmembers on the barque *Senator* moored in Port Melbourne deserted repeatedly after a strike over poor rations had failed.[1] Most were recaptured, fined and sent on board.

While informal organisation was often marked by a single instance of collective action, as the last case indicates it was not uncommon for a succession of actions to occur. By the mid-1820s in towns like Launceston, groups of convicts from the same gang were being tried for neglect or refusing to work every few days. Similar patterns can be found outside towns. On 28 and 29 November 1841 two groups of convicts absconded from the Browns River Probation Party south of Hobart; some were quickly apprehended but others remained at large for over two months during which time other groups absconded from the party.[2] Court records indicate collective prosecution of workers was often interspersed with trials involving individual workers symptomatic of a wider dispute. In January 1849 the English ship *Maitland's* crew struck over poor rations. One seaman charged the captain with ill-treatment while two others were tried for attempted desertion and threatening the captain. Dissent on the *Maitland* kept Port Melbourne magistrates busy for almost three months, illustrating the complex array of actions involved in protracted struggles.[3] Finally, but not least, this chapter examines formal organisation and its relationship to informal organisation.

The Overall Extent of Worker Mobilisation

The database records 6426 instances of worker organisation prior to 1851, 29 between 1788 and 1800, 68 in 1801–10; 173 in 1811–20; 1767 in 1821–30; 2763 in 1831–40 and 1629 in 1841–50. In addition there was at least one union peak body and over 20 instances where workers mobilised politically (Chapter 11). As noted earlier the 6426 figure represents my best estimate of around 60–70% of worker organisation for which written evidence survives. Most instances of organisation were small and confined to a single workplace. There is evidence of 135 formal organisations/unions (Table 3.1).

The oldest and then largest colonies of NSW (4052 or 63.4%) and VDL (1990 or 31%) dominate instances of worker organisation followed by Victoria (212 or 3.1%), South Australia (99 or 1.5%), Queensland (40 or 0.6%), Western Australia (36 or 0.6%) and what became the Northern Territory (1). While instances of organisation outside NSW and VDL can be identified from the 1820s (like an instance of collective absconding in the short-lived Port Phillip colony of 1803), it only became substantial in the decade to 1850 at 18.2% of total organisation. If comparison is confined for free workers the figure almost doubles to 34.6%. The rise of organisation in Victoria and South Australia is even more pronounced if only formal organisation is considered (Table 3.2). Interrogation of additional court records may increase these colonies' relative significance.

Another spatial dimension is the extent worker organisation was concentrated in urban centres. Figure 3.1 differentiates organisation occurring in each colony's capital/principal town from that outside it (data for 1851–1900 is less complete but indicative). From 1819 organisation outside colonial 'capitals' grew sharply to establish a gap but this entirely reverses in the early 1840s, a situation maintained until the 1880s when unions formed branches in many regional towns. Not surprisingly, urban centres were critical for formal organisation. Of 135 known unions only 9 were established (or attempted) outside the principal town/city of each colony—one in Maitland; four in Launceston, two in Geelong, and two in regional Western Australia (Table 3.1). More so than North America or even Europe, despite the spread of settlement, the colonies' population urbanised with a large part living in in each colony's principal town/capital (Sydney, Hobart, Adelaide, Perth, Melbourne and Brisbane). With a few exceptions like Maitland, Geelong and Launceston, regional towns remained small and of these only Launceston—founded 1806 and the only town to rival a colonial capital—was the home to more than two unions (four) prior to 1851.

It is important to distinguish organisation by free workers or convicts (Figure 3.2). There were 5047 instances of organisation by convict workers and 1379 by free workers. Organisation by free workers is evident from 1790 but only grew strongly from the late 1820s and by 1841–50 had outstripped organisation amongst convicts. There were 389 instances of organisation by

Table 3.1 Formal Worker Organisation by Occupation and Duration in Australia 1825–50

Year	New South Wales	Van Diemen's Land	Victoria	Western Australia	South Australia	Total
1825	1. police (1825)					1
1828	2. stonemasons (1828)					1
1829		1. printers (1829–38)				
1830	3. shipwrights (1830– 1980)			1. shepherds, domestics? (1830)		2
1831	4. carpenters (1831) 5. bootmakers (1831)					2
1833	6. cabinetmakers (1833–46) 7. curriers (1833)	2. carpenters, joiners (1833) 3. tailors (1833–34)				4
1834	8. coachmakers (1834) 9. carpenters (1834)	4. sawyers (1834) 5. bakers (1834)				4
1835	10. printers (1835–40) 11. tailors (1835–38) 12. carpenters (1835–37) 13. joiners (1835–41)	6. carpenters, joiners (1835–37)				5
1836	14. curriers (1836) 15. bakers (1836)	7. painters, glaziers (1836)				3
1837	16. coachmakers (1837–41) 17. seamen, labourers (1837) 18. blacksmiths (1837) 19. coopers (1837–43)					4
1839	20. pressmen (1839) 21. seamen (1839–45)	8. sawyers (1839–52) 9. wheelwrights, coachmakers (1839)			1. building trades (1839–46) 2. tailors (1839–46)	6

(*Continued*)

Table 3.1 (Continued)

Year	New South Wales	Van Diemen's Land	Victoria	Western Australia	South Australia	Total
1840	22. sawyers (1840–47) 23. tailors (1840–46) 24. engineers, moulders (1840) 25. carpenters (1840–45) 26. painters, plumbers, glaziers (1840) 27. bootmakers (1840–44) 28. stonemasons (1840–49) 29. blacksmiths (1840) 30. bakers (1840–41) 31. assistant-drapers (1840–42)	10. bakers (1840) 11. Launceston bakers (1840) 12. Launceston whalers (1840)	1. bakers (1840) 2. bricklayers (1840) 3. carpenters, joiners (1840–41) 4. tailors (1840)		3. stonemasons (1840)	18
1841			5. assistant-drapers (1841) 6. sawyers (1841) 7. printers (1841) 8. stonemasons, bricklayers (1841) 9. brickmakers (1841) 10. assistant grocers (1841) 11. paviors (1842)			5
1842	32. plasterers (1842–47) 33. bricklayers (1842–44) 34. slaters, shinglers (1842)	13. tailors (1842)				5

1843	35. weavers (1843–50?) 36. labourers (1843)	14. bootmakers (1843) 15. joiners, cabinetmakers, coachmakers, turners (1843)	12. bootmakers (1843)	2. shepherds (1843)	6
1844	37. port j watermen (1844–60) 38. watermen(2) (1844–49) 39. assistant-drapers (1844–45) 40. clerks (1844–50) 41. bakers (1844)	16. butchers (1844)	13. stonemasons (1844–47) 14. bricklayers (1844) 15. printers (1844–46)		9
1845	42. millwrights etc (1844–50) 43. wool-staplers (1845) 44. carpenters (1845–46) 45. brickmakers (1845–49)		16. tailors (1845–47)	4. water-carriers (1845–50)	6
1846	46. nailers (1846) 47. bakers (1846–47)	17. tailors (1846–55) 18. seamen (1846)	17. police constables (1846) 18. assistant-drapers (1846) 19. grocer's assistants (1846) 20. bootmakers (1846–55) 21. tailoresses, dressmakers (1846) 22. carpenters, joiners (1846–48)	5. assistant-drapers (1846) 6. carpenters, joiners (1846–51) 7. bootmakers (1846) 8. blacksmiths, wheelwrights (1846–47)	14

(Continued)

Table 3.1 (Continued)

Year	New South Wales	Van Diemen's Land	Victoria	Western Australia	South Australia	Total
1847	48. tailors (1847) 49. painters, glaziers (1847) 50. gardeners (1847–49)	19. mercantiles assistants (1847–55) 20. Launceston shop-assistants (1847) 21. Campbell Town shop-assistants (1847) 22. bootmakers (1847–48) 23. shipwrights (1847)	23. assistant-drapers (1847) 24. water-carriers (1847) 25. blacksmiths, wheelwrights (1847–48) 26. saddlers (1847) 27. Geelong water-carriers (1847) 28. Geelong shop-assistants (1847) 29. sawyers (1847–55)		9. bakers (1847)	15
1848	51. assistant-drapers (1848–49) 52. carpenters (1848–49)	24. tanners, fellmongers (1848) 25. printers (1848)	30. bricklayers (1848) 31. assistant-drapers (1848) 32. curriers (1848)		10. miners (1848–49)	8
1849	53. joiners (1849) 54. bakers (1849–50) 55. fellmongers, woolsorters (1849)	26. Launceston printers (1849–54) 27. public servants (1849)	32. assistant-drapers (1849)		11. curriers (1849)	7

1850	56. bakers (1850–51)	33. assistant-drapers (1850) 34. carpenters, joiners (1850–53) 35. tailors (1850–52) 36. stonemasons (1850–53)	12. shop-assistants (1850) 13. tailors (1850)	7
	27	37	2	13
Total	56			135

Table 3.2 Number of Workers Involved in Organisation by Period, Australia 1788–1850

Worker Numbers	1788–1800	1801–10	1811–20	1821–30	1831–40	1841–50	Total
Convict workers							
Raw Numbers	92	167	494	6297	8705	2663	18418
Median members	3	3	3	3	3	3	
Zero reporting organisations	1	1	10	49	89	36	
Additional numbers based on median*	3	3	30	147	267	108	
Estimated Total	97	170	524	6444	8972	2771	18978
Free workers—informal							
Raw Numbers	69	109	157	255	1577	5144	7311
Median Members	6	4	4	4	4	3	
Zero reporting organisations	1	3	4	25	79	157	
Additional numbers based on median*	4	12	16	100	316	471	
Estimated Total	73	121	173	355	1893	5615	8230
Free workers—formal							
Raw Numbers				9	574	1822	2405
Median Members				9	36	45	
Zero reporting organisations				2	32	76	
Additional numbers based on median*				18	1152	3420	
Estimated Total				27	1726	5242	6995
All workers totals							
Raw Numbers	161	276	651	6561	10856	9629	28134
Estimated Total	170	291	697	6826	12591	13628	34203

* number of zero membership reporting organisations multiplied by median membership

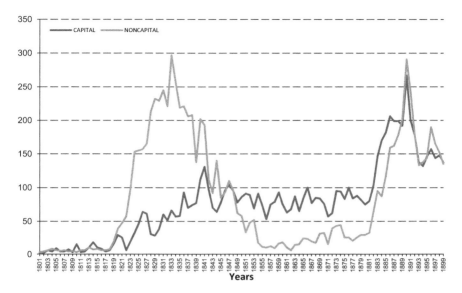

Figure 3.1 Instances of Worker Organisation by Capital/Non-Capital Location

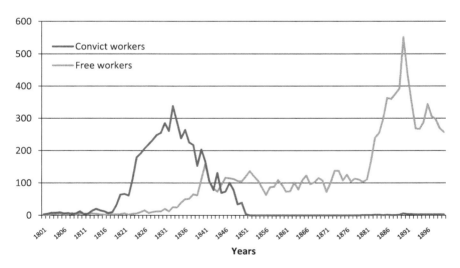

Figure 3.2 Instances of Convict and Free Worker Organisation in Australia 1801–
1900

free-labour in 1831–40 (compared to 2374 by convicts) and 849 in the following decade (compared to 780 organisations involving convicts). Hence
the growth of free-labour organisation paralleled a sharp decline in convict
organisation, marking the wind-down in transportation and growth of the

free-labour colonies. Formal organisation wasn't an option for convicts, although ticket-of-leave holders and emancipated convicts joined unions.

Combined action by convict and free workers occurred but was rare and largely confined to ticket-of-leave holders. On 27 May 1835 two free workers and two ticket-of-Leave holders were prosecuted for collective action at William Kermode's Mona Vale Estate near Tunbridge VDL.[4] Ticket-of-leave holders were permitted to work in sealing/whaling, and in February 1850 five were charged with breaching their agreement aboard the colonial whaling brig *Prince of Denmark*.[5] The rarity of combined action by convicts cannot be explained by race, ethnic or class divides but rather the combination of regulatory/employment segregation. This raises questions about studies of free and unfree-labour that ignore or downplay these elements.

Another important distinction can be made between formal and informal organisation. Figure 3.3 provides a breakdown of formal and informal organisation by year (1801–1900), highlighting the slow transition to formal organisation. There were 29 known instances of informal organisation prior to 1801—all occurring in Sydney or its environs. Instances of informal organisation exceed formal organisation until 1868 and union numbers only surge in the 1880s.[6] As expected, Figure 3.3 indicates greater volatility amongst informal organisations in any given year. While there some matching in short-term peaks and troughs (suggesting economic fluctuations affected both) from the 1840s, a longer term substitution effect is apparent especially after 1880 though informal organisation doesn't disappear.

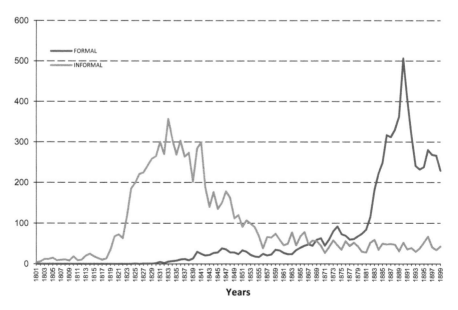

Figure 3.3 Instances of Formal and Informal Worker Organisation: Australia 1801–1900

While the emergence of unions after 1825 might owe something to repeal of the UK *Combination Acts* (1824), the growth more closely matches the transitioning to free-labour and a critical mass effect amongst trades in larger towns. Local labour market volatility rather than political repression also explains why unions were often short-lived (see Chapters 7 and 8). The 135 unions identified are conservative given fragmentary surviving sources. Formal bodies were identified via their title (like society, association, institution, union, club or committee) or whether formal organisation was essential to their activities (like mutual insurance, a House-of-Call or reaching signed agreements with employers). Organisations like the Australian Union Benefit Society (established in Sydney, 1834) and the Maitland Trades Union Benefit Society (established 1838) were excluded as generic friendly societies of working people. Instances of multi-workplace organisation, like Sydney printers and carpenters strikes in December 1829 may have entailed formal organisation but as yet lacks evidence. At worst these combinations were precursors to formal organisation (see later chapters). The 135 unions represent around 2.1% of worker organisations or 4% if organisations are weighted by years of existence.

About 74% were trade societies formed by printers, tailors, cordwainers, carpenters, stonemasons, bricklayers, coachmakers, wheelwrights, blacksmiths, curriers and other trades drawing on long-established models of organisation (see Chapter 1). Craft bodies exploited their geographic remoteness that made obtaining substitute labour difficult but were small and vulnerable to economic downturns. Most collapsed after a few years—a pattern of organisational turnover continuing long after 1850.[7] The remaining unions (35 or 26%) were non-trade bodies (Table 3.1). Most conspicuous were shop-assistants (16 bodies) followed by water-carriers (3), seamen and whalers (3), police constables (2), watermen (2), shepherds (2), labourers (2) and wool-staplers, clerks, gardeners, junior public servants, dressmakers and miners (all 1). Fittingly for a penal colony, the first known union was a Sydney police constables benefit society established in 1825—three years before Sydney stonemasons formed the first craft union. Both organisations of shepherds occurred in Western Australia, then a free colony. Again, most were short-lived with longer surviving bodies including Sydney Watermen, Hobart Mercantile Assistants and Port Jackson Coasting Seamen. They too drew on customary modes of organisation and contemporary UK developments like the early-closing movement.

Organisation by Duration and Size

Other dimensions for assessing organisation include duration and size. The database records first and last known dates for organisations, with best-estimates for a small number of ambiguous cases. Reporting-gaps sometimes made it difficult to establish if a union had continued or was succeeded by a new body, but changes in name, meeting place or officials; retrospective news items or other sources often clarified this. Data may still understate longevity. The vast majority of organisations were informal and short-lived. Workers typically came together for a single act or several closely-timed actions, often then being brought to trial, which played out over a few days or week although a few extended over six months or longer. Unions typically lasted far longer though many collapsed within a year of being established. Table 3.1 indicates that 27 survived between two and five years, 22 between five and ten years, seven over 10 years and one (Sydney Shipwrights) over 100 years. Newly formed bodies were highly vulnerable to adverse circumstances—the massacre of the innocents noted in organisational ecology literature.[8] Over half unions surviving a year stayed in operation five or more years.

As later chapters demonstrate, informal organisation facilitated union formation and, in turn, even a year's survival represented a substantial advance on the former. Pre-1851 unions were not failed experiments preceding a more important wave of union formation. There was direct carryover of organisations into the 1850s. With notable exceptions, like the UK-based Amalgamated Society of Engineers, unions formed in the two decades after 1850 were similar to earlier bodies, experiencing frequent setbacks/collapses even as unionism slowly consolidated. Further, organisational turnover, before or after 1850, didn't preclude some continuity. This is evident in successive attempts to form unions in particular trades involving the same individuals (see Chapter 7). Examining interactions between formal and informal organisation over time provides a better understanding of the development unions and worker mobilisation more generally.

Regarding size, the database includes the number of workers involved in each organisation where known. Figures were unavailable for some organisations, with numbers being more typically reported where organisation was informal and small (below 10 workers). Amongst unions, membership was reported at general meetings or in annual reports. Numbers attending meetings provided additional evidence. Total worker involvement was estimated by assigning median membership for each decade to organisations without reported membership (Table 3.2). Distinguishing convict and free workers, and separating out formal and informal organisation of free workers, limited over-generalisation as well as revealing important changes in worker organisation, especially the shift to free-labour and the effects of formal organisation. Tabulating numbers by decade better accommodated data gaps and indicated changes over time. Counting involvement by year doesn't mean workers were active all year. Union membership can more be readily presumed to have lasted for a year but not always given organisational volatility.

Table 3.2 indicates rapid increases in total worker involvement after 1820. Mobilisation by free-labour (including ex-convicts) after 1830 is apparent though more than offset by a sharp decline in convict worker involvement in the decade after 1840, reflecting both the transitioning of the labour market and poorer economic conditions. The growing importance of unions is evident in the fact they account for almost half free-labour involvement in the decade to 1850. Union membership ranged from eight (Launceston Printers) to 343 (Burra Miners). Numbers involved in informal organisation ranged from two to around 1,000 (including women at a Female Factory) with the vast majority under 12 workers. Given the caveats mentioned above counter-posed against the incompleteness of the database (Chapter 1), Table 3.2 provides a conservative baseline for growing worker mobilisation.

Organisation by Industry, Occupation and Gender

Another way of scoping organisation is the breakdown by industry, occupation and gender. Totals in Tables 3.3 and 3.4 exceed 6426 because they are weighted by the number of years an organisation survived (acknowledging an important effect of formal organisation) and because some organisations covered more than one occupation. Table 3.3 indicates organisation occurred in all industries but was concentrated in government (53.4%) followed by rural/farming (21.4%), maritime (12.3%), manufacturing (or 4.2%), services (2.6), mining (2.3%) and retailing (0.4%). This pattern reflects both the dominance of the state and key activities within colonial economies, and the strategic positioning/capacity of specific workers to combine (Chapter 1). Whalers and sealers were included under maritime rather than a farming/fishing and forestry industry designation (as would occur today) because this more accurately reflected the nature and regulation of their work (see Chapter 5). If the industry breakdown is confined to convicts, a different pattern emerges, with 65.2% in government, 24.1% of organisation in rural/farming, 3.3% in manufacturing, 2.8% in personal services, 2.7% in mining, 0.4% in maritime and 0.3% in retailing (1.7% were unknown). This reflects their significance in government infrastructure-building and, as assigned-convicts, to pastoral and manufacturing employers. Female convicts were predominantly engaged in personal service.

Table 3.4 provides an occupational breakdown. As with industry, it indicates the wide array of workers taking collective action including clerks, cooks, domestic servants and teachers. Construction and general labourers (overwhelmingly convicts) constituted the single biggest category of worker organisation (46.2% of the weighted total), followed by rural/farmworkers (22.2%), seamen (11.4%), miscellaneous unskilled (4.2% including police and military), cooks/domestics (2.9%), miners (2.4%), sealers/whalers (2%), sawyers (1.2%) and cab-drivers/carters (1%). The number of organisations involving unskilled-workers—free and convict—reinforces the need to consider all organisations not just unions. All craft groups combined account for about 6.4% of organisation though most formal organisation. Collective action was spread across a wide spectrum of the colonial workforce rather than being confined to a few groups. Distinguishing convict and free-labour reveals that convicts constituted 99% of organisation amongst

Table 3.3 Worker Organisation by Industry, Australia 1788–1850

Industry	1788–1800	1801–1810	1811–1820	1821–1830	1831–1840	1841–1850	Total	As % of all organisation
Building & construction	2			6	28	38	74	1.2
Building materials	1			8	26	30	65	1
Clothing, boots & apparel				9	36	34	79	1.2
Commercial services	1		2	14	117	36	170	2.6
Food manufacture				7	28	28	63	1
Government & community service	9	35	135	1394	1359	498	3430	53.4
Maritime & sealing/whaling	5	24	19	34	252	456	790	12.3
Metal manufacture				1	4	8	13	0.2
Mining				1	108	42	151	2.3
Miscellaneous manufacturing	1			4	15	20	40	0.6
Printing & publishing				2	11	11	24	0.4
Retailing			1	1	12	19	33	0.5
Road transport						9	9	0.1
Rural & farming	9	6	11	263	715	371	1375	21.4
Unknown	1	3	5	22	52	32	115	1.8

Table 3.4 Worker Organisation by Occupation, Australia 1788–1850

Occupation	1788–1800	1801–1810	1811–1820	1821–1830	1831–1840	1841–1850	Total*	As % of all organisation
Bakers				3	8	10	21	0.3
Bootmakers				1	16	17	34	0.5
Bricklayers	3		1		3	5	12	0.2
Brickmakers	2	2	5	11	21	7	48	0.7
Misc Build trades-				2	2	5	9	0.1
Butchers					3	10	13	0.2
Cab-drivers/carters			6	21	25	10	62	1.0
Cabinetmakers				3	15	8	26	0.4
Carpenters	2	1	4	2	12	13	34	0.5
Clerks					2	7	9	0.1
Clothing trades				11	27	15	53	0.8
Cooks & domestics	1		5	16	122	40	184	2.9
Coachmakers					5	6	11	0.2
Coopers			1	1	2	1	5	0.1
Construct labour	4	15	56	822	968	294	2159	33.6
General labourers	5	10	23	425	279	67	809	12.6
Leather trades					3	7	10	0.2
Miners			1	4	105	43	153	2.4
Metal trades		1	2	2	8	14	27	0.4
Misc skilled/profn		1	15	4	1	4	25	0.4
Misc unskilled		2	19	54	92	104	271	4.2
Painters, plasterers & plumbers			1	1	7	8	17	0.3
Printers				2	11	12	25	0.4
Letter carriers						1	1	0

(Continued)

Table 3.4 (Continued)

Occupation	1788–1800	1801–1810	1811–1820	1821–1830	1831–1840	1841–1850	Total*	As % of all organisation
Retail workers			2	1	13	20	36	0.5
Rural/farm labour	10	7	12	318	709	373	1429	22.2
Sawyers	1		6	14	28	21	75	1.2
Sealers & whalers		8	1	6	49	67	126	2.0
Seamen	5	18	23	42	222	423	733	11.4
Shearers					1	10	11	0.2
Shipwrights	1		2	2	1	6	12	0.2
Stonemasons			2	2	10	9	23	0.3
Teachers						1	1	0
Wharf-labourers				3	8	5	16	0.2
Unknown	1	4	5	11	39	24	84	1.3

* Total exceeds 6426 because some organisations involved multiple occupations

construction labour, 97% amongst general labourers, 90% of rural labour, 87% of cooks and domestics (overwhelmingly female) and 60% of miscellaneous unskilled workers (including women in Female Factories). Amongst trade workers, the numbers are more evenly split. For seamen and sealers/whalers, the situation is reversed with free workers constituting 90% of organisation and convicts largely confined to customs and other boat crews servicing ports given the risk of escape.

For a gender breakdown three categories were used, male only, female only and organisations involving both men and women. Worker organisation was male-dominated (96.2% of 6426) but there were 246 instances where women organised, 154 times by themselves and 92 cases alongside male colleagues. Convicts account for most female-only organisation (94.2%) and organisations involving both men and women (81.3%). Women account for 3.8% of worker organisations but 7.7% of total workers involved. The congregation of convicts in Female Factories, stronger collaborative networks and shared experiences (including bonding during voyages to the colonies) contributed to a greater willingness/capacity to act collectively (see Chapters 9 and 10).[9] Free women employed as domestics, laundresses and dressmakers also engaged in collective action, including a Melbourne Dressmakers/Tailoresses Union (Chapters 8, 9 and 10).

Organisation by Objectives and Methods

Worker organisation was examined in terms of objectives and methods. Objectives and methods were largely deduced from the collective action of organisations as well as formal aims, government and rules in the case of unions. Benefits covering funerals, sickness, unemployment or loss of tools clearly indicated the union pursued mutual insurance. Rules or practices restricting access into a trade indicated craft controls. Unions also sought to maximise members' employment through devices like the House-of-Call. For informal organisation in particular it was possible to deduce aims and methods through reports of action or subsequent court proceedings. The evidence is incomplete. Unions may have pursued issues not identified and collective action commonly arises from multiple causes. Nonetheless, evidence affords valuable information on issues and methods used.

Table 3.5 summarises evidence on objectives/issues for 6426 organisations. Percentages exceed 100% because many organisations, especially unions, pursued multiple objectives. Unions were counted for each year of their existence—a weighting already discussed. Most issues like wages, working conditions, management behaviour, hours of work and safety were identical to those involving individual workers brought before the courts (Chapter 2). However, other objectives required formal organisation including craft control, mutual insurance and practices like the House-of-Call.

Almost 80% of organisations were concerned with working conditions—a necessarily generalised notion though more specific detail exists for a

Table 3.5 Worker Organisation by Objectives/Issues Pursued in Australia 1788–1850

Issue	1788–1800	1801–1810	1811–1820	1821–1830	1831–1840	1841–1850	Total	% of 6426 worker orgs
Wages/remuneration	3	1	8	24	111	225	372	5.8
Working conditions	17	40	144	1587	2337	990	5115	79.6
Management behaviour	2	2	2	35	198	199	438	6.8
Hours of work	2	5	6	103	292	364	772	12.0
Jobs/employment				8	63	77	148	2.3
Health & safety	4	4	7	66	227	215	523	8.1
Skill/trade control				2	20	64	86	1.3
Subcontracting					2	7	9	0.1
Mutual insurance				4	29	54	87	1.3
Unionism				1	7	11	19	0.4
Other*						2	2	0
Unknown	1	23	15	59	55	89	242	3.7

* One instance each of race and gender-based exclusion

significant minority (like workloads and work methods). This was followed by hours (12%), health and safety (8.1%), management behaviour (6.8%), wages (5.8%), jobs/employment (2.3%), craft control and mutual insurance (both 1.3%). The low ranking of wages/remuneration reflects regulatory restrictions on convict-pay and the capacity of free workers, especially rural workers and seamen, to bargain over wages. Like other objectives—notably jobs/employment, trade control, mutual insurances and unionism—the growing importance of wages from the 1830s onwards was associated with the emergence of unions (Table 3.5). On the other hand, OHS maintains its importance throughout—and after 1850—something that reflects poorly on the preoccupations of labour/industrial relations historians.[10] Health and safety was an issue for many informally organised workers but especially convicts and seamen dependent on rations. For unions, mutual insurance entailed important health objectives like providing accident/sickness benefits.

Table 3.6 provides a breakdown of methods. As with objectives, some organisations employed multiple methods, especially unions where some used eight of more. The Hobart Town Journeymen Tailors Benefit Society (1846–1855) provided friendly benefits, used trade-based controls (including apprentice/journeymen ratios), imposed compulsory unionism, struck work and its members' assaulted strike-breakers. Even amongst informal organisations, multiple methods weren't uncommon. In March 1827 assigned-convicts at John Raine's Darling flour mill Parramatta conducted a go-slow, abused their overseer, struck work and one (John Picket) tried to sabotage machinery.[11] Absconding after a failed strike was also common.

Table 3.6 indicates collective absconding was the commonest method used by 59.6% of organisations (overwhelmingly informal) followed by strikes (26.8%), go-slows (6.9%), misconduct (4.3%), insolence/abuse (3.2%), court action (2.4%), made demands (1.5%), mutual insurance (1.3%), assault (1.3%), petition (1.1%), craft control (1.1), threats (0.9%), larceny (0.9%), sabotage (0.8%), public demonstration (0.8%) and political agitation (0.7%). Collective stealing from employers, like seamen 'broaching' cargo, was common but only cases where a work connection is evident (stealing food to supplement rations) were included. The third-party settlement case involved the Governor appointing a panel of magistrates to investigate complaints by 87 convicts on the Sydney Harbour hulk *Phoenix* in November 1825.[12] This early instance of third-party dispute settlement—later a defining feature of Australian industrial relations—reflected the prominence of the state role from the country's beginnings.

Distinguishing between convict and free-labour significantly alters the ranking. Around 70.9% of convict organisation involving absconding, followed by strikes (19.1%), neglect/go-slows (7.1%), misconduct (4.1%), insolence/abuse (3.7%), assaults (1.2%), larceny (1%), sabotage (0.9%), court actions (0.8%), threats (0.8%), made demand/complaint (0.6%), riots (0.3%) and petitions (0.1%). For free workers strikes were the most

Table 3.6 Worker Organisation by Methods Used, Australia 1788–1850

Methods	1788–1800	1801–1810	1811–1820	1821–1830	1831–1840	1841–1850	Total	% of 6426 worker orgs
Strike	9	17	26	222	637	809	1720	26.8
Mass Absconding	7	41	133	1407	1775	473	3829	59.6
Made Demands		1	2	10	26	60	99	1.5
Court Action	2	2	4	14	56	77	153	2.4
Petition			3	7	18	45	73	1.1
Deputation					2	5	7	0.1
Go-slow	12	6	3	87	239	111	446	6.9
Insolence/abuse	2	2	0	16	108	78	204	3.2
Threats		1	1	5	27	21	55	0.9
Assault		0	1	5	43	35	84	1.3
Misconduct	2			12	129	137	278	4.3
Larceny		2		12	31	11	54	0.9
Sabotage			1	8	24	16	49	0.8
Bans				2	8	21	31	0.5
Mutual insurance				4	30	52	86	1.3
Unilateral Regulation					8	18	26	0.4
House-of-Call					13	16	29	0.5
Closed shop				1	1	2	4	0.1
Strike-fund					4	8	12	0.2
Craft/Skill control					18	50	68	1.1
Public Demonstration					15	38	53	0.8
Political agitation				1	15	32	48	0.7
Collective bargaining				1	4	7	12	0.2
Riot	1	1	0	4	2	5	13	0.2
Cooperation					2	1	3	0.1
Other*				1				0
Unknown		4	2	36	29	25	96	1.5

important method (54.7%) followed by absconding (18.9%), court actions (7.8%), mutual insurance (6.2%), go-slow (5.7%), misconduct (5.4%), made demands (5%), craft control (4.9%), petition (4.8%), public demonstration (3.8%), political agitation (3.5%), House-of-Call (2.1%), unilateral regulation and bans (both 1.9%), assault (1.7%), threat (1.2%), strike-fund (0.9%), deputation (0.5%) and sabotage (0.4%). Aside from the greater propensity of free workers to strike, a number of these differences are directly attributable to the methods (like craft control and mutual insurance) only available to formal organisation. Table 3.6 reiterates the importance of considering all methods not just strikes.

Collective absconding—the single most important method used by convicts but was also common amongst free workers like female domestics, seamen, whalers, rural and indentured workers—warrants comment. Records were more complete for convicts because their absconding was subject to tighter government oversight and public reporting, whereas reports of absconding by free workers was dependent on employers placing advertisements in newspapers or the workers being apprehended and tried. As other evidence makes clear, these reports only capture a fraction of the instances of absconding. Even with convict records there are gaps because those apprehended within days of deserting (not uncommon) were not included in formal government notices. From the late 1820s NSW Government Notices did include apprehension reports. Thus, the report for 9 May 1829 included two groups of absconders, from Berry and Wollstonecraft's Estate and the No. 22 road-gang respectively, apprehended before notice of their absconding was published.[13] Even when absconding and apprehension reports were both published, they cannot be viewed as exhaustive. Interrogation of additional records will add to our understanding, but is unlikely to alter the ratio of absconding to other forms of collective action by more than a few percentage points.

Absconding/desertion was a very old form of collective action, being utilised by bound-rural workers and others exploiting labour shortages that followed the Black Death in Europe. It was also well-suited to non-unionised workers who couldn't bargain with their employer and were subject to lengthy engagements. In the Australian colonies widespread absconding was enormously costly to individual employers and the state because it deprived them of labour on a longer term basis than strikes, and explains why such efforts were taken to combat it. Absconding illustrates the importance of not confining analysis of collective action to strikes but considering all forms of action. This, in turn, has global implications for understanding the origins and development of worker organisation.

Taking rations and the possession of money (not uncommon amongst convicts unlike slaves) facilitated escapes as did the fact that compared to many slaves, convict absconders weren't readily distinguishable in the communities they 'disappeared' into under an assumed name. Unlike slaves on small islands, the vastness and slow communications in Australia also aided absconding. The vast majority of absconders sought employment elsewhere (see Chapter 2). Some tried to escape the colonies altogether, mostly by secreting themselves on ships or working as seamen, though there were a few instances of groups engaging in planned and sometimes violent piratical seizure of boats and ships. Group absconding was especially prevalent amongst convict gangs peaking in 1833, after which instances declined sharply in NSW partly in response to changes in policy regarding the use/administration of gangs as well as distinctive attire/slops and more secure housing of road-gangs with military guards making escape more difficult.[14] There was no similar tail-off in group absconding from farms/estates. In 1823 there were over 30 instances of collective absconding from Emu Plains (west of Sydney) alone involving groups of up to 22 workers (groups of 6–8 were more typical). While pull factors like seasonal peaks in labour demand exerted an influence, push factors (poor conditions, harsh discipline) were more critical, evident in the fact that absconding occurred at all times of the year and evidence given by absconders when brought to trial. Especially harsh conditions on some gangs also helps to explain why they experienced higher rates of absconding, although other factors playing a role included the relative ease or difficulty of absconding from particular locations.

In remote penal stations (like Moreton Bay and Macquarie Harbour), gangs and farms collective absconding was more viable if not essential. Collective absconding commonly entailed a degree of planning and coordination to deal with encumbrances like chains, provide sustenance/funds, determining an escape route/destination and timing. In December 1838 five members of the Campbell Town chain-gang were charged with aiding and abetting the escape of another prisoner.[15] Without narks, proving such claims was difficult and in this case the charges failed. As this case indicates, the divide between collective and individual absconding could be blurred. Moreover sequential absconding was common with one group's departure from a gang or farm being followed by others. On occasion those absconding on different days were recaptured together. Sequential absconding by small groups may have been planned to maximise chances of evading recapture. On 19 April 1833 three men absconded from the No.10 road-gang (NSW) followed by another group of five on the 26th, while three small groups absconded from the No.13 road-gang over a four-day period from 28 May.[16] In October 1833 three members of the No.9 road-gang absconded on the 6th, six more on the 7th and another three on the 11th.[17] These examples are illustrative of hundreds of similar cases.

While absconding was generally confined to a single workplace, coordinated multiple-workplace escapes did occur. Hindmarsh describes such a case in VDL in March in 1826 and on occasion absconding notices make explicit reference to such incidents.[18] In October 1843 the NSW *Government Gazette* reported Anne Russell had absconded from Captain Bull, accompanying two men who had absconded from the Twenty Mile Hollow Stockade.[19] More typically reports of rural workers absconding from neighbouring farms/estates on the same day suggest a degree of collusion as do court records where absconding workers from several farms were caught and tried on the same day.[20] On 4 February 1834 four convicts absconded from HC Sempill's Segenhoe Estate as did William Shearman from Potter Macqueen's neighbouring estate.[21] Servants of both Alfred Kennedy and Mrs Lowe at Bringelly absconded on the same day and a similar incident occurred at Lanyon and Wright's Limestone-Plains estates on 1 November 1836.[22] It was common for workers on neighbouring estates to socialise. There was also dialogue between convicts in gangs, stockades or Female Factories and those outside, notwithstanding efforts by authorities to prevent it. This undoubtedly facilitated coordinated absconding.

For convicts, absconding offered a chance of obtaining freedom or escape from a detested employer or overseer. Both influences help explain repeated attempts by individuals and groups to abscond from gangs or farms. In 1836 and 1837 John Garner and William Smith made repeated attempts to desert H Hall's Yass estate and Jane Mack and Mary Greenwood were equally committed to escaping their assignment to Mary Reynolds in Sydney. These examples were by no means exceptional. Larger absconding groups seem to have split up into smaller groups or individuals subsequently to minimise the chances of detection. Larger escapes were easier in summer when roving groups of harvest workers (reapers and shearers) made them less conspicuous—and employers desperate for labour more willing to allay their suspicions. In early May 1832 six convicts absconded from the No. 21 road-gang in regional NSW, most being recaptured within a week but at least one—Michael Carty—remained at large until August.[23] This wasn't an isolated case. Of a group of nine convicts absconding from the No. 23 road-gang in March of the same year, most were quickly recaptured but others remained at large over five months.[24] At least six workers absconded from EJ Eyre's Molonglo estate between June 1836 and February 1837 with four listed as still being at large in March 1837.[25] Notwithstanding control measures, a significant number of convicts appear to have evaded recapture. Seamen, whose desertion was abetted by organised crimping networks in every major port, were if anything more successful.

Including absconding with other forms of collective action provides a more informed picture of dissent in particular workplaces. In October 1833 newspapers reported that Dr Robert Wardell prosecuted convicts assigned to his estate at Petersham (now a suburb of Sydney) for both striking and neglecting work.[26] What they failed to report were instances of collective absconding in March and May as well as repeated absconding by William Francis, Thomas Connors and five others in the months before and after the October disputes, including a failed attempt at collective absconding in December.[27] Clearly, issues had been festering before Wardell's servants struck work, involved over twice as many workers as those prosecuted and continued after those involved in striking/neglect had been lashed. Co-founder (with WC Wentworth) of the *Australian* newspaper in 1824 and recklessly courageous, Wardell fought two duels and died less than a year later while attempting to apprehend three bushrangers. Two of the convicts (John Perry and James Reilly) involved in the explosive fracas at James Mudies' Castle Forbes Estate in November 1833 had tried to abscond three months before this.[28] Another nine of Mudie's workers absconded from Castle Forbes in the six months following the incident. It is entirely possible there would have been more violent confrontations like Castle Forbes had efforts to suppress absconding been more successful.

Aside from absconding, other methods favoured by informally organised workers included making a demand or expressing dissent collectively. This could be especially important for workers with little capacity to impose sanctions like public servants. For convicts particularly, making a collective demand or expressing dissent was readily construed as insolence. Some employers used insolence as a back-up when other charges against collective action failed, as Captain James Dixon's overseer Robert Crawford did against ringleader William Smith (60 days' hard-labour).[29] Today workers making demands or complaints still risk retribution even in democracies with well-established unions. For convicts and many free workers, petitions and lodging complaints before courts represented the only legitimate mechanisms for pursuing complaints. Both entailed supplicating before authorities. Petitioning was a centuries-old method of asking authorities for redress using subordinating language like 'your petitioners humbly beseech', 'graciously favour them' and 'in duty bound will ever pray.' Petitioning Governors/Legislative Councils over employment conditions was principally undertaken by convicts or government employees. In contrast, privately-employed free workers mainly used petitions for political purposes like restricting immigration or requesting import duties. Court actions largely concerned unpaid wages and ill-treatment/poor rations. Seamen and rural workers constituted the largest groups of free workers complaining about ill-treatment/poor rations. Other methods informally organised workers were more likely to use, seemingly out of frustration, were threats, assaults on overseers/employers and sabotage. Use of these methods is considered in more detail in Chapter 4.

Table 3.6 (mostly the second half) also identifies an array of methods connected to unions including craft control, the closed shop, unilateral regulation, deputations, imposing bans and collective bargaining. Mutual insurance was important, reflecting the vagaries of life without a welfare state and giving unions a sustaining activity that would, unlike strikes, attract approbation in colonial society. Registration as a friendly society also gave the union's constitution some legal standing and helped secure their funds. Mutual insurance wasn't confined to craft unions, being adopted by others including police, clerks, seamen and general labourers. Some, like the Port Jackson Society of Coasting Seamen (1839–45) and Australian Clerks Provident Society (1844–50), survived over five years. While formal and informal organisation both used petitions, deputations were more firmly tied to the former and were increasingly used after 1850.[30] Other activities more aligned to formal organisation were public demonstrations (like marches and mass/public meetings) and letters/notices/advertisements in the press to garner community support (like assistant-drapers pursuing early-closing) or to justify collective action. Occasionally informal bodies used letters/notices. In January 1835 journeymen cabinetmakers at J W Woolley's Macquarie St Hobart manufactory published a letter disputing Woolley's claims about their wage demands, his advertisement for 'six good cabinetmakers' and telling the Immigration Committee he was 'at the mercy of his journeymen'.[31] Nonetheless, unions dealing with multiple employers and having funds to pay for advertisements could more readily use the device.

Craft unions agitated politically, including campaigning against convict transportation/assignment and assisted-immigration (Table 3.6 doesn't include political mobilisations, addressed in Chapter 11). While largely composed of immigrants, craft unions were sensitive to government-sponsored labour importation and misleading newspaper reports or job advertisements they labelled 'gulling'. In addition to direct lobbying via petitions/memorials/deputation, unions wrote to their UK counterparts warning of unfavourable job prospects, as the Sydney Stonemasons Society did in 1842.[32] They also placed statements/notices in colonial newspapers known to be read in Britain or whose contents were summarised in the UK press. In May 1838 the Australian Society of Compositors published a statement responding to an advertisement for 30 to 40 compositors in *The Australian* telling 'brother workmen' in Britain and Ireland no such jobs existed and some colonial journeymen were already under-employed.[33]

Customs, Meeting Points, Networks and Other Sources of Solidarity

Beyond the quantitative data, it is important to make observations about shared experiences, solidarity and networks facilitating/shaping worker organisation. Chapter 1 identified centuries-old traditions and methods used by craft workers to uphold their interests as well as a heritage of collective action amongst miners, seamen, seasonal labourers and others. Some actions were of more recent origins like food riots mirrored in some colonial protests, most notably several incidents in Female Factories like that in Hobart in 1829 and at the Parramatta factory two years earlier.[34] Convicts and emigrant workers brought this social DNA to the colonies, many having prior knowledge of, if not involvement in, collective action.

The vast majority of transported convicts were not career criminals, but impoverished working people who had committed opportunistic crimes during the upheaval of the first industrial revolution (Chapter 1). Selection for transportation took account of vocational skill sets needed in the colonies as did the provision of passage assistance to poor emigrants. Emigrant workers expected higher living standards and were prepared to pursue this collectively. Influential union/political activists like Adelaide shoemaker George Wells[35] and Hobart cabinetmaker William Jeffrey clearly had prior experience. Jeffrey ultimately left VDL for the mainland (reinforced by the death of his wife) but his contribution to Tasmanian unionism may have been recalled, with a William Jeffrey Cup featuring in an organised-labour race meeting a century later. More idiosyncratic examples include Worthy Worthington George Nicholls (1808–49), an avowed socialist who spoke regularly at political gatherings of Adelaide workers, assisted the poor and was a dissident member of the Adelaide water-carriers union before becoming a Burra mines carter. Nicholls committed suicide in 1849.[36] Some emigrants were probably escaping retribution after involvement in strikes, like engineers who formed the first Australian branch of the Amalgamated Society of Engineers in 1852 while travelling to Sydney.[37]

There is evidence of prior involvement amongst convicts, with a significant minority (Rudé estimated between 783 and 968) being transported for crimes related to industrial or associated political dissent. Amongst these were 1797 naval mutineers, Luddites, radical Scot weavers (1820), Cato Street conspirators (1820), radical Yorkshire weavers (1821), Captain Swing rioters, machine-breakers and arsonists, participators in the Bristol (1831) and Welsh riots (1835, including two women), the six Tolpuddle Martyrs, and 102 Chartists.[38] Available evidence indicates the vast majority remained in the colonies, the conspicuous exception being the Tolpuddle martyrs whose return fares were paid by the British Government after a concerted public campaign.[39]

Evidence of dissenters' subsequent behaviour in the colonies is fragmentary and mixed. A few were offered positions of responsibility due to their education/perceived honesty (like Tolpuddle martyr George Loveless) or succeeded in business, the professions (like surgeon William Redfern), trade or farming. Others became constables, gang overseers or led relatively quiet lives as workers. Political activist and machine-breaker, James Pumphrey— a surveyor—was placed in charge of the No.10 road-gang (Great Western Road) but court records and evidence of another transportee (Captain Swing protester Thomas Cook) indicates he abandoned his radicalism/humanity. In 1833, 51 gang-members were charged with refusing work, absconding, neglect, insulting Pumphrey or making a complaint. Pumphrey fulfilled expectations in his new role and was rewarded with a conditional pardon by 1837 notwithstanding his sentence of transportation for life.[40] Surviving letters from protesters to UK family members describe colonial work/living conditions but make no reference to collective action—hardly surprising given likelihood their letters would be read by authorities.[41]

Brown found Captain Swing rioters like William Jeffries (a blacksmith) and shepherd Isaac Hurrell accumulated numerous convictions for workplace dissent, others a few and some none.[42] Machine-breaking transportees Anne Entwistle and Mary Hindle were active in Female Factory protests.[43] Robert Barrett, transported for machine-breaking and riotous assembly in Wiltshire, had his sentence extended a year for inciting fellow servants to mutiny at James Gordon's Sorell farm in April 1832. John Archer described machine-breaking ploughman John Ingram as the most troublesome convict he ever had. Amongst other things Ingram organised a petition from Archer's servants requesting tickets-of-leave. Ploughman John Seaman was convicted for creating a riot amongst his fellow servants at George Rayner's Upper Derwent estate.[44] Another prominent activist was Chartist William Cuffay (1788–1870). Born to a West Indian father, Cuffay, an active unionist, helped form the Metropolitan Chartist Tailor's Association (1839) and was elected to the Chartist National Executive (1842). Part of a group tried for conspiring to levy war against Queen Victoria, Cuffay was sentenced to 21 years' transportation to VDL. At his trial Cuffay lambasted the government for rapidly enacting laws to ensure a conviction.

> The New Act is disgraceful, and I am proud to be the first victim of it, after the glorious Mitchell. Every good Act was set aside in Parliament. Everything that was likely to do any good to the working class was either thrown out or postponed; but a measure to restrain their liberties would be passed in a few hours.[45]

Soon after arriving in Hobart (1849), Cuffay played a leading role in campaigns against convict transportation and oppressive master and servant laws in the 1850s.[46] Joined by his wife in 1853, he died in poverty but was not forgotten in 1870. Overall, it appears radical industrial activists were no more conspicuous in colonial workplace dissent than the spectrum of behaviour found amongst other convicts, which is consistent with more resent research pointing to the broader base of collective action and networking underpinning the Captain Swing and other outbreaks as well as the arbitrariness of those transported.[47]

Some transported for property crimes had industrial experience which they used after arriving, a notable example being London-born Peter Tyler, secretary of the Sydney Compositors Society in the 1830s.[48] The database includes names of office-holders/activists that could assist further research on these connections. British craft workers also brought trade-based customs that reinforced a sense of shared identity. Journeymen printers held an annual 'wayse goose' dinner, providing a meal for their master and this custom continued in Australia.[49] The same applied to shoemakers' annual feasts to celebrate their patron saint St Crispin. It is perhaps more than coincidental that Adelaide cordwainers used the St Crispin dinner venue (the *Royal Oak* in Hindley St) to establish their society and at least one of its leaders, George Wells, was an organiser of this customary celebration.[50]

Other points of social intercourse facilitated collectivism. Drawing on long-established traditions in Britain, trade/calling-based pubs were to be found in colonial towns catering for a vocational clientele or working people living in close proximity or passing by. Sydney examples included the *Stonemasons Arms* located in George Street and the *Shipwrights Arms*, *Whalers Arms* and *Watermen's Arms*, all close to dock/ship-repair activities in the Rocks. These hotels were hubs for exchanging information on work and wages, coordinating industrial and political action, establishing unions and serving as the union's 'office'. In 1847 shipwrights formed a union at the *Shipwrights Arms* hotel Battery Point Hobart close to Peter Degraves' shipbuilding slipways. Other hotels without vocational names served a similar role like the *Orient* (a haunt of seamen in the Rocks) or the *Royal Oak* in Hindley St Adelaide and the *Jolly Hatters Inn* in lower Melville St Hobart—both meeting places for unions.[51] Hotels also formed a hub for more illicit collective action like the crimping tunnel connecting the *Hero of Waterloo* hotel and nearby *Whalers Arms* in the Rocks. In smaller towns or on major thoroughfares pubs, a few with vocational titles like the *Shearer's Arms*, served as meeting places for reapers, shearers, dray-drivers or working people more generally. Carpenters used Holdstock's *Cricketer's Arms Hotel* in Maitland to organise a strike in 1846.

Some hotels became hiring points for workers. Early trade societies established a House-of-Call (see Chapters 8 and 9) but the practice also operated informally and included other callings. In 1834 the *Somerset Arms* in Elizabeth St Hobart advertised itself as a House-of-Call for the drivers of teams taking loads up country as did the *Golden Fleece Inn* in Brickfield Hill, Sydney.[52] Day labourers too had recognised pick up points. Labourers seeking work from the Sydney City Council collected outside a York Street pub in 1846.[53] Shop-assistants tended to avoid pubs because it conflicted with temperance elements whose support they needed for early-closing. Hotels remained a hub for union activity for much of the 19th century before the building of Trades Halls and union-offices/halls. Reflecting this, in 1849 the Sydney Brickmakers Friendly Society petitioned the NSW Legislative Council opposing a clause in the *Licensed Victuallers Act* prohibiting friendly societies meeting in public-houses.[54]

Hotels were also a venue for sharing views on work via anecdotes, stories and irreverent songs penned locally. Thus, lice-infested food on a colonial whaleship earned a tune with the refrain 'Shout Boys, Hurrah Boys; We welcome it—Godspeed; We've had 18 months starvation; In the lousy *Runnymede*.' A more sombre song lamented the loss of a whaleboat-crew from the brig *Grecian* 'We sailed to the east and also west; And north and south where we thought best; No tale nor tidings none did hear; Of Marney's crew or boat or gear.'[55] Other callings shared songs away from the prying eyes of their masters. Colonial sawyers had one with the verse:

> Come all ye sawyers stout and bold, whose hearts are on these gum
>   trees sold
> And list while I a tale unfold, of the poor down-trodden sawyer, Fol,
>   de rol etc
> When we work and cut the stuff, the buyers come and treat us rough
> And swear the measure's not enough, and rob the weary sawyer.[56]

Like other songs this one captured sentiments that could only be expressed in safe company. When passholder George Palmer accused his master, Peter Roberts Esq, of cheating his sawyers, he rapidly found himself brought before the Oatlands Bench and remanded to stand trial.[57] Directly affronting the sensitivities of those who ruled them was dangerous.

Convicts on road-gangs also used songs as a form of collective affirmation and protest. William Romaine Govett, Assistant Surveyor on the Western Road to Bathurst, noted convicts singing around the camp-fire and as they marched to work in the 1830s.[58] When another assistant surveyor and magistrate John Nicholson banned the practice, the convicts responded by singing a defiant song immediately after passing his tent. According to Rosen, 'Nicholson immediately halted the gang, found the man who instigated the chorus and, forgoing the formality of a trial, had him flogged on the spot.'[59]

Another tool affirming collective identity was satirical mimicry. Some vivid examples involved women. A *Cornwall Chronicle* correspondent described how a group of women at the Launceston Female Factory lampooned their betters' pretences:

> On . . . being allowed to walk for their amusement in the courtyard to give them air and exercise, they mimicked their late mistress; the chief actor has a rug placed across her shoulders quite NEGLEGEE, in imitation of an Indian shawl, and with a piece of a square board under her arm to imitate a novel. She walked with "solemn steps and slow" across the area, followed by her maids of honour, and affected all the sentimental airs of a boarding school Miss, perusing, for the first time, the Sorrows of Werter; at every turn looking behind to see how she was supported in the rear, and drawing a deep sigh, as if her heart would break.[60]

Women in the factories also used music and dance as a form of protest. In September 1827 a group of women in the Hobart Female Factory were convicted for singing 'obscene songs.' On 23 August 1842 a group in the Crime Class Yard of the Cascades Female Factory refused contact with men working on the building 'started dancing and singing, refusing to desist . . . their riotous behaviour' until Superintendent Hutchinson sent for police constables.'[61]

Convict men and women used language itself as a tool of resistance and identity affirmation, constructing a 'dialect' designed to affront their 'betters' but also disguise the true meaning of their barbs. Known as 'talking flash' or using flash language, women in Female Factory protests were especially adept in its use, including overtly sexual overtones they knew would affront their often religiously-moral superintendents. Masters, superintendents and overseers could be in no doubt they were being lampooned/belittled or criticised but in ways difficult to untangle either the meaning or the precise target. Charging several members of the New Norfolk Public Works gang with insolence, overseer Lachlan White complained 'they behave in a most insulting way towards me, their language they use is flash and sometimes directed at me tho' not to me.'[62] Like their descendants a century later, free workers too used the tactic of making critical statements/mumblings amongst themselves which their employers could hear but not prove were directed at them.

Only fragments survive of what was undoubtedly a rich culture of working-class language, songs, rhymes, satirical mimicry and doggerel confirming collective experiences of work. Maxwell-Stewart and Hindmarsh point to narratives of convict oppression (some transcribed from oral tales) by Davis, McNamara and others. As in plantation slave societies, convicts used dissenting storytelling and songs portraying injustice, venal and stupid elites as well as power reversal, retribution or divine judgement in the future.[63] The songs sung by convicts in gangs or on farms and those of other workers drew directly on the rich tradition of plebeian music from Britain, Ireland and Scotland they brought with them. Gregory examines working-class culture in far greater depth than is possible here, pointing to how protest songs like those on poaching written in the UK referred to transportation to Australia while colonial ballads alluded to both abusive local conditions and injustice in Britain. An example of the latter was a ballad commemorating the seizure of the brig *Cyprus* by 31 convicts in Recherche Bay when bound for Macquarie Harbour in 1829 which included the stanzas:

> Come all ye sons of freedom, a chorus join with me/I'll sing a song of heroes and glorious liberty/Some lads condemn'd from England sailed to Van Diemen's shore/Their country, friends and parents, perhaps never to see more/When landed in this colony to different masters went/ For trifling offences to Hobart Town Gaol were sent/A second sentence being incurr'd we were ordered for to be/Sent to Macquarie Harbour, that place of tyranny.[64]

Other factors shaping collective identity included the close confinement/ accommodation of convicts, including women in Female Factories, and some groups of free workers like seamen and whalers. Solidarity was by no means unproblematic. Convicts brought elaborate status divisions that marked Britain as well traditions of plebeian revolt. Nonetheless, despite powerful incentives to break ranks (which some did) a strong anti-dobbing sentiment prevailed along with more explicit refusals to assist masters in sanctioning other servants.[65]

As Babette Smith, Maxwell-Stewart and others have shown, in addition to time on Hulks prior to transportation, the four-month or more voyage to the colony built bonds amongst convicts that survived for years after.[66] There is evidence these bonds translated to collective action in the colonies. When 10 convicts absconded from four different employment locations in a boat on 16 January 1819, seven came from just three ships (the *Morley*, *Hadlow* and *Tottenham*).[67] Three assigned-convicts absconding from Captain Robert Lethbridge's Maitland estate in June 1835 arrived on the same ship (*Georgiana*) as did three who absconded from Goat Island in March 1837 (*Lady Kennaway*) and eight of ten who deserted A & T R Campbell's Brisbane Water estate in September 1843 (*Captain Cook* 3rd voyage).[68] Similarly, when three women absconded from the Parramatta Female Factory in February 1833, two (Bridget Lehane and Catherine Hurbey) had arrived on the same ship (*Southworth*).[69] Notwithstanding efforts by authorities to avoid such congregations, these examples are indicative of numerous others and which warrant more detailed research.

There were a number of attempted revolts by convicts during voyages to the colonies, the first recorded on the *Scarborough* in 1790 followed by the *Albermarle* in 1791.[70] On occasion a degree of solidarity emerged between convicts, merchant seamen and even members of the military escort, especially when harsh punishment was meted out by the ship's officers. These groups shared similar socio-economic backgrounds, were subject to stringent disciplinary regimes and lived in close confinement on institutional food. However, fears of revolt also sparked hysterical responses. On 26 July 1817 the convict transport *Chapman* arrived in Sydney from Ireland reporting that seven convicts had been killed in a daring mutiny. However, subsequent information painted a more disturbing picture of privations on board, including some convicts being kept in double-irons for much of the voyage, others being punished for coughing and a seamen being keel-hauled—by this time an unlawful brutal punishment.[71] During the alleged revolt—no evidence for which was uncovered—soldiers fired indiscriminately into the grating above the convicts, ignored cries for mercy, and the wounded were left unattended for days amidst unreasoned panic amongst some ship-officers including the surgeon.[72] As news filtered out, anger spread throughout Sydney. Governor Macquarie established a Committee of Enquiry which became divided and several officers and soldiers whose behaviour was the subject of damning evidence escaped punishment when the matter went before the judicial system in England.

As an untouchable group in the eyes of polite society, convicts tended to socialise together. Free settlers and governors were riven between those prepared to associate with emancipated convicts like Governor Macquarie and those (including landholders like the Macarthur's) who eschewed social acceptance even for those few who became extraordinarily wealthy like Samuel Terry. For the many it was simpler to associate amongst themselves and with free workers from similar humble origins. Ticket-of-leave holders also exploited government-mandated musters to swap information and coordinate collective action. In 1817, for instance, concern was expressed that Sunday Musters of convicts was being used by them to combine to raise wages.[73]

Shared origins and a long sea voyage to Australia could also build bonds amongst free workers. In 1833 150 skilled building mechanics arriving in

Hobart on the immigrant ship *Strathfieldsaye* formed a union and struck for higher wages. Giving evidence to the Immigration Committee, one master-builder (Chapman) employing 32 tradesmen complained of the combination—views echoed by several other masters.[74] Two days later Governor Arthur wrote a despatch to the Secretary of State for the Colonies in London urging caution in selecting mechanics to avoid 'political effects'.[75] For their part, the *Strathfieldsaye* mechanics believed they were victims of inflated reports of colonial wages, job prospects and cheap food (especially meat) that ignored higher clothing and accommodation costs.

Finally, but not least the experience of lopsided laws and courts stacked against them reinforced workers sense of identity/injustice and, as later chapters will illustrate, the attractiveness of collective action which presented employers with greater logistical difficulties.

Conclusion

Considering informal and formal organisation, and convict and free-labour, affords a different perspective on worker mobilisation in terms of the numbers involved, who took action and why. It reveals the actions and significance of neglected groups like women and convicts. While there is only evidence of one attempt at unionisation, both free and unfree women accounted for a small but still significant level of collective action. Convicts engaged in a substantial level of collective action especially mass absconding. There are striking parallels with at least some slave societies in this regards. For example, in 1830 bi-weekly government notices reported 70 to 80 absconding slaves from sugar plantations in Mauritius.[76] At the same time, organisation involved more workers from a wide array of occupations. Industry-patterns reflected the nature of colonial economies, including the dependence on maritime transport. Informal organisation by free and unfree can be seen as an extension of far more numerous collisions between individual workers and employers in the courts, the first attempt to mount some countervailing power based on shared interests. Informal organisation typically involved fewer workers. But taken as whole or within particular industries, it was important in terms of scale and as a small step to formal organisation. Unions themselves were often short-lived—a pattern that continued long after 1850. Later chapters will examine the progression from informal to formal organisation in greater depth.

This chapter also examined the spatial and size dimensions of organisation, issues and methods and the impact of formal organisation in this regard. Formal organisation enabled workers to pursue objectives and deploy methods not available to informally organised workers. Finally, the chapter explored the origins of collectivism beyond labour market conditions drawing on some themes identified in Chapter 1. This included social bonding and networking amongst convicts, the prior industrial experience of convicts and emigrants, spatially-defined working communities, occupational and social networking in pubs, and the songs, parody and satire working people used to assert their own identity and critique those seen to oppress them. The next chapter examines collective action in more detail.

Notes

1 *Port Philip Gazette* 8 November 1848 and *Melbourne Argus* 21 November 1848.
2 LC247-1-9 Hobart 2 and 30 December 1841 and 6 February 1842.
3 *Melbourne Daily News* 10, 13 and 17 January 1849, 28 and 31 March 1849.
4 LC83-1-1 Campbell Town 27 May 1835.
5 LC247-1-17 Hobart 15 February 1850.
6 A surge first examined by Markey. Markey, R. (2002) Explaining Union Mobilisation in the 1880s and Early 1900s, *Labour History*, 83:19–42.
7 Quinlan, M., Gardner, M. and Akers, P. (2003) Reconsidering the Collective Impulse, 137–180.
8 Baum, J. and Shipilov, A. (2006) Ecological Approaches to Organizations, in Clegg, S., Hardy, C., Lawrence, T. and Nord, W. eds. *The Sage Handbook of Organization Studies*, Sage Publications, London, 55–110.
9 Oxley, D. (1996) *Convict Maids: The Forced Migration of Women to Australia*.
10 For evidence of its significance in other countries, see Quinlan, M. (2013) Precarious and Hazardous Work: The Health and Safety of Merchant Seamen 1815–1935, *Social History*, 38(3):281–307.
11 *Sydney Gazette* 22 March 1827.
12 *The Australian* 17 November 1825.
13 *Sydney Gazette* 12 May 1829.
14 Karskens, G. (1984) The Convict Road Station Site at Wisemans Ferry: An Historical and Archaeological Investigation, *Australian Historical Archaeology*, 2:17–26; Karskens, G. (1986) Defiance, Deference and Diligence; Rosen, S. (2006) That Den of Infamy, the No. 2 Stockade Cox's River, 1.
15 LC83-1-3 Campbell Town 26 December 1838.
16 *NSW Government Gazette* 8 May 1833 and 12 June 1833.
17 *NSW Government Gazette* 30 October 1833.
18 Hindmarsh, B. (2001) *Yoked to the Plough: Male Convict Labour, Culture and Resistance in Rural Van Diemen's Land, 1820–40*, Ph.D. Thesis, University of Edinburgh, 149–150.
19 *NSW Government Gazette* 20 October 1843.
20 See for example LC362-1-4 Longford 29 July 1839.
21 *NSW Government Gazette* 12 February 1834.
22 *NSW Government Gazette* 22 October 1834 and 16 November 1836.
23 *NSW Government Gazette* 8 and 15 May 1832 and 16 August 1832.
24 *NSW Government Gazette* 29 August 1832.
25 *NSW Government Gazette* 8 March 1837.
26 *Sydney Gazette* 10 and 24 October 1833.
27 *NSW Government Gazette* 20 March 1833; 17 and 24 April 1833; 8, 15 and 29 May 1833; 12 June 1833; 20 and 30 October 1833, 13 November 1833, 4 and 24 December 1833.
28 *NSW Government Gazette* 31 July 1833.
29 LC83-1-10 Campbell Town 3 May 1850.
30 Quinlan, M., Gardner, M. and Akers, P. (2003) Reconsidering the Collective Impulse, 137–180.
31 *Colonial Times* 20 January 1835 and TAHO CSO 1/528/11502.
32 These links warrants further research. Leeson, R. (1980) *Travelling Brothers*, 137 and 191.

108   *Overview of Worker Organisation, 1788–1850*

33 *Sydney Gazette* 10 May 1838.
34 Hendriksen, G., Liston, C. and Cowley, T. (2008) *Women Transported: Life in Australia's Convict Female Factories*, NSW Parramatta Heritage Centre/University of Western Sydney, 43.
35 For a discussion of the proclivity for political activism amongst shoemakers see Hobsbawm, E. and Wallach Scott, J. (1980) Political Shoemakers, *Past and Present*, 89:86–114.
36 Gibbs, R. (2005) Nicholls, Worthy Worthington George (1808–1849), *Australian Dictionary of Biography*, National Centre of Biography, Australian National University, http://adb.anu.edu.au/biography/nicholls-worthy-worthington-george-13128/text23757
37 Buckley, K. (1968) The Engineers and Emigration 1851–1887, *Labour History*, 15:31–39.
38 Rudé, G. (1978) *Protest and Punishment: The Story of the Social and Political Protesters Transported to Australia, 1788–1868*, Oxford University Press, Melbourne, 9–10.
39 Hobsbawm, E. and Rudé, G. (1972) *Captain Swing*, 232–240.
40 Rosen, S. (2006) That Den of Infamy, the No. 2 Stockade Cox's River, 244–245.
41 Rudé, G. (1978) *Protest and Punishment*, 182–228.
42 Brown, B. (2004) *The Machine Breaker Convicts from the Proteus and the Eliza*, M.A. Thesis, University of Tasmania.
43 Hendriksen, G., Liston, C. and Cowley, T. (2008) *Women Transported: Life in Australia's Convict Female Factories*, 20–21.
44 Brown, B. (2004) The Machine Breaker Convicts from the Proteus and the Eliza, 212, 256, 283.
45 Gammage, R. (1976) *History of the Chartist Movement, 1837–1854*, facsimile of 1894 edition, Merlin Press, London, 340.
46 *Colonial Times* 28 February 1851.
47 Walsh, B. (2007) Heartbreak and Hope, Deference and Defiance on the Yimmang.
48 Tyler, who arrived on the *Grenada*, was listed as absconding from the Hyde Park Barracks in March 1829, a charge refuted by his employer *Monitor* editor ES Hall who alleged the action was being used to punish him for criticising the government. Tyler married another convict Anne Currier/Carrier (transported in 1829) and died on 6 July 1842. *Sydney Gazette* 31 March 1829, *Monitor* 11 April 1829 and Smith, B. (2008) *A Cargo of Women: Susannah Watson and the Convicts of the Princess Royal*, Allen & Unwin, Sydney, 252.
49 See for example in Hobart and Melbourne respectively *Colonial Times* 12 September 1837 and *Argus* 20 October 1846.
50 There is reference to a Benefit Society of St Crispin which may have been a precursor to the cordwainers society. *South Australian Register* 18 October 1843 and 15 October 1845; and *Adelaide Observer* 28 October 1843 and 19 October 1844.
51 Quinlan, M. (1986) Hotels and Early Australian Trade Unions: The "Jolly Hatters" Inn, *Heritage Australia*, 5(2):40–41.
52 *Hobart Town Courier* 8 August 1834 and *Sydney Gazette* 18 October 1834.
53 *Bell's Life of Sydney* 28 February 1846.
54 *Melbourne Argus* 16 August 1849.
55 Lawson, W. (1986) *Blue Gum Clippers and Whaleships of Tasmania*, D&L Book Distributors, Launceston, 65-73.
56 This song survived because it was favoured by widely-read and humane Tasmania shipbuilder John Wilson. Reproduced in Lawson, W. (1986) *Blue Gum Clippers and Whaleships of Tasmania*, 130.

57 LC390–1–1 Oatlands 23 August 1845.
58 Govett, W. (1977) *Sketches of New South Wales: Written and Illustrated for the Saturday Magazine 1836–37*, Gaston Renard, Melbourne, 49–50.
59 Rosen, S. (2006) That Den of Infamy, the No. 2 Stockade Cox's River, 240–241.
60 *Cornwall Chronicle* 11 August 1838.
61 Hendriksen, G., Liston, C. and Cowley, T. (2008) *Women Transported: Life in Australia's Convict Female Factories*, 56, 62.
62 LC375–1–2 New Norfolk 20 October 1837.
63 Hindmarsh, B. (2001) Yoked to the Plough, 220–222.
64 Gregory, M. (2014) *Australian Working Songs and Poems-A Rebel Heritage*, Ph.D. thesis, University of Wollongong, 32.
65 Hindmarsh, B. (2001) Yoked to the Plough, 252.
66 Smith, B. (2014) *Luck of the Irish*, Allen & Unwin, Sydney; Walsh, B. (2007) Heartbreak and Hope, Deference and Defiance on the Yimmang, 232.
67 *Sydney Gazette* 30 January 1819.
68 *New South Wales Government Gazette* No.175, 8 July 1835; No.272, 19 April 1837 and No.75, 8 September 1843.
69 *New South Wales Government Gazette* No.50, 13 February 1833.
70 See *HRNSW* Vols. 2, 1793–1795, 447, 762, 781, 819–820, 857; Maxwell-Stewart, H. "Those lads contrived a plan": Attempts at Mutiny on Australian Bound Convict Vessels, *International Review of Social History*, 58(s21):177–196.
71 AONSW CSO August/September 1817 Reel 6020 9/2639, 97, 173–174.
72 AONSW CSO 20 August 1817 Reel 6020 9/6239, 30–422.
73 AONSW CSO 24 November 1817, Reel 6047; 4/1739, 15–21.
74 TAHO CSO 1/528/11502.
75 TAHO GO 38.
76 *Hobart Town Courier* 17 July 1830.

4   Analysing the Components
of Organisation

Introduction

This chapter examines characteristics of collective action 1788–1850 (afore-mentioned caveats about the database continue to apply). Like slaves societies in the Americas, there were instances of violent revolts and riots by convicts, but these were relatively rare and typically confined to a single workplace. One exception occurred in 1804 when hundreds of convicts rebelled against colonial authorities before being defeated in a battle at Castle Hill (24 convicts died in the battle or were subsequently executed). While Irish transportees and nationalism was conspicuous, English convicts too were involved, indicating it entailed wider issues. Most violent riots occurred on penal stations notorious for their poor rations, harsh punishment and difficulty of escape, particularly Norfolk Island. In September 1826 for instance around 150 Norfolk Island convicts rioted, raided the Commissariat store and some attempted to escape, resulting in the death of one soldier and the execution of some of the instigators.[1] Poor food and accommodation also sparked riots on convict road-gangs like that at Mount Victoria in the early 1830s.[2] The Parramatta and Cascades (Hobart) Female Factories were also the sites of a number of riots like one by about 50 women at the Cascade Factory on 4 May 1839. Violent revolts also occurred amongst assigned rural workers, most notably perhaps at Bathurst in September 1830.[3]

More typical was widespread absconding, though this too could take a violent turn as occurred in February 1803 when 15 convicts escaping from Castle Hill robbed two settlers of food and arms but were captured at the foot of the Blue Mountains (two were hung).[4] The transition from absconding to bushranging, that was more common prior to 1820, indicated the blurring of workplace dissent and property crime. Incendiarism and physical assaults were other measures used by convicts (and free workers) to exact revenge on their masters. While important, the vast majority of collective action including those involving convicts didn't involve or transition to violence, robbery or incendiarism. While violent incidents, like slave revolts, have attracted deserved attention from historians, they need to be situated within a wider context of protest if their origins and significance is to be understood. Informal and formal action by different groups of workers also needs to be examined and compared. This chapter attempts this task.

Overall Patterns of Collective Action

Figure 4.1 charts the number of strikes and non-strike forms of collective action (NSCA) by year, 1801–1900. Again, data for 1851–1900 is incomplete but indicative of later trends, helping put the earlier period into context. Strike numbers vary substantially by year including clear peaks and troughs like the well-known 1890 strike wave. Strike waves are a characteristic feature identified in other countries and for other periods. Ignoring the period prior to 1825 where numbers are small and may represent reporting effects, there are discernible strike waves in 1826 (all informal) and 1840 with a minor peak in 1847. The 1840 peak coincided with labour shortages and rising prices. Like that in 1890, it followed a period of capital inflow and was succeeded by a depression. The number of NSCA between 1801 and 1900 indicates a conspicuous peak in 1833. After this, trends broadly match those of strikes apart from 1844. As with subsequent tables, Figure 4.1 demonstrates the importance of considering all forms of collective action, not just strikes, in terms of understanding worker mobilisation.

Collective Action by Convict/Free Status, Location and Formal/Informal Status

Table 4.1 breaks down strikes and NSCA by colony. The oldest/largest colonies of NSW and VDL account for over 90% of strikes and NSCA.

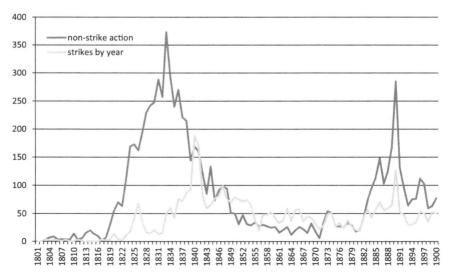

Figure 4.1 Strikes and Non-Strike Collective Action (NSCA) Australia 1801–1900

Table 4.1 Strikes and Non-Strike Collective Action (NSCA) by Colony in Australia 1788–1850

Jurisdiction	1788–1800	1801–1810	1811–1820	1821–1830	1831–1840	1841–1850	Total
Strikes							
New South Wales	7	16	26	117	172	124	462
Van Diemen's Land		1	1	108	494	581	1185
Victoria					14	80	94
South Australia					5	47	52
Queensland						8	8
Western Australia					9	5	14
Total	7	17	27	225	694	845	1815
Non-Strike Collective Action							
New South Wales	22	41	137	1446	1795	301	3742
Van Diemen's Land		7	13	140	501	396	1057
Victoria		1			17	102	120
South Australia					8	38	46
Queensland				3	23	10	36
Western Australia				2	13	8	23
Total	22	49	150	1591	2357	855	5024
Grand Total	29	66	177	1816	3051	1700	6839

Interrogation of additional records might reduce this dominance somewhat (although NSW court records will add more strikes). Confining the comparison to the decade 1841–50 indicates the growing importance of Victoria and South Australia which together account for 15% of strikes and 16.4% of NSCA—a trend that continues in subsequent decades. Queensland only grew significantly in the decades after 1850 and growth was even later (the 1880s) in Western Australia.

Convicts account for most strikes but strikes by free-labour become increasingly important, outstripping those by convicts in the decade to 1850. The vast majority of strikes still didn't involve formal organisation. Unions only accounted for 3.1% of strikes and 1.1% of NSCA, and 4% of strikes and 4.7% of NSCA in the decade to 1850 (Table 4.2). The proportion of strikes involving unions slowly increased over time but didn't exceed informally organised strikes until almost two decades after 1850. Of course, union-organised strikes and NSCA were on average far larger. Regarding location, the principal town of each colony (including regions that became colonies) accounted for 40.1% of strikes and 22% of NSCA.

There were significant differences between convicts and free-labour regarding modes of collective action. Convicts were involved in 1029 strikes and 4425 other forms of collective action, predominantly absconding (4033 instances) while free workers took part in 786 strikes and 598 other types of collective action, including 267 instances of group absconding. Strikes constituted 18.9% of collective action by convicts, while collective absconding represented 73.9%. In contrast, strikes represented 56.8% of collective action by free workers while collective absconding represented only 19.3%. Even so, absconding was significant for free-labour (seamen, whalers and rural workers), and these figures probably understate its incidence because absconding by convicts was more systematically documented/reported. The importance of collective absconding declined in the decades after 1833 but didn't disappear. Strikes seem to have become the most prevalent form of collective action in the four decades after 1840 (needs verification). However, the rise of formal organisation saw other types of NSCA (like demands, deputations and bans) grow in importance, in combination outstripping strikes after 1880, even during strike waves like 1890 (Figure 4.1).

Collective Action by Size and Duration

The database enabled calculations regarding the size of strikes/NSCA in terms of the number of workers and workplaces involved. Important caveats apply. While numbers of workers involved was obtained for 87.4% of strikes and 92.5% of NSCA, these understate total, average and median worker involvement for several reasons. Most important, sources typically reported precise numbers where strikes/NSCA involved a few workers in a single workplace (often when tried in court). The bigger a strike/NSCA— a ship's crew and more especially workers at multiple workplaces—the

Table 4.2 Summary of Collective Action in Australia 1788–1850

Type of Action	1788–1800	1801–1810	1811–1820	1821–1830	1831–1840	1841–1850	Total	Percentage
Strikes								
Convict or free-labour								
Convict	5	8	18	184	466	348	1029	56.7
Free-labour	2	9	9	41	228	497	786	43.3
Total	7	17	27	225	694	845	1815	
Formal/informal								
Formal				1	22	34	57	3.1
Informal	7	17	27	224	672	811	1758	96.9
Total	7	17	27	225	694	845	1815	
Capital/non-capital								
Capital	6	12	16	75	250	382	741	40.1
Non-capital	1	5	11	150	444	463	1074	59.9
Total	7	17	27	225	694	845	1815	
NSCA								
Convict or free-labour								
Convict	14	29	128	1555	2199	500	4425	88.1
Free-labour	8	20	22	35	158	355	598	11.9
Total	22	49	150	1591	2357	855	5024	

(Continued)

Table 4.2 (Continued)

Type of Action	1788–1800	1801–1810	1811–1820	1821–1830	1831–1840	1841–1850	Total	Percentage
Formal/informal								
Formal				1	14	40	55	1.1
informal	22	49	150	1590	2343	815	4989	98.9
Total	22	49	150	1591	2357	855	5024	
Capital/non-capital								
Capital	12	34	76	261	415	317	1105	22
Non-capital	10	15	74	1330	1942	538	3909	78
Total	22	49	150	1591	2357	855	5024	

less likely numbers were reported. Instances where only ringleaders' stood trial represents another (subsidiary) source of under-reporting. Trying ringleaders is made clear in some cases as in June 1839 when William Dudeny was tried for insolence and insubordination in Hobart after the crew of the barque *Augustus Caesar* had demanded an additional grog allowance.[5] However, prosecutions targeting only ringleaders undoubtedly went unreported. Therefore, data is biased towards understating numbers involved in strikes/NSCA. Nonetheless, the data provides a conservative baseline for mobilisation and also highlights that many strikes/NSCA prior to 1851—and several decades thereafter—were indeed small, an outcome of informal organisation.

Table 4.3 provides a breakdown for total and average involvement strikes/NSCA by decade. Raw numbers have been used to provide a conservative estimate of total involvement by assigning averages to unknowns. Total worker numbers involved in strikes/NSCA grew strongly after 1830 and average strike involvement grew after 1840—trends that continue after 1850. While some convict strikes were relatively large, both their total and average involvement was smaller than for free workers (Table 4.3). The rise of formal organisation and trend to larger NSCA/strikes almost certainly means the degree of understatement is larger for later periods. Unlike strikes, total convict involvement in NSCA is much higher than for free-labour (in large part due to absconding), although the situation reverses in 1841–50 and average involvement growth is only discernible for free-labour. The rise in 1841–50 appears to reflect the growth of unions—a point reinforced when number of workplaces involved is considered (Table 4.4).

Another measure of strike/NSCA size is the number of workplaces involved. Workplace rather than employer was deliberately chosen. Prior to 1851 most employers operated a single workplace, but there were conspicuous exceptions especially colonial governments with multiple post-offices, courts, administrative offices and police stations. Strikes/NSCA involving multiple workplaces, whether single or multiple employers, were identified. Identifying single workplace strikes/NSCA generally presented no difficulty but with multiple-workplace strikes/NSCA the precise number of workplaces was often not specified. More typically reports referred to workers, like carpenters or shearers, taking action in several workplaces, an entire town or region. Table 4.4 therefore divides strikes/NSCA into three categories, single-workplace, multi-workplace and town/region. While crude, this breakdown provides a guide to relative size. Strikes and NSCA in one town/region occasionally flowed onto other towns/regions. The small number of colony-wide strikes/NSCA didn't warrant a separate category.

The vast majority of strikes and NSCA were confined to a single workplace, especially with regard to convicts (Table 4.4). For convicts, instances of multiple-workplace actions were probably the tip of wider informal networking. Multiple-workplace strikes/NSCA was more common amongst free workers and grew over time, paralleling but not confined to the

Table 4.3 Number of Workers Involved in Strikes and NSCA by Period, Australia 1788–1850

Worker Numbers	1788–1800	1801–10	1811–20	1821–30	1831–40	1841–50	Total
Strikes by Convict Workers							
Raw Numbers	18	32	49	742	1555	1858	4236
Average	3.6	4	2.7	4	3.3	5.3	
Zero reports			2	22	27	15	
Adjusted missing estimate (rounded)*			5	88	89	80	
Estimated Total	18	32	54	830	1644	1938	4516
Strikes by Free Workers							
Raw Numbers	11	32	27	198	1211	3508	4987
Average	5.5	3.5	3	4.8	5.3	7.1	
Zero reports		2	6	12	53	84	
Adjusted missing estimate (rounded)*		7	18	58	281	596	
Estimated Total	11	39	45	256	1492	4104	5947
All Worker Strike Totals							
Raw Numbers	29	64	76	940	2766	5962	9223
Estimated Total	29	71	99	1086	3136	6042	10463
Non-Strike Collective Action by Convict Workers							
Raw Numbers	68	124	441	5560	7111	1569	14873
Average	4	4.3	3.4	3.6	3.2	3.1	
Zero reports	1	3	6	28	70	110	
Adjusted missing estimate(rounded)*	4	13	20	101	224	341	
Estimated Total	72	137	461	5661	7335	1910	15576
Non-Strike Collective Action by Free Workers							
Raw Numbers	58	77	127	96	637	2294	3289
Average	7	3.9	5.8	2.7	4	6.5	

Zero reports	1	2		11	44	100	
Adjusted missing estimate (rounded)*	7	8		30	176	650	
Estimated Total	65	85	127	126	813	2944	4160
All Worker NSCA totals							
Raw Numbers	126	201	568	5656	7748	3863	18162
Estimated Total	137	222	588	5787	8148	5773	19736
All Workers Combined Strike and NSCA totals							
Raw Numbers	155	265	644	6596	10514	9825	27385
Estimated Total	166	293	687	6873	11284	11815	30199

* number of zero involvement reporting organisations multiplied by involvement average

Table 4.4 Strikes and NSCA by Period and Number of Workplaces Involved, 1788–1850

Period	Single workplace	Multiple workplaces	Entire town or region	Unknown	Total
Convict Strikes					
1788–1800	5				5
1801–10	6	2			8
1811–20	18				18
1821–30	177	7			184
1831–40	461	5			466
1841–50	344	2			346
Total	1011	16			1027
Percentage	98.4	1.6			100%
Free-Labour Strikes					
1788–1800	2				2
1801–10	9				9
1811–20	9				9
1821–30	36	3	2		41
1831–40	202	8	17		227
1841–50	463	11	21		495
Total	718	22	40		780
Percentage	92.1	2.8	5.1		100%
All Strikes Total	95.6				
Convict Non-Strike Collective Action					
1788–1800	14				14
1801–10	28	1			29
1811–20	123	5			128
1821–30	1459	4			1463
1831–40	2193	3			2197

1841–50	496	3	499
Total	4389	16	4405
Percentage	99.6	0.4	100%

Free-Labour Non-Strike Collective Action

1788–1800	7		1	8
1801–10	20	1		20
1811–20	21	2		22
1821–30	32	8	1	35
1831–40	142	17	8	158
1841–50	300	28	38	355
Total	522	28	44	594
Percentage	87.8	4.7	7.4	100%

emergence of formal organisation. Consistent with Shorter and Tilly (Chapter 1), unions account for 75% of town/region-wide strikes and 84.2% of town/region-wide NSCA. Multi-workplace collective action, especially that encompassing a town or region, required coordination and resourcing more readily accomplished by unions. Informal multi-workplace strikes were sometimes a precursor to formal organisation. Melbourne bricklayers struck in 1840 and tried to form a benefit society with stonemasons the following year.[6] Strikes by unions could also encourage similar actions in another town. In August 1846 a wages strike by the Sydney Society of Carpenters and Joiners was followed by carpenters and joiners in Maitland (160 km north) 11 days later.[7]

Unions were more capable of organising multi-workplace strikes, but even those with strike-funds found a prolonged confrontation rapidly depleted their resources (Chapters 7 and 8). Unions often preferred to exert pressure/resist attacks through single workplace strikes or other forms of collective action. Even as unions grew in the second half the 19th century, single-workplace withdrawals still constituted the vast majority of strikes in Australia.[8] Table 4.4 indicates multiple-workplace disagreements amongst free workers were more likely to entail non-strike action (12.1% of NSCA) than strikes (7.9% of strikes). For shop-assistants pursuing early-closing or government clerks dissatisfied with their pay, taking collective action at a single workplace made little sense. These and other differences are examined in later chapters.

Another measure of strikes/NSCA is duration. A start and end date was recorded for every strike/NSCA in the database, for the vast majority with some precision, though most absconding cases without trial records understate times and a small number of other strikes/NSCA were a best-estimate based on sources. Duration data was representative and provided further evidence on worker mobilisation. Table 4.5 summarises average, median and total duration. Median duration of strikes is several days as expected, given the vast majority were informal, involving a handful of workers in a single workplace. There is no clear trend in average duration over time. Median strike duration is shorter than for NSCA. The difference is more pronounced regarding average duration. Strikes were more likely to be resolved in a shorter timeframe through winning, losing/lapsing or workers being prosecuted. Long duration strikes were exceptional.

However, when workers petitioned, made a demand, imposed a ban or pursued a pledge-based agreement, the process could extend over weeks or months. Similarly, apprehending mass absconders might take weeks, months or even years. Six convicts absconded from a gang near Hobart on 11 November 1841, were apprehended on 23 December at Woolnorth on the far side of the island, and it took another seven weeks before they removed to Hobart, tried and sentenced to two years at Port Arthur.[9] This helps explain why whereas, consistent with Shorter and Tilly, the median

Table 4.5 Strikes and NSCA by Average, Median and Total Duration 1788–1850

Period	Total/Average Involvement	Average Duration	Median Duration	Total Duration	Total Working Days Involved*
Convict Strikes					
1788–1800	18 (3.6)	1.6	2	8	29
1801–10	32 (4)	1.9	2	15	60
1811–20	54 (2.7)	2.1	1	38	103
1821–30	830 (4)	9.5	1	1754	7016
1831–40	1644 (3.3)	1.7	1	803	2650
1841–50	1938 (5.3)	1.4	1	476	2523
Total	4516	3			12381
Free-Labour Strikes					
1788–1800	11 (5.5)	2	2	4	22
1801–10	39 (3.5)	1.9	2	32	112
1811–20	45 (3)	11.9	2	145	435
1821–30	256 (4.8)	9.1	2	2130	10224
1831–40	1492 (3.3)	6.1	2	2205	7277
1841–50	4104 (5.3)	6.9	2	3883	20579
Total	5947			8399	38649
All strikes Total	10463				51030
Convict Non-Strike Collective Action					
1788–1800	72 (4)	4.7	2	66	264
1801–10	137 (4.3)	12.1	5	352	1514
1811–20	461 (3.4)	40	13	5121	17411
1821–30	5661 (3.6)	19	7	29801	107284
1831–40	7335 (3.2)	26.7	8	58527	52607
1841–50	1910 (3.1)	34.6	5	16970	179080
Total	15576				

(Continued)

Table 4.5 (Continued)

Period	Total/Average Involvement	Average Duration	Median Duration	Total Duration	Total Working Days Involved*
Free-Labour Non-Strike Collective Action					
1788–1800	65 (7)	5.6	2	45	315
1801–10	85 (3.9)	8	3	59	230
1811–20	127 (5.8)	10.4	3	229	1328
1821–30	126 (2.7)	143.1	5	5007	13519
1831–40	813 (4)	9	2	1409	5636
1841–50	2944 (6.5)	18.3	3	6487	42166
Total	4160			13336	63194
All NSCA Total	19736				242274

* average involvement in strikes and NSCA multiplied by total duration

duration of union-strikes were longer than informal strikes (three days compared to one day), there is no difference for the median duration of NSCA and average duration of informal NSCA was far longer (40 days compared to 16 days).

Total duration provides another measure of worker mobilisation, combining numbers and duration. Total duration of strikes and NSCA grows over time, especially between 1831 and 1850. Incomplete data indicates total duration of NSCA increases after 1850 but not substantially until 1871–1880. For strikes total working days lost were estimated by multiplying the average number involved by total duration (Table 4.5). While probably understated given the bias in strike size, it provides a baseline. Overall, total working days lost grew rapidly after 1820, although for convicts it peaked in 1821–30 (annual figures varied markedly of course). Total working days lost were not inconsiderable, especially for the decade to 1850. Total involvement in NSCA is almost five times higher but doesn't translate into lost working days although some actions had similar effects. Mass absconding imposed a cost on affected-employers though other employers might gain the absconders' services aside from those who left the colonies, were incarcerated or took up bushranging. Go-slows, sabotage and other of non-cooperative behaviour imposed serious though hard to measure costs. The importance of not confining analysis to strikes is reinforced, not to mention the cost of extensive worker resistance described in Chapter 2.

Collective Action by Industry, Occupation and Gender

Table 4.6 confirms the wide dispersal of collective action by industry even if in some it was fitful and embryonic. Three industries account for over 78% of strikes—maritime/whaling, rural/farming and government. Government and rural/farming accounted for 85.8% of NSCA with maritime/whaling contributing another 4.9%. Distinguishing between convict and free-labour, 390 convict strikes (37.9% of the total of 1029) occurred in rural/farming followed by government (34.3%), mining (11.6%) and services (2.9%). Amongst free workers, maritime/whaling dominates, accounting for 582 strikes (74%) followed by rural/farming (6.7%), building (3.4%), clothing (3.1%) and government (2.9%). With regard to NSCA, government dominates for convicts (72.1%) followed by rural/farming (20.2%), services (2.6%), mining (2.2%), and clothing (0.5%). For free workers, maritime again heads the list (243 NSCA or 40.6%) followed by rural (17.7%), building (3.3%), building materials (3%) and retailing (2.8%).

Workers in a wide array of occupations went on strike (Table 4.7) although again numbers are often small. Seamen accounted for 29.1% of strikes followed by rural/farmworkers (23%), construction and general labourers (16.6%), miners (7.1%), sealers/whalers (4.8%), cooks and domestics (2.4%), clothing trades (1.6%) and sawyers (1.2%). All trades

Table 4.6 Strikes and NSCA by Industry and Period in Australia 1788–1850

Industry	1788–1800	1801–10	1811–20	1821–30	1831–40	1841–50	Total	Percentage of Total
Strikes								
Building & construction				2	13	17	32	1.8
Building materials				3	11	15	29	1.6
Clothing, boots & apparel				8	16	24	48	2.6
Commercial & personal services	1	0	0	5	19	17	42	2.3
Food manufacture				4	11	7	22	1.2
Government & community service		4	14	105	140	112	375	20.7
Maritime & sealing/whaling	2	9	9	29	179	368	596	32.8
Metal manufacturing					1	6	7	0.4
Mining					96	30	126	6.9
Miscellaneous manufacturing				3	9	6	18	
Printing & publishing				1	5	3	9	0.5
Retailing			1	1	5	2	9	0.5
Road transport						4	4	0.2
Rural & farming	4	2	1	55	171	211	444	24.5
Unknown		2	2	9	18	23	54	3.0
Total	7	17	27	225	694	845	1815	
Non-Strike Collective Action								
Building & construction	1			2	10	10	22	0.4
Building materials	1	0	0	6	16	9	32	0.6
Clothing, boots & apparel				3	22	14	29	0.6
Commercial & personal services			2	10	99	18	129	2.6
Food manufacture				3	12	14	29	0.6
Government & community service	9	29	124	1327	1392	432	3313	65.9
Maritime & sealing/whaling	3	16	11	8	86	124	248	4.9
Metal manufacturing				1			1	0

							Total	%
Mining				1	80	26	107	2.1
Miscellaneous manufacturing					4	5	10	0.2
Printing & publishing					6	4	10	0.2
Retailing					6	19	27	0.5
Road transport						3	3	0.1
Rural & farming	6	4	10	216	589	173	998	19.9
Unknown	1	0	3	14	35	7	60	1.2
Total	22	49	150	1591	2957	855	5024	

Table 4.7 Strikes by Occupation and Period in Australia 1788–1850

Occupation	1788–1800	1801–10	1811–20	1821–0	1831–40	1841–50	Total	As % of Total
Bakers				2	1	2	5	0.3
Bootmakers				1	6	13	20	1.1
Bricklayers					2	2	4	0.2
Brickmakers			3		3	4	10	0.6
Misc Build trades-					1		1	0.1
Butchers					2	3	5	0.3
Cab-drivers/carters					1	5	6	0.3
Cabinetmakers				1	4	4	9	0.5
Carpenters				1	4	9	14	0.7
Clerks					1		1	0.1
Clothing trades		0	0	8	12	9	29	1.6
Cooks & domestics	1			5	19	20	44	2.4
Coachmakers					1	1	2	0.1
Coopers				1	1		2	0.1
Construct labour	1	1	3	80	109	77	270	14.9
General labourers		2	8	9	7	4	31	1.7
Leather trades					3	4	7	0.4
Miners			1	2	95	30	128	7.1
Metal trades			1		5	4	10	0.6
Misc skilled/profn				1		3	4	0.2
Misc unskilled				6	26	18	50	
Painters, plasterers & plumbers					2	2	4	0.2
Printers				1	5	3	9	0.5
Postal workers					2	2	2	0.1
Retail workers			1	5		3	10	0.6
Rural/farm labour	3	2	1	57	166	206	435	23

Sawyers			1	2	10	9	22	1.2
Sealers & whalers		3	1	4	30	50	88	4.8
Seamen	2	6	8	31	152	330	529	29.1
Shearers						2	2	0.1
Shipwrights				2	3	1	6	0.3
Stonemasons					1	1	2	0.1
Teachers								
Wharf-labourers				3	6	4	13	0.7
Unknown		2	2	5	15	15	39	2.1

combined account for 8.9% of strikes. Previous histories of pre-goldrush labour organisation focused on craft unions, but examining strikes by occupation paints a different picture, with tradesmen but part of a far wider array of collective action. Wharf-labourers only successfully unionised from the 1870s but engaged in 13 strikes comparable in size to those by journeymen prior to 1851. Even cooks and domestics—many of them women—engaged in 44 strikes though most very small.

As with strikes, Table 4.8 indicates a wide distribution of non-strike collective action by occupation, but with a different ranking headed by construction/general labourers (57%) then rural workers (20.9%), seamen (4.8%), miscellaneous unskilled (4.2%), cooks/domestics (2.7%), miners (2.1%) and sealers/whalers (1%). Much collective action by these groups consisted of absconding/desertion with the exception of miscellaneous unskilled workers which largely consists of government workers, including police, engaging in activity like go-slows or petitioning. Convicts dominate the categories of labourers (especially convict gangs), rural workers and domestics, helping to explain the occupational skewing. Nevertheless Table 4.8 demonstrates the importance of looking beyond strikes. For example, retail workers undertook 10 strikes (almost all in a single workplace) but 25 other types of collective action, mostly multiple employer campaigns for shorter hours at least comparable in size to larger strikes by craft workers. Some occupations were more predisposed to particular types of collective action. For others like miners, there is a fairly even split between strikes and NSCA.

Regarding gender, the database contains 22 strikes involving both men and women—one in the decade 1821–30, 8 for 1831–40 and 13 for 1841–50. There were 26 female-only strikes, four in 1821–30 and 13 in 1831–40 and 9 in 1841–50. In total women were involved in 2.6% of strikes, including a number of relatively large ones at Female Factories. For NSCA there is evidence of 70 involving men and women, one in 1788–1800 (1798), three in 1811–20, eight in 1821–30, 45 in 1831–40 and 13 in 1841–50. There were 142 female-only NSCA; one in the decade to 1810, 21 in 1811–20, 29 in 1821–30, 73 in 1831–40 and 18 in 1841–50. In total women were involved in 4.2% of NSCA (2.8% if women-only NSCA are considered). Again a number were relatively large, although the vast majority involved five or fewer workers.

Most strikes and NSCA involved female convicts assigned as domestic servants or in Female Factories. Convicts account for 81.3% of strikes involving women or 92.3% of women-only strikes, and 90% of NSCA involving women or 95% of women-only NSCA. Collective absconding was by far the most frequent action taken by female convicts, accounting for over 90% of their NSCA while only accounting for 46.6% of NSCA by free women (though caution is required due to small numbers). Larger female protests, including strikes and riots, also tended to involve convicts although there were exceptions. Hundreds of Sydney laundresses petitioned the NSW Legislative Council against convict competition in 1843.[10]

Table 4.8 Non-Strike Collective Action by Occupation and Period in Australia 1788–1850

Occupation	1788–1800	1801–10	1811–20	1821–30	1831–40	1841–50	Total	As % of Total
Bakers				1		3	5	0.1
Bootmakers					10	6	16	0.3
Bricklayers	3				2	1	6	0.1
Brickmakers	2	2	5	9	16	1	35	0.7
Misc Build trades-				1	1	1	3	
Butchers					1	5	6	0.1
Cab-drivers/carters			6	21	12	3	42	0.8
Cabinetmakers				3	12	2	17	0.3
Carpenters	1	1	3	1	3	3	12	0.2
Clerks					1	5	6	0.1
Clothing trades				4	13	8	25	0.5
Cooks & domestics			5	11	103	20	139	2.7
Coachmakers					1	1	2	
Coopers			1		1		2	
Construct labour	3	13	51	758	1008	250	2083	41.5
General labourers	3	6	12	411	278	61	779	15.5
Leather trades					1		1	
Miners				3	76	27	106	2.1
Metal trades		1	1	2	1		5	0.1
Misc skilled/profn		1	19	7	1		28	0.6
Misc unskilled		2	6	44	74	87	213	4.2
Painters, plasterers & plumbers					2	1	3	
Printers					6	5	11	0.2
Postal workers								
Retail workers			1		8	19	28	0.5

(Continued)

Table 4.8 (Continued)

Occupation	1788–1800	1801–10	1811–20	1821–30	1831–40	1841–50	Total	As % of Total
Rural/farm labour	6	5	11	271	579	179	1051	20.9
Sawyers	1		5	10	18	8	42	0.8
Sealers & whalers		6	1	2	19	21	49	1.0
Seamen	3	12	14	15	80	119	243	4.8
Shearers					2	6	8	0.2
Shipwrights	1		2	0	0	3	6	0.1
Stonemasons			3	1	3	3	10	0.2
Teachers					1	1	1	
Wharf-labourers							1	
Unknown	1		3	7	24	8	42	0.8

Collective Action by Issue

Table 4.9 provides a breakdown of strikes/NSCA by issue. As many involved multiple issues, total percentages exceed 100%. Issues of poor working conditions often overlapped with health and safety or management behaviour. Trying to identify a primary issue would paint a misleading picture of industrial conflict which often entails multiple causes. Surviving records only partially capture this complexity but are still valuable. Table 4.7 indicates working conditions was an issue in 49.3% of strikes followed by working hours (39.8%), health and safety (17.5%), management behaviour/discipline (13.1%), wages/remuneration (8.9%), jobs/employment (2.7%) and work methods (1.7%). Unionism and legislation were insignificant, being strongly linked to formal organisation. Wages assumed greater importance after 1830 as colonies transitioned to free-labour. For NSCA the ranking differs. Working conditions dominate (90.6%), in large part because it is the one generalised complaint linked to mass absconding by convicts. Evidence from well-documented cases indicates other issues like harsh discipline and poor food also drove absconding, but there is insufficient evidence to attribute them in the vast majority of cases. Other issues in NSCA were management behaviour (5.6%), wages (4.4%), health and safety (4.4%) and hours (1.7%).

Distinguishing convict and free-labour reveals several differences. For convicts working hours were an issue in 52.6% of strikes, followed by working conditions (43.6%), health and safety (15.2%), management behaviour (12.4%), wages (1.7%) and jobs/employment (0.5%). Amongst free-labour, working conditions were an issue in 57% of strikes followed by hours (23%), health and safety (20.6%), wages (18.3%), management behaviour (14%), jobs/employment (5.6%) and work methods (3.6%). For convict NSCA the leading issue was working conditions (95.6%) followed by management behaviour (5.2%) and health and safety (3.5%). For free workers the leading issues were working conditions (53.8% of free NSCA), wages (32.3%), health and safety (11.5%), management behaviour (8.5%), hours (6.4%) and jobs (6.2%). Some differences are readily explainable. Convicts had fewer opportunities to debate wages and job insecurity was hardly an issue. There are, however, similarities too including the importance of strikes/NSCA over OHS, reinforcing its neglect as a mobilisation point by historians raised in Chapter 3.

The greater proportion of strikes over hours compared to NSCA is largely explained by the nature of claims and who was undertaking it. Many of these strikes were seamen, domestic servants and others like convicts seeking recreation/time-off (see Chapter 2). Some employers condoned temporary absences, others didn't, and it was an ongoing source of friction/tacit negotiation. When Simon Fraser reprimanded his convict shoemakers for being absent without leave on Boxing Day night 1836, Joseph Ball responded that asking his permission was worthless as 'you would not have given it.'[11] Craft

Table 4.9 Strikes and NSCA by Issues and Period in Australia 1788–1850

Issue	1788–1800	1801–10	1811–20	1821–30	1831–40	1841–50	Total	% of Total*
Strikes								
Wages/remuneration	4	8	1	10	52	98	161	8.9
Working conditions		1	16	93	344	430	895	49.3
Management behaviour		1	1	15	114	107	238	13.1
Hours of work	1	4	5	98	281	333	722	39.8
Jobs/employment				5	17	27	49	2.7
Health & safety	1		2	42	145	128	318	17.5
Work methods & subcontracting				5	19	22	35	1.9
Unionism					2	3	5	0.3
Legislation						1	1	0.1
Unknown	1	5	6	12	7	6	38	2.1
Non-Strike collective action								
Wages/remuneration	3	1	7	17	71	124	223	4.4
Working conditions	17	32	133	1540	2206	622	4550	90.6
Management behaviour	3	2		23	122	131	281	5.6
Hours of work			2	5	38	39	84	1.7
Jobs/employment	2			3	20	17	40	0.8
Health & safety		4	5	37	97	76	221	4.4
Work methods & Subcontracting			1	6	14	14	35	0.7
Unionism						2	2	
Legislation					1	1	2	
Unknown		16	9	22	28	64	149	3.0

* Percentages for issues will both total more 100% due to multiple issues in single strike or NSCA.

unions didn't pioneer the eight-hour day movement until the mid-1850s. Prior to this, the principal organised push for shorter hours was the early-closing movement amongst shop-assistants which began in 1840 following earlier UK initiatives. Their main tactic was seeking a pledge/agreement signed by multiple employers backed by moral suasion, adverse publicity directed at 'renegades' and consumer pressure/bans (see Chapter 10).[12] Management behaviour typically entailed allegations of harsh discipline or punitive harassment. Convicts in particular could feel trapped with a master they loathed. In January 1837 several assigned-convicts absented themselves from farmer Louis Beaumaris with James Cater telling Beaumaris he 'would leave his service even if he was hanged for it' (transportation sentence extended nine months).[13]

Collective action over workloads, discipline/supervision, hours and other issues should be seen as responses to inequality at work. Employers commonly demanded unquestioning obedience, to work hard and long, under wages and conditions they deemed fit. For convicts especially masters could intrude in their every waking moment, impeding the simplest pastimes and social discourse. North Midlands (VDL) landholder Captain James Dixon prosecuted four assigned-servants for playing cards in their hut and later the same year (1848) prosecuted another group for having strangers in their hut.[14] Some landholders placed overseer's accommodation close to their servants' to maintain close oversight. However, as with Jamaican slave quarters, convicts viewed their huts/accommodation as personal space—something not all employers contested.[15] Workers had their own views on what constituted reasonable effort, rewards and loyalty. The resulting tensions played out continuously (see Chapter 2), with workers turning to their only sanction, collective action. Of necessity the collective impulse began on a small scale, but its historical significance should not be underestimated.

Collective Action by Outcome and the Role of the Courts

The outcome of collective action warrants consideration. For each strike/NSCA an outcome was recorded as win (including partial-win), loss, draw or unknown. Outcomes were identified for the vast majority of strikes and about half NSCA because the outcome was reported in the press, absconders were reported as apprehended, workers brought before the courts or took court action themselves (4.4% of all cases—see Table 4.10). When prosecuted the vast majority of workers were found guilty. While important for understanding collective action court outcomes aren't entirely representative because where workers took action and employers conceded, or didn't take it to court, the incident or its outcome was seldom reported. Acknowledging this reporting bias, it is still worth examining what surviving records show.

Table 4.10 indicates only 2.2% of strikes by convicts and 12.1% by free workers succeeded, with 1.3% and 3.4% respectively drawn. The higher

Table 4.10 Strikes and NSCA by Period and Outcome, Australia 1788–1850

Period	Won	Lost	Draw	Unknown	Total
Convict Strikes					
1788–1800				5	5
1801–10		6		2	8
1811–20		18			18
1821–30	4	166	1	13	184
1831–40	10	437	5	14	468
1841–50	8	326	6	8	350
Total	22	953	12	34	1021
Percentage of Total	2.2	93.3	1.2	3.3	
Free-Labour strikes					
1788–1800		1		1	2
1801–10		5		4	9
1811–20		3		6	9
1821–30	5	24	2	10	41
1831–40	29	145	9	45	228
1841–50	60	348	16	73	497
Total	94	526	27	138	785
Percentage of Total	12.1	67	3.4	17.6	
Convict NSCA					
1788–1800		1		13	14
1801–10		14		15	29
1811–20	1	26	7	94	128
1821–30	19	232	18	1286	1555
1831–40	16	1117	122	944	2199
1841–50	20	322	23	135	500
Total	56	1712	170	2487	4425
Percentage of Total	1.3	38.9	3.8	56.2	
Free-Labour NSCA					
1788–1800				8	8
1801–10	1	3	1	15	20
1811–20		3		19	22
1821–30	3	12	2	18	35
1831–40	23	72	4	59	158
1841–50	74	142	4	137	357
Total	101	232	11	256	600
Percentage of Total	16.8	38.7	1.8	42.7	

number of unknowns for free workers might affect the disparity. The disparity between convict and free workers in terms of NSCA outcomes was more pronounced (1.3% compared to 16.8%), although the high proportion of unknowns (largely the result of absconding cases) adds a note of caution. The lower apparent success rate for convict NSCA than strikes is almost certainly misleading as successful absconding is difficult to determine because those escaping apprehension simply disappear from the record. Further, long periods at large, months or years, was a victory of sorts though counted as a loss in the database. The improving success rate of free-labour NSCA is not aberrant. The trend continues after 1850, reflecting the growth of formal organisation and the deployment of specific modes of action in different circumstances (see later chapters). Of 55 strikes, unions won 19, lost 13 and for 23 outcomes are unknown, while for 57 NSCA unions won 16, drew 1, lost 15 and for 25 outcomes are unknown. Given small numbers caution is required, but these results suggest formal organisation significantly improved outcomes for workers. It is likely many workers were aware of this, encouraging those that could to form unions.

Another dimension for assessing outcomes is to examine the role of the courts. Chapter 2 argued that a meaningful account of worker mobilisation must consider the pivotal role of the state and its judicial apparatus. This chapter reinforces this point, demonstrating how courts were used to entrench inequality at work by suppressing worker dissent. Between 1788 and 1850, there is evidence of 4899 court actions, involving a total of 9968 workers (6905 convicts and 3063 free workers), concerned with collective action. Instances of collective action often involved multiple court actions. Even so, these figures are significantly understated. In addition to caveats already mentioned, while government notices on convict absconding did include some information on those subsequently apprehended, it was only possible to cross-match this with court proceedings in a minority of cases. Convicts dominate litigation in the 1820s and 1830s but in 1841–50 the numbers almost equalise (involving 2301 convicts and 2027 free workers), demonstrating the courts' centrality in suppressing collective action by free workers.

Importantly, unions—or rather their members—were only involved in court proceedings (overwhelmingly as defendants) on 31 occasions, nine times in 1831–40 and 22 times in the following decade. This amounts to 0.6% of all court cases whereas unions constituted 2.1% of worker organisations even ignoring their greater longevity. Overall, 23.3% of unions were involved in court proceedings compared to 76.1% of informal organisations. Convicts were more likely to be prosecuted for collective action than free workers (except seamen) and workers in unions were least likely to be prosecuted. The relative scarcity of tradesmen was undoubtedly a factor. As noted in Chapter 1, historians have pointed to the use of courts against unions and this is important. Nonetheless, past research hasn't compared formal and informal organisation in this regard and evidence here suggests forming unions actually made workers less likely to face court for collective action—a finding that warrants further investigation in other countries and at earlier times.

Figure 4.2 tracks convict and free-labour court appearances between 1801 and 1900, highlighting disparities but at least one parallel peak in the early 1840s. Previously mentioned caveats apply to the post-1850 period

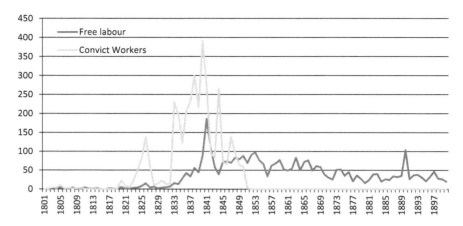

Figure 4.2 Court Appearances Involving Collective Action by Convict and Free-Labour, 1801–1900

but Figure 4.2 demonstrates that the judicial apparatus continued to be deployed against worker organisation.

Table 4.11 summarises litigation by issue/charges, either used by workers or more commonly against them. The total exceeds 4899 because in 12.9% of cases employers charged workers with multiple offences, including ringleaders marked out for more serious charges like conspiracy/mutiny in the case of seamen. Worker-initiated cases constituted only 4.4% of cases. Very few succeeded though outcomes were somewhat better for unpaid wages claims. This mirrors workers' limited legal avenues for redressing grievances. The vast majority of employers' charges were identical to those used against individual workers (Chapter 2) but about 4% were specific to collective action (combination/conspiracy/mutiny and picketing).

The number of prosecutions for collective absconding is understated for reasons already mentioned, although it still indicates the greater difficulties posed for employers compared to strikes or neglect where resort to the courts and rapid punishment was more certain. Sabotage also posed difficulties. In January 1826 Michael Newman, William Mahoney, John Fish, Andrew Moore, and Michael Murphy, five convicts at Sydney's Carters Barracks, were charged with cutting the handles of government hammers. Four received 30 lashes while Mahoney escaped with 25.[16] However, other types of sabotage were difficult to prove. In August 1841 four members of the Campbell Town (VDL) Gaol Gang were reprimanded for breaking a hand cart with which they were working.[17] Sabotaging machinery or tools was more easily proved than the capital offence of incendiarism. In May 1826 four assigned-convicts charged with setting fire to a barn on Dr Elyard's Stonequarry Estate were acquitted for want of evidence.[18] However, even

Table 4.11 Court Actions by Issue/Charge and Period, Australia 1788–1850

Issue	1788–1800	1801–10	1811–20	1821–30	1831–40	1841–50	Total*	Percentage**
Worker-Initiated Claims								
Unpaid wages or remuneration	2		3	6	20	58	89	1.8
Health & safety/ill-treatment		2	2	21	54	45	124	2.5
False imprisonment					1	2	3	
Unfair dismissal							1	
Total*	2	2	5	27	75	105	217	4.4
Charges Laid Against Workers								
Strike/refusing work	7	14	23	319	1082	1111	2556	52.2
Absconding/desertion	4	21	7	46	353	340	731	14.9
Neglecting work, misconduct etc	14	7	8	175	733	406	1343	27.4
Insolence & abuse	2	5	4	31	177	145	364	7.4
Conspiracy/combination	1	6	8	42	56	80	193	3.9
Assaults & threats on master, others		1	2	10	97	76	186	3.8
Picketing						7	7	0.1
Felony/not resisting bushrangers				2	1	2	5	
Larceny/stealing food		2	1	8	37	17	65	1.3
Sabotage/incendiarism				3	32	11	46	0.9
Loitering & vagrancy					1		1	
Unknown		1		2	1	7	11	0.2
Total*	18	50	53	638	2569	2203	5531	

* exceeds 4899 due to multiple charges laid in the same court proceedings
** exceeds 100% because some employer-initiated cases involve multiple charges

where sabotage couldn't be proved other charges could sometimes suffice. In August 1848 when the Hobart Bench failed to convict six of James Wilson's convict servants of wilfully destroying rations, he charged them with misconduct (wasting their bread) and they were gaoled for a month.[19]

While court action occurred in all industries and almost all occupations, the distribution was uneven. Government workers (mainly convict gangs) were involved in 1756 court cases (involving 3718 workers), followed by rural/farming (1174 cases involving 2264 workers), maritime (929 cases and 2290 workers), mining (542 cases and 783 workers), commercial and personal services (mainly domestics, 115 cases and 167 workers), clothing manufacture (mainly tailors, 82 cases and 145 workers), food (mainly bakers, 60 cases and 133 workers) and building materials (mainly sawyers, 47 cases and 103 workers). Overall, government workers accounted for 37.3% of those before the courts followed by maritime (23%), rural/farming (22.7%) and mining (7.8%). Notably, maritime workers were probably more likely given their relative numbers to be brought to court as convict workers. Mining, which included many convicts, is also conspicuous given its relative modest workforce during this period.

Even rare victories in court could be offset by defeat in another claim or risked retribution. In January 1834 the *Sydney Herald's* journeymen compositors successfully defended a claim they had refused work, arguing their contract had expired. However, their counter claim for unpaid wages was rejected by the same Bench.[20] Some wins were pyrrhic. In 1835 Henry Cape, master of the Sydney whaleship *Cape Packet*, transferred a crewmember (Lewis) to *HMS Alligator* allegedly to pre-empt a revolt off New Zealand. Lewis took a charge of false imprisonment to the NSW Supreme Court, which after six months pondering found for him but awarded derisory damages of one farthing.[21] In 1838 Cape was again before the Supreme Court after another disagreement with his crew, charged by James Macintyre with abandoning him on shore—a clear breach of both UK and NSW maritime laws. Like Lewis, Macintyre got nowhere, charges being dismissed due to a technical flaw.[22] Collective complaints of ill-treatment were also fraught with risk of retribution. When three convicts tried to complain about food supplied by their Bruny Island master in January 1834, it was labelled pretence, they were charged with absconding and flogged.[23]

Another measure of judicial repression was the punishments inflicted on workers engaging in collective action. Table 4.12 summarises a range of penalties by period, differentiating convict and free-labour. Convicts were already under sentence, making gaol terms of imprisonment not comparable. They were also subject to a number of additional penalties not imposed (with isolated exceptions) on free workers. Table 4.12 doesn't include some additional penalties (like being convicts being worked in chains or sent to a gang), the imposition of hard-labour or solitary confinement (on both convict and free-labour) or fines like forfeiting wages (predominantly free-labour) but is sufficient for the purposes of this book.

Table 4.12 Court Penalties Imposed on Workers Taking Collective Action by Decade

Sentence (in days)	1788–1800	1801–10	1811–20	1821–30	1831–40	1841–50	Total/Average
Convict Workers							
Total Number of Cases		31	24	417	1916	1213	3598
Cases where additional confinement recorded		6	4	71	873	727	1681
Average sentence (days)		165	17	23	61	70	
Median sentence term (days)		913*	14	14	30	30	
Total additional sentence duration		5110	407	9398	117601	84458	216974
Average involvement		2.7	1.7	2.4	1.8	1.9	
Estimated total time		13797	691	22555	211682	160470	409195
Number sent to penal settlement			2	36	75**	22	135
Transportation sentence extended			1	1	73	63	137
Number placed in stocks				1	35	8	44
Number flogged/lashed		35	46	412	915	148	1556
Cases where number of lashes unknown		9	5	2	1	1	18
Total Number of lashes		4200	1425	16866	31,879	5108	59,478
Average number of lashes		120	31	41	35	35	45
Death (where known commuted)		4		8	16 (3)	17 (12)	45
Free-Labour							
Total number of cases		18	18	49	332	857	1274
Number of cases where gaol sentence recorded			1	19	115	396	531
Average sentence (days)			1.7	78	16	28	
Median gaol sentence (days)			30	14	30	30	
Total duration of gaol sentences			30	3813	5228	23,896	32,967
Average involvement in court cases		3.3	5	2.6	2.2	2.4	
Estimated total gaol days based on average involvement			150	9914	11,501	57,350	78,915
Death					25 (25)		25

* Too few cases to be meaningful; ** includes 40 women removed from Parramatta to Newcastle

Imprisonment is emblematic of the intensity of work-related struggles at this time and severe penalties imposed on dissent. The total duration of court sentences imposed on convicts amounted to 216,927 days (or 409,195 days if multiplied by average involvement, Table 4.12), with construction/general labourers (convict gangs) accounting for 131,000 days (60.4%) followed by rural workers (52,346 or 24.1%). Total duration for free workers was 32,967 days (or 78,195 if multiplied by average involvement) with seamen accounting for 19,103 days or 58%, which rises to 69% if sealers/whalers are added. While sentencing was used in every industry and almost all occupations to subordinate free and convict workers who dared to dissent, these figures indicate its particular use in activities pivotal to colonial economies. It also paints a rather different picture of worker mobilisation than would one focusing on unions.

As Table 4.12 indicates, convicts engaging in collective dissent risked additional penalties, with 135 being sent to penal stations like Port Arthur, 137 having their transportation sentence extended, and 44 being placed in stocks. When four convicts working on Mr Hollis's North Midlands estate took Saturday afternoon off in October 1838, three were reprimanded but James Twigg was ordered to be placed in the stocks after completing his work until sundown each day.[24] Special punishments were reserved for women in the Female Factories (Illustration 4.1). In December 1825 six women who absconded from the Hobart Female Factory had their hair shorn and were forced to wear an iron collar for a week in addition to being confined in cells on bread and water.[25] Head-shaving was particularly loathed and sparked a number of riots like that at the Parramatta Female Factory in March 1833.

The most brutal 'routine' punishment, with grisly outcomes (Chapter 2) and all the markings of slavery, was use of the lash. In September 1805 eight threshers at Castle Hill were charged with refusing work and inciting others to join them. The ringleaders (Fitzwilliam and Akroyd) received 100 lashes while the others were admonished.[26] In early NSW convicts were not the only ones flogged. In April 1806 three seamen of 16 who deserted the *Tilicherry* were given 'corporal punishment' before being sent to a gaol gang and three months later four crewmembers of the colonial vessel *Governor Hunter* were flogged for mutiny.[27] Table 4.12 indicates that 1556 convicts (somewhat fewer as a minority received several doses) received a total of 59,478 'stripes' between 1801 and 1850 for their involvement in collective action, most cases occurring between 1821 and 1840. There were another 18 cases involving over 50 workers where the number of lashes inflicted could not be identified. Both the number flogged and the number of lashes declined after 1840, but its use continued especially in VDL. In June 1842 Henry Johnson, George Powell and John Singleton received 50 lashes on two occasions for repeated absconding from the New Town Government Farm, two on the breech because their scarified backs were not fit for another round. Singleton and Johnson refused to be cowered and absconded (with others) in early July, were apprehended and received another 50 lashes in front of their gang.[28]

205

RULES & REGULATIONS

FOR THE

MANAGEMENT

OF THE

FEMALE CONVICTS

IN THE

NEW FACTORY AT PARRAMATTA.

31st JANUARY, 1821.

SYDNEY:

PRINTED BY ROBERT HOWE, GOVERNMENT PRINTER.

1821.

Illustration 4.1 Rules and Regulations, Parramatta Female Factory
Source: State Library of NSW

Revolt/piracy, incendiarism, murder and, for convicts, assault occasioning grievous bodily harm were capital offences. Ten groups of convicts and three groups of seamen involved in collective action were sentenced to death (Table 4.12). Thompson and Hay demonstrated by the late 18th century a raft of property offences in England were capital crimes.[29] Consistent with this, stealing sheep attracted severe penalties in the Australian colonies. In June 1807 four convict shepherds assigned to Richard Partridge were charged with stealing and consuming a sheep in Partridge's flock belonging to another sheep-owner—James Lara. Benjamin Yeats and Robert Murray were sentenced to death. Timothy Mulahay and Isaac Tibbs received 500 lashes and were sentenced to a gaol gang for 12 months.[30] A fifth man William Bagnell escaped their fate by testifying for the Crown. In several cases convicts assaulting their masters/overseers were hanged even when those assaulted were not killed and there were mitigating circumstances, as at James Mudie's Castle Forbes estate in 1833 (see Chapter 6). Less than two years after Castle Forbes, Maitland Quarry gang-members Patrick Cassidy and William Bagley were charged with assaulting and inflicting grievous bodily harm on overseer, Hugh McIntyre. Other gang-members testified McIntyre had treated Cassidy and Bagley harshly, repeatedly bringing them to court for punishment. The Supreme Court found this and McIntyre's survival was immaterial, sentencing them to death which was duly carried out.[31] Upholding the authority of even tyrannical overseers was paramount notwithstanding public acknowledgement of widespread mistreatment in chain and road-gangs.

In contrast, assaults by seamen on ship's officers, while severely punished, rarely entailed the death penalty unless those assaulted died or it was associated with piratical seizure of the ship. A total of 25 crewmembers on three ships, the *Isabella* (1832), whaler *Harmony* (1832) and *Amelia Thompson* (1839) were sentenced to death for mutiny at sea but reports make it likely their sentences were commuted.

Conclusion

This chapter reinforced points made in Chapter 3. Incorporating a consideration of small-scale action and all modes of action provides a very different picture of the extent of collective action, who undertook it and when compared to an analysis confined to formal organisation, free-labour or strikes. Strikes were a common form of collective action but not for all groups of workers. Other forms of collective action, especially absconding and go-slows were also widely used. In the 1830s absconding was more common than other forms of dissent and was arguably more costly and difficult for private employers and government authorities to manage than strikes. Confining analysis to strikes provides a unrepresentative view of collective action in this period and more generally. Effort-bargaining go-slows by workers also presented difficulties, though it is just as important to recognise that multiple methods interacted and even merged on occasion. Frequent resort to the courts was indicative both of the State's central role in subordinating labour but also the limitations of such measures to suppress resistance, becoming a source of antagonism in its own right.

This chapter's findings also raise important questions about the scale of collective action and preferred modes of dissent amongst slaves and bonded and free-labour elsewhere. For example, absconding seems to have been a preferred mode of protest amongst these groups in the Americas and elsewhere at this time. Absconding was more likely to succeed where absconders were not too physically 'conspicuous', had resources to aid their escape and where there were places to 'disappear' to where there were jobs or opportunities to escape the jurisdiction altogether. Notwithstanding an extensive surveillance regime for convicts and seamen, the size of the continent, slow communication, local demands for labour and possessing resources were more conducive to success (even if many were apprehended fairly rapidly) than may have been the case with slaves on small islands like Mauritius and in the Caribbean although Jamaica which was larger and had a free black community was somewhat different. Similarly prior to the Civil War, free black communities in the South were small—meaning absconding slaves needed to travel large distances. These speculations regarding the comparative dynamics of absconding warrant more detailed comparative research.

Observations were also made about issues and other characteristics of collective action and their outcomes, including the effects of formal organisation. Many issues subject to litigation involving individual workers (Chapter 2)—like wages, hours and management were also the subject of collective action. Nonetheless, collective action altered how some issues were presented or enabled other issues to be pursued. For example, aside from complaints about rations and ill-treatment, some OHS-issues like manning levels or unseaworthy ships could only be effectively raised collectively (see Chapter 5). Some goals/issues could only be pursued through methods available to formal organisation including mutual insurance, trade-controls and early-closing. The chapter pointed to differences in capacity/preferences of specific groups to use particular types of collective action.

The next six chapters examine worker organisation in a number of industries, each subject to particularities of the colonies' political economy, more closely. Using quantitative and more qualitative analysis, the aim is to explore the nature and characteristics of worker organisation in these industries. Again, a central theme is how and why workers combined, and the relationship between formal and informal organisation. Each chapter begins by briefly describing the political economy and dominant modes of production as well as other characteristics shaping worker organisation.

Notes

1 *Sydney Gazette* 6 April 1827.
2 Rosen, S. (2006) That Den of Infamy, the No. 2 Stockade Cox's River, 137–138.
3 *Sydney Gazette* 5 October 1830 and *Sydney Monitor*12 January 1831.
4 *HRNSW* 1803–1805, 28 February 1803, 58 and *Sydney Gazette* 15 and 19 March 1803.
5 LC247–1–7 Hobart 19 June 1839.

6 *The Colonist* 13 May 1840 and *Port Philip Herald* 9 July 1841.
7 *Maitland Mercury* 9 September 1846.
8 Quinlan, M., Gardner, M. and Akers, P. (2003) Reconsidering the Collective Impulse, 137–180.
9 LC247–1–10 Hobart 9 February 1842.
10 *Australasian Chronicle* 23 December 1843.
11 LC247–1–6 Hobart 27 December 1836.
12 Quinlan, M., Gardner, M. and Akers, P. (2005) Failure of Voluntarism: Shop-assistants, the Early-closing Movement and the Struggle to Restrict Work and Trading Hours in the Colony of Victoria 1850–1885, *Labour History*, 88:161–178.
13 LC247–1–6 Hobart 24 and 25 January 1837.
14 LC83–1–8 Campbell Town 9 and 15 May 1848, 25 and 27 July 1848.
15 McDonald, R. (1993) *The Economy and Material Culture of Slaves; Goods and Chattels on the Sugar Plantations of Jamaica and Louisiana*, Louisiana State University Press, Baton Rouge.
16 *Sydney Gazette* 1 February 1826.
17 LC83–1–5 Campbell Town 5 August 1841.
18 *Sydney Gazette*10 May 1826.
19 LC247–1–16 Hobart 17 August 1848.
20 *Sydney Gazette* 1 February 1834.
21 *Australian* 25 September 1835.
22 *Sydney Herald* 13 August 1838.
23 *Colonial Times* 28 January 1834.
24 LC83–1–3 Campbell Town 8 October 1838.
25 Hendriksen, G., Liston, C. and Cowley, T. (2008) *Women Transported: Life in Australia's Convict Female Factories*, 56.
26 *Sydney Gazette* 22 September 1805.
27 *Sydney Gazette* 13 April and 13, 20 July 1806.
28 LC247–1–10 Hobart 16 and 29 June, 14 July 1842.
29 Hay, D. et al. (1977), *Albion's Fatal Tree*.
30 *Sydney Gazette* 28 June 1807.
31 *Sydney Herald* 6 August 1835.

5   Organisation in Transport and Maritime Activities

Introduction

Prior to 1851, the merchant-marine and whaling accounted for far more strikes than was proportionate to its workforce size, perhaps 10% at very most of total employment.[1] Several factors help explain this, including their pivotal economic role, distinctive features of shipboard work, and centuries-old customs. Convicts played little role apart from pilot/customs boats, loading/unloading ships and sealing. The regulatory/industrial struggle of maritime workers has been the subject of more published research than other industries.[2] This chapter focuses on points critical to the broader purposes of the book, including aspects that have received less attention like dockwork and land transport.

The Political Economy of Transport

Modes of transport in the colonies were shaped by climate, topography, settlement patterns/sparse population, technology and distance to markets. As the most arid inhabited continent with an old and weathered topography, Australia lacked extensive freshwater lakes and large inland rivers. River-based ports were focal points for settlement for reasons of transport and providing a supply of fresh water. The only substantial inland river system (tiny by North American standards) was the Darling River flowing from Queensland through NSW before being joined by the Alps-fed Murray River and flowing onto South Australia. It didn't become important for navigation until after 1850. Some of the string of rivers—navigable to some degree—flowing east to the sea from the Great Dividing Range formed the base for early settlements including the drowned river-valley of Port Jackson (Sydney), Maitland and Newcastle on the Hunter River, and Brisbane and Ipswich on the Brisbane River. Two important rivers (the Derwent and Tamar) at the southern and northern end of VDL Island were the base for Hobart and Launceston respectively. Rivers on VDL's west coast were ignored apart from the short-lived penal settlement at Macquarie Harbour.

Victorian settlement was primarily initiated from the mouth of the small Yarra River (Melbourne) flowing into Port Philip Bay with another town

(Geelong) close to the Bay's entrance and smaller settlements further west on Victoria's southern coast (Portland and Port Fairy). Adelaide (South Australia) was established on the small Torrens River (the Murray River's mouth was a good deal further east). In the southwest of Western Australia Fremantle and Perth were established on the small Swan River. Settlements were attempted in northern Australia at Fort Dundas (Melville Island) in 1824 and Port Essington (near present-day Darwin) in the 1840s. Both failed due to the harsh climate and disease.

Early settlement huddled the coast and relied on maritime transport. International shipping was a lifeline for the colonies, importing goods and people and exporting goods to remote markets in the UK (like wool, whale-oil, copper and tallow), India (like sandal wood, flour, copper, wine and horses), China and the Americas.[3] By the 1830s Australia was integral to the great circle of global shipping. It became an increasingly significant destination for Britain's manufactured goods, ranking seventh overall by 1850.[4] This and the remoteness of Australia encouraged local ship-repair/refitting facilities along with shipbuilding predominantly to serve intra and inter-colonial trade. Ships ranged from larger vessels (mostly British or overseas owned) used in international trade with more lightly-manned barques, brigs, schooners and ketches used in intra-colonial and inter-colonial transport. Sail remained dominant but steamers were increasingly used, especially for the short-haul people movement as between Sydney and Newcastle.

Land transport relied on roads (using drays) radiating from ports for moving goods to and from the expanding pastoral districts. Water was used wherever possible to move bulky goods because it was cheaper—initially wheat was moved from Windsor/Richmond to Sydney via the far longer Hawkesbury River/Pacific Ocean route—and roads were often poor. Colonial governments only began building railways after 1850.

Two other maritime-related activities were important to colonial economies, sealing and whaling (Chapter 1). Killing seals for their pelts rapidly decimated the large populations around the south of the continent, to the point of extinction with elephant seals on King Island. Hunting deep sea whales for their oil (rendered from blubber in large try-out pots for use in lighting and as lubricants), bone (used in corset stays, whips and umbrellas) and ambergris (used to make perfume) lasted far longer. Sydney and Hobart became major hubs of southern-hemisphere whaling, with their own fleets (38 whaleships were based in Hobart in 1848) and servicing whaleships from other countries.[5] Bay whaling using small boats from land-bases to catch whales migrating along the coast began in the 1820s in NSW and VDL (with 35 alone in 1841) before spreading to South Australia and Western Australia.[6] Pelagic or deep sea whaling relied on robustly-built schooners, brigs and barques normally carrying twice the crew of a merchant vessel, provisioned for a long voyage and having between two and four boats to chase and harpoon whales. Narrow, light, pointed at both ends and just over 7 metres in length, these boats carried a crew of six, a boat-steerer, four rowers and a captain/headsman.[7] Initially rivalling wool, in 1850 combined NSW and VDL exports of whale products still totalled £4.2 million.[8] However, the industry was already in long-term decline due to over-exploitation and whale-oil substitutes. Whaleships relied on crews drawn from all corners of the globe, including Tasmanian Aboriginal William Lanney. As with the merchant-marine, it was a physically-hard, poorly-paid, dangerous and insecure life as tiny whalers' cottages in now-trendy Battery Point, Hobart attests.[9]

Patterns of Organisation in Maritime Transport and Sealing/whaling

Table 5.1 summarises organisation and collective action amongst maritime workers. It includes a separate count of collective action by convict transport workers engaged by government which is excluded from the industry count but is indicative of the conspicuous role of the state in maritime activities. Analysis of strikes by year identified a peak of 88 strikes in 1841 overshadowing all other years (the next highest being 41 in 1845). There were no prominent peaks in NSCA. Aside from strikes, mass absconding was the most frequent type of collective action by maritime industry workers, followed by court actions and petitions. Seamen made more use of courts to pursuing collective claim than any other group of workers. Of 87 claims, 50 concerned unpaid wages (won 25, lost 17, one draw and seven unknowns), while 37 concerned poor rations, ill-treatment/assaults by officers or the safety of the ship (won 10, lost 20, one draw and six unknowns). Other forms of protest, like sabotage, were rare. Crewmembers of the barque *Alfred* threw cargo into Sydney harbour in 1842 and four years later crewmembers on an unnamed US ship were accused of arson during a revolt on the high seas.[10]

Table 5.2 indicates working conditions was the most important issue for both strikes and NSCA. For strikes this is followed by OHS, hours, management behaviour, wages and jobs/employment. The rank-ordering for NSCA of wages, management behaviour, OHS, jobs/employment and hours differs slightly. Most hour-related strikes entailed seamen going/staying ashore without permission while work methods actions often entailed disagreements over task allocation. Wages rank higher in NSCA largely due to seamen's court actions to recover unpaid wages. The strictures of seamen's articles made absconding preferable to demanding better wages. Consistent with this, most jobs/employment-related actions were attempts to win a discharge from the ship. With regard to safety, all NSCA represent court claims, though seamen frequently struck over this issue too. Many OHS disputes also entailed claims of management behaviour/harsh discipline reflecting the particularly authoritarian structure on ships and seamen's inability to escape supervisory oversight.

From settlement discord amongst seamen aroused concern amongst commercial/shipping interests and government authorities. In June 1822 nine

Table 5.1 Summary: Organisation/Activity in Maritime/Whaling and Road Transport 1788–1850

Nature of activity	1788–1800	1801–10	1811–20	1821–30	1831–40	1841–50	Total	Percentages
Maritime/Whaling								
All Organisation	5	24	19	35	252	457	792	
Formal Organisation					3	4	7	
Involvement	20	97	73	169	1232	2238	3829	
Adjusted involvement*	25	105	89	219	1456	2542	4436	
Strikes	2	9	9	29	179	368	596	70.6
NSCA	3	16	11	8	86	124	248	29.4
Total	5	25	20	37	265	492	844	
Absconding	3	14	9	3	50	68	147	
Court actions		1	2	7	30	47	87	
Petitions		1		1	2	11	15	
Press Letters						1	1	
Sabotage						2	2	
Bans				1	1		2	
Road Transport								
All Organisation						9	9	
Formal Organisation						3	3	
Strikes						4	4	
NSCA						3	3	
Total						7	7	
Court actions								
Petitions						3	3	
Press Letters						1	1	
Mass meetings						1	1	

Government-Engaged Convicts

Boatmen/crew

Organisation	3	14	22	33	72
Strikes		9	8	18	35
NSCA	2	7	15	16	40
Total	2	16	23	34	75
Absconding	2	3	9	7	21

Wharf-Labourers

Organisation		2	4	2	8
Strikes		2	3	2	6
NSCA			1		1
Total		2	4	2	8
Absconding			1		1

Carters

Organisation	6	21	12		39
Strikes			1		1
NSCA	6	21	12		39
Total	6	21	13		40
Absconding	5	21	12		38

* Estimate based on adding median membership to zero count organisations

Table 5.2 Strikes and Non-Strike Collective Action by Issue in the Maritime/Whaling Industries 1788–1850

Nature of activity	1788–1800	1801–10	1811–20	1821–30	1831–40	1841–50	Total*	Percentage*
Strikes								
Wages/remuneration	1			2	16	25	43	7.2
Working conditions	1	4	7	15	121	247	395	66.3
Management behaviour		1	1	4	39	58	104	17.4
Hours of work		3	1	4	29	90	127	21.3
Jobs/employment				3	12	19	34	5.7
Health & safety			1	9	52	75	137	23
Work methods				1	7	11	18	3
Unionism						1	1	0.2
Legislation								
Unknown		2	1	2	6	2	13	2.2
NSCA								
Wages/remuneration	1	1	2	3	28	29	63	25.4
Working conditions		6	3	4	46	76	135	54.4
Management behaviour	2			2	12	22	38	15.3
Hours of work					1	5	6	2.4
Jobs/employment				1	8	5	14	5.6
Health & safety	1	1	1	3	11	20	37	14.9
Work methods					3	2	5	2
Unionism								
Legislation								
Unknown		9	5	1	17	20	52	

* exceeds total for strikes (596) and NSCA (248) and 100% because of multiple issue strikes/NSCA.

shipmasters in Sydney petitioned the Governor to deal with insubordination amongst merchant ship crews.[11] In July 1824 consideration was given
to reducing pay on colonial vessels in exchange for increased allowances to
discourage desertion from European ships but deemed impractical.[12] Disparities between international, inter-colonial and coastal wages were not
the only factors contributing to desertion/insubordination. Others included
shipboard conditions and higher colonial wages. Mercantile/shipping interests repeatedly lobbied government for additional regulatory and policing
measures to combat dissent.[13] Insubordination amongst whalers formed
part of this debate. Three colonies (VDL, South Australia and Western Australia) introduced separate laws to regulate whalers, but as with merchant
seamen the regulatory struggle was ongoing.[14] On occasion, the conduct
of masters of whaling vessels was referred to government authorities, as
occurred in NSW in 1810 and again 1820.[15]

Informal Shipboard and Sealing/Whaling Protests

Strikes, mutinies and mass absconding were a common occurrence in the
European mercantile marine—and not unknown in navies—from the
17th century if not before. Rediker identified 60 revolts at sea in the Anglo-
American trade between 1700 and 1750, while Dobson identified 37 strikes
by seamen and ships carpenters in UK ports between 1717 and 1800.[16] These
figures may prove conservative as further sources are examined. Rediker
identified ritual forms of protest including the round robin petition (with
signatures in a circle) designed to prevent victimisation of ringleaders—a
practice not confined to seamen (see Chapter 7).[17] Port hotels were important meeting places for seamen, also serving as venues for recruitment and
crimping networks.

These practices rapidly took hold in the Australian colonies, aided by
the global nature of the industry and its workforce. In 1790 the crew of the
convict transport *Neptune* complained about poor rations and ill-treatment,
two years later the crew of the *Kitty* struck, and in 1797 the crew of another
convict transport protested harsh discipline.[18] Shipboard protests grew in
number over succeeding decades, most occurring in port in part because
strikes at sea risked charges of mutiny. By the mid-1830s shipboard strikes
and collective desertion were a regular occurrence in ports like Sydney,
Hobart and Launceston and a decade later this pattern had extended to
Fremantle, Melbourne, Adelaide and Brisbane and was also occurring in
regional ports like Geelong.

Sealers based on Bass Strait islands also took collective action. Paid according on a lays system, earnings in no way matched the value of seal pelts and
were reduced further by inflated deductions for food and clothing analogous
to the truck system. Groups were left at remote islands to fend for themselves for months. Some were marooned when a ship returned late or sank,
living off food they could catch and suffering scurvy. In November 1804

seven sealers absconded from Cape Barren Island—the sealer settlement there later being notorious for abducting Aboriginal women.[19] A year later eight sealers picked up by the *Sophia* brought a court action in Sydney, arguing they had been left to starve.[20]

Collective action was more frequent amongst pelagic and bay whalers. In 1807 the whaleship *Elizabeth's* crew was charged with mutiny. Instances of collective action grew and by the 1830s whalers were regularly being tried in Sydney and Hobart, with similar cases in other ports like Fremantle.[21] Like sealers, whalers were paid on the lays system based a share of returns which varied according to the task—masters getting the biggest share followed headsmen/harpooners (say an 11th lay), boat steerers, carpenters/ coopers and other seamen depending on skill and experience (say between a 48 and 50th lay). Erratic/low returns from a poor voyage/season were frequent sources of disagreements, as was voyage duration, choice of hunting grounds/port stopovers and OHS. Deductions for items like clothes, shoes, tobacco and soap could be considerable, for example amounting to between £3/5/- and £6/6/9 for the schooner *Eliza's* crew on its 1845 voyage.[22] Like seamen, whalers receiving advances to cover clothing expenses and travel to bay whaling stations often absconded like four at a Recherche Bay whaling station in July 1833.[23] Others absconded to obtain higher wages. In 1837 whalers at the Point Rosetta station absconded to seek higher wages in Adelaide. The Colonial Secretary lamented one of the absconders from VD Land (unclear if intentional pun) had infected the local Aboriginal population with venereal disease, making their departure opportune.[24]

Harsh discipline and hazards also sparked collective action. In February 1837 the whaleship *Alexander Henry's* crew was charged with mutiny after striking, and demanding the second officer be sent ashore due to his frequent intoxication.[25] In June 1838 whalers at the Kingscote Bay whaling station combined over poor rations and harsh working conditions.[26] The prominence of management behaviour/discipline and not-unrelated OHS-issues reflected rigid shipboard authority, ever-present dangers to life and limb, and cost-cutting on crew-numbers and provisions. Court records capture some of this but logbooks afford more detailed evidence and also demonstrate that not all disputes ended up in court. Ships were required to keep daily logs recording weather conditions, the ship's location/condition and crewmember activities like repairs, caulking, cleaning, painting and pumping. Logbooks offer insights into workplace conflicts rarely found in other industries.

The voyage of Hobart whaling barque *Marianne* (November 1834 to September 1836) illustrates a progressive breakdown of relations between the crew and some officers with the master, Robert Lincoln. On 28 January 1835 James Creed refused to stop smoking his pipe on deck and was chained to the quarterdeck on 15 March for mutinous language. On April 2 Charles McBride threatened the chief mate. Relations between Lincoln and other officers also deteriorated. On 22 April 1835 Lincoln ordered one

(Walker) below for being asleep on duty and a week later another officer (Harvey) held Lincoln by the throat saying he was neither 'a whaler nor a sailor.' There were further disputes, involving a number of seamen and the ship's carpenter including refusals to work over the next six months. In May 1836 Arthur Elmsley and several colleagues deserted the ship in a boat after another dispute with Lincoln. Lincoln and the chief mate tried to launch boats in pursuit but the remaining crew responded in a dilatory fashion indicating prior knowledge of and sympathy with the escape. When Lincoln called them to account for their neglect, Harvey gave him 'a great deal of insolence and was ordered to his cabin.'[27] Desertion so late in a voyage that had caught whales (thereby losing all pay) was indicative of the state relations had reached. For the remainder, neglect was a safer option than outright refusal that risked a charge of mutiny.

The brig *Marianne* (different vessel) whaling off New Zealand a decade later experienced similar issues. On 9 August 1845 George Harris was ropes-ended for being 'dilatory and insolent.' Six days later Harris and several others took a boat and tried to desert at Pidgeon Bay near Lyttelton, New Zealand. They were apprehended despite calculated lethargy by other crewmembers called out in pursuit. Several ringleaders, including Thomas Wilkinson, were put in chains. When the vessel reached Jervis Bay south of Sydney on 21 October 1845, another crewmember (Wells) absconded but was returned by local Aborigines. Given Wells's and others' determination to desert, the master offered to allow crewmembers to leave but without their clothes. The offer was renewed the following day but so many accepted the captain nominated just eight he would allow to go. These men refused to leave without their clothes. The captain relented on condition they helped get the vessel underway and signed an agreement clearing all future claims against the shipowners. After reaching Sydney on 30 October 1845, three crewmembers (George Perry, James Deane and James Young) struck and demanded a discharge but were persuaded to resume work. On 31 October Jack Rice also refused work using 'the most insolent language. The next day a boat came alongside to take five crewmembers aboard a Man-O-War they had agreed to join. Only Rice was denied because he was under arrest.[28]

Some shipmasters, like AW Murray on the brig *Esperanza*, were more accommodating. Murray's log records on 7 August 1847 several seamen and the carpenter went ashore without leave and returned tipsy 'at their own pleasure.' Three were still drunk the next day, the carpenter didn't return until August 11th and was too drunk to work. By this time another seaman (Sprout) had gone absent, not returning until the 13th. Six weeks later on 29 September Murray noted the ship was detained in Hobart 'the hands not being on board.' Despite being drunk on other occasions, Murray reported the carpenter undertaking important repairs while at sea. Murray discharged a seaman (Miller) 'at his own request', recorded another (James Kenny) refusing to work for two days (25–26 December 1847) before resuming duty and two other seamen going absent when the ship returned to Hobart in late January 1848.[29]

Only one seaman (Rice) was prosecuted for dissent on these three ships. The Crowther Collection's more than 100 logbooks (a tiny surviving fragment of logs), suggest around one-fifth of Hobart-based vessels experienced some form of collective action, a magnitude higher than hundreds of cases brought to court. Cooper-Busch's examination of US whaleship logbooks identified a similar pattern of collective dissent.[30] Not surprisingly colonial logbooks suggest a higher win/draw ratio for seamen than court records. While maritime dissent levels were atypical, logbooks and other sources like diaries (see Chapter 6) point to a significant level of collective action in other industries that went unrecorded.

Provisions were often of poor quality, spoiled or sometimes in short-supply, with coopers making new kegs at sea in an effort to rescue deteriorating food stocks. On 29 January 1814 the master of the sealing schooner *Mary and Sally* recorded the need to shorten bread rations.[31] In December 1820 Andrew Haigh, master of the *Snipe*, recorded scurvy amongst crewmembers notwithstanding a monthly allowance of lime juice.[32] The log of the barque *Sarah and Elizabeth* on its South Sea whaling voyage of July 1839 to September 1840 repeatedly records barrels of pork and ship biscuit either in poor condition or condemned outright.[33] Fresh water was also an issue. There are no colonial figures on maritime/whaling fatalities, but newspapers regularly reported ships lost/disappearing in storms, and fatalities arising from seamen lost overboard, falling from rigging or into holds. The toll certainly numbered in the thousands and surviving logbooks reinforce this grim toll. On 13 July 1837 William Fletcher fell overboard from the whaler *Prince of Denmark* and drowned.[34] The whaling barque *Sarah and Elizabeth* logbook records James Parker dying after falling from the top gallant on 10 October 1839, two days later another crewmember (Evers) died, a fire erupted during trying-out (rendering blubber) on the 15th, and the second mate fell down the aft hold two months later.[35] On 5 December 1846 a boat from the barque *Fortitude* capsized after harpooning a whale, five drowned and the captain barely survived by clinging to the upturned boat for four hours.[36] Dragged out of sight or rammed by an injured whale, some boats simply disappeared. Heavy clothing and cold water made survival unlikely even if seamen were able to swim—most couldn't. Along with ship losses, close calls were also common. Returning from Mauritius in January 1840 amidst heavy seas, the leaking brig *Esparanza* was only saved by continuous pumping and tossing 140 bags of sugar overboard.[37]

Health and safety was the single most important source of collective shipboard protests. Analysis of a dataset of over 1900 cases between 1790 and 1900 found OHS far outstripped management and wages. The main issues—which didn't alter significantly over time—were harsh discipline/assault/ill-treatment (35.3% of 567 OHS-related protests) followed by poor rations (30.4%), unseaworthy vessels (16.1%), illness/clothing/quarters

(14%), overwork/fatigue (8.3%), short-handed crew (7.6%), drunk/incompetent officers (6%) and other (1.5%). Of 567 court cases seamen were prosecuted in 83.7% for their actions, while in the remainder they lodged complaints. Prosecuted seamen were convicted in 86.7% of cases with 79% of those convicted being gaoled. Outcomes remained consistent only improving slightly after 1880.[38]

Formal and Port-Wide, Multi-Ship and District-Based Informal Organisation

Substantial in scale, collective action by seamen/whalers was overwhelmingly confined to a ship or bay-station. The globally dispersed nature of the industry and a mobile workplace made wider alliances more difficult except in ports. There are hints of colonial multi-ship networking by the 1820s (if not before) but from the 1830s the evidence is unambiguous. Port-wide combinations of seamen working in a particular trade (like colliers) or for a specific company like the Dutch East India Company had been occurring in Europe since the early 17th century.[39] Colonial seamen engaging in multi-ship or port-wide combinations were following well-established customs, drawing on social networks in port-pubs/sailor-towns like Sydney's Rocks.

In February 1837 merchant seamen, whalers and labourers outfitting whaling vessels in Sydney combined to raise wages. This involved strikes and mass desertion from ships, one newspaper alleging the action was timed to exploit the seasonal peak in activity. 'A lover of justice' claimed the *Andromeda's* crew told those on the *Sir George Murray* not to ship for less than £3 per month.[40] Whalers demanded increased lays and ship-labourers 4s per-day. Coopers and shipwrights were claimed to receive 7s and 10s per-day respectively while the Coopers' Society was alleged to have sent a report to a Glasgow newspaper that their members were earning only 2s 3d per-day.[41] On March 14 a meeting of shipowners, merchants (like Campbell & Co) and other interested parties resolved to reject the increases sought.[42] Most Sydney newspapers supported the shipowners but the *Sydney Monitor* dissented, arguing wages were low and accusing shipowners of conspiring to supress wages.[43] There is no evidence workers involved were prosecuted and some whaleship owners at least acceded to the demands.[44] The combination highlighted close connections between merchant seamen, whalers and those like coopers fitting out vessels.

In late February 1839 seamen in the port of Launceston also combined to raise their wages. The *Cornwall Chronicle* reported that Captain Walmsley (the *Henry*) had only completed his complement by paying £4 10s per month as 'a result of a combination of the seamen in the port.'[45] Others involved crews on the schooner *Munford* loaded with sheep for South Australia and the government cutter at Georgetown.[46] Like the Sydney combination, those involved were not prosecuted.

Aside from informal multi-ship/port combinations, there were attempts to establish unions. Formal organisation had a long history in Europe, taking different forms including semi-religious fraternities and from the 17th century port-based insurance boxes of seamen or seamen's boxes. Earlier bodies had provided mutual insurance to ordinary seamen, including for capture by Barbary pirates, but seamen's boxes were exclusively devoted to this task. For a subscription, seamen could access funds when shipwrecked, captured or injured.[47] By the early 19th century mutual insurance morphed into benefit/benevolent societies (often formed in taverns) of mariners (including fishermen) to provide funeral funds and other support, like the Seamen's Loyal Standard Association of North-East England founded in 1824.[48] Early colonial unions followed suit. In 1839 seamen sailing out of Sydney formed the Port Jackson Coasting Seamen's Mutual Benefit Society. In additional to mutual insurance, the union established a House-of-Call and survived until August 1845 at least.[49] This more than matched most craft unions of the period, though it was another three decades before Australian seamen managed to establish permanent bodies, around the same time as their UK counterparts.

There is more ambiguous evidence of organisation in VDL—the other major maritime colony. In November 1840 a meeting at Henry Readings *Edinburgh Castle* hotel established the Launceston Whalers Benevolent Society for the relief of distressed whalers and their families.[50] Worker involvement in this body is unclear. While the title indicated philanthropy rather than mutual insurance, at least eight other unions (including the Sydney carpenters' union formed in 1834) used 'benevolent' in their title and others referred to benevolent activities in their aims. In 1846 a Merchant Seamen's Institution/Society was formed in Hobart, establishing a pension scheme based on a small monthly subscription.[51] Hobart's Port Officer Captain William Moriarity (1792–1850) was the prime mover and it enjoyed the Governor's support. Like the Launceston Whalers Benevolent Society, it was short-lived. Employer/government involvement in both questions their unionate status, although it should be noted that similar involvement/sponsorship occurred in other industries like retailing and employer involvement reflected recognition that moderating insecurity benefited the industry by providing a more reliable/sustainable workforce.

Dockworkers and Other Maritime Workers

Two other categories of maritime workers were watermen and dockworkers/wharf-labourers. Watermen were self-employed skilled boatmen rowing people and merchandise between ships and docks or across short bodies of water like between Dawes Point and Milson's Point in Sydney. Given potential involvement in smuggling and crimping, watermen were regulated through licensing like ex-London waterman (Badge No. 5704) John Smith Glover. The *Watermen's Arms* in the Rocks probably served as a meeting point and possibly a House-of-Call. Wharf-labourers were involved in the loading/unloading of vessels and were only emerging as a specialised work-force at this time.

Informal Collective Action at Workplace Level

Early collective action by wharf-labourers mainly involved convicts. In June 1826 three convicts assigned to Cooper and Levey refused to unload wheat from the brig *Venice* in Cockle Bay Sydney after sunset. Ringleader Thomas Butler received 10 days on the treadmill and returned to government.[52] Messrs Wright and Long based at Millers Point repeatedly pros-ecuted their assigned-convicts for dissent, including collective action—one for unauthorised absence (1834) and another for refusing to move a punt and 'impertinent language' (1836) where ringleader John Welsh received 25 lashes.[53] Similar incidents occurred in other colonies. In November 1840 Thomas Rann hired to Mr DeLittle was charged with disobedience after he and two assigned-convicts adjourned from unloading a lime boat to a nearby public-house, believing they'd 'done as good a day's work as any gentleman in the island would look for.' Rann received 30 days hard-labour on the Launceston Treadmill. The convicts got two hours in the stocks.[54] In January 1846 wharf-labourers loading wool on the British barque *Duke of Richmond* Geelong struck over bad meat in their rations. Four ringleaders were sentenced to 30-days imprisonment.[55]

Multi-Workplace Action and Formal Organisation

Watermen also took informal action; although being self-employed, it was often directed at government. In 1839 Fremantle boatmen struck for a wage increase.[56] In 1847 Launceston watermen petitioned the government against a ticket-of-leave holder using probation labour to move timber in boats con-trary to government regulation.[57] In June 1850 Hobart watermen also took jobs-related action, petitioning the government for a clause in the *Police Act* restricting license-holder numbers and keeping license fees to £5 per-year.[58] Four months later watermen in Williamstown, Victoria struck against a reduction in their government-mandated scale of fares.[59]

Sporadic instances of wider organisation also occurred amongst wharf-labourers as several examples illustrate. In February 1823 a Sydney trader complained that 20 to 30 wharf-labourers refused to load wheat onto carts for five shillings per-day. However, another correspondent argued the strike had more to do with the trader wanting to pay in kind not cash.[60] In August 1837 the *Cornwall Chronicle* complained of a wage-hiking combi-nation amongst free-labourers on the Launceston wharves, although a dis-senting correspondent argued the issue had more to do with misuse of the convicts to unload ships.[61] In December 1849 wharf-labourers in the same port struck for a 6d increase in daily wages to 3s 6d.[62] The ongoing use of convicts to suppress free-worker organisation became more evident six months later when 50 petitioned the government in protest at the gaoling (for three months) of three men for 'loitering' while seeking work, and alleging probation-passholders were being preferred for jobs.[63] In Port Adelaide wharf-labourers struck for increased wages in January 1846.[64] Unlike their Launceston compatriots, they couldn't be replaced with convicts.

There is evidence of formal organisation of Sydney watermen concerned with mutual insurance. In April 1844 the Port Jackson United Watermen's Benefit Society obtained registration as a friendly society, surviving until at least 1860.[65] A related body, the United Watermen's Birmingham Benefit Society Sydney was also separately registered in 1844, surviving until at least 1849. As Friendly Society records haven't survived, their relationship cannot be clarified. Newspaper reports indicate they initially met at the *New York Hotel*, later Kettle's *Star of the East* in George St (1844), the *Kings Head Inn* in lower George Street (1849) and by 1851 the *Watermen's Arms* in Harrington Street.[66] Their activities included arranging the funeral of members like Isaac Johnson, in 1848.[67]

Land-based Transport

Without steam railways and canals, roads were the only means of moving goods and people inland. Heavy/bulky goods (like bales of wool, wheat and furniture) were moved by bullock-drawn drays to or from the closest navigable river or port. Dray-drivers had meeting points at strategically-located pubs but evidence of organisation wasn't uncovered. From the 1830s coaches moved people between major settlements like Hobart and Launceston, operations being small family businesses until the arrival of American Freeman Cobb in the 1850s. In towns, self-employed drivers of horse-drawn cabs (like watermen licensed with fees mandated by government) did organise as did self-employed port, ore and water-carriers—the latter vital prior to reticulated water systems. Tables 5.1 and 5.2 indicate limited organisation amongst land transport workers from 1840—a trend that accelerated in succeeding decades. The primary issue for strikes and NSCA were wages/remuneration followed by management behaviour and legislation. The latter reflected the importance of regulation affecting the working conditions of cab-drivers and water-carriers, as did the use of petitions.

Informal Workplace-Based Collective Action

Single-workplace collective action appears rare amongst dray-drivers, carters and cab-drivers, not surprising given many were self-employed and engaged multiple clients. In January 1834 when Captain Coghill admonished his draymen for being 'so long on the road with his wool . . . they threw down their whips, and said he had better drive the drays himself.'[68] In January 1850 dray-drivers engaged by Matthew Morgan to supply firewood to the *Thames* steamer in Geelong were charged with disobedience and threatening language after they refused work and demanded their wages when a bushfire approached the drays.[69]

Multi-Workplace Action and Formal Organisation

In terms of wider actions water-carriers predominated. In addition to an ambiguous report of water-carriers striking during a Hobart fire in 1841,[70] there is evidence they organised in Adelaide, Melbourne and Geelong. In December 1845 Adelaide water-carriers formed a society and petitioned the government about regulated charges/access to water holes—issues subject to further protests in 1846 (involving 50 drivers) and 1850 (another petition).[71] In Melbourne water-carriers petitioned over poor road conditions in 1845, formed a society in May 1847 and then combined to raise their remuneration/charges.[72] Geelong water-carriers rapidly followed suit, seeking increased cartage rates and establishing a benefit/benevolent society.[73] Geelong carriers struck again for increased remuneration in September 1850.[74] Unlike Adelaide water-carriers, the Melbourne and Geelong unions appear short-lived

Illustration 5.1 Lower Murray St Cab-Drivers 1848

Source: John William Newland (?–1857) Murray Street 1848 Full plate daguerreotype 15 × 20cm. Presented by Mrs M Walker, 1937 Collection: reproduced with permission of Tasmanian Museum & Art Gallery

Other carriers to take collective action included those driving carts between Port Adelaide and Adelaide. They struck for increased cartage rates in February 1846 and also lodged complaints with the government over road conditions.[75] Burra ore drivers organised in 1846 and also became enmeshed in a major dispute at the mine when, like the miners, their remuneration was cut.[76] Organisation amongst cab-drivers was exceptional but became common in later decades. In November 1848 Hobart cab-drivers struck work after the *Cab Regulation Act* was amended giving passengers the option of paying by the distance travelled or time.[77] An 1848 photograph of cab-drivers in lower Murray Street Hobart (Illustration 5.1) represents the earliest known depiction of workers who took collective action in Australia.

Conclusion

Examining the Anglo-American merchant-marine of the early 18th century, Rediker argued seamen were amongst the first wage labour to mobilise. Seamen and whalers were equally prominent in the Australian colonies between 1790 and 1850, with almost 800 instances of informal organisation. As Rediker has argued, maritime workers warrant a more conspicuous place in the history of worker mobilisation. By the 1820s, strikes and other collective dissent were regular occurrences on ships in colonial ports and, like convicts, seamen were prosecuted in large numbers. Collective dissent was also common at bay whaling stations. The pivotal role of maritime transport and whaling to the colonies economically along with the closely confined, hazardous and insecure nature of work helps explain this. While colonial labour markets were conducive to organisation, widespread insubordination and calls for stringent regulation were common across the British Empire and beyond, often coinciding in particular periods/years.[78]

As in Europe, seamen belonging to multiple ships in particular ports took collective action or tried to form unions. Explicit alliances were exceptional but the scale and patterns of shipboard protests indicate a degree of networking, hardly surprising given the congregation of seamen near the docks with well-known meeting places like the *Orient*, *Hero of Waterloo* and *Whaler's Arms* hotels in the Rocks, Sydney. There is also evidence of informal collective action amongst wharf-labourers and waterman, the latter forming benefit societies like their counterparts in London had for many centuries. Watermen were self-employed as were many land-based transport workers who organised, most notably water-carriers. Prior to 1851, collective action was sporadic and the issues rather different to those affecting seamen, including government-mandated remuneration.

Notes

1 Broeze, F. (1981) The Seamen of Australia, *Push from the Bush*, 10:78–105.
2 Quinlan, M. (1992) Making Labour Laws Fit for the Colonies; Quinlan, M. (1996) Industrial Relations Before Unions; Quinlan, M. (1997) Balancing Trade

and Labour Control; Quinlan, M. (1998) Regulating Labour in a Colonial Context; and Quinlan, M. (2012) The Low Rumble of Informal Dissent.

3 Dyster, B. (1979) Argentine and Australian Development Compared.
4 Bach, J. (1981) *A Maritime History of Australia*, Pan Books, Sydney, 56.
5 *Andrew Haigh Journal* 6 February 1842, TAHO Crowther Collection, Logs Box 30, SD_ILS 549158.
6 For further evidence on VDL whaling, see Dakin, W. (1963) *Whalemen Adventurers*, Sirius Books, Sydney, 43 and 111.
7 de Oliveira Torres, R. (2016) Seafaring Life, Shipboard Routine and Temperance Propaganda in Nineteenth Century American Whaling Communities as Depicted in Francis Allyn Olmsted's *Incidents of a Whaling Voyage (1841)*, *International Journal of Maritime History*, 28(3):550–558.
8 Bach, J. (1981) *A Maritime History of Australia*, 23.
9 Quinlan, M. (2013) Precarious and Hazardous Work, 281–307.
10 *Sydney Morning Herald* 14 January 1843 and 20 October 1846.
11 AONSW CSO 14, 15 June 1822 Reel 6055 4/1760, 126–127.
12 AONSW CSO 13 July 1824 Reel 6064 4/1777, 173 and 173a.
13 See Quinlan, M. (1996) Industrial Relations Before Unions, 269–293; Quinlan, M. (1997) Balancing Trade and Labour Control, 19–56; and Quinlan, M. (1998) Regulating Labour in a Colonial Context, 303–324.
14 Quinlan, M. (1992) Making Labour Laws Fit for the Colonies, 19–37.
15 AONSW CSO 2 July 1810 Reel 6042 4/1725, 33–34 and 14 September 1820 Reel 6007 4/3502, 261.
16 Rediker, M. (1987) *Between the Devil and the Deep Blue Sea*; and Dobson, C.R. (1980) *Masters and Journeymen*.
17 Davids, K. (1994) Seamen's Organisation and Social Protest in Europe, c. 1300–1825, *International Review of Social History*, 39(Supplement):158.
18 Christopher, E. (2004) Ten Thousand Times Worse That the Convicts: Rebellious Sailors, Convict Transportation and the Struggle for Freedom, *Journal of Australian Colonial History*, 5:30–46.
19 Johnson, M. and McFarlane, I. (2015) *Van Diemen's Land: An Aboriginal History*, UNSW Press, Sydney, 116–118.
20 *Sydney Gazette* 11 November 1804 and 3 November 1805.
21 O'May, H. (1957) *Wooden Hookers of Hobart Town and Whalers out of Van Diemen's Land*, Government Printer, Hobart.
22 TAHO, Crowther Collection Logs box 6, Log Schooner *Eliza* SD_ILS:504684.
23 *Trumpeter* 12 July 1833.
24 AOSA CO GRG 24/90/366 John MacFarlane to Edward Stephens 28 June 1837.
25 *The Australian* 17 February 1837.
26 AOSA CO BRG 42 7 June 1838.
27 TAHO Crowther Collection Logs Box 10 Log Barque *Marianne* 11 November 1834 to 29 September 1836, SD_ILS:548316.
28 TAHO Crowther Collection Logs Box 10 Log Brig *Marianne* 17 March 1845 to 27 January 1846, SD_ILS548319.
29 TAHO Crowther Collection Logs Box 6 Log brig *Esperanza* 12 February 1847 to 17 August 1848, SD_ILS:550504.
30 Cooper-Busch, B. (1994) *Whaling Will Never Do For Me*.
31 TAHO Crowther Collection Logs Box Log colonial schooner *Mary and Sally* SD_ILS:551083.
32 TAHO Crowther Collection Logs Box 30 Log brig *Snipe* 1820–1823, SD_ILS: 549156.
33 TAHO Crowther Collection Logs Box 13 Log Barque *Sarah and Elizabeth* 10 July 1839 to 20 September 1840, SD_ILS:546383.

34 TAHO Crowther Collection Logs Box Log colonial schooner *Prince of Denmark*, SD_ILS:547396.
35 TAHO Crowther Collection Logs Box 13 Log Barque *Sarah and Elizabeth* 10 July 1839 to 20 September 1840, SD_ILS:546383.
36 The long voyage also proved financially unsuccessful only yielding 12 tonnes of sperm oil. TAHO Crowther Collection Logs Box 17 Log Barque *Fortitude* 13 January 1843 to 31 December 1848, SD_ILS550034.
37 TAHO Crowther Collection Logs Box 6 brig *Esperanza* 12 February 1847 to 17 August 1848, SD_ILS:550504.
38 Quinlan, M. (2012) The Low Rumble of Informal Dissent, 131–155.
39 Davids, K. (1994) Seamen's Organisation and Social Protest in Europe, 157–160.
40 *Sydney Gazette* 1 March 1837.
41 *Sydney Herald* 16 March 1837.
42 *The Australian* 17 March 1837 and *Sydney Gazette* 21 March 1837.
43 *Sydney Monitor* 17 March 1837.
44 Dakin, W. (1963) *Whalemen Adventurers*, 53–54.
45 *Cornwall Chronicle* 23 February 1839.
46 *Hobart Town Courier* 8 March 1839.
47 Davids, K. (1994) Seamen's Organisation and Social Protest in Europe, 152–154.
48 Davids, K. (1994) Seamen's Organisation and Social Protest in Europe, 146, 163–164.
49 *Commercial Journal* 27 February 1839; *Sydney Gazette* 17 December 1839; and *Port Philip Patriot* 20 August 1845.
50 *Cornwall Chronicle* 25 and 28 November 1840.
51 *Launceston Advertiser* 11 June 1846.
52 *Sydney Gazette* 14 June 1826.
53 *Sydney Herald* 17 April 1834 and *Sydney Monitor* 31 August 1836.
54 *Cornwall Chronicle* 11 November 1840.
55 *Geelong Advertiser* 21 January 1846.
56 *Perth Gazette* 28 September 1839.
57 TAHO CSO 24/26/693 2 September 1847.
58 *Hobart Town Courier* 27 June 1850.
59 *Geelong Advertiser* 26 October 1850.
60 *Sydney Gazette* 13 and 20 February 1823.
61 *Cornwall Chronicle* 5 and 26 August 1837.
62 *Cornwall Chronicle* 8 and 15 December 1849.
63 TAHO CSO 24/139/4752 petition to Lt Governor, 19 June 1850.
64 *South Australian* 13 November1846 and *South Australian Gazette* 14 November 1846.
65 Terry, D. (1951) The Development of the Labour Movement in New South Wales 1833–1846, 13; *Sydney Morning Herald* 2 April 1849; Folder 459 of the Register of Friendly Societies including 1858 rules.
66 *Sydney Morning Herald* 1 August 1844.
67 *Sydney Morning Herald* 26 September 1848 and 22 June 1849.
68 *Sydney Monitor* 14 January 1834.
69 *Geelong Advertiser* 26 January 1850.
70 *Van Diemen's Land Chronicle* 24 December 1841.
71 *South Australian Register* 6 December1845; *Adelaide Observer* 28 February 1846; *South Australian* 30 April 1850.
72 *Port Philip Patriot* 17 July 1845; *Port Philip Herald* 4 May 1847; *Argus* 11 June 1847.
73 *Geelong Advertiser* 30 July 1847.

74 *Geelong Advertiser* 17 and 21 September 1850.
75 *Adelaide Observer* 13 May 1846; *South Australian* 23 May 1846.
76 *South Australian Register* 4 November 1846 and 15 November 1848.
77 *Sydney Morning Herald* 14 November 1848.
78 See for example *Sydney Herald* 30 June 1836.

6 Organisation in the Rural and Extractives Sectors

Introduction

Climate, topography, soils, population and remoteness shaped rural/agricultural activities. While Australia includes considerable well-watered land ranging from the hot tropics to cool temperate zones, much of the continent is arid and unsuitable for intensive agriculture. An old and weathered continent, with substantial exceptions like the along the Great Dividing Range, soils are generally poor. Remoteness meant food production was largely confined to local demand although grain exports grew from the 1840s. The only areas remotely suitable for labour-intensive plantation-based production in Queensland were largely unsettled prior to 1851 (sugarcane growing began in the 1860s). Exports had to be non-perishable and of sufficient value to cover expensive transport costs. Thus, climate and modes of production helped to dictate primary products, most notably fine wool but also tallow to exploit growing herds prior to refrigeration. Extensive areas of undulating and lightly wooded country—the result of Aboriginal firing practices to promote game—were well-suited to sheep and cattle raising. Wool exports grew from less than 200,000 lb (or 90 metric tonnes) in 1821 to over 41 million lb (18,597 tonnes) by 1850.[1]

Rapid pastoral expansion took little account of climate, preserving water-course and rich native grasses, or fragile soils that had never experienced cloven-hoofed animals. Lands were over-cleared especially after American practices of ring-barking and burning replaced more labour-intensive methods of tree removal. This, and over-stocking in marginal rainfall areas, magnified the effects of periodic droughts and flooding rains (that settlers viewed as aberrant not the norm) causing serious erosion/land degradation still evident today.[2] It also reduced habitat for pest-predators. Spreading settlement stole Aboriginal lands and destroyed their food sources, leading to resistance (attacks on isolated farms and shepherds/hutkeepers), disease, poisoning flour/infected blankets, reprisals and massacres involving rural workers like that at Myall Creek in January 1838.[3] At times intense conflict in particular regions led to strikes or the escalation of wage rates.[4] Aboriginals were used in some pastoral activities and to aid landholders apprehend absconders, something requiring further investigation.[5]

Land grant/sale and squatting practices favoured large-scale rural activities that were capital intensive in terms of land and stock with relatively small labour needs (Chapter 1). More remote landholdings, often in harsher climates, were ever larger in scale, with a small core workforce and reliant on seasonal labour during shearing. Wool was subject to volatility arising from droughts, fluctuations in British demand and colonial business cycles that affected labour demand, wages and work practices.[6]

Like grains, wool production was seasonal. In summer, just as reapers migrated from farm to farm, so too bands of shearers moved from one sheep-station to the next. These groups formed bonds and, just as convicts demanded extra indulgences/wages at harvest time, sought to bid-up wages. Shearers were paid according to a daily tally of the number of sheep shorn. Good hands might shear between 80 and 130 sheep per-day though the *Perth Inquirer* believed the average was around 60.[7] Before shearing, sheep had to be washed in dips, the washers paid on a daily rate based on expected numbers. Shorn wool was graded and pressed into bales for shipment to port and export. In peak season woolsheds became factories, with dozens (later hundreds) of workers congregating together if only for a few weeks (later the basis for union organisation).

Convict labour was pivotal to early pastoral/agricultural development, clearing land, building roads and providing labour to farmers and pastoralists including remote leases free-labour shunned. At least food-wise conditions were often better than for agricultural workers in Britain. The *Launceston Advertiser* complained the deterrence of transportation was undermined by letters from convict agricultural labourers describing their situation 'in the most favourable light.'[8] The expansion of settlement had complex—even contradictory—effects on labour relations. A squatter from outside the 'western boundary' in NSW complained labour shortages put employers 'wholly in the power of our servants, whether free or bond. They well know we cannot punish them . . . not having hands to supply their places.'[9] However, in more densely-settled districts prosecutions could be swift. A Longford District landholder (Haslewood) tried five servants for disobedience committed earlier that day, the court imposing an array of penalties on each tailored to his wishes.[10] While convict and later free-labour proved profitable, some landholders were ever looking for cheaper options, including indentured servants from India and China (Chapter 1).

Patterns of Organisation and Collective Action

There were conspicuous spikes in combined strikes/NSCA in 1824 (60 instances), 1836–37 (both 118), 1840 (80) and 1847 (54). For convicts there were 1214 instances of organisation, entailing 387 strikes and 792 NSCA, with 677 instances of collective absconding (excluding 65 instances of organisation on government farms like that at Emu Plains). There were 152 instances of organisation amongst free workers, entailing 53 strikes and 106 NSCA. Absconding accounted for over 85% of convict NSCA and 47.2% of free-labour NSCA, or over half all collective action (Table 6.1). Far behind but still significant were lodging complaints with magistrates and sabotage. Apart from two wages cases (both won), the remaining 33 convict complaints concerned health, typically failure to provide adequate rations or clothing, with claimants winning 12, losing 14 and an unknown outcome in seven cases. Of the 21 court actions taken by free workers, 14 concerned unpaid wages (won five, drew one, lost four with three unknown), while 7 concerned poor rations/ill-treatment (lost three and four unknown). Other methods were rarely used, some requiring formal organisation while others, like letters to the press, were difficult outside large towns.

Strikes and absconding were largely confined to a single workplace, but there are instances of workers absconding from neighbouring estates or being arrested as absent/out after hours in town on the same day implying a degree of collusion.[11] Absconding peaked in summer when labour was in highest demand as did other forms of dissent. Nonetheless, in rich agricultural districts like the Norfolk Plains conflict was relatively continuous, especially during the convict period, with prosecutions of male and female servants dominating local court sittings, including numerous instances of small-scale collective action. This doesn't include instances when landholders simply became exasperated, returning servants deemed 'useless' to government as William Brumby did with three assigned-convicts in June 1836.[12]

Sabotage, mostly burning barns, wheat stacks and hayricks, was conspicuous compared to other industries. It was an effective and costly form for revenge. In October 1829 Joseph Archer wrote to the colonial secretary alleging four assigned-servants on his Panshanger Estate (northern VDL) had fired a stack of oats and barley the day after he had cut their allowances for insolence. The Archer family held a number of large estates in northern VDL and their born-to-rule hardnosed approach resulted in numerous prosecutions of their servants, no more so than Joseph who tried workers for collective dissent on at least six occasions prior to the 1829 incendiarism incident. Like many others, Archer's suspicions foundered on the difficulty of proving such acts weren't accidental unless directly witnessed. Two years later he experienced an even more costly fire destroying £500 of wheat. The suspected culprits (one had allowances removed and another had requested clothing refused) again escaped conviction. In other regions too, like the Upper Hunter, convict workers used incendiarism against despised landholders like Edward Cory and William Dun, driving the latter close to bankruptcy.[13] Incendiarism often succeeded where other protests failed, and as Hindmarsh observes, could also be expressed/compounded by slovenly efforts to assist masters in extinguishing a fire.[14]

As in the UK other rural sabotage, like wilfully breaking tools or ill-treating animals, was more commonly committed by individuals and also easier for masters to secure a conviction.[15] In 1836 Edward Archer charged two servants with wilfully mismanaging two valuable bullocks drowned in a river.

Table 6.1 Summary: Organisation/Activity in Rural Industry 1788–1850

Nature of activity	1788–1800	1801–10	1811–20	1821–30	1831–40	1841–50	Total	Percentages
Convict Workers								
All Organisation	5	5	8	258	688	255	1214	
Involvement	19	32	23	740	1846	682	3342	
Adjusted Involvement*	19	32	23	776	1922	706	3478	
Strikes	3	2	1	55	161	168	387	32.8
NSCA	2	3	7	211	571	98	792	67.2
Total	5	5	8	266	732	236	1179	
Absconding		1	6	178	456	36	677	
Court actions				11	17	7	35	
Petitions				1	1		2	
Sabotage			1	7	16	4	28	
Bans				1	2		3	
Free Workers								
All Organisation	4	1	3	5	27	116	152	
Formal Organisation					1	2	3	
Involvement	46	3	43	19	102	499	646	
Adjusted Involvement*	46	3	43	22	114	551	779	
Strikes					10	43	53	34.9
NSCA	4	1	3	5	18	75	106	65.1
Total	4	1	3	5	28	118	161	
Absconding	2	1	2	2	12	33	50	
Court actions	1		2	1		17	21	
Petitions				1			1	
Sabotage						4	4	
Press Letters						2	2	

* Estimate based on attributing median membership to zero count organisations

Evidence presented indicated antagonism between master and men, with one (John Hudson) allegedly refusing to join efforts to rescue the bullocks. Conviction was secured but the sentence of solitary confinement (21 days for James Sweeting and 7 for Hudson) suggests they were too valuable to be sent to a road-gang.[16] The charge of 'wilfully mismanaging work' was used repeatedly by the Archers and others before Longford magistrates in an effort to curb behaviour deemed beyond neglect.[17] In 1847 a Campbell Town District landholder named Palmer urged the Bench to provide a constable to protect his property from depredations after prosecuting several servants.[18] His fears were not unfounded. Four months later William Davey, passholder at another Palmer estate near Bagdad, was committed to trial for setting fire to a wheat stack valued at £500.[19]

Incendiarism caused alarm amongst landholders and government with substantial rewards being offered for information leading to the apprehension of perpetrators. In May 1844 Richard Styles offered a £50 reward and the government another £20 or a conditional pardon after an attempt to burn a barn and office at his Reevesdale Bungonia Estate (NSW).[20] However, even substantial rewards generally failed to uncover culprits setting fire to sheaves/stacks and built infrastructure—probably because it was a capital offence, sympathy for the action/perpetrators and fears any informant would become a pariah in the community. Most known collective sabotage incidents involved convicts, and like riots, seem to cluster around employers noted for harsh discipline and breaching accepted norms like working them on Sundays. Nonetheless, the practice had been common amongst UK agricultural workers, in areas like East Anglia, since the 18th century if not before.[21]

The ranking of issues causing strikes is headed by hours followed by working conditions, OHS, management behaviour and wages, while NSCA is headed by working conditions followed by OHS, management behaviour, wages and hours (Table 6.2). Short-term 'recreational' absences largely explain the significance of hours-related strikes while absconding— permanent withdrawal—explains the heavy preponderance of working conditions-related NSCA. The growth of wage-related actions is evidence of the transition to free-labour and payments to convict workers under the probation system in the 1840s.

Informal Workplace-Based Collective Action

With regard to informal collective action at single farms/estates, there were distinctive aspects for different categories of labour, so the examination distinguishes convicts, indentured non-European and European indentured/free-labour. As in other industries, much collective action involved a handful of workers at single workplace and should be viewed as an extension of the individual disputes described in Chapter 2. Indeed individual and collective action often occurred in quick succession, indicative of a more generalised

Table 6.2 Strikes and Non-Strike Disputes by Issue in the Rural Industry 1788–1850

Nature of activity	1788–1800	1801–10	1811–20	1821–30	1831–40	1841–50	Total*	Percentage*
Strikes								
Wages/remuneration	2			1	3	17	21	4.7
Working conditions	1	1		27	75	77	182	40.1
Management behaviour				3	29	18	51	11.5
Hours of work	1			19	106	130	256	57.5
Jobs/employment				1	1	1	3	0.7
Health & safety	1			17	20	26	64	14.4
Work methods & Subcontracting				2		2	4	0.9
Unionism								
Legislation				1			1	0.2
Unknown		1	1	2			4	0.9
NSCA								
Wages/remuneration	2		1	8	12	29	51	5.7
Working conditions	4	4	10	207	553	119	897	99.5
Management behaviour				10	36	29	75	8.4
Hours of work				3	14	18	25	2.8
Jobs/employment					1	2	3	0.3
Health & safety	1		1	17	29	28	76	8.5
Work methods				2	1	6	9	1
Unionism								
Legislation								
Unknown				1	4	11	16	

* exceeds totals of 445 strikes 898 NSCA and 100% because of multiple issues in some strikes/disputes

dispute. For example, in two months from late January 1843 and again between mid-July and mid-September 1843, landholder Simeon Lord Jnr in the Fingal District prosecuted his workers for two strikes and two go-slows. On each occasion only two or three servants were tried. Other workers may have been involved and these court actions were interspersed with prosecutions of individual workers for essentially similar offences (neglect, disobedience and insolence). Lord's overseer, Edward Kearney, was less successful when he prosecuted cook Sarah Fletcher for telling other servants he didn't work her too hard because he 'humps me.' Lord went before the courts at least 12 times in this four-month period.[22] Considering all these incidents provides a more comprehensible picture of worker dissent and similar cases involving indentured and free rural workers will be cited below.

Convict Rural Servants

In 1798 Annandale landholder George Johnston charged four assigned-convicts with neglecting work and disobedience.[23] Such incidents became increasingly common. By the 1820s collective absconding was rife. Despite large numbers of constables, hefty financial rewards and severe penalties, apprehension proved difficult. It took almost two months to recapture eight convicts who deserted (then splitting into smaller groups) Dr Sherwin's Mulwaree Ponds estate in September 1835.[24] Many remained at large far longer, some escaped altogether and even recapture didn't end the issue. On 11 December 1834 three convicts absconded from George Campbell Curlewis's landholding south of Goulburn. Quickly apprehended, they promptly absconded again along with five others on 1 January 1835.[25] Employers could dispense with troublesome servants but difficulties arose at harvest/shearing time or where the worker concerned possessed scarce skills/expertise.

For aggrieved convicts lodging a complaint before a local magistrate was problematic (Chapter 2). Some sought a more impartial hearing elsewhere. Groups of convicts on Archer family estates walked over 180 km to Hobart to lodge complaints in December 1826 and again in September 1830. The first group went before the Hobart Bench, all four complaining they were supplied with insufficient blankets and soap. Further, Peter Chambers alleged being struck by Archer and his overseer while William Bridgewater complained of receiving unwarranted punishment from the Launceston Bench. They were returned to Launceston with a copy of the proceedings detailing their ill-treatment.[26] In the second incident John Welsh, Emanuel Lowen, Charles Fitten and Shadrach Fennell—assigned to William Archer's Longford estate—tried to lodge a complaint with the Superintendent of Convicts in Hobart but Governor Arthur ordered a return to their master. They refused to go before the Norfolk Plains Bench close to Archer's estate and were sentenced to two years' hard-labour because their actions set a dangerous 'example to the prisoner population.'[27] Perceived magisterial bias wasn't helped by revolving-bench situations as when Richard Barker JP prosecuted two servants for neglect on 26 November 1838, then resumed the Bench to adjudicate the very next case.[28]

As with the military and seamen, rations were a frequent source of dissent. In February 1832 seven convicts on Peter Lette's White-Hills estate complained of continual abuse, ill-treatment and insufficient food and clothing. With supporting evidence from an ex-overseer, Lette was directed to 'remedy the evils complained of.'[29] Three years later a northern Midlands landholder (Massey) returned two servants to government, after four complained about not receiving rations. The two remaining servants subsequently absconded to lodge a complaint of being threatened—six months' hard-labour on the roads, then returned to Massey.[30] When tea became expensive in Hobart in 1825, James Sutherland offered his servants roasted wheat as coffee— they refused.[31] Refusing bad or substituted ration items could have severe consequences. In 1834 Merton (now Denman) landholder William Ogilvie had his assigned-servants punished for refusing rye in place of wheat, even though it breached the rules on substituting ration items.[32] New Norfolk landholder William Bannon prosecuted four servants who complained about bread made using a maize/wheat flour mix, two receiving 50 lashes and the ringleader (John Bateman) also getting six months' hard-labour in the Hulk chain-gang.[33] Similarly, a Richmond (VDL) District landholder had two ringleaders gaoled for six months, charging them with wilfully destroying his property—namely bacon six men in the hut deemed 'bad'.[34]

Disputes also occurred over workloads. Workers had clear views of what constituted a fair day's work. In October 1836 George Robinson alleged that when ordered to undertake another task after planting a field of potatoes his men responded 'they knew when they had done a day's work as well as any bloody man in the country.' As in many other cases, issue of deference/control were also involved. When Robinson told the men not to swear in his presence, he claimed they responded 'why not?'[35]

Working conditions and hours were another source of disagreement. Reflecting customary practice, refusals to work before sunrise or after sunset were common. In midwinter 1836 one Norfolk Plains landholder (Fletcher) prosecuted six servants for not rising til almost 8 am, while on a nearby estate (of William Archer) William Rogers, the ringleader of a group who had left off work at sunset, received 50 lashes for saying in front of the other men he'd be damned if he would work after sundown.[36] Similarly, in August 1838 North Midlands landholder Robert Taylor's servants refused to start work until the sun had risen. Taylor's overseer (Walton) alleged ringleader Charles Edwards told him they knew convict regulations on working hours and to go 'fuck himself'.[37] Like their township counterparts, rural convicts took regular absences to visit pubs or friends on neighbouring estates. Viewed as a right, efforts to prevent it aggravated relations, leading to verbal exchanges and even violent confrontations. When James

Smith challenged George Matthewson and James Bate returning to his farm drunk, they assaulted him—two years' hard-labour in chains at Port Arthur. Another servant Thomas Smith, who failed to come to his master's assistance, received 12 months' hard-labour and was removed to the other side of the country.[38]

Echoing 'Saint Monday' disputes in Britain dating back to the Middle Ages, claimed-holidays were another source of friction, exacerbated by the intransigence of some employers. In December 1838 North Midlands landholder Robert Kermode prosecuted three assigned-convicts for being absent on Christmas Eve and Christmas Day.[39] The following year another northern VDL employer Thomas Walker charged seven servants with the same offence, but interceded to prevent the ringleader being flogged.[40] Others were not so lenient. In 1835, 40 convicts at Circular Head (Stanley) refused to work on New Year Day. They escaped with a magisterial reprimand to the considerable annoyance of Van Diemen's Land Company principal manager, Edward Curr.[41] Court cases likely represented but a tiny fraction of the instances where workers took time off around Christmas/Boxing Day and New Year. Indeed, to cement paternalistic bonds, some masters extended customary practices for agricultural workers in Britain to the colonies. James Sutherland provided his servants with an additional roast-joint, pudding and bottle of rum on Christmas Day 1825, a bottle of rum on New Year's Day and a glass of whisky to celebrate the birth of his daughter. However, as Hindmarsh observes, sharing a drink with servants on Christmas Day was deemed contrary to perceived good order/discipline. William Allardyce had his convicts withdrawn for this in March 1829. Joseph Archer was at no risk of getting close to his servants, prosecuting seven including two females for holding a party on Christmas Day 1834.[42] Similarly, six Longford District employers prosecuted groups of their workers for absence on 24–26 December 1839 and as many groups belonging to other employers were prosecuted for being absent/drunk and disorderly in the town.

Taking time off on royal birthdays and Good Friday were also common and subject to contestation. Six convicts who refused to work on the Kings Birthday at Mrs Harriet Oakes' Goat-Hills farm received 36 hours' solitary confinement on bread and water. The ringleaders of a group refusing to work on Good Friday at Mr Lawrence's Norfolk Plains estate got seven days' solitary.[43] Similarly in 1838, convicts at James Atkinson's Paterson's Plains estate were prosecuted for refusing to work on Good Friday.[44] Another landholder (Adam Beveridge) in court during their trial, observed his men 'never thought of asking him for a holyday on a Good Friday.'[45] Beveridge's convict management was nothing to skite about, entailing repeated collisions. In June 1838 Beveridge charged seven convicts with insubordination after they struck because their rations were stolen by an absconder.[46] Rural workers used religious time for other purposes. Four of James Dunn's Breadalbane Plains ticket-of-leave and passholders were charged with unauthorised absence after being found in a pub during Divine Service on Sunday 1 March 1846.[47]

Regular absences with no claim to pious motivation and refusals to do anything work-related on Sunday were also common. In April/May 1834 Mrs Oakes prosecuted three groups of servants for being absent without leave, the New Norfolk Bench recording she had made frequent complaints in this regard.[48] Convicts at Frederick Houghton's Georgetown estate refused to receive their rations on a Sunday, arguing they should be left alone.[49] Convicts also exploited temporary absences by their masters (like going to town or social events) to take time off or slow the pace of work, though the presence of overseers could make this more difficult.[50]

Convicts exploited harvest/shearing peaks of activity. Demands for additional rations (tea and sugar) and alcohol during heavy tasks quickly became the norm. Employers refusing them encountered resistance like four of Adam Beveridge's convicts who refused to wash sheep unless supplied with wine or spirits.[51] Others made wage demands, especially probation-passholders seeking increases over their specified rate like those at a New Norfolk farm in 1844.[52] Harvest demands encouraged groups of probation-ers to 'hire' themselves as reapers even when they lacked the skills. Some then refused work while others were prosecuted by disgruntled employ-ers, exemplified by a series of cases before the Richmond Bench in Janu-ary 1847.[53] While probationers were entitled to an annual wage, it was well below the prevailing (free-labour) rate and took no account of particular tasks, so probationers had no incentive to exert themselves. In January 1846 Thomas Burbury prosecuted six passholder reapers for idleness stating they had only cut a sheaf each in half an hour.[54] Threats of prosecution seemingly had little effect. Claiming three reapers had only completed a sixth of the work they should have, West Tamar landholder F Y Wilmore ordered them to 'do better' only to be told by one that he 'could do no better.'[55] Others refused to engage at the designated wages as a Jericho (VDL) landholder (Coyle) discovered when he sought men for haymaking at the Oatlands Hir-ing Depot in January 1848.[56]

Employers with a reputation of harsh treatment, like John Macarthur's (1767–1834) nephew Hannibal Macarthur (1788–1861), experienced repeated dissent. In late December 1821 two assigned-servants tried to lodge a complaint in Sydney but were referred back to the Liverpool Bench. They hadn't expected a fair hearing and weren't disappointed, being convicted for absenting themselves on the charges of Macarthur.[57] Less than a month later another assigned-servant James Straiter was charged with:

> exciting his master's servants to combine, for the purpose of obliging him to raise their wages and increase their rations, or otherwise to destroy their master's property, in sheep entrusted to their care; and with violently resisting the orders of Mr. Charles Macarthur, and setting at defiance all those in authority on the establishment.[58]

Giving evidence Hannibal's brother, Charles, stated Straiter had told him:

> If the men were all of my mind, you would be obliged to give more rations. I know the value of that flock of sheep as well as you do. I know what every pound of wool on their backs is worth, and you can afford to give us what we want.-Look at them; they were a d—d set of rips when I took them; now they are worth looking at . . . I've been in gentlemen's service before, but I'll be d—d if I'm in gentleman's service now. I was drawing 17lbs of flour from Government, when I had Major Druitt's sheep, and your brother sent for me, and puts me upon nine. He is no gentleman to do such a thing. I'll sooner be d—d and hanged than stay in such an out-of-the-way starve-gutted place. The men are cheated of their wages. You tell me I'm in debt, the things are charged at such a price they are always in debt, though you never give one of us a farthing in money. Two, three, four hundred pounds is soon lost in the lambing-down; if they would be of my mind and stick out, you must give us what we want.

Charles admitted his brother had promised Straiter £15 wages per-annum plus a £5 premium and two shillings and sixpence for every lamb above 300-on a flock of 350 ewes.[59] The case provides clear evidence of effort-bargaining, convicts comparing working conditions/rations at different establishments, and their awareness of the value of their labour. The last point is reinforced by promised wages, exceeding the then stipulated rate but disregarded by employers when it suited them, especially during harvest, lambing and shearing. Also notable is reference to the truck system of levying exorbitant charges on workers for purchases from the estate store—a practice confirmed by freeman John Cronin who worked for Macarthur. Macarthur's overseer Barzillah Bensley testified to absconding by other men on the estate. The Bench found Straiter warranted a signal punishment given 'the mutinous and atrocious conduct of the prisoner, and the dangerous consequences likely to result to the Community there from.'[60] He was ordered to receive 500 lashes, one month's solitary confinement on bread and water, and to serve the remainder of his sentence at the Port Macquarie penal settlement.

On 3 April 1826 Hannibal Macarthur prosecuted four servants on a range of charges relating to a protest. One received 50 lashes for absconding and travelling to Sydney without a pass. Three others were charged with insolence and neglect of duty. One was ordered to work in irons for three months. Another (John Neeves) deemed to have been deluded by the others was 'admonished to be more circumspect in future.' John Middleton was initially sentenced to 75 lashes. Telling the court he would never return to Macarthur was deemed contempt and the punishment increased to 100 lashes.[61] There was clearly more to this dispute than what was reported, but it does capture workers' views of Macarthur. Macarthur later served on the

NSW Legislative Council, part of the Tory landholder-faction whose efforts to enhance their wealth and privileges at the expense of labour earned enduring ire from both convicts and free workers (see Chapter 11).

James Meehan also experienced repeated dissent at his Ingleburn farm southwest of Sydney. First reported by Bigge (see Chapter 1) Meehan's problems continued into the 1820s.[62] After several earlier incidents in 1827, he brought Henry Bicknell before the Liverpool Bench for being 'frequently disobedient and mutinous, and particularly in jeering the other men, and instigating them to disobedience with insolence, saying they were not of such game as he was.'[63] Bicknell refused his rations saying he wouldn't work for his master—returned to government and sentenced to one month in irons. A similar pattern can be found in Van Diemen's Land. The Fingal District Bench Books of the 1840s show landholders like Captain Robert Hepburn and Simeon Lord Jnr (son of a convict) repeatedly before the courts trying their servants for insolence, idleness, neglect of duty, mismanaging their work, refusing work, absence, disobedience and other offences associated with collective action.

The partnership of Alexander Berry (1781–1873) and Edward Wollstonecraft (1783–1832, nephew of Mary) came to prominence over their treatment of convicts and free workers. Berry had built a fortune from business ventures in partnership with Wollstonecraft. Berry was granted 10,000 acres south of Sydney with 100 convicts, later leasing parcels to Scots and Scots-Irish tenant farmers like James Moffitt at Crooked River Gerringong. Berry also held a monopoly on the cedar trade—a native timber prized because it resembled mahogany. There were inklings of animosity amongst their convicts in 1825 when Dennis Keefe was charged with setting fire to two wheat stacks at their Shoalhaven farm—acquitted owing to informality in the indictment.[64] However, things erupted in May 1832 when newspapers reported four assigned-servants at their Shoalhaven estate—Charles Dunn, John McCudden, James Bevistock and William Lahee—had repeatedly complained about bad rations and failure to provide slops (cheap clothing), soap and other essential items. One claimed he had requested a new blanket for three years. Dunn asked his overseer's (Campbell) permission to lodge a complaint before Wollongong Police Magistrate Lieutenant Sleeman. Repeatedly denied, he left without leave. Wollstonecraft despatched a convict constable (John Mathews) who returned Dunn to Shoalhaven where he was imprisoned in a log-gaol built on their estate. McCudden too sought leave to lodge a complaint. Being refused, McCudden travelled to Wollongong where Sleeman heard the grievance before returning him to the estate where he was promptly imprisoned like Dunn. Sleeman informed Wollstonecraft he would consider complaints of both parties in Kiama the following Tuesday. Before this could occur, Wollstonecraft instructed Constable Mathews to escort the men to Sydney on Berry and Wollstonecraft's barge (the *Experiment*) for trial for absconding and refusing work. Unlike instances where convicts sought another jurisdiction, the Sydney Bench heard the case. However, things didn't quite go to plan as damning evidence of the men's mistreatment emerged. McCudden testified Wollstonecraft stated they were being sent to Sydney so that 'his friend Mr. Rossi' (the Sydney Police Magistrate) might punish them.

This wasn't the first instance of injustice on Berry and Wollstonecraft's estate. In June 1831, 18 assigned-convicts and free orphan apprentices were refused passes to lodge complaints over a lack of clothing, soap and other items. They absconded, going to see Magistrate Sleeman. Sleeman ordered them back to work until he could hear their case in Shoalhaven. Returning to the estate, they refused work until they got their slops. Sleeman ordered the ringleaders flogged when he arrived. The *Sydney Monitor* was outraged at the treatment of apprentices and the hypocrisy of the Church responsible for their care:

> The orphan-boys, apprenticed by Archdeacon Scott, were treated like the convicts. Thus Mr. Scott's Church and School Corporation, which expends £20,000 a-year in teaching humanity, and in curing souls . . . virtually transported the free male orphan-boys to Shoalhaven, without a trial, to be brought up amongst thieves . . . they were made to sleep in the same huts with the men, and like them, were not supplied with necessaries. Was this the way for the Corporation to look after those poor lads?[65]

The Dunn et al. case was referred to the Secretary of State for the Colonies in London. Wollstonecraft died in the interim and the incident didn't damage Berry. He continued as an appointed member to the NSW Legislative Council (1829–61) where he stoutly opposed moves to democracy and local government.

Like slaves, convicts experiencing sustained ill-treatment sometimes violently revolted as a group of starving convicts did in Bathurst in 1830.[66] Three years later a more publicised incident occurred at ex-Lieutenant (but titling himself major) James Mudie's Castle Forbes estate. Mudie (1779–1852) was a pompous man full of his own importance—not uncommon amongst middling to large landholders who took an imperious approach to his workforce that breached customary conditions like working on Sundays. Following an undistinguished military career (ending in 1808) and a failed business venture, Mudie and his family received free passage to NSW and a 2000-acre Hunter Valley land grant in 1822. He employed fellow Scot John Larnach as his overseer. Larnach married Mudie's daughter Emily in 1827 and proved as gift-less in 'people-management' as his father-in-law. Appointed a magistrate by Governor Ralph Darling, Mudie inflicted harsh penalties on convicts brought before the Maitland bench, seeing this as essential to counter the overly lenient policies of Governor Richard Bourke, Darling's successor.

A generally overlooked prior incident warrants mentioning. In December 1832 a servant was charged on his own confession with setting fire to

Mudie's dwelling after Dr Coleman refused to accept his claim of illness, thereby relieving him from work. Given hot weather and harvested grain stored in the barn, the fire could have consumed the house and spread disastrously but for concerted actions by Mudie's other servants. The *Sydney Monitor* praised them as 'good Christians and faithful servants in putting out the fire, and we feel assured, they will not lose their reward.'[67] If these were the same servants involved in the 1833 revolt, their reward was not what the *Monitor* imagined.

Floggings, poor rations and threats of being punished were a regular occurrence at Castle Forbes. In November 1833 one of the aggrieved convicts was delegated to lodge a complaint with the Governor, but this was 'not received'. The convicts mutinied, releasing three convicts (including two from Castle Forbes) on their way to chain-gang and capturing and threatening Emily and a maid and saying they would have 'settled' Mudie had he been around.[68] They shot at Larnach who was at the sheep-wash, calling out 'I shall take care you never punish another man' before escaping into the bush. The six men were eventually caught at Lamb Valley after a shootout with mounted police and settler Robert Scott. Tried in Sydney, evidence of their ill-treatment got a rare public airing, causing a mixture of outrage and discomfort. Nonetheless, five were sentenced to death and executed. David Jones, held to be least culpable, was transported to Norfolk Island for life. Amidst symbolism redolent of those described in *Albion's Fatal Tree* (the men travelling to the gibbet on a cart with their coffins), two were executed close to Castle Forbes on 23 December 1833 while the others were publicly executed in Sydney. The prescribed rituals were marred by delays in removing the men's leg irons prior to hanging, and the absence of Reverend Cowper to minister to those executed at Castle Forbes. One of the condemned, John Poole, complained bitterly about this.

Amidst a public outcry, Governor Bourke ordered a detailed investigation of convict treatment at Castle Forbes and more generally which heard damning evidence. Some newspapers and their correspondents acknowledged convict ill-treatment was not isolated, especially on road-gangs. Others, including Hunter Valley landholders, continued to champion the cause of 'firm-discipline', warning of widespread convict insubordination—especially absconding.[69] The investigation found that Mudie hadn't treated convicts with the consideration of his neighbours but many claims were unfounded. In the community however Mudie became a pariah. He was not reappointed as a JP in 1836, soon after sold Castle Forbes and retuned to Britain. Mudie published a self-justifying book, *The Felonry of New South Wales*, criticising those who had disagreed/opposed him and labelling colonial society as indelibly criminally-tainted which lost his few remaining friends. Coming back to NSW in 1840, Mudie found he was unwanted—being horsewhipped by the son of a judge insulted in his book. He returned to England two years later, dying in 1852. Larnach, Emily and Mudie's other children had remained in the colony, Larnach dying at his Rosemount estate in 1869.

Mudie was a stupid short-sighted man, not simply a product of his times—endless gene-pool there it seems. Some landholders more adeptly managed their workforce, convict or free. However, Mudie was not exceptional. The volatility of the industry, an amass wealth quickly mentality, landholder belief in their innate superiority, and a lopsided regulatory regime combined to encourage practices Mudie took to excess. Despite the public gnashing of teeth, Castle Forbes had limited effect on the treatment of convicts in rural districts as evidenced by another incident soon after. In February 1834, the Supreme Court with a military jury sentenced two female convicts, Sarah McGregor and Mary Maloney, to death for wilful murder of Illawarra landholder Captain Charles Waldron. Waldron died from a stroke during an altercation with them after finding fault with Maloney's cleaning. Like Mudie, Waldron was an ex-military man who took up land and was a local JP in the Illawarra District. While not as harsh as Mudie, Waldron had expressed his determination to suppress the spirit of insubordination amongst convict servants.[70] McGregor and Maloney were eventually reprieved after a year awaiting their fate.[71] Two of four male convicts who allegedly refused to come to Waldron's assistance were charged with perjury.

Indentured Non-European Workers

As transportation wound down, employers looked to other perceived sources of cheap subordinate labour in India, China and the Pacific. Indentured under conditions well below those of free European workers, these workers didn't prove as tractable as hoped. In 1846 Captain Robert Towns imported 30 (some sources suggest 17) Indian 'coolies'—as newspapers labelled Indian and Chinese labourers—under four-year indentures. The workers struck on their arrival in Sydney, demanding higher wages before they would proceed to Town's sheep-station. They complained about rations and ill-treatment on the voyage, having to work pumps on the *Orwell* to pay for their passage.[72] In a test case, Towns prosecuted one, 'Purseen', for refusing work. The Sydney Bench dismissed the case, not because of Purseen's counter-claims of ill-treatment—similar claims generally failed whatever the worker's origins or status—but because Towns couldn't provide evidence of the agreement signed in Calcutta. Town's initiative had been a joint venture with local worthies W C Wentworth and Robert Campbell, who imported labourers in the same shipment.[73]

In November 1846 five Indian shepherds on H. Scott's Glendon estate near Singleton were gaoled for refusing to work without a new suit of summer clothes. The agreement didn't stipulate summer clothes, but they were seeking conditions comparable to other workers. The *Maitland Mercury* reported their response as 'gaol very good, no work gaol.'[74] Another settler (Ayers) bringing 'coolies' to his Moreton Bay estate was charged with severe ill-using one of them. Eighteen travelled to Brisbane complaining of being 'beaten most unmercifully, besides having their rations and clothing withheld, in violation of the terms of their agreement.'[75] Whaling/business entrepreneur Benjamin Boyd also experienced difficulties when he imported Pacific Islanders as labourers/shepherds to his southern NSW property. Complaining of poor working conditions and cold, 16 struck in May 1847 and tried to walk to Sydney along the coast—a demanding feat.[76] Later the same year 42 others absconded, arriving at Albury 140 miles from the station starving. Boyd prosecuted the absconders but the Albury magistrates ruled they lacked jurisdiction. Even the *Geelong Advertiser and Squatters Advocate* expressed sympathy for the Islanders, reporting that they swore if they caught 'Captain Kirsopp they will eat him for bringing them to this country'.[77] Kirsopp may have escaped this fate, but Boyd didn't, being killed on Guadalcanal in 1851. Pacific islanders weren't the only ones to find the weather disagreeable. A Geelong District settler's (Johnstone) Malay servants struck work for this reason in January 1850—sentenced to a month in Melbourne's House of Correction.[78]

William Lawson (1774–1850), part of the trio to first cross the Blue Mountains in 1815, experienced ongoing dissent from Chinese servants at his Veteran Hall estate Prospect. In September 1849 Lawson prosecuted nine for refusing work, the Chinese complaining about their rations and of being under-paid. The Parramatta Bench retuned them to Lawson, the second time it had so ordered.[79] Shortly after Lawson's death (1850), two Chinese servants were prosecuted, one charged with threatening Lawson's son and the other with refusing work. The latter argued Lawson's death ended his agreement, which if upheld would have had affected the others. This helps explains why the court discharged the man who threatened Lawson's son, but gaoled the one refusing work for 30 days.[80] In 1850 William Walker too experienced repeated work refusals and absconding from Chinese (and one Afghan) servants at his Botany estate, resulting in multiple court appearances over two weeks. One worker told the Bench 'in very unmistakeable English, that he was no "nigger" and do what they might, he would not return to Mr. Walker's service'.[81] The racist reference to Black slaves was commonly used at the time to refer to unacceptable workloads/ work intensity and not just by European workers. As in other instances newspapers muttered darkly about how rapidly non-European workers were apprised of 'acceptable' wages and working conditions.

These cases illustrate key tensions in the indenturing of non-European workers. They were introduced under long-term engagements at wages and conditions well below those of European workers (indentured or free) and even convicts when it came to rations/clothing. They were treated abysmally even by the standards of the time, but the contrast shouldn't be overdrawn since treatment of other rural workers was hardly exemplary. Social isolation and information on better wages/conditions provided through informal networks fomented dissent but the legal apparatus kept them vulnerable. The exploitation contributed to fears of non-European workers being used to flood the labour market and undermine conditions that have received much attention from historians. Without denying the racist element, the structural conditions shouldn't be ignored or employers' clearly racist presumptions that they could (and did) exploit these workers more intensively than their European counterparts. This is identical to employer use of guest-worker/ temporary visa-holders and undocumented workers today, but employers' racist presumptions are seldom confronted in policy debates. Ironically, the combination of cheaper transport, governments creating a dodgy assembly of short-term/manipulated work visas, weakened labour laws and unions, global temporary employment agencies covering both ends of the supply chain, and debt networks to cover travel costs, now provide agriculture in Australia and elsewhere with a ready supply of hyper-exploitable foreign workers Towns and Boyd could only dream about.[82]

European Free-labour

In Western Australia economic and labour market conditions oscillated widely, as did the experience of particular employers. Some like George Fletcher Moore complained workers they imported under indenture had too much bargaining power. On the other hand, one of the colony's largest employers, Thomas Peel, failed spectacularly, leaving 11 indentured servants petitioning the Governor that being left unpaid and with inadequate rations they were starving.[83] In NSW early hopes the shift to free-labour would bring more subordinate and productive workers were rapidly overwhelmed by complaints about their absconding and dissent. Some turned to indentured European workers. Indenture-agreement wages were superior to those signed by non-Europeans and those of agricultural/rural workers in Britain/ Ireland. Nonetheless, disparities with prevailing colonial wages and shorter-term engagements induced considerable disaffection. In March 1841, five Irish labourers were prosecuted for refusing to proceed to J B Bettington's estate. One, Michael Maher, told the Sydney Bench wages were 'too small and that since they had arrived, they had been told, by some gentlemen who had come to see them, that they would not be able to live on their rations, as the allowance to convicts was more and better than they were to get.'[84] Notwithstanding efforts by employer's agents to escort new arrivals inland, others either absconded immediately or took collective action after reaching their master's farm/sheep-station. In June 1841 seven farm labourers and shepherds indentured to Bathurst District landholder John Street absconded after arriving on the *Moffatt*. Published notices warning others not to engage them over the next three months suggest they were never caught.[85]

In 1846 Morpeth landholder John Eales imported 18 indentured farm-workers (free and ex-convicts) from the closer (cheaper passage costs of £3 each) and economically struggling VDL, but 13 quickly absconded and another (Joseph Greenham) refused work.[86] In Greenham's case the Maitland Bench refused to rule on agreements made in another colony.

Greenham then took a complaint of unpaid wages and poor rations before the Sydney Bench which, in a wondrous piece of judicial innovation, gaoled him for six weeks under the *Vagrancy Act*.[87] Like some others, Eales was repeatedly before the courts prosecuting workers or answering claims for unpaid wages, including a strike by several ticket-of-leave holders in 1850.[88] Similar disputes occurred elsewhere, including the Port Phillip District. In February 1842 two Werribee District landholders (Forlonge and Wells) prosecuted groups of their men, one group with refusing to separate their flocks while the other struck 'on the frivolous excuse that they had been kept twenty four hours without tea and sugar.'[89] Three years later Highett and Haines published a reward notice after five servants they paid passage to Geelong failed to 'appear'.[90]

In addition to indenture-specific tensions, free workers often took action for reasons similar to convicts like six working for William Archer— prosecuted for being absent over Christmas 1844.[91] In addition to being gaoled, free workers risked forfeiting their wages and being returned to their master. In January 1843 R C Gunn's three hired farm servants forfeited their wages plus court costs for 'absenting themselves'.[92] Rations were another source of unrest. In September 1841 shepherds at Messrs Manifold's Weerite estate between Geelong and Colac absconded after not receiving their tea allowance. The ringleader was fined £5 and his agreement cancelled at his master's request.[93] Similarly, six men absconded from James Purves's Pleasant Bank estate, claiming the meat supplied was bad.[94] In September 1847, 13 men working at Alexander McGilveray's Cape Otway Corio estate lodged a complaint about poor rations. This was dismissed. McGilveray's counter-charge of absconding upheld, and 10 were sentenced to three months' imprisonment.[95]

Unlike convicts, wage disagreements were common amongst free-labour. In February 1844 shepherds at Henry Darlot's Mount Macedon estate refused to take the sheep out to pasture unless he acceded to their wage demands.[96] Piecework, customary payments and related questions of work quality were a particular source of friction. In November 1848 Mooringa (SA) landholder Christopher Bagot was embroiled in a dispute with sheep-washers over tasks they would perform if the weather didn't permit washing and the quality of their work. The washers took Bagot to court for unpaid wages. After considering complex evidence, the Adelaide Magistrates Court awarded different amounts to each worker involved.[97] Masters often refused or discounted wages when unhappy with work quality, for repeated misconduct/disobedience or because they had suffered a loss. In 1841 three shepherds failed to secure unpaid wages from Messrs Brodie Blackwood Vale, the court ruling non-payment was justified because they had lost 93 sheep.[98] Likewise, when labourers and shearers at John Ellis' Port Gawler station struck and tried to recover unpaid wages, the local Bench halved the amounts claimed because their work was poor. They appealed to the Adelaide Court of Quarter Sessions but lost there too.[99] Counter-arguments often worked for employers like Ellis, but seldom for workers. Some workers were obliged to take collective legal action to recover wages from a bankrupt employer, usually with a poor or mixed outcome. This was the case at James Triffett's farm at Emu Bottom VDL in 1843, where those on longer engagements won their case but weekly contract workers didn't.[100] Whether any actually received their money is unknown—still an issue.

Formal and District-Wide Informal Organisation

Collective action by rural/farmworkers during this period was overwhelmingly informal. There is evidence of attempts at formal organisation in Western Australia—then a free colony. In December 1831 pioneer settler George Fletcher Moore's diary recorded:

> Great visitings among the neighbouring servants, seven or eight of them patrolling about . . . They talk of forming a 'club'! They have too much control over their masters already and club law would be a terrible exercise and increase their power.[101]

Moore's servants told him they wouldn't remain after their contracts expired unless he matched higher wages paid by another master. In other entries Moore lamented the expense of indentured English labourers compared to Aborigines he paid with rice but then somewhat inconsistently wanted to hire indentured workers on longer contracts (five years) even if obliged to pay £5 for their passage. Discipline was also an issue, with Moore lamenting he could gaol a servant 'yet cannot afford to lose the advantage of his time, and pay £30, besides diet, to another in his place.'[102] Other settler diaries warrant investigation.

In January 1843 the *Perth Gazette* carried an advertisement for the Western Australian Shepherds Club and Mutual Protection Society formed by shepherds in the York, Toodyay and Northam Districts in response to recent changes to the *Master and Servant Act* and to provide mutual insurance for sickness or 'dismissal from service by caprice.'[103] A meeting was to be held on 1 February 1843 at the York Hotel to elect office-bearers. Another newspaper, the *Inquirer*, stated the organisation had been concocted by 'a few discontented spirits, for the wicked purpose of disturbing that good understanding between masters and servants.'[104] This was the last newspaper report on the society which was probably short-lived. There are no known unions of rural/agricultural/horticultural workers in the other colonies aside from a Sydney Friendly Society of Free Gardeners (1847–49).[105]

Even if unions remained a bridge too far, there is evidence of multi-workplace disputes amongst convicts from neighbouring farms/estates as well as references to customary conditions in single workplace disputes. In September 1840 the day after a farmer (Rowcroft) prosecuted four workers with disobedience and insolence, a number of his convicts joined those at a neighbouring farm in 'tumultuous proceedings'. Ringleaders from both farms were charged with insubordination and other offences, including insolence and harbouring absentees.[106] Wider alliances over wages also occurred as in Bathurst in 1835 with the *Monitor* complaining:

> Customary assistance rendered to settlers by government, for . . . securing the harvest, has been much curtailed this season owing to reduced . . . gangs on the road, and those distributed appeared to have entered into a combination to annoy their employers . . . Since the commencement of the harvest the Bench of Magistrates have a quadruple daily duty trying whole squads . . . for insolence, negligence and frequent positive refusals to labour. Although proverbially troublesome, no former season has been marked by such a display of insubordination notwithstanding the scourge.[107]

Reinforcing the point about wider networks, there is substantial evidence of informal multi-workplace/regional organisation and bargaining amongst free and semi-free workers. The first—a 1795 combination of Sydney District reapers—induced a Government Order to suppress such actions and set maximum wage rates.[108] The Order was re-issued/re-published regularly for over two decades thereafter, suggesting harvest workers continued to informally bargain for higher wages. After publishing Governor Macquarie's 1816 Order in 1818, VDL Lt Governor Sorell issued his own General Order stating that following excessive wage demands by ticket-of-leave holders during the last harvest, magistrates and police should refer those 'refusing to accept work at a just and reasonable rate' to authorities so their ticket could be cancelled. The Order specified payments for different tasks, including burning-off, clearing, planting and fencing.[109] As in NSW its effectiveness seems limited. In 1827 a virtually identical notice was published in *Bents Almanack* urging employers to act in unison against excessive wage demands and refusals to work amongst crown prisoners.[110]

Landholders sought government intervention to weaken worker bargaining power. In 1823 the Agricultural Society of NSW memorialised the Governor on wages and victualling, clothing and paying assigned-convicts.[111] Four years later fixing wages was advocated in VDL.[112] In October 1834 NSW landholders petitioned for additional assigned-convicts at harvest time. This didn't prevent a combination amongst Bathurst District convict-shearers the following December/January.[113] In July 1843 landholders in Ross (VDL) memorialised the Governor, for wage-controls given a want of 'firmness' in masters resisting labourers' demands. They were hankering for a return to General Orders, reflecting an earlier era of magistrate-regulated wages in the 17th and 18th centuries. The Governor was unsympathetic given the rapidity with which landholders broke these when it suited them.[114] Landholders employed their own combinations. In VDL regional agriculturalist associations, like the Brighton Union Club (Agriculturalist) and the Midland Agricultural Association, set wages for different categories of labour, invariably below the 'going rate' indicated in returns from Police Magistrates.[115] These measures could backfire if pressed. In 1847 a VDL correspondent lamented, employers couldn't get their sheep shorn until they agreed to pay 9s per 100 with shearers avoiding one recalcitrant altogether while good farm labourers voted with their feet by leaving for the mainland.[116]

Landholders repeatedly sought other government measures—accessing additional labour, more punitive laws and extra court/police resources to enforce them. These often proved self-defeating but help explain why worker organisation remained informal. While landholders exercised considerable power in colonial society, they couldn't prevent rural workers using informal networks to both bargain and inform new arrivals of 'agreed' benchmarks. In 1837 a Hunter River farmer complained time-served convicts were exploiting the abundant crops between Maitland and Invermein, demanding 'exorbitant wages and an extra quantity of ardent spirits, and many have ceased to work upon being refused spirits.'[117] Tacit and not so tacit bargaining became more evident in the 1840s. The *Portland Guardian* reported that responding to a rapid ripening of crops, South Australian reapers 'have come to the determination to demand higher wages than hitherto.'[118] Similar demands occurred in the following year (1843). Reapers reinforced their claims by striking at particular farms, as occurred at Manfull's Chellaston Grove estate near Adelaide and J White's Brown Hill Creek farm.[119] By 1842 newspapers were discussing promising labour-saving machinery like Ridley's reaper, but it took over a decade to supplant reapers.[120] In January 1848 Port Philip District reapers were reportedly 'demanding most unreasonable prices, and in some instances are obtaining ten shillings per-diem.'[121]

Workers also resisted wage cuts during slack periods or poor seasons, much to the chagrin of landholders.[122] In November 1844 the *Maitland Mercury* bemoaned that notwithstanding depressed conditions, Singleton District reapers 'are demanding singularly exorbitant wages—so high, indeed, that some of the farmers declare that they will be compelled to allow part of their crops to remain uncut.'[123]

Shearers and shepherds/hutkeepers too bargained over wages at multiple workplaces and district level. In March 1840 Western Australian settler G F Moore recorded wage increases were being sought by servants at his and several other establishments.[124] Five years later the *Perth Gazette* reported shepherds 'over the hills' were seeking additional wages plus rations.[125] In August 1847 the *Geelong Advertiser* reported wages of £26 for shepherds and hutkeepers within 100 miles—servants refusing less and also resisting employer requests to enter engagements longer than three months.[126] Like reaping, seasons commenced with district-level bargaining over rates. In November 1840 Murrumbidgee-District workers were demanding 6d per score for shearing and 7s 6d per day for washing the sheep.[127] In the Port Philip District the shearing-rate 'acceded to by flock-masters' in October 1845 was 12s per 100 sheep or two shillings over the previous year's rate.[128] Two years later the *Geelong Advertiser* reported shearers were demanding 16 shillings per hundred and 'sheer necessity will compel the settlers to submit to something like twelve shillings per hundred.'[129]

Like reapers, shearers and sheep-washers reinforced demands or resisted attempts to remove customary entitlements by striking at specific workplaces. In November 1847 Mr Sturt's Mount Gambier station sheep-washers struck over working conditions and failure to provide their grog allowance.[130] In succeeding decades pastoral unions would transform the coincidence of district/general demands with specific workplace strikes into a planned strategy targeting key sheep-stations like Jondaryan on the Darling Downs. In another precursor to later developments shearers not adhering to the 'going rate' were targeted. In 1841 shearers in the Geelong District demanded a rate of 20 shillings per hundred from local landholders and threatened shearers who had engaged at 15 shillings. Four of the ringleaders (William Gallagher, David Mahony, John Cockerell and John Ward) were committed to stand trial on the charge of conspiracy to raise wages, but the trial was abandoned due to the absence of two witnesses—presumably two of the threatened shearers.[131] Workers were also quick to apprise emigrants of the 'going rate' to pre-empt undercutting. In 1849 Ragged School emigrants were engaged as shepherds and hutkeepers in the Geelong District 'considerably under the current rate of wages' causing animosity amongst 'old hands' who endeavoured to make them 'dissatisfied with their employment and their employers.'[132]

Evidence of district-wide bargaining over wages is hardly surprising. Many landholders had an interest in paying a uniform rate, even if they wanted lower one than workers. In a volatile industry bargaining flourished in favourable economic conditions, but was difficult during downturns as even large and relatively well-resourced pastoral unions found in the 1890s.

Mining

While mining became a major industry in the 40 years after substantial gold discoveries in NSW and Victoria in the early 1850s, it assumed some importance prior to this. Coal mining commenced in the Hunter Valley in 1798, tapping reserves that are still globally significant and from the 1830s a number of mines also opened in VDL. Originally for local demand, Governors cognisant of the need for colonial exports encouraged exports. Initially convicts were used to mine under the direction of experienced miners.[133] Conditions were primitive and dangerous. The first recorded death at the Nobby's mine was in 1816 and over the next 200 years over 1800 men and boys (the youngest 13 years) would die in 'accidents' in the Hunter and northern NSW District—far more would perish from work-diseases like pneumoconiosis.

Coal production grew from 150 tonnes in 1805 to 3915 tonnes in 1820 but stagnated until the Australian Agricultural Company was granted a monopoly of the Hunter coal trade in 1833, with coal output reaching 40,000 tonnes by 1842.[134] Nonetheless, the AA Company's initial preference for assigned-convicts (who promptly left when they received their tickets-of-leave), and primitive mining methods, hampered growth.[135] From 1847 the AA Company's monopoly was breached by other operators. Coalmining in VDL also began as a small-scale government operation in the early-1830s on the Tasman Peninsular near Port Arthur, with further small mines opening up at Recherche Bay and Schouten Island in the 1840s. The latter didn't use convicts. Metalliferous mining commenced in NSW in the late 1840s, but more significant development occurred in South Australia where large copper deposits were discovered. Mines near Gawler and more especially at Burra, using experienced miners from Cornwall, made a substantial contribution to global copper supply in the second half of the 1840s—export value briefly rivalling wool in the colony.[136] Cornish miners brought customary modes of work organisation and payment, including the tribute (paying a share of ore value) and tutwork (piecework payment-by-weight) systems. Remnants of these operations including flooded pits, smelter buildings, miners' houses and a countryside deforested for fuel are evident today.

Patterns of Collective Active Action

There is evidence of 151 instances of organisation. Only 14 involved free workers, though these were larger on average including one union at Burra. It's also possible Newcastle coalminers had some form of organisation. Table 6.3 indicates a relatively even split between strikes and NSCA. The figures for convicts include both those working in private and government mines. In this case government convicts were included in mining rather under the government industry category because combining them provided a more meaningful picture of mining activities. Interrogation of additional sources will almost certainly uncover more instances of collective action, especially in South Australia and NSW—including the period prior to 1830. Unlike rural workers and seamen, mass absconding was less common amongst miners though still significant, especially with regard to convicts. Letters to the press were predominantly associated with a copper miners' union in Burra, as were mass meetings and one of the petitions.

Working conditions, especially efforts to restrict output, were significant issues in both strikes and NSCA followed by health and safety, hours of work (strikes only), management behaviour and wages (Table 6.4). The low ranking of wages reflects that convicts were formally precluded from payment (though they did get additional rations), while convicts 'absenting themselves' accounts for most strikes over hours.

Table 6.3 Summary: Organisation/Activity in Mining Industry 1788–1850

Nature of activity	1788–1800	1801–10	1811–20	1821–30	1831–40	1841–50	Total	Percentages
Convict Workers								
All Organisation				1	107	29	137	
Involvement				3	615	157	775	
Adjusted involvement*				3	633	161	794	
Strikes					95	24	119	54.6
NSCA				1	80	18	99	45.4
Total				1	175	42	218	
Absconding				1	24	6	31	
Sabotage					6	1	7	
Free Workers								
All Organisation					1	13	14	
Formal Organisation						1	1	
Involvement					30	514	544	
Adjusted involvement*					30	1114	1144	
Strikes					1	6	7	46.7
NSCA						8	8	53.3
Total					1	14	15	
Absconding					1	1	2	
Court actions					1	1	1	
Petitions						2	2	
Press Letters						4	4	
Mass meetings						5	5	

* Estimate based on adding median membership figure to zero count organisations

Table 6.4 Strikes and NSCA by Issue in the Mining Industry 1788–1850

Issue	1788–1800	1801–10	1811–20	1821–30	1831–40	1841–50	Total*	Percentages*
Strikes								
Wages/remuneration					1	6	7	5.6
Working conditions					40	24	64	50.8
Management behaviour					12	4	16	12.7
Hours of work					31	2	33	26.2
Jobs/employment					1		1	0.1
Health & safety					38	5	43	34.1.
Work methods					1		1	0.1
NSCA								
Wages/remuneration					1	7	8	7.5
Working conditions				1	64	20	85	79.4
Management behaviour					5	5	10	9.3
Hours of work								
Jobs/employment								
Health & safety					22	1	23	21.5
Work methods					3	1	4	3.7
Unionism								
Legislation								
Unknown								

* exceeds total for 126 strikes and 107 NSCA because of multiple issue strikes/NSCA

Informal Mine Specific Collective Action

Organisation was overwhelmingly informal and confined to a single mine. There were frequent instances of collective absconding by convict miners at the AA Company's Newcastle mines from the early 1830s (and probably from government mines before this). In 1836 the AA Company's Newcastle convict miners imposed a go-slow, protesting a government directive replacing monetary incentives with orders redeemable for goods from local shopkeepers.[137] The AA Company began importing mineworkers under lengthy indentures, but like their rural counterparts they became disgruntled after comparing their terms (seven years' duration at £1 per week plus rations/board) to prevailing colonial agreements. In 1840 they struck and after a prolonged struggle the AA Company agreed to pay them piece-rates (per skip-load). During the confrontation, four men were gaoled for breaching their agreement, strike-leader John Griffith was prosecuted and 24 miners absconded—12 remaining at large two months later.[138] In 1842 introduction of a larger skip (affecting pay) caused further action, with its leader overman James Birrell from Fife successfully suing the company for unpaid wages. The issue re-ignited in 1844 with Birrell again leading court actions to recover wages.[139]

In VDL convicts worked coalmines on the Tasman Peninsular and at Recherche Bay south of Hobart. As in the Hunter Valley, absconding was an ongoing problem. In December 1840 (twice) and February/March and June/July 1841, groups of convicts were punished after absconding from the Recherche Bay mines.[140] In October and November 1841 groups of convicts apprehended after absconding from the Browns River gang were sentenced to work in the Recherche Bay coalmines, probably in part to replace those who had absconded.[141] Other absconders like John Porter and Philip Ayres were sent to the Tasman Peninsular mine, as well as receiving 75 and 100 lashes respectively as a warning to others.[142] And it wasn't just collective absconding. In March 1841 three Recherche Bay miners were charged with insubordination, ringleader Joshua Hodges receiving 12 months in Port Arthur in chains.[143]

A narrow and closely guarded isthmus (with savage dogs) made absconding difficult from the Tasman Peninsular mines, but miners still 'defaced' their irons to escape and some made a break though most seem to have been quickly caught.[144] If absconding was difficult, surviving court records demonstrate collective action and individualised dissent was endemic. Between February 1836 and July 1841, well over 100 instances of collective dissent were tried, mostly strike and go-slows. Indeed, at times including much of 1840, strikes were occurring on a weekly basis. Organised pilfering of food (typically bread, vegetables, fish and meat) by hungry mineworkers was also common even though, as in NSW, convict mineworkers were issued with additional rations, perhaps indicative of corruption amongst officials. The AA Company protested this practice when it took over the NSW mines from government, arguing task-work of 2.5 tonnes per-day per workers didn't warrant 50% additional rations. In a heroic piece of logic the company argued its own miners would become insubordinate unless government-stipulated miner rations were cut.[145] At the Tasman Peninsular mines suspending extra rations was used to punish dissent. In May 1839 three miners had their rations cut to the 3rd scale for idleness when sinking a new shaft.[146] Attempts to obtain additional food, possessing food or cooking materials (like tinder), or cooking food privately were also subject to harsh punishments as happened when four mineworkers were caught making a damper in July 1838.[147]

Refusals to work based on physical incapacity or inexperience was common, typified by a strike by 10 mineworkers on this ground in October 1837.[148] Effort-bargaining was also pervasive with groups of mineworkers being prosecuted for neglect, not reaching their task-targets, being caught falsifying coal tallies, or engaging in labour-saving sabotage. In March 1836 three miners were charged with neglect in breaking two buckets, with two receiving seven days' solitary confinement.[149] Others went a more dangerous path by taking coal from the sides of mine roads—shortcuts to obtain 'easy coal' were (and remained a century later) an endemic problem connected to tally-based systems—with 14 being charged with this offence in September 1837.[150] Sawyers and stonecutters engaged in building mine infrastructure like timber support-beams also engaged in collective neglect, absence (including time collecting extra food) and cooking food in their huts.

There were recurrent tensions between mineworkers and their overseers, resulting in the former being charged with using abusive or improper language. On occasion tensions erupted into violence. In September 1837 Thomas Cooper was ordered to receive 50 lashes for striking his overseer with a wooden mallet during a dispute involving several miners, and four months later William Hewitt received 25 lashes for throwing a stone at his overseer.[151] In July 1844 Thomas Smith (a wheelwright by trade) and James Boyle pushing a coal cart became involved in an argument with their overseer (Perry) which culminated in them bludgeoning him with a pickaxe. They were tried, convicted and executed in Hobart on 7 August 1844.[152] While the pernicious conditions at the Tasman Peninsular mines help explain the dissent, collective action was of a type common in British coalmines at the time, whilst also highlighting the 'difficulties' associated with dragooning an unfree workforce including many lacking mining experience.

In South Australia expanding copper-mining operations soon experienced strikes/NSCA. In June 1844 miners at Rapid Bay demanded a wage increase, followed by miners at Burra in November 1845, Paringa in 1846 and Mount Remarkable in 1847.[153] Several strikes were associated with agitation involving multiple mines.[154] Reporting the Paringa miners' strike for 42 shillings per week in December 1846, one newspaper observed many miners were 'requiring 40s and a not a few have been earning considerably more on tutwork and tribute.'[155] When economic conditions deteriorated in the late-1840s, strikes became defensive like one against a wage cut by Port Lincoln miners in May 1850.[156]

Pastoralist William Suttor (1805–77), who controlled 13,446 acres by 1838 (vastly more by the 1860s), opened a lead mine at Brucedale near Bathurst in 1849 but soon experienced labour difficulties. After working for rations-only while developing the mine, miners struck against a wage cut in January 1850.[157] A month later, Cornish miners at the Summer Hill copper mine near Bathurst struck work when water-inrush from an underground spring affected a verbal agreement over payment and work methods. Given the shaft's narrowness, miners rejected an offer of additional men and were summonsed before the Bathurst Bench. After hearing technical evidence in Cornish, the case was adjourned for several days, but resolved in the interim when the parties negotiated a compromise.[158]

Formal Organisation and Multi-Mine Site Collective Action

In the Hunter Valley coalminers were organising on a multi-mine and district-wide basis by the late 1840s. In July 1850 all AA Company pits struck for a 6d per-ton increase in the hewing rate (piecework). They succeeded but not before several were prosecuted for breaching their agreement and John Dyer sentenced to six weeks in Maitland Gaol.[159] In a courtroom crowded with miners, the Bench imposed the gaol-time to discourage collective action. It signally failed. Over the next few years between June and August, coalminers throughout the Hunter Valley took collective action over wages, job security and OHS.[160] This was the precursor to formal organisation. Like those that followed, the 1850 strike reflected the growing importance of coalmining including exports to the Americas. In the NSW Legislative Council employer representatives claimed the strike indicated the capacity of the labouring classes to injure their interests and demanded substantial increases in assisted-immigration.[161]

In contrast, the South Australian copper-mining boom subsided in the late 1840s. The combination of an economic downturn and overly optimistic management came to a head at the largest—the 'Monster' Burra mine. On 12 August 1848 miners petitioned the Board to modify the assay method adversely affecting their earnings. Getting no response, around 400 miners struck work in September. One miner, William Sprague, was convicted of using threatening language to the mine secretary and two strike-breakers, and gaoled until the fine was paid. Two other miners were fined for picketing—the Kooringa Bench labelling combinations to prevent work 'improper'.[162] The Burra Board agreed to modify the assay method, but success proved short-lived.[163] Within days Directors imposed across-the-board wage cuts of 4s (to 21s per week) for less skilled workmen and 5s (to 30s) for skilled miners. On October 2nd miners again struck, eventually capitulating after over three months—amounting to around 38,000 working days lost. Twenty-seven activists were refused re-employment and blacklisted from other mines.[164] Courts played only a tangential role in this strike. An assayer discharged by the Burra Board (believing his incompetence led to the strike) claimed unfair dismissal in the Supreme Court and was awarded considerable damages.[165]

Aside from being notable for its size, the Burra strike was associated with the first known miners' union. During the first strike, a Burra Burra Metal Miners Committee was established. This broadened into the Colonial Miners' Friendly Society that continued after the second strike collapsed. In July 1849 following a mass meeting, the Society sent a letter with over 300 signatures calling on the company to employ a second doctor. They complained the company had reneged on an agreement negotiated in 1848 for doctors to treat miner's families on the basis of fees already paid.[166] The outcome of this dispute is unknown. After experiencing industrial defeat, mutual insurance was pivotal to the Colonial Miners' Friendly Society survival (last mentioned in September 1849), although this was difficult for workers in insecure occupations.

Conclusion

Prior to 1851 and for many years thereafter, rural/farming activities were a cornerstone of colonial economies. The industry, especially vital wool exports, was essentially kick-started by unfree-labour, followed by waves of free and semi-free workers. Even accounting for the sizable workforce, there was considerable single-workplace collective action by convicts and free-labour responding to ill-treatment, poor rations, no/low wages and employers wedded to a one-sided legal code. Many single-workplace actions also drew on wider understandings/comparisons and customary conditions. While there were few short-lived attempts at formal organisation, multi-workplace/regional bargaining exploiting seasonal labour demand and drawing on information networks about of acceptable practices is evident by 1795 and became more pervasive by the 1840s. These set a foundation for growing attempts to form unions in succeeding decades.

This pattern and the intensity of the conflict should come as no surprise. Seasonal bargaining by agricultural workers had already been going on for centuries in Europe. Many rural workers—both convict and free—came from regions affected by Captain Swing or other protests, some being directly involved. What they encountered in the colonies was an equally exploitive production regime, dominated by large landholders demanding subordination in a rather different labour market. The imprint of both older and contemporary experiences can be seen in some methods used like incendiarism, strikes and mass absconding. Organisation might have been informal but it was sufficient to exercise the wits of colonial legislators, courts and bodies representing agricultural/rural interests.

As another primary extractive industry dominated by large capital, mining began early but only commenced to assume importance in late 1830s. It was also marked by widespread workplace-based dissent, but one that also transitioned into wider informal organisation. Collective action by miners also drew on longstanding customs/traditions and by the late 1840s, a trajectory towards formal organisation is evident.

Notes

1 Bach, J. (1981) *A Maritime History of Australia*, 20–21.
2 Made worse where single-crop agribusiness displaced the family-based mixed farming model that could adapt to vagaries of climate and shifts demand for wool, wheat, cattle and sheep meat.
3 Millis, R. (1994) *Waterloo Creek: The Australia Day Massacre of 1838, George Gipps and the British Conquest of New South Wales*, UNSW Press, Sydney.
4 Clements, N. (2013) *Frontier Conflict in Van Diemen's Land*, Ph.D. Thesis, University of Tasmania and *Sydney Morning Herald* 31 January 1848.
5 Walsh, B. (2007) Heartbreak and Hope, Deference and Defiance on the Yimmang, 170–188.
6 *Sydney Morning Herald* 18 November 1848.
7 *Perth Inquirer* 17 April 1850.
8 *Launceston Advertiser* 3 July 1834.
9 *The Australian* 10 November 1838. For other examples, see *Sydney Gazette* 17 May 1834 and 16 June 1836.
10 Longford LC362–1–4 27 August 1840.
11 See for example LC362–1–6 Longford 18 March 1846.
12 LC362–1–3 4 Longford June 1836.
13 Walsh, B. (2007) Heartbreak and Hope, Deference and Defiance on the Yimmang, 224–225.
14 Hindmarsh, B. (2001) Yoked to the Plough, 139–143.
15 LC362–1–2 Longford 19 October 1830; LC362–1–3 16 January 1836; 7 November 1836 and 15 June 1839.
16 LC362–1–3 Longford 19 and 21 September 1836.
17 For another case involving William Archer (Edward's brother), see LC362–1–4 Longford 13 February 1840.
18 *Cornwall Chronicle* 6 and 16 January 1847.
19 *Hobart Town Courier* 26 May 1847.
20 For this and other incendiarism reward advertisements cases, see *New South Wales Government Gazette (NSWGG)* 28 May 1844; 18 February 1845; 8 July 1845; 31 October 1845; 6 February 1846; 20 February 1846; 10 July 1846; 1 January 1847; 26 January 1847; 5 February 1847; 30 April 1847; 20 March 1849; 3 April 1849; 22 June 1849; 9 November 1849.
21 Hobsbawm, E. and Rudè, G. (1972) *Captain Swing*; and Hindmarsh, B. (2001) Yoked to the Plough.
22 LC143–1–1 *Fingal* 26 January, 21 and 25 February, 20 July, 1, 16 and 28 August, 1 and 13 September 1843.
23 Cited in Roberts, A. (2008) *Marine Office-Convict Wife: The Johnston's of Annandale*, Annandale Urban Research Association, Sydney, 38.
24 *NSWGG* 23 September 1835, 21 October 1835, 4 November 1835 and 11 November 1835.
25 *NSWGG* 24 December 1834, 14 January 1835.
26 LC247–1–1260 Hobart 22 December 1826.
27 *Colonial Times* 17 September 1830.
28 LC375–1–2 New Norfolk 26 November 1838.
29 *Launceston Advertiser* 22 February 1832.

30 LC83–1–1 Campbell Town 21 July and 19 August 1835.
31 Hindmarsh, B. (2001) Yoked to the Plough, 165.
32 *Sydney Monitor* 5 July 1834.
33 LC375–1–1 New Norfolk 27 October 1834.
34 LC445–1–1 Richmond 27 January 1847.
35 LC247–1–6 Hobart 8 October 1836.
36 LC362–1–3 Longford 2 July 1836.
37 LC83–1–3 Campbell Town 8 August 1838.
38 LC83–1–4 Campbell Town 24 and 28 October 1840.
39 LC83–1–3 Campbell Town 27 December 1838.
40 Hindmarsh, B. (2001) Yoked to the Plough, 218.
41 *Hobart Town Courier* 27 March 1835.
42 Hindmarsh, B. (2001) Yoked to the Plough, 218–220.
43 LC 362–1–3 Longford 2 April 1836.
44 *Launceston Advertiser* 26 April 1838.
45 *Cornwall Chronicle* 28 April 1838.
46 *Cornwall Chronicle* 10 February 1838 and 16 June 1838.
47 *Cornwall Chronicle* 4 March 1846.
48 LC375–1–1 New Norfolk 30 May 1834.
49 *Cornwall Chronicle* 6 May 1837.
50 Hindmarsh, B. (2001) Yoked to the Plough, 103.
51 *Launceston Advertiser* 3 November 1836.
52 *Launceston Examiner* 9 March 1844.
53 LC445–1–1 Richmond 7, 9 and 19 January 1847.
54 LC390–1–2 Oatlands 29 January 1846.
55 LC156–1–2 George Town 15 January 1848.
56 LC390–1–2 Oatlands 3 January 1848.
57 *Sydney Gazette* 11 and 25 January 1822.
58 *Sydney Gazette* 1 March 1822.
59 *Sydney Gazette* 1 March 1822.
60 *Sydney Gazette* 1 March 1822.
61 *The Australian* 15 April 1826.
62 Hirst, J. (1983) *Convict Society and Its Enemies*, 184.
63 *Sydney Gazette* 20 February 1823 and 19 February 1827.
64 *The Australian* 20 October 1825.
65 *Sydney Monitor* 12 May 1832.
66 *Sydney Monitor* 12 January 1831.
67 *Sydney Monitor* 15 December 1832.
68 There are numerous accounts of the incident. See for example Walsh, B. (2007) Heartbreak and Hope, Deference and Defiance on the Yimmang, 244–245.
69 Walsh, B. (2007) Heartbreak and Hope, Deference and Defiance on the Yimmang, 248.
70 *Sydney Gazette* 9 July 1833.
71 *Sydney Herald* 27 February 1834.
72 *Morning Chronicle* 4 April 1846.
73 *Sydney Morning Herald* 4 April 1846.
74 *Maitland Mercury* 11 November 1846.
75 *Maitland Mercury* 18 October 1845.
76 *Sydney Morning Herald* 27 October 1847.
77 *Geelong Advertiser* 22 October 1847.
78 *Geelong Advertiser* 10 January 1850.
79 *Sydney Morning Herald* 12 September 1849.
80 *Sydney Morning Herald* 4 July 1850.
81 *Bell's Life of Sydney* 10 and 24 August 1850.

82 Toh, S. and Quinlan, M. (2009) Safeguarding the Global Contingent Work-force? Guestworkers in Australia, *International Journal of Manpower*, 30(5):453–471; Underhill, E. and Rimmer, M. (2016) Layered Vulnerability: Temporary Migrants in Australian Horticulture, *Journal of Industrial Relations*, 58(5):608–626.
83 Crowley, F. (1949) Working Class Conditions in Australia, 1788–1851, 395–397.
84 *Sydney Herald* 31 March 1841.
85 *Sydney Herald* 26 June 1841, 17 July 1841, 21 August 1841 and 4 September 1841.
86 *Sydney Morning Herald* 3 September 1846.
87 *Bell's Life of Sydney* 5 September 1846.
88 See *Maitland Mercury* 4 April 1850 and 8 June 1850.
89 *Geelong Advertiser* 21 February 1842.
90 *Geelong Advertiser* 29 October 1845.
91 LC362–1–6 Longford 27 December 1844
92 *Launceston Examiner* 25 January 1843.
93 *Geelong Advertiser* 4 September 1841.
94 *Melbourne Courier* 13 October 1844.
95 *Geelong Advertiser* 24 September 1847.
96 *Port Philip Gazette* 10 February 1844.
97 *South Australian Register* 2 December 1848.
98 *Port Philip Patriot* 12 December 1841.
99 *South Australian* 26 October 1847 and 17 December 1847; and *South Australian Register* 1 December 1847.
100 *Launceston Examiner* 22 July 1843.
101 Moore, G.F. (1884) *Diary of Ten Years Eventful Life of an Early Settler*, 91.
102 Moore, G.F. (1884) *Diary of Ten Years Eventful Life of an Early Settler*, 60, 88–91, 101.
103 *Perth Gazette* 21 January 1843.
104 *Inquirer* 1 February 1843.
105 *Sydney Morning Herald* 22 June 1849.
106 LC362–1–4 and LC362–1–5 Longford 14 and 22 September 1840.
107 *Monitor* 10 January 1835.
108 AONSW CSO Government and General Order re control of wages determined by settlers 14 April and 18 September 1797 Reel 6037 ML Safe 1/18b.
109 *Hobart Town Gazette* 12 January 1822.
110 *The Tasmanian Almanack for the Year 1827*, Andrew Bent, Hobart, 57–58.
111 AONSW CSO Reel 17 July 1823 6056 4/1765, 177–9a.
112 *Hobart Town Gazette* 25 August 1827.
113 *Sydney Gazette* 11 October 1834 and *Sydney Monitor* 10 January 1835.
114 TAHO CSO 8/91/1897.
115 See for example *The Colonist and VDL Advertiser* 8 January 1835; *The Tasmanian* 31 January 1838; *Hobart Town Courier* 28 July 1843; and *Launceston Examiner* 25 September 1844.
116 *Colonial Times* 23 April 1847.
117 *The Australian* 8 December 1837.
118 *Portland Guardian* 17 December 1842.
119 *South Australian Register* 29 November 1843; *Southern Australian* 1 December 1843.
120 See for example the *South Australian* 2 January 1849.
121 *Maitland Mercury* 12 January 1848.
122 *Adelaide Observer* 26 August 1843.

123 *Maitland Mercury* 23 November 1844.
124 Moore, G.F. (1884) *Diary of Ten Years Eventful Life of an Early Settler in Western Australia*, 406.
125 *Perth Gazette* 21 February 1845.
126 *Geelong Advertiser* 21 August 1847.
127 *Sydney Herald* 28 November 1840.
128 *Launceston Examiner* 15 October 1845.
129 *Geelong Advertiser* 21 September 1847.
130 *Geelong Advertiser* 26 November 1847.
131 VPRS 109 Unit 1, p525; Willis' Case Book No.12, 29 and Port Phillip Gazette 16 October 1841 cited in Mullaly, P. (2008) *Crime in the Port Phillip District 1835–51*, Hybrid Publishers, Melbourne, 717.
132 Reproduced in the *South Australian* 8 May 1849.
133 *HRNSW 1803–1805*, 2 May 1804, 369, 418.
134 Turner, J. (1982) *Coal Mining in Newcastle, 1801–1900*, City Council of Newcastle, Newcastle, 17.
135 For evidence of recurring labour issues, see *In the Service of the Company: Letters of Sir Edward Parry, Commissioner to the Australian Agricultural Company*, Australian Nation University e-press, Canberra, 2005.
136 Bach, J. (1981) *A Maritime History of Australia*, 23.
137 Turner, J. (1982) *Coal Mining in Newcastle, 1801–1900*, 40, 142.
138 Turner, J. (1982) *Coal Mining in Newcastle 1801–1900*, 41–42 and 143; *Sydney Herald* 9 January 1841.
139 Turner, J. (1982) *Coal Mining in Newcastle 1801–1900*, 42–43.
140 LC247–1–8 Hobart 12 and 21 December 1840, 18 March 1841, 10 June 1841 and 13 July 1841.
141 See for example LC247–1–9 Hobart 11 November 1841.
142 LC247–1–9 Hobart 2 December 1841.
143 LC247–1–8 Hobart 19 and 22 March 1841.
144 TAHO A584–1–1 Port Arthur Coal Mines 25 November 1839.
145 *In the Service of the Company: Letters of Sir Edward Parry, Commissioner to the Australian Agricultural Company*, 155.
146 See for example TAHO A584–1–1 Port Arthur Coal Mines 10 May 1839.
147 TAHO A584–1–1 Port Arthur Coal Mines 25 July 1838.
148 TAHO A584–1–1 Port Arthur Coal Mines 25 October 1837.
149 TAHO A584–1–1 Port Arthur Coal Mines 3 March 1836.
150 TAHO A584–1–1 Port Arthur Coal Mines 29 September 1837.
151 TAHO A584–1–1 Port Arthur Coal Mines 1 September 1837.
152 *Colonial Times* 13 August 1844.
153 *Adelaide Observer* 15 June 1844; *South Australian Register* 12 November 1845; *Bell's Life of Sydney* 9 January 1847; and *South Australian Gazette* 6 February 1847.
154 *South Australian* 25 December 1846.
155 *Bell's Life of Sydney* 9 January 1847.
156 *Adelaide Times* 25 May 1850 and 31 May 1850.
157 *Bathurst Advocate* 10 February 1849 and 12 January 1850.
158 *Bathurst Free Press* 16 February 1850.
159 *Sydney Morning Herald* 6 July 1850; *Maitland Mercury* 17 July 1850 and 20 July 1850; and Turner, J. (1982) *Coal Mining in Newcastle, 1801–1900*, 58–59.
160 *Geelong Advertiser* 5 June 1851; *Empire* 19 June 1852; and *Maitland Mercury* 20 August 1853.
161 *Maitland Mercury* 31 July 1850 and 7 August 1850.

162 *South Australian* 22 September 1848.
163 *South Australian Register* 20 September 1848 and *South Australian* 22 September 1848.
164 *South Australian* 14 November 1848 and *Sydney Morning Herald* 10 May 1851.
165 *Adelaide Observer* 4 November 1848.
166 *Adelaide Observer* 14 July 1849.

7 Organisation in Construction and Building Materials

Introduction

Increasing population, economic expansion and no pre-existing built infra-structure created strong demand for residential, farm and public build-ings (like schools and court houses) and infrastructure (roads, bridges, wharves) as well as materials for this (dressed stone, bricks, lime, sand, timber, lead, slate and shingles). Private building activity was susceptible to business cycles, volatility accentuated by speculative waves of building grand houses in/near towns like Sydney and Adelaide or on rural estates. Much construction prior to 1840, especially labouring, was undertaken by government-engaged convicts. Of the 74 instances of organisation by pri-vate construction industry workers only nine involved labourers (all free-labour) including one formal union (Table 7.1). Even in free colonies, government played a pivotal role to civil construction. Public works were also used to support the jobless during economic downturns. This chap-ter also examines organisation amongst workers manufacturing building materials (stonecutters, brickmakers, lime-makers and pipe-makers) and furniture (cabinetmakers, carvers), given close links between the two activi-ties. Building materials were often manufactured close to construction sites and were equally susceptibility to boom/bust cycles in colonial economies.

Building/Construction

Overview of Organisation

Tables 7.1 and 7.2 summarise organisation in construction and building materials by decade as well as organisation amongst all construction work-ers, including those—especially convicts employed by government, who will be examined in chapter 9. Although numbers are small Table 7.1 indi-cates strikes were a more common device than non-strike action in both industries. Workers in both also used petitions, public notices/letters and mass meetings. This, use of the House-of-Call, and the large number of workers per organisation reflects the greater capacity of skilled workers to

Table 7.1 Summary: Organisation/Activity in Construction and Building Materials 1788–1850

Nature of activity	1788–1800	1801–10	1811–20	1821–30	1831–40	1841–50	Total	Percentages
Construction								
All Organisation	2			6	28	38	74	
Formal Organisation				1	13	23	37	
Involvement	6			13	215	591	825	
Adjusted Involvement*	6			26	501	2041	2574	
Strikes				2	13	17	32	59.3
NSCA	2			2	10	10	22	40.7
Total				4	23	27	54	
Absconding					4		4	
House-of-Call					5	10	15	
Court actions						1	1	
Petitions				1	3	3	7	
Press Letters					7	6	13	
Mass meetings						1	1	
Marches						1	1	
Building Materials and Furniture								
All Organisation				8	26	30	64	
Formal Organisation					4	7	11	
Involvement				14	136	451	601	
Adjusted involvement*				19	192	644	855	
Strikes				3	11	15	29	48.3
NSCA				6	16	9	31	51.7
Total				9	27	24	60	
Absconding				4	6	2	12	
House-of-Call					1	1	2	
Court actions	1				1		2	

Petitions				3	3	6	
Deputations					1	1	
Press Letters				4	2	6	
Mass meetings				4		4	
Bans				1		1	
All Construction including Government-engaged Convicts and Free Unemployed Relief Workers							
Organisation	9	25	1262	1293	409	3082	
Involvement	36	113	4720	5393	2570	13097	
Strikes	3	12	92	136	103	346	10.5
NSCA	9	20	1194	1321	329	2943	89.5
Total		23	1286	1457	432	3289	
Absconding	2	18	1127	1193	255	2671	

* Estimate based on adding median membership figure to zero count organisations

Table 7.2 Strikes and NSCA by Issue in Construction and Building Materials 1788–1850

Nature of activity	1788–1800	1801–10	1811–20	1821–30	1831–40	1841–50	Total*	Percentage*
Construction								
Strikes								
Wages/remuneration				1	10	13	24	75
Working conditions				1	3	2	6	18.8
Hours of work				1	2	2	5	15.6
Health & safety					2	1	3	9.4
Work methods						1	1	3.1
NSCA								
Wages/remuneration				2	6	7	15	68.2
Working conditions	2			1	3	1	7	31.8
Hours of work						1	1	4.5
Jobs/employment						1	1	4.5
Health & safety						1	1	4.5
Work methods						2	2	9.1
Unionism						1	1	4.5
Unknown					2		2	9.1
Building Materials and Furniture								
Strikes								
Wages/remuneration	1			1	5	4	11	35.5
Working conditions				2	4	6	12	38.7
Management behaviour					1		1	3.4
Hours of work					4	8	12	38.7
Jobs/employment				1			1	3.4
Health & safety					1		1	3.4

Work methods	1		1	2	6.9
Unionism		1		1	3.4
NSCA					
Wages/remuneration	1	3	4	8	25.8
Working conditions	5	10	5	20	64.5
Management behaviour		1	1	1	3.2
Hours of work	1	1		2	6.5
Jobs/employment	1	1	1	3	9.7
Health & safety		3	2	5	16.1
Work methods	2			2	6.5

* Exceeds totals strikes/NSCA and 100% because of multiple issue strikes/NSCA bargain over their conditions, establish multi-workplace organisation and form unions. In contrast, there were relatively fewer instances of collective absconding—largely by convicts. Notable in terms of the ranking of strike/ NSCA issues for both industries, but especially construction, is the significance of wages compared to maritime and rural workers, and the relative insignificance of management behaviour, both indicative of greater bargaining power and formal organisation (Table 7.2).

Notwithstanding periodic collapses, unions in some building trades tended to survive longer or were quickly revived in major towns. This was the case with carpenters and joiners and stonemasons in Sydney from the early 1830s. Unions formed by Sydney painters, plasterers and plumbers in the early-1840s survived much of that decade and a bricklayers' society lasted at least three years. Bodies representing more specialist building trades like a slaters and shinglers society (established 1842) seem to have been short-lived. In Hobart a relatively successful carpenters' union was formed in 1833 but this early promise was swamped by a flood of convicts after transportation to NSW ended (1840). In Melbourne bricklayers, stonemasons and carpenters made repeated (at least three each) attempts to organise between 1839 and 1850. Most lasted less than three years. Unions established by carpenters and stonemasons in 1850 were more successful.[1] Unlike Sydney, there is no evidence of even informal organisation amongst painters, plumbers and plasterers but a paviors society existed in 1842.[2] In Adelaide a combined building trades union was established in 1839, followed by separate unions of stonemasons (1840) and carpenters (1846).[3] Adelaide bricklayers (1844, 1846 and 1847), plasterers (1847) and plumbers, painters and glaziers (1848) also organised informally. There is no evidence of unions in Western Australia or Queensland.

Some unions may have reorganised rather than collapsed. The Hobart Carpenters and Joiners Institution met at the *Lamb Inn*, as initially did its successor body the Hobart Carpenters and Joiners Benefit Society two years later.[4] Reorganisation sometimes went unreported in newspapers. An Account Book of the Sydney Progressive Society of Carpenters and Joiners (1849–58) documents attempts to establish unions in 1849 and 1851 involving the same core of activists before a successful effort in 1854. Originally belonging to an earlier (1846) carpenters' union, the book was donated along with some cash affording further evidence of continuity/ ongoing networks.[5]

Organisation was typically confined to a single trade or related trades (like carpenters and joiners) along British lines. On occasion, insufficient numbers led several closely-aligned trades to combine or (more rarely) for workers to be offered on a self-employed basis. The Hobart Carpenters and Joiners Institution (1833) offered cabinetmakers as well as carpenters, and workers who could supervise their own work, from its House-of-Call at the *Lamb Inn*.[6] As economic conditions deteriorated in VDL, a short-lived attempt was made to establish a benefit society involving cabinetmakers, carpenters, joiners, coachmakers and turners in 1843.[7] Multi-trade bodies were still being formed in Hobart as late as the 1880s.[8] In other colonies early attempts at multi-trades unions like Adelaide builders (1839) and Melbourne stonemasons and bricklayers (1841) soon gave way to separate bodies. In Sydney, painters, plumbers and glaziers formed a union in 1840, but wider collaborations were rare in larger, more prosperous towns.[9]

Informal Single Workplace Organisation

Informal organisation amongst unskilled construction workers was considerable but dominated by government-engaged convicts (see Chapter 9). There were instances of collective action by free-labourers. In June 1831 contractors and labourers building a canal in Perth (WA) struck for increased rates, claiming they had to cut more yards than originally estimated.[10] In 1844 labourers repairing the Supreme Court building in Sydney petitioned the government for work after they were discharged.[11] Informal single-workplace action amongst building tradesmen was also comparatively rare, especially after unions formed. In December 1834 a Brickfields Hill plumber and glazier named Gould prosecuted his assigned-tradesmen for demanding rump steak in addition to their other rations.[12] In 1847 bricklayers stopped work on an Adelaide building site over concerns with unsafe scaffolding and work methods and subsequently attempted to recover their wages.[13]

Informal Multi-Workplace Activity and Formal Organisation

Informal multi-workplace typically involved wage claims, like those by Sydney shinglers in August 1829 and Adelaide bricklayers in October 1846.[14] It extended to second-tier towns where unions were slower to form, examples including strikes for increased wages by carpenters and joiners in Maitland (September 1846) and Portland (April 1847).[15] Construction labourers sometimes joined these multi-workplace strikes, like those (over a currency switch/wage cut) in Sydney in December 1829 and in Melbourne (for a wage increase) a decade later.[16] On occasion, issues more typically associated with unions were pursued. In 1837 Hobart stonemasons petitioned government over competition from convict labour as did Maitland building operatives six years later.[17] In 1844 a group of Adelaide bricklayers disputed the *South Australian Register's* claim that work in the trade was 'plentiful' and 'remunerative'.[18] Similarly, in May 1848 plumbers, plasterers and glaziers met at the *Globe Inn*, Rundle Street, Adelaide to protest advertisements 'which might lead to the belief that there is a scarcity of hands.'[19]

Compared to workers in most other industries, informal organisation in the building trades rapidly transitioned into unions especially in larger towns. In Sydney general labourers too established a benefit society in the early 1840s which, while exceptional, was indicative that mutual insurance was important to many workers, not simply tradesmen.[20] Colonial tradesmen drew on centuries-old organisation and methods (Chapter 1) to establish unions and communicate with unions in other colonial towns and the UK. This included restricting trade entry to time-served journeymen, limiting apprentice numbers in workshops, imposing rules on demarcation (the scope of work covered by a trade) and work methods, and establishing a House-of-Call.[21] The House-of-Call was a conveniently located tavern serving as a meeting place/union office where employers were encouraged to hire members at the union-rate. Some, like the Adelaide Carpenters and Joiners Society (1846–51), also used its House-of-Call at the *Black Horse Inn*, Leigh St, to implement unilateral regulation. The selling point to masters was they would get fully-qualified workers, some unions indemnifying against poor workmanship.[22] However, as Dyster notes, industry volatility meant employers could easily bypass the House-of-Call during downturns.[23]

The pub/tavern also served as a recreational meeting place where traditions of annual feasts/dinners were held, reinforcing shared identity, aspirations and solidarity. In June 1836, 45 members of the Hobart Carpenters and Joiners Benefit Society sat down to dinner at the *Jolly Hatter's Inn* consisting of 'two enormous pieces of beef, two hams, turkeys, geese, ducks, fowl and several other substantial dishes . . . followed by two plain puddings of enormous size, moulded in imitation of Mount Wellington and Mount Nelson.'[24] This was followed by toasts with colonial whisky-punch and songs extolling pride in being free-born Britons, of liberty, freedom of the press, the prosperity of their adopted island home and the civilising effects of bodies like their own. While these statements seem ironic for a colony where half the population were ex/serving convicts, they reflected widely held sentiments repeated at union and political gatherings throughout the colonies.[25] Coming together in isolated settlements on a remote continent reinforced affinities and customary values along with determination to reject the stultifying subservience their 'betters' wished to replicate.

Another centuries-old function was the provision of friendly benefits covering accidents/illness and funerals.[26] Virtually all building trades unions pursued mutual insurance, some compensating for loss of tools through fire, theft or accident—then as now essential to earning a livelihood.[27] Mutual insurance, and slogans like 'united to help not combined to injure' weren't there just to cast unions in a positive light, although several sought sanction from the Governor as the Sydney Stonemasons Benefit Society did in 1828.[28] Mutual insurance sustained organisations and met important member needs. The first step towards recognition as a friendly society and protecting the union's funds was having its rules and regulations recognised by the Court of Quarter Sessions, as the Sydney Operative Joiners Society did in 1841.[29] Recognition was not automatic. The Sydney Plasterers were rebuffed two years later as too small to make mutual insurance viable when it lodged rules with the Register of Friendly Societies.[30] Registration didn't mean all rules could be enforced. The Carpenters and Joiners rules on loss of tools required claimants have an affidavit witnessed by a magistrate, but some magistrates refused to do this.[31]

Union-funded funeral processions/burials were lauded by newspapers, but economic downturns and building industry volatility challenged their capacity to maintain mutual insurance. In September 1843 Secretary James McEvoy gave notice the Society of Operative Bricklayers was withdrawing its funds from the Savings Bank of Sydney and holding a general meeting.[32] Four months later the *Sydney Record* reported the carpenters and bricklayers' societies had suffered considerable membership losses because many couldn't pay their weekly subscriptions. Unfinancial members couldn't access benefits. One union had accumulated funds of £300 but only 20 financial members.[33] In June 1845 the Friendly Society of Carpenters and Joiners dissolved—another union was formed within three months.[34]

Emigrant-plasterer George Kershaw's diary provides further insights. Kershaw joined the Sydney Plasterers Society, becoming its president in 1842 but when he fell ill it lacked funds to recompense him.[35] Kershaw's fate was probably not uncommon. Membership losses dried up funds even if the society didn't immediately collapse. Workers joined because they had done the same in the UK, believed unions would survive, and there were no alternatives aside from general friendly societies. Many early societies were too small to be actuarially sound. Unlike federated general friendly societies, like the Manchester Unity of Oddfellows, they had a finite number of contributors, many of who might suffer in a downturn, couldn't spread risk across an array of occupations or transfer benefits when members moved. Some staunch unionists like George Kershaw joined a general friendly society too, in an effort to safeguard his family but neither survived the 1840s depression.[36] Nonetheless, bodies like the Sydney Carpenters and Joiners Society were able to provide mutual insurance for five to ten years or longer as the NSW Friendly Society Register attests. In VDL deteriorating economic conditions in the 1840s undermined trade society-based mutual insurance.

Unions also kept strike-funds—a device dating from the 18th century.[37] Lis and Soly argue that from the 16th century unions favoured shop by shop strikes over multiple workplace strikes. This was both a response to legal measures suppressing strikes and because the growing division of labour created small and large employers, which suited targeting specific employers and playing some off against others.[38] Societies with strike-funds included the Sydney Carpenters and Joiners (1845–46), Sydney Stonemasons (1840–49) and Melbourne Stonemasons (1844–47). Funds could sustain longer strikes or, like the Sydney Carpenters in 1846, send some members to another town during a strike.[39] In 1847 Melbourne Carpenters reportedly 'had sufficient resources to maintain a strike for some time to come.'[40]

Unions used strike-funds or collections to support other unions. The *Sydney Morning Herald* noted the Stonemasons were assisting the Sydney

Carpenters in 1846.[41] A rare surviving union document demonstrates this was but a fraction of what was occurring. Records of an earlier Sydney carpenters' union detail payments made to at least 90 men on strike between August and mid-September 1846, funds subscribed by other trade societies and repayments made when the strike ended. Supporting unions included the journeymen tailors, sawyers, cabinetmakers, bakers, stonemasons and nailers—some refusing repayment of their donation.[42] Unions also used funds to publish newspaper notices justifying their actions and countering criticism by employers or others. In September 1846 the Sydney Carpenters' Executive Committee responded to a correspondent signing himself 'screwdriver', arguing they had a perfect right to strike for a fair wage comparable to other workers, given the cost of living, and carpenters' wages in Britain and Ireland. They argued employers had combined to screw down wages and in Britain 'to put on the screw is a byword for oppression.'[43]

Other methods included negotiating an increase backed by a strike-threat or unilateral regulation. In April 1840 Sydney Operative House Painters demanding eight shillings per-day resolved not to engage below the new rate (unilateral regulation). When several employers responded by advertising for painters, the society published its own notices, stating those needing painters:

> to execute their work in a proper workmanlike manner, either by contract or measurement, or at eight shillings per diem, which, in rate with other trades, is only a fair equivalent for their labour. If the public would favour the trade with any work, they may have it done in a superior style, on application to Mr Craig, *Rob Roy* Pitt-street.[44]

Society members also wrote a letter refuting the 'gulling' job advertisements of individual masters. In August the union thanked master builders and others for the 'liberal patronage' given to their House-of-Call now moved to John Collins' *Governor Macquarie* Pitt Street.[45]

On occasion disagreements were resolved amicably, some of which probably went unreported. In October 1846 Sydney master plasterers 'kindly agreed' to increased wages to cover rising provision costs.[46] In other cases, as with Melbourne journeymen carpenters in 1850, extended negotiations eventually failed leading to a strike.[47] However achieved, some agreements held for a year or more.

Two practices identified by the Webbs were important, the common rule (establishing a minimum set of wages and conditions applying to all employers) and unilateral regulation (rules requiring members to refuse to engage or work below union-set wages and conditions). Unilateral regulation had been used by European craft unions since the 16th century, with Lis and Soly arguing it was a response to legal measures to inhibit strikes by requiring workers to fulfil their contracts. This requirement became less effective when workers 'refused to sign a new contract or to offer their skills to other employers.'[48] It is arguable unilateral regulation imitated guild price-setting practices—still used by professional associations. In June 1835 journeymen carpenters in Sydney passed resolutions

> similar to those forming the principle of the Trades' Unions in England; viz. for regulating the rates of wages to be taken by them in future, for providing the means of supporting those losing employment, and for compelling refractory master carpenters to accede to their terms.[49]

The Australian urged government to investigate this 'unlawful combination' and for the Emigration Committee to obtain more labour to break it. Similarly in Melbourne in 1840 and again in 1846 various trades were 'forming themselves into Trade Societies for the better regulation of the scale of charges.'[50]

Unilateral regulation hinged on tightly controlling labour supply. Colonial unions were advantaged by their remoteness from alternative labour sources. Hostility to convict transportation and assisted-immigration also made sense, strengthening their capacity to implement unilateral regulation. In May 1841 Sydney joiners criticised an employer deputation to the Governor requesting the appointment of a recruiting agent to obtain building tradesmen in Britain. Refuting claims of a labour shortage, the union argued any advantage in reduced wages would soon be lost as masters undercut each other and, prefiguring Keynesianism, reduced spending amongst the 'working classes' would induce economic stagnation.[51]

Building Materials Manufacture

Overview

Manufacturing building materials including lime (by burning sea-shells), quarrying stone, brickmaking and timber-work (tree felling and sawing) was often small scale and conducted close to construction. Like construction, much building materials manufacturing was initially undertaken by government-engaged convicts like a group of New Norfolk sawyers repeatedly prosecuted for not completing their allotted tasks between January and March 1835.[52] After 1830 three trade-based groups were prominent in informal activity and forming unions—sawyers, brickmakers and cabinetmakers (Table 7.1). Brickmakers were often self-employed. There was a roughly even split between strikes and NSCA. While numbers are small, use of mass meetings, letters and petitions reflected the degree both trades formally organised. The most frequent issues in strikes were wages/remuneration followed by working hours, management behaviour, work methods, jobs and OHS. For NSCA management behaviour ranked highest followed by wages, jobs/employment and OHS (Table 7.2).

Informal Single Workplace Organisation

From the 1830s assigned-convict and free sawyers engaged in collective action including absconding like those at Berry and Wollstonecraft's Shoalhaven estate in early 1833 and men working for John Tunks, Parramatta in April and September 1835.[53] These groups may have escaped but two probationers working for Captain Robson at Port Sorell in 1844 were apprehended, complaining bitterly of being 'hard-worked' and given scanty rations at their trial.[54] Sawyers also struck work, like those who demanded wage increase from Thomas Watt (Port Philip District) in February 1838.[55] On Boxing Day 1837 three workers at Jackson and Addison's Hobart timberyard were sentenced to the treadmill for being absent and too 'celebratory' on Christmas day. Two assaulted a constable trying to arrest them.[56] Four years later 'free emigrants' at Spencer's timberyard York St, Launceston received one month with hard-labour for 'contumacious behaviour'.[57] In 1846 five passholder sawyers at Kangaroo Bottom near Hobart struck for an increase in their rates per-yard cut. Prosecuted for neglecting work, the case was dismissed because their employer (Hecksher) had previously agreed to pay more than was stipulated under probation regulations.[58]

Brickmakers, who typically worked in groups at particular sites like what is now Brickfields Park, Launceston, also took collective action. Like sawyers the earliest instances involved government-engaged convicts. After 1830, collective action involved assigned-convict and free brickmakers. In 1834 Thomas Agar, engaged in clay tempering, was charged with 'poisoning the minds of his fellow servants.' The case became enmeshed in competing claims of Agar and his Hobart master (Pendlebury) about who abused who and the provision of additional indulgences like a pair of shoes for better behaviour, highlighting ongoing bargaining between masters and their workers. Pendlebury's prosecution collapsed when it was revealed Agar had been lent by another master.[59] In 1840 the Campbelltown Bench imposed 36 lashes on two convicts refusing work and insulting their master T R Brennan Esq.[60] In another typical case free brickmakers working for Hunter Valley landholder John Brown were fined 10 shillings plus costs for refusing work after claiming the clay was unfit for purpose.[61]

Others producing building materials took collective action. In July 1835 four convict lime-burners working for Cleary and Davis near Hobart were prosecuted for demanding money.[62] In June 1850 timber-cutters workers engaged at Pine River (north of Brisbane) by John Beard successfully sued for their wages plus court costs after part of the load was lost in transit when the boat grounded.[63] There is little evidence of collective action amongst stonecutters/quarrymen until after 1850, probably reflecting the use of convicts in this task.

There were also 21 single workplace disputes involving cabinetmakers (including apprentices) in Sydney and Hobart, the earliest in 1821 though most occurred after 1835. Of these 13 involved convicts. There was also a protest over bedding and rations by convict carvers and framemakers in Hobart in 1839.[64]

Multi-Workplace Informal Organisation and Formal Organisation

Like construction, building materials was sensitive to economic conditions. In January 1835 Perth District sawyers petitioned the government to order timber giving them work.[65] In June 1845 Melbourne District sawyers combined to raise their wages allegedly to 14s per-day. Five years later they were petitioning the Governor about being undercut by timber imported from VDL. When this measure failed, 200 struck following a substantial cut to their wages.[66] The Melbourne Sawyers Society was probably involved.

From the late 1830s, sawyers formed unions in several colonies. In May 1839 the Hobart Town Sawyers Benefit Society was established, submitting its rules to the Chief Police Magistrate, and a month later petitioning the Governor in protest at convict competition.[67] The union operated a House-of-Call, initially the *Sawyers Arms* Murray St and from 1841 William Champion's *Jolly Hatters Inn* Melville St.[68] Thereafter, the society's activities became increasingly confined to mutual insurance like paying benefits to member's widows, even widening its membership to remain viable.[69] Sydney District sawyers established a union in 1840, striking twice over wages in three months.[70] Along with providing mutual insurance, the society continued to take industrial action, most notably in July 1847 which may have precipitated its collapse.[71] The Melbourne Sawyers Society (established 1841) also combined mutual insurance with wage bargaining. During a strike at Kemmis & Co, six members were charged with unlawful combination but discharged when the 'round robin' they had signed (see Chapter 5) went missing from documents tended in court. The Bench warned the missing document saved them a year's gaol and the society should be more cautious in future.[72] Two strikers (Connell and Dove) refused to return to work and forfeited their wages for breaching the *Master and Servant Act*.[73] This union seems to have been short-lived, but the Melbourne Sawyers Society (1847–55) lasted longer, registering under the Friendly Societies Act.[74]

Brickmakers also took informal multi-workplace action, including a joint strike over wages with shinglers in Sydney in April 1830 and negotiating improved wages a decade later.[75] In December 1834 Hobart brickmakers petitioned against public auctions of convict-produced bricks, part of Governor Arthur's efforts to suppress free-labour combinations.[76] By 1841 Melbourne brickmakers formed a society with Charles Latrobe (Port Philip District Superintendent and later Governor of Victoria) as their patron. Demonstrating the importance of hotels as union meeting places, a deputation asked the Melbourne Police Magistrate (Major St John) not be turned out from *Grant's Bird in Hand* Hotel for disorderly behaviour.[77] In 1845 Melbourne brickmakers combined to increase wages and Sydney brickmakers formed a union at the *Victoria Inn* Parramatta Road which registered as a friendly society and survived until at least 1849.[78]

Sydney cabinetmakers formed a trade society (1833–46) which established a House-of-Call and was relatively successful in regulating wages. In 1839 it became involved in a dispute over piecework and use of the London book of prices as reference point. An aggrieved journeyman complained employers commonly stated piecework in misleading terms because unlike much British furniture, colonial furniture was made solid and didn't use veneers.[79] In the other major cabinetmaking centre, Hobart, convict competition made the formation of a stand-alone cabinetmakers union more difficult, leading to allied bodies with carpenters (including a House-of-Call in 1833 and 1843). Import competition was a more pressing issue in Sydney. During the early 1840s, depression master and journeymen cabinetmakers organised public meetings and a joint-petition calling for a 15% duty on imported furniture.[80]

Like building unions, brickmakers, sawyers and cabinetmakers societies pursued a mixture of mutual insurance, industrial action and political agitation. In VDL convict competition inhibited unions. In South Australia limited timber resources probably had the same effect on sawyers and cabinetmakers.

Conclusion

As in manufacturing (Chapter 8) once free tradesmen in construction and building materials reached barely sufficient numbers in major towns, there was a fairly rapid translation into unions. These small bodies remained vulnerable to business-cycle shifts and to VDL convict competition. Their organisation and methods mirrored those in the UK with some local adaptations. Convicts undertook most construction labouring in NSW and VDL. This and succeeding waves of emigrants made it difficult for labourers to organise, although one society was formed in Sydney. This examination has focused on aspects central to the purposes of the book. There is scope for further research on pre-goldrush trade societies drawing on a more forensic exploration of sources (like government and court records, local and genealogical histories, business records and diaries) which may provide further insights into their activities, the origin and fate of officials, continuity and other questions. The next chapter examines informal and formal organisation in manufacturing. To avoid repetition, parallels with building unions are identified along with evidence on the rules and governing structures of trade societies.

Notes

1 They were adversely affected by the labour market turmoil associated with the Victorian gold rushes but were soon replaced by longer lived bodies.
2 *Port Philip Patriot* 4 August 1842.

3 *South Australian Register* 21 November 1840.
4 *Cornwall Chronicle* 13 June 1836.
5 Sydney Progressive Society of Carpenters and Joiners 1849–1858, Account Book, Mitchell Library.
6 *Hobart Town Courier* Friday 8 March 1833.
7 *Murrays Review* 27 October 1843.
8 *Southern Australian* 3 April 1839; Port Philip Herald 9 July 1841; *Tasmanian News* 1 October 1885.
9 *Sydney Monitor* 8 April 1840.
10 AOWA CSO 1956.
11 *The Australian* 11 October 1844.
12 *Sydney Gazette* 13 December 1834.
13 *South Australian Register* 30 October 1847.
14 *Sydney Monitor* 1 August 1829, 4 and *Adelaide Observer* 3 October 1846.
15 *Maitland Mercury* 9 September 1846 and *Port Philip Patriot* 15 April 1847.
16 *The Australian* 12 December 1829 and *The Colonist* 2 November 1839.
17 TAHO CSO 22/62/1416; *Trumpeter* 17 March 1837 and *Australasian Chronicle* 27 December 1843.
18 *Adelaide Observer* 15 June 1844.
19 *South Australian Register* 24 May 1848.
20 *Sydney Morning Herald* 28 September 1843.
21 Lis, C. and Soly, H. (1994) An Irresistible Phalanx: Journeymen Associations in Western Europe, 1300–1800, *International Review of Social History*, 39(Supplement):18–19.
22 See for example the Sydney carpenters and joiners (1845–1846), *Sydney Morning Herald* 27 September 1845.
23 Dyster, B. (1989) *Servant and Master: Building and Running the Grand Houses of Sydney 1788–1850*, University of New South Wales Press, Sydney, 127.
24 *Cornwall Chronicle* 13 June 1835.
25 See for example *Australasian Chronicle* 18 February 1841.
26 Materne, J. (1994) Chapel Members in the Workplace: Tension and Teamwork in the Printing Trades in the Seventeenth and Eighteenth Centuries, *International Review of Social History*, 39(Supplement):62–65.
27 *Australasian Chronicle*13 December 1842.
28 *The Australian* 27 June 1828.
29 *Sydney Gazette* 25 November 1841.
30 Dyster, B. (1989) *Servant and Master*, 126–127 and Register of Documents Lodged with the NSW Register of Friendly Societies.
31 Dyster, B. (1989) *Servant and Master*, 127.
32 *Sydney Morning Herald* 2 September 1843.
33 *Sydney Record* 27 January 1844.
34 *Sydney Morning Herald* 7 June 1845.
35 Dyster, B. (1989) *Servant and Master*, 126–127.
36 I am profoundly indebted to Barrier Dyster for this information and other insights critical to this book.
37 Lis, C. and Soly, H. eds. (1994) An Irresistible Phalanx, 11–52.
38 Lis, C. and Soly, H. (1994) An Irresistible Phalanx, 32–33.
39 *Citizen* 29 August 1846.
40 *Port Philip Patriot* 21 January 1847.
41 *Sydney Morning Herald* 3 September 1846.
42 Sydney Progressive Society of Carpenters and Joiners 1849–1858, Accounts Book, Mitchell Library.
43 *Sydney Morning Herald* 5 September 1846.
44 See for example *Sydney Herald* 8 May 1840.

45 *Sydney Gazette* 25 April 1840 and *Sydney Herald* 12 August 1840.
46 *Sydney Morning Herald* 29 October 1846.
47 *The Argus* 25 September 1850; *Sydney Morning Herald* 5 October 1850.
48 Lis, C. and Soly, H. (1994) An Irresistible Phalanx, 32–33.
49 *The Australian* 19 June 1835.
50 *Sydney Morning Herald* 19 November 1846.
51 *Sydney Monitor* 1 May 1840.
52 LC375–1–1 New Norfolk 31 January, 2 and 9 March 1835.
53 *Sydney Gazette* 2 March 1833 and 25 April 1835; and *Sydney Monitor* 12 September 1835.
54 *Cornwall Chronicle* 18 September 1844.
55 Historical Records of Victoria IV Melbourne Court Registry 14 February 1838.
56 *Colonial Times* 2 January 1838.
57 *Cornwall Chronicle* 16 October 1841.
58 *Colonial Times* 15 May 1846.
59 *Colonial Times* 2 September 1834.
60 *Sydney Monitor* 13 April 1840.
61 *Maitland Mercury* 3 June 1848.
62 *Colonial Times* 14 July 1835.
63 *Moreton Bay Courier* 15 June 1850.
64 *Colonial Times* 19 November 1839.
65 AOWA CSO 37/47 14 January 1835.
66 *Port Philip Patriot* 30 June 1845; *Melbourne Daily News* 17 October 1850; *Argus* 27 November 1850.
67 TAHO CSO 5/201/462 and 5/201/4879.
68 *Colonial Times* 14 September 1841.
69 *Colonial Times* 10 February 1846.
70 *Sydney Herald* 10 April 1840.
71 *Sydney Morning Herald* 3 July 1847.
72 *Port Philip Patriot* 3 and 10 June 1841.
73 *Port Philip Herald* 15 June 1841.
74 In 1849 a member was tried for assaulting another member during a meeting. *Argus* 16 February 1849.
75 *Sydney Gazette* 29 April 1830.
76 TAHO CSO 1/774/16539; *Colonist* 24 February 1835.
77 *Port Philip Gazette* 8 December 1841.
78 *Port Philip Patriot* 7 July 1845 and Index to Register of Documents Lodged with the NSW Register of Friendly Societies.
79 *Sydney Herald* 4 and 9 September 1839.
80 *Sydney Morning Herald* 26 January 1843.

8   Organisation in Manufacturing and Related Trades

Introduction

Prior to 1810 manufactured goods were largely imported apart from pro-cessing food and beverages and building materials (see last chapter). By the 1820s manufacturing included breweries, distilleries, flour mills, tanneries, printing, foundries, soap and candle making, wool-cloth, tailoring, boot and hat-making. Maritime activities encouraged shipbuilding, ship-repair and associated manufacturing including rope, sails, mast-blocks and bar-rels to store whale-oil. In succeeding decades manufacturing diversified to include cooperages, fellmongering, potteries, dyers, coachmakers, furri-ers, engineering, tobacco/snuff, textiles and sugar refining. Though small in scale, manufacturing became increasingly important economically and employment-wise.[1]

Initially mills for grinding grains were wind-powered (examples survive in Brisbane, Launceston and Oatlands) or water-powered especially in VDL where climate and topography more closely resembled Britain (impressive examples survive in Richmond, Carrick and Launceston). Increasing use was made of steam-powered mills. A rare surviving beam-engine at the Syd-ney Powerhouse Museum was imported for a Southern Highlands mill in the 1830s. Milling and other operations required engineering and foundries to service and maintain machinery. By the 1840s small engineering works were producing machinery including steam engines. Growing population, remoteness and availability of raw materials encouraged import replace-ment in areas like clothing, shoes and other apparel. Production occurred in small workshops run by a master tradesmen (commonly also a sales outlet) employing journeymen (initially convicts living on the premises) in major towns. In many respects colonial manufacturing reflected a model fast receding in Britain and some areas faced competition from mass-produced imports. There were also the beginnings of mechanised production, taking advantage of local raw materials, including woollen-cloth manufacturers in Sydney, Newcastle (Stockton) in NSW and other colonies using imported machinery.[2]

Overview of Organisation

Table 8.1 summarises organisation and collective action in manufacturing, with only one instance prior to 1821, reflecting government dominance of manufacturing. There were nine instances of collective action by government-employed convicts (blacksmiths, nailers, shipwrights, coopers and flour millers) all but one—mass absconding from blacksmiths' gang on Goat Island in 1839—being before 1821.[3] Overall there is evidence of 220 instances of organisation, 105 strikes and 90 NSCA. There were no notable peaks of action apart from 1840. As with building, the craft base of much manufacturing assisted a rapid transition to formal organisation in the 1830s and strong association between collective action and unions. Unlike the rural and maritime industries, there were few instances of group absconding and worker-initiated court actions (three concerning OHS—all lost—and three over unpaid wages with one win/two losses). More frequent use of petitions, letters to the press/advertisements and mass meetings/marches than industries previously examined is indicative of greater formal organisation. Workers taking collective action were also dragged before courts less frequently. By a range of measures, including numbers of workers involved and capacity to sustain organisation, manufacturing was a significant area of worker mobilisation prior to 1851.

Hours and wages ranked highest in terms of strikes followed by working conditions while working conditions ranked highest for NSCA followed by wages, jobs/employment, health and safety and hours (Table 8.2).

Informal Action Confined to a Single Workplace

Prior to 1830 assigned-convicts accounted for most informal collective action. In 1821 Benjamin Helsten and 12 others each received 25 lashes for refusing to work before 6 am (the starting time for government-convicts) at Simeon Lord's clothing factory at Botany.[4] In December 1825 a George St master baker (Carmichael) prosecuted several men for neglecting work, one receiving 60 lashes for 'indecorous references' to Carmichael's family. Two years later Carmichael was again before the courts charging men with unauthorised absence.[5] In VDL this type of conflict continued well into the 1840s. In late March 1848 a Campbell Town master, William Tarrant, charged three of his shoemakers with neglect. Two, John Rusden and Charles Wittick, were acquitted. In what may have been revenge and certainly indicative of a breakdown in relations, they were prosecuted for absence on a Friday night two weeks later and sentenced to one month hard-labour.[6]

While most disputes involved journeymen, others took action. Three convicts working for Sydney brewer J T Hughes were charged with absenting themselves in November 1834.[7] In 1837 John Maynes assigned to a Sydney soap-boiler (Aspinall) received 50 lashes for insolence, refusing work and encouraging other servants to misbehave.[8] Some employers were repeatedly

Table 8.1 Summary of Organisation and Activity in Manufacturing 1788–1850

Nature of activity	1788–1800	1801–10	1811–20	1821–30	1831–40	1841–50	Total	Percentages
Clothing, Footwear and Textiles								
All Organisation	1			23	95	101	220	
Formal Organisation				1	24	40		
Involvement	4			84	521	644	1253	
Adjusted Involvement*	4			110	612	988	1714	
Strikes				17	42	46	105	53.8
NSCA	1			7	44	38	90	46.2
Total				24	86	84	195	
Absconding					14	6	6	
House-of-Call					5	9	11	
Court actions					5	2	3	
Petitions					6	4	7	
Deputations				1	1	1	1	
Press Letters					18	42	46	
Mass meetings					2	1	8	
Marches						2	2	
Bans					1	3	2	
Sabotage					3	1	4	

* Median membership added to zero reporting organisations

Table 8.2 Strikes and NSCA by Issue in Manufacturing 1788–1850

Nature of activity	1788–1800	1801–10	1811–20	1821–30	1831–40	1841–50	Total*	Percentage*
Strikes								
Wages/remuneration				4	13	19	36	34.3
Working conditions				2	10	9	21	20
Management behaviour					4	1	5	3.8
Hours of work				10	23	24	57	54.3
Jobs/employment					2	5	7	6.7
Health & safety					1	1	2	1.9
Work methods				1	1	2	4	3.8
Unionism				1			1	0.9
Unknown				1		2	3	2.9
NSCA								
Wages/remuneration				1	9	18	28	31.1
Working conditions	1			2	38	13	54	60
Management behaviour					3	3	6	6.7
Hours of work					3	3	6	6.7
Jobs/employment					9	4	13	14.4
Health & safety				2	5	1	8	8.9
Work methods					2	1	3	3.3
Unionism						1	1	1.1
Legislation					1		1	1.1
Unknown						1	1	1.1

* Exceeds totals 105 strikes and 90 NSCA and 100% because of multiple issue strikes/NSCA

before the courts. In June 1835 Peter Degraves charged five assigned-servants with neglecting duty at his Hobart brewery.[9] This seemed to spark further unrest amongst brewery workers resulting in 15 collective disputes and numerous court cases over the next nine years. Degraves was atypical in having several manufacturing interests including shipbuilding. He was not alone in resorting to the courts on multiple occasions, reflecting ongoing struggles in particular workplaces (Chapter 2).

Free workers also took collective action. In 1824, coopers working for Icely and Hindson Macquarie St Sydney were remanded to stand trial for combination and conspiracy after demanding increased wages and allowances.[10] Free workers took informal collective action even after unions were established. The *Sydney Examiner* and venerable *Sydney Gazette* both failed during the 1842 downturn and their journeymen sought unpaid wages. The *Gazette* printers struck while those at the *Examiner* took court action—neither succeeded.[11] Informal single-workplace action remained the norm for non-craft workers, and for craft workers in smaller towns. In 1844 nine workers at Mark Riddel-Thompkin's Windsor flour mill successfully sued for unpaid wages.[12] In February 1846 three tobacco twisters at Walthall's West Maitland tobacco factory were imprisoned for a month for trying to persuade (offering free accommodation and food) another worker Rees Jones to join a strike. The other strikers escaped with a reprimand.[13]

Indentured non-European workers also combined. In early 1838, 15 Indian labourers absconded from William Abercrombie's Glenmore Distillery in Woolloomooloo. Apprehended and tried, they complained of being starved, beaten and receiving neither clothing nor wages in breach of their agreement. They were told to resume work and bring their complaints before the courts.[14] When two labourers did this, the Bench dismissed the case, accepting Abercrombie's argument that the agreement required payment and clothing provision on an annual not six-month basis, and ignoring testimony of beatings altogether.[15]

Multi-Workplace Informal Collective Action and Formal Organisation

While few unions survived over five years duration, this varied by trade, reflecting differences in labour market conditions, competition amongst employers and capacity to organise. Journeymen bakers were amongst the first to establish societies but more so than others their unions were short-lived even in large and prosperous towns. This pattern continued long after 1850. In Sydney a society and House-of-Call was established at the *Robin Hood* hotel in June 1836 with further bodies being formed in November 1840, November 1844, August 1846, July 1849 and December 1850. Only two (established in 1840 and 1846) are known to have survived over a year. They were also the only ones to strike over wages, the first opposing a wage cut in 1841.[16]

While bakers were especially susceptible, regular churning of unions only slowly declined over the course of the 19th century. Early unions were small and often overwhelmed by circumstances. Emigrant-mechanics brought strategies and organisational techniques from Europe and their accoutrements, including membership cards and testamurs. The Sydney Compositor's Society's membership cards were lauded as one of the 'neatest specimens of engraving we have witnessed in the colony.'[17] Detailed record keeping and support for other trades societies should also be recalled in this regard (Chapter 7).

Mutual Insurance, Jobs/Employment and the House-of-Call

As in building, manufacturing unions pursued mutual insurance and operated a House-of-Call. Mutual insurance was used in virtually all trades including bakers (in Hobart [established 1834], Sydney [1840–41, 1846–47, 1850–51]); blacksmiths (Sydney 1840); bootmakers (Sydney [1831], Hobart [1843, 1847] and Melbourne [1846]); butchers (Sydney [1851 but possibly earlier], Hobart [1844]); cabinetmakers (Sydney [1833]); coachmakers (Sydney [1837], Hobart [1839, 1843]); coopers (Sydney [1837]); curriers, fellmongers et al. (Sydney [1833, 1836], Hobart [1848], Melbourne [1847]); engineering/metal trades (Sydney [1840, 1845]); printers (Sydney [1835], Hobart [1829], Launceston [1849], Melbourne [1841, 1844]); shipwrights (Sydney [1830], Hobart [1847]); and tailors (Sydney [1835, 1840], Hobart [1833, 1842, 1846], Melbourne [1845, 1850]). Some, if not most, sought registration as a friendly society before the Court of Quarter Sessions, one of the earliest being the United Friends Benefit Society of Shipwrights in 1831.[18] Others include the Sydney Millwrights and Engineers Benevolent Society in 1847 and the Melbourne Operative Cordwainers in 1849.[19] Safeguarding union funds in a savings bank account was important as the Melbourne Cordwainers were all too aware, losing over £40 when its room at the *Farmers Hotel* in Collins Lane was burgled in 1847.[20]

Mutual insurance helped protect members from the vagaries of work, including sickness/illness/accident, unemployment and loss of tools. Rule 21 of the Sydney Compositors' Society entitled members to between 10/6 and 11/6 weekly (depending on when they joined) if unemployed not through neglect or drunkenness but being 'tyrannically discharged.' Rule 22 required members to refer grievances to the Committee of Management before resigning their job.[21] The rules of the Port Philip Printers Benefit Society established a decade later provided 12 to 15 shillings per week for legitimate cases of distress (sickness, unemployment) and a death benefit of £5 paid to the widow.[22] The paucity of union records makes it difficult to assess the effectiveness of these activities. As in building, prolonged unemployment could lead to exclusion from the society and its benefits. Some societies gave opportunities for lapsed-members to become financial again, as the Sydney Coachmakers did in 1841.[23] Periodic collapse of societies also deprived members of benefits. Those announcing their demise, like the Sydney Millwrights and Engineers Benevolent Society, were exceptional.[24] On a more positive note, even the tiny Launceston Printers Benefit Society survived over six years, although it relied on public support in 1850.[25] The Melbourne *Argus* was impressed by Operative Cordwainers Friendly Society's (1846–55) capacity to provide physicians for sick members and organise funerals. In 1846 it provided eight weeks' medical assistance and a dignified funeral for one member.[26] Two years later similar support was afforded John King, a young VDL-born shoemaker, with 200 journeymen and several masters attending his funeral.[27]

Unions operated a House-of-Call in many trades including bakers (Sydney [1836, 1850–51], Hobart [1840]), bootmakers (Hobart [1847]); butchers (Hobart, 1844); engineers (Sydney, 1840); printers (Sydney, 1835); and tailors (Sydney [1847], Hobart [1846], Adelaide [1839], Melbourne [1845, 1850]).[28] The Sydney Society of Engineers, Millwrights, Founders and Smiths (1840) advertised a register of qualified jobless workmen was kept by the secretary at its House-of-Call which prospective employers could inspect.[29] Reinforcing the advantages of hiring at union-regulated wages, the Hobart Journeymen Tailors Benefit Society (1846–52) amongst others indemnified masters against poor workmanship.[30] Promoting jobs/employment was an objective for most societies including bakers (Sydney [1836, 1840, 1849]); blacksmiths (Sydney [1837], Adelaide [1846], Hobart [1837]); bootmakers (Sydney [1840], Hobart [1837, 1847]); butchers (Adelaide [1848]); coopers (Sydney [1837]); engineers and other metal trades (Sydney [1840]); fellmongers and woolsorters (Sydney [1849]); printers (Sydney [1835]; Hobart [1848]); saddlers (Melbourne [1847]); tailors (Sydney [1840]; Adelaide [1850], Hobart [1838], Melbourne [1845,1850]); wheelwrights (Adelaide [1846]); and wool-staplers (Sydney [1845, 1847]). With few exceptions, like printers, trades attempted to establish a House-of-Call at least once. The House-of-Call was also used to regulate wages in conjunction with unilateral regulation, the common rule, strikes and efforts at collective bargaining. The House-of-Call was also one of several measures used to ensure only duly-apprenticed tradesmen were employed.

Other measures to protect jobs included political agitation, countering claims of labour shortages, and on occasion trying to change conditions of employment. In November 1839 Sydney shipwrights struck for a wage increase and better job security.[31]

Wages, Unilateral Regulation and the Common Rule

The vast majority of societies sought to regulate wages including bakers (Sydney [1840, 1846]); blacksmiths (Sydney [1837, Melbourne [1847]], Hobart [1837, 1847], Melbourne [1847]); bootmakers (Sydney [1831, 1840], Adelaide [1846], Melbourne [1843, 1846]); butchers (Melbourne, 1850); coachmakers (Hobart [1843]); coopers (Sydney [1837], Hobart

[1836]); nailers (Sydney[1846]); printers (Sydney [1835], Adelaide [1850]); saddlers (Melbourne [1847]); tailors (Sydney [1840], Adelaide [1850], Hobart [1846], Melbourne [1840, 1845, 1850]) and wheelwrights (Melbourne [1847]). As in building, trade societies maintained strike-funds including the bakers, nailers and tailors in Sydney and tailors in both Melbourne and Hobart.

An important goal was enforcing uniform rates across all workshops in a town/region, expressed as daily/hourly rate—the common rule—to prevent undercutting. Piecework wasn't favoured—a stance that strengthened during the 19th century—though it was common in bootmaking and tailoring. In these trades establishing a uniform rate meant also setting payment for tasks (linked to prices of the final product) usually drawing on UK models. In 1846 the Adelaide Tailors' Society disputed the time to make garments based on London-standards.[32] As elsewhere, attempts to establish uniform rates predated unions—illustrated by a strike by printers and other trades in Sydney in December 1829.[33] Nonetheless, the common rule was central to union regulation of wages with unions repeatedly advocating its benefits to masters in terms of limiting competition and retaining better workmen. Adelaide journeymen tailors' president (Palmer) told a meeting at the *Norfolk Arms* Hotel Rundle St 'a common rate of wages would protect the masters as much it would the men.'[34]

Behaviour consistent with unilateral regulation also predated unions. In January 1834 *Sydney Herald* printers left their job rather than accept a wage cut—a year before the compositor's society was formed.[35] The Sydney Tailors Benefit Society (1835–38) used unilateral regulation, a journeyman charged with absconding stating he was simply adhering to a trade regulation.[36] Its successor, the Phoenix Benefit Society of Tailors, fined members hiring to an employer without its permission.[37] The Hobart Journeymen Tailors' Benefit Society (1846–52) too resisted attempts by two employers (Roberts and Lightfoot) to cut rates in 1846 and 1847 respectively and regulated wages until 1852.[38] Displaying inter-colonial solidarity, it refused to supply strike-breakers to a Melbourne master in 1846.[39] Unilateral regulation relied on 100% unionisation and was especially vital for those like the Hobart Tailors threatened by convict competition. Shipwrights at Andrew Summerbell's Sydney shipyard struck in December 1840 when a newly hired foreman (Patterson) refused to join the union.[40] The Melbourne Journeymen Tailors Society (1845–47) took action against employers undermining its regulated wages as did the Adelaide Printer's Society. The *South Australian's* printers gave their notice when the proprietor tried to cut wages—they won.[41]

To advance wages societies usually made demands, backed by a strike-threat rather than resigning. Whether the society was pursuing an increase, a common rate or both is sometimes unclear, especially in trades where piecework prevailed. Societies often justified their actions through newspaper letters/advertisements. In October 1831 Edward Gregory, representing the Working Boot and Shoemakers of Sydney Friendly Society, countered claims by employer Henry Sloman.[42] Sloman's ongoing resistance to uniform rates led to strikes (April 1840 and January 1841) by members of the reformed union (Society of Operative Cordwainers).[43] During the second strike, Sloman had a picket cockatoo (lookout) named Palmer arrested, but with union support Palmer prosecuted Sloman for false imprisonment and was awarded substantial damages of £25.[44] Other societies publishing newspaper refutations of employer claims included Sydney Coopers in 1837, Adelaide Journeymen Tailors (1846) and Melbourne Journeymen Saddlers (1847).[45] During prolonged confrontations, like strikes by tailors in Sydney in 1840 and Hobart in 1846, an extended string of competing claims in newspapers was common. Both sides tried to manipulate labour market conditions with Adelaide master-tailors placing job advertisements to encourage emigrants after the Adelaide Journeymen Tailors Society won a wage increase in mid-1846.

Town/region-wide wage demands and strikes coincided with periods of inflation/labour demand like 1840. Sometimes masters readily conceded as was the case with the Melbourne journeymen tailors' claim for uniform rates and no outwork/taking work home in 1845.[46] However, strikes seem more common. The Sydney Phoenix Benefit Society of Tailors struck twice for increased wages in January 1840 and July 1840. The second was prolonged, with the union publishing detailed cost-of-living and itemised clothing prices to bolster its case. In September around 100 men were still out, straining union-resources, notwithstanding a strike-fund.[47] Prolonged strikes could also bankrupt individual members. When Charles Brown came before the Insolvent Debtors Court, the presiding judge (Stephen) grilled him, determined to punish any journeyman made insolvent through striking. Brown escaped Stephen's wrath because he had earned comparable money by jobbing (self-employment) during the strike and had already offered to partially pay his debts. Much of Brown's debt (£30 of £50) was for passage to the colony being repaid in weekly instalments to his employer (Melzier). Brown was discharged on undertaking to repay his other creditors five shillings per week.[48] This case affords a rare insight into the financial impact of prolonged strikes (especially where journeymen were indebted for passage costs) and punitive judicial views on strikes.

Lengthy strikes were exceptional as were two or more multi-workplace strikes in the same year. The Melbourne Operative Cordwainers Friendly Society struck twice over wages in May and December 1846. Outraged, the *South Australian Register* castigated Melbourne as 'chiefly remarkable for a species of trades-union combination' that raised wages to ruinous levels and put restrictions on masters that must be resisted.[49] During downturns strikes commonly targeted the first employer to introduce cuts to avoid a more costly general action. This wasn't always possible. In 1843 the Melbourne Journeymen Shoemakers Trade Society struck against a wage cut, lost and the union collapsed.[50]

Apprenticeship, Skill and Control of the Trade

Craft control was the raison d'être for trade societies, including maintaining admission through apprenticeship. The Sydney Wool-staplers' Society established in 1845 aimed to ensure members served a seven-year apprenticeship.[51] Another device was limiting the number of apprentices any master could engage—something originally stipulated by medieval guilds to restrict competition.[52] As the division of labour grew, masters had less interest in restricting access to cheaper/additional labour. In contrast, journeymen were concerned to maximise their bargaining power by fixing the ratio of apprentices per workplace or the ratio of apprentices to journeymen in larger workplaces.

In 1840 Sydney compositors were involved in a dispute over apprentice numbers as were their Launceston counterparts a decade later.[53] Similarly, in April 1846 Melbourne master Michael McNamara's tailors struck when he breached the union's rule of one apprentice per workshop. Unable to get replacements, McNamara prosecuted four journeymen. This failed, the union's legal counsel mounting a successful technical challenge that the men were back at work when charges were laid.[54] Aggrieved, McNamara hired six VDL journeymen. When they arrived at Port Melbourne, pickets endeavoured to persuade them not to proceed. They also debated throwing McNamara—there to meet his recruits—off the pier. McNamara charged five journeymen (Gurney, Rourke, Higgins, Hornblower and Johnstone) with putting him in bodily fear. They were bound over to keep the peace at £20 plus two sureties of £10 each and 10/6 for court costs. The society's ability to meet these costs was testament to its resources, while large numbers of journeymen and masters attending court was indicative of the dispute's wider implications.[55] McNamara's court victory proved pyrrhic. Within a week he charged two of his newly arrived journeymen (John Gould and John Wall) with absconding.[56] The men may have felt misled or had second thoughts. Trade societies commonly published advertisements in other colonies' newspapers warning of a strike in progress. Melbourne and Adelaide societies targeted VDL newspapers because less favourable conditions there encouraged a steady drift of workers to the mainland.

Craft controls also excluded other workers from tasks reserved for the trade and safeguarded trade knowledge. At a meeting of the Port Philip Journeymen Printers Benefit Society in 1841, there was a call to expel any member revealing trade secrets.[57] Another perceived threat was competition from women in trades like tailoring. In 1850 Adelaide tailors decried competition from needlewomen. In April 1846 their Melbourne counterparts struck when a master engaged women to make vests. A month later Melbourne dressmakers clubbed together, striking for increased wages.[58]

By the 1840s UK tailors were increasingly threatened by mass-produced clothing. This helps explain why tailors were especially numerous in the colonies. However, the colonies were at best a temporary sanctuary, with growing clothing imports (some known as slops) pressuring local masters. Some masters tried cutting costs. Others saw advantages in uniform costs with Melbourne journeymen claiming several helped form their union.[59] Craft-based organisation of tailors and bootmakers was threatened by imports and mechanised production. Efforts to form societies in already endangered-trades were exceptional and short-lived. The Sydney Society of Weavers, Spinners and Warpers (established 1843) may have been a case in point, although a letter attacking power-looms from 'the Handloom Weavers of Sydney' in June 1850 indicates it could have survived seven years.[60]

Although apprentices were excluded from societies until they qualified, this didn't prevent collective dissent. In November 1828, 12 apprentices received 10 days' solitary confinement for absenting themselves to attend a boxing match.[61] In October 1840 two apprentices complained their Sydney master (Vercoe) wasn't teaching them the trade and he countered with a charge of absconding.[62] In 1848 several apprentices at *The Australian* refused to work at night unless they were paid like journeymen.[63]

Hours of Work, Subcontracting and Sweating

Notwithstanding commonalities just described, there were trade differences regarding issues, campaigns and methods. Prior to the pioneering eight-hour crusade in 1855–56, demands for shorter hours were uncommon, perhaps indicating that unlike the United States, trades had adopted UK shorter hour arrangements.[64] In June 1847 Melbourne saddlers struck for increased wages and one less hour per-day.[65] However, the major exception was journeymen bakers and butchers where, as in the UK, hours were an important issue. Most worked in small establishments, where working-time was tied to trading hours. Journeymen bakers began agitating against extended hours due to the British/early colonial practice of using bakers' ovens to cook family roasts on Sunday. In December 1844 journeymen petitioned the NSW Legislative Council for a law prohibiting bakehouses cooking dinners on Sunday. Reverend Dr Lang supported legislation stopping a 'flagrant breach' of the Sabbath, but his motion was defeated by a large majority.[66] In March 1847 journeymen bakers petitioned the Melbourne Town Council to pass an ordinance banning Sunday baking but this too failed.[67] Journeymen bakers continued to agitate for shorter hours—now framed in general terms.[68]

As in Britain, bakers' long hours were seen as health-impairing. In 1849 the *Sydney Morning Herald* summarised a report by William Guy in the *Journal of Public Health*:

> From an authentic statistical table, it appears that even compared with tailors (whose trade is unwholesome) the bakers lose . . . a quarter of a year of life each year! There are few old or middle-aged men amongst them. Few of them enjoy robust health . . . They were peculiarly liable

to disease of the chest, and spitting of blood–arising from long hours & work, great muscular efforts, exposure to the heat, the inhalation of particles of flour etc. The author advocates the abolition of night work, which is peculiarly injurious to health . . . one which now exacts a practical answer at the hands of the public and the legislature: Is there to be free trade in health and life, as well as in food and clothing![69]

Guy's argument that markets shouldn't be permitted to trade off life and advocacy of regulatory intervention was prescient of debates over working hours/labour standards that continue to the present.

Competition between bakehouses contributed to long hours and also made it difficult for journeymen to improve wages. As a result, journeymen sought or supported agreements amongst masters fixing bread prices in return for agreed wages, with examples occurring in Hobart (1834), Launceston (1840) and Melbourne (1840). In the Melbourne case several journeymen and masters were charged with entering into an unlawful combination to raise wages and the price of bread after a master (Taylor) who refused to join was threatened. Given the repeal of the 1799/1800 combination acts in 1824, the charges were apparently laid under a wage combination statute of Edward VI (1547–53). At the trial before the Court of Quarter Sessions, the masters' leader William Overton was sentenced to one month gaol and fined £100, while the journeymen's leader John Henderson received 14 days and a fine of £50. Several other conspirators were fined £5 and two acquitted. John May, another journeyman actively involved, escaped apprehension by leaving the colony. Tried upon his return, May was discharged, the Bench determining the 'ends of justice were sufficiently attained'.[70]

Journeymen butchers were in a similar position to bakers when it came to hours and doing price/wage-fixing deals. Melbourne journeymen butchers agitated over hours in May 1847.[71] These efforts at price/wage combinations became more frequent after 1850. Other health and hours-related concerns were evident in tailoring, including opposition to outwork. In 1850 Adelaide tailors resolved work should be carried out in employers' 'well-ventilated premises' at wage rates and set hours to prevent 'sweating'. As with long hours amongst bakers and butchers, opposition to sweated labour in the clothing, boot and other trades would grow in succeeding decades.[72]

Public Demonstrations and Political Agitation

Trade societies were also politically active, which continued after 1850. It was a logical response to the prominence of the state in colonial economies and raises wider questions about homogeneity in union development.[73] Like their 18th century predecessors, societies used petitions to seek political remedies.[74] Less supplicating devices like deputations, marches and public meetings were used and became dominant in the decades after 1851.

Convict competition was a key target of political protest. In 1834 Hobart tailors petitioned against convict assignment and between 1836 and 1848 they were joined by other Hobart trades including coopers, bootmakers, bakers and printers.[75] In Sydney the Compositors' Society petitioned twice in 1840, the second after the *Sydney Herald* tried to obtain convict strike-breakers.[76] The Sydney Journeymen Bakers' Society too sent a deputation to the Governor after Hughes and Hosking sought convict strike-breakers.[77] Like others, the VDL Boot and Shoemakers Benevolent Society used public meetings and newspaper letters to oppose convicts/promote free-labour.[78] This agitation didn't mean ticket-of-leave holders or emancipated convicts were excluded from unions. The Hobart Journeymen Tailors Benefit Society (1846–1852) included ticket-of-leave holders and wage-entitled probationers in its ranks.

Another target of political agitation was jobs/immigration. In May 1841 Adelaide Journeymen Tailors memorialised for government work. In 1842 Sydney Operative Cordwainers president Patrick White wrote several newspaper letters refuting employer evidence to the Immigration Committee.[79] Countering over-favourable representations of labour conditions, along with regulating wages, were central to Adelaide cordwainers unionising in 1846.[80] Similarly, in March 1849, 21 Adelaide printers published letters denying there was a labour shortage, before forming a union.[81] Unions sent letters to trade societies, friends and newspapers in Britain. As in building, these and colonial newspaper notices were used to combat 'gulling' job advertisements or other practices threatening job prospects, wages and conditions. The Sydney Compositors did this at least three times—1838, 1839 and 1840. On occasion, trade societies allied with employers, with Sydney tanners and curriers petitioning for import duties in 1846.[82]

Punitive legislation was also targeted. An 1840 compositors strike escalated when several at the *Sydney Gazette* office were gaoled for unauthorised absence under the *Masters and Servants Act*. The union unsuccessfully challenged the decision, claiming printers were skilled artisans not covered by the Act. Later the same year three printers at the *Sydney Herald* were convicted of neglecting work.[83] Melbourne printers and Sydney shipwrights also mounted unsuccessful challenges to the legislation.[84] Despite these failures, unions continued to challenge the law's jurisdiction over the next 20 years, as well as campaigning to abolish these laws.[85]

These examples demonstrate the close nexus between the industrial and political spheres which made political agitation by unions essential—not an optional extra.

Governing Structures, Office-Holders and Workshop Organisation

Surviving evidence permits some observations about the governing structures of trade societies. Building-trades societies were included to avoid repetition, and there are many similarities with benefit societies formed by clerks, labourers, seamen and others. The typical governing structure consisted of a president, secretary, treasurer, steward, trustees and committee of management elected for terms of between three months and a year. Membership subscriptions were payable on a weekly or monthly basis. General

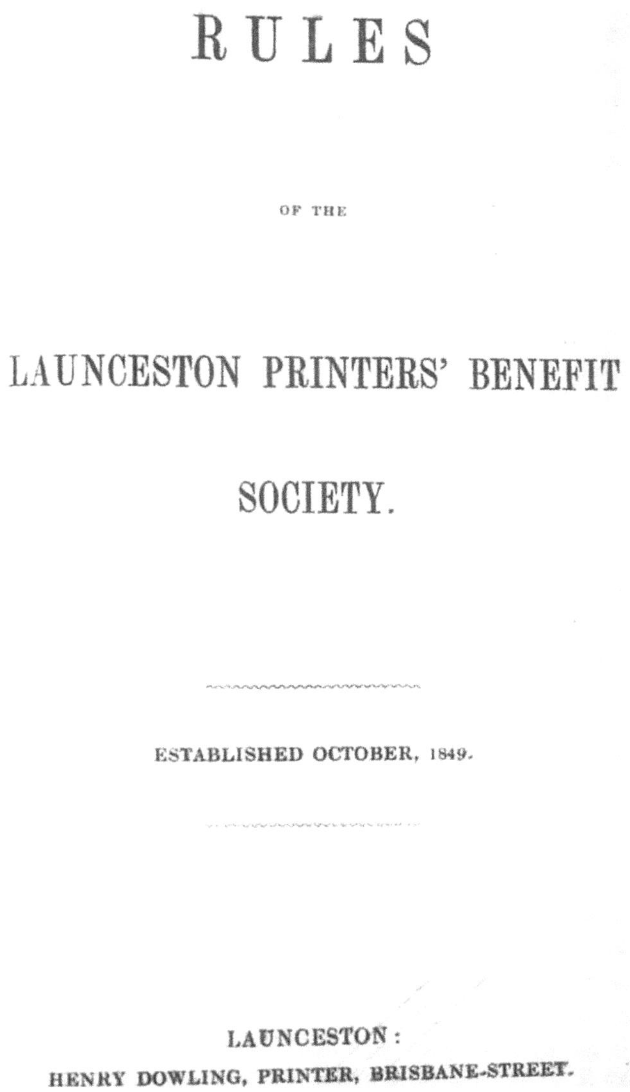

RULES

OF THE

LAUNCESTON PRINTERS' BENEFIT

SOCIETY.

ESTABLISHED OCTOBER, 1849.

LAUNCESTON:

HENRY DOWLING, PRINTER, BRISBANE-STREET.

Illustration 8.1 Launceston Printers Rules Title Page

[Pamphlet, Launceston Printers' Benefit Society]; call number DSM/042/P383, State Library of New South Wales.

meetings were held fortnightly or monthly with more significant meetings (including the election of officers) held at six-month/annual intervals. Rules of the Friendly Operative Society of Carpenters and Joiners (formed 1840) stated it was established to provide relief for members in the case of sickness or loss of tools by fire or robbery. Under Rules 2 and 3 office-holders consisted of a president, treasurer, secretary, steward, three trustees and a committee of five. The president was to receive 2/6 for chairing quarterly and half-yearly meetings. Trustees' tasks included depositing funds in the bank, while the steward was to receive all fines, visit the sick and deliver summonses. The steward and committee of management members were elected every three months while other office-holders had six-month terms (Rules 3 and 4). Other rules dealt with petty cash funds (Rule 5); entry and subscription fees (15s and 1s per week respectively), nomination for membership and procedures governing benefits for sickness (Rules 6–11); loss of tools (Rules 12–13); death (Rules 14–15), benefits limited to the colony (Rule 16); recall of funds (Rule 17); order in meetings (Rule 18); benefits-exclusion and expulsion of unfinancial members (Rules 19–20); meeting non-attendance fines (Rules 21–22); secretary to prepare accounts statement (Rule 23); members lodging complaints (Rule 24); expulsion of members convicted of criminal offence (Rule 25); collection of fines (Rule 26); president to quit chair if charged with an offence (Rule 27); notification/evidence supporting claim for benefits (Rules 28–29); and procedures governing dissolution (Rule 30).

Aside from loss of tools, similar rules and governing structures operated in other bodies like the Launceston Printers Benefit Society (Illustration 8.1) and were clearly modelled on UK societies. With a few exceptions, like the Tasmanian Tailor Benefit Society (1842) membership was confined to a particular town or its immediate vicinity.[86] Printers' unions used a form of workplace organisation, the chapel with its father and other office-holders located in each establishment harking back to the religious origins of printing.[87] A surviving minute book (1848–66) of the *Sydney Morning Herald* Chapel includes a list of members, rules and information on other chapels.[88] This record suggests workplace organisation survived the compositors' society's collapse in 1844, carrying over to its successor—the Sydney Typographical Association established in 1851. While comparatively little is known about union leaders and activists, the database records names where known and could assist future research.

Conclusion

As in other industries there is evidence of a progression from informal single-workplace organisation through to multi-workplace collective action and then unions, especially in NSW and VDL. Most early workplace organisation involved assigned-convicts who couldn't form unions. However, the transition to unions was rapid once there were barely enough free workers belonging to a trade and there were relatively few informal disputes once unions were established in a town. The relatively rapid shift to unions in the trades was not surprising given centuries-old experience and their generally stronger bargaining power. Wages and mutual insurance were important rallying points as were jobs/employment even where convict competition wasn't an issue. Other issues included the pernicious *Masters and Servants Act*. Societies continued to collapse and be revived periodically, but there were a core of extant unions in any given year from the mid-1830s in Sydney and Hobart and from 1840 in Melbourne and Adelaide. There is also evidence of growing industrial and political collaboration amongst trade societies and the first steps towards inter-colonial cooperation.

Trade societies tried to influence the labour market through friendly benefits, regulating wages, craft controls and compulsory union membership—centuries-old methods brought from Britain. Even when convict competition wasn't an issue, they were sensitive to business-cycle volatility and the potential for an even modest increase in immigration to affect labour conditions. Imperial and colonial authorities' involvement in labour flows helps explain why colonial trade societies were so engaged politically. Employers understood this connection only too well and lobbied heavily. On occasion temporary alliances formed over import duties—something that recurred over a century in sharp contrast to the export-orientated rural and mining sectors where no such synergies existed.

Beyond these generalisations, differences between particular manufacturing subsectors affected issues and methods deployed. Some were in a stronger position while others, as in Britain, experienced increasing challenges. Journeymen tailors formed some of best-organised societies, but they were increasingly threatened by mass-produced clothing and associated cost-cutting changes (subcontracting-based sweated labour). Female seamstresses/dressmakers had also begun to organise. They would come to dominate the clothing workforce as trade-based production was superseded.

Notes

1 See Butlin, N. (1994) *Forming a Colonial Economy: Australia 1810–1850*, 166–180.
2 Like that for tweed-manufacturing in Port Philip. *South Australian* 8 May 1849.
3 *New South Wales Government Gazette* 5 June 1839.
4 Byrne, P. (1993) *Criminal Law and the Colonial Subject*, 33.
5 *Sydney Gazette* 15 December 1825 and 6 April 1827.
6 LC83–1–8 Campbell Town 27 and 29 March and 14, 18 and 19 April 1848.
7 *Sydney Monitor* 5 November 1834.
8 *Sydney Monitor* 2 August 1837.
9 *Colonial Times* 16 June 1835.
10 *Sydney Gazette* 24 June 1824.
11 *Australasian Chronicle* 29 October 1842; *Sydney Morning Herald* 24 November 1842.
12 *Parramatta Chronicle* 3 August 1844.
13 *Maitland Mercury* 18 February 1845.
14 *Sydney Monitor* 28 February 1838.
15 *Sydney Monitor* 12 March 1838.

16 *Sydney Herald* 4 May 1841; *Australasian Chronicle* 22 May 1841.
17 *Sydney Monitor* 13 June 1835.
18 *Sydney Monitor* 7 May 1831.
19 Index of Register of Documents Lodged with the NSW Register of Friendly Societies and Argus 10 October 1849.
20 *Argus* 23 April 1847.
21 *Sydney Gazette* 7 April 1836.
22 *Morning Chronicle* 21 May 1845.
23 *Sydney Herald* 31 May 1841.
24 *Sydney Morning Herald* 13 September 1850.
25 *Launceston Examiner* 22 November 1850.
26 *Argus* 18 August 1846.
27 *Argus* 26 May 1848.
28 *Sydney Morning Herald* 16 June 1836, 20 August 1840, 22 June 1842, 18 May 1847, 13 July 1847; *Hobart Town Courier* 8 March 1833, 13 March 1840; *Sydney Morning Herald* 2 December 1850; *Colonial Times* 13 February 1844, 6 March 1846; *The Australian* 26 March 1840; and *Argus* 9 October 1850.
29 *Sydney Monitor* 13 May 1840.
30 *Hobart Town Courier* 15 April 1846.
31 *The Australian* 21 November 1839.
32 *Adelaide Observer* 27 June 1846 and *South Australian* 3 July 1846.
33 *Sydney Gazette* 1 December 1829.
34 *South Australian Register* 18 September 1850. See also *Sydney Herald* 9 September 1839.
35 *Sydney Gazette* 1 February 1834.
36 *The Australian* 11 November 1838.
37 *The Australian* 1 August 1840.
38 *Colonial Times* 19 June 1846 and 30 November 1847.
39 *Colonial Times* 29 May 1846.
40 *Sydney Monitor* 3 December 1840.
41 *Adelaide Times* 27 April 1850.
42 *Sydney Monitor* 12 October 1831.
43 *Australasian Chronicle* 23 January 1841.
44 *Sydney Monitor* 6 August 1841.
45 *Sydney Monitor* 24 March 1837; *South Australian* 3 July 1846; and *Argus* 8 June 1847.
46 *Port Philip Patriot* 4 October 1845.
47 *Sydney Monitor* 3 August 1840 and *Sydney Herald* 6 September 1840.
48 *Sydney Herald* 18 September 1840.
49 *South Australian Register* 23 May 1846.
50 *Port Philip Herald* 4 April 1843; *Port Philip Gazette* 22 April 1843.
51 *Sydney Morning Herald* 4 August 1845.
52 Lis, C. and Soly, H. (1994) An Irresistible Phalanx, 22.
53 *Australasian Chronicle* 21 January 1840; *Launceston Examiner* 8 May 1850.
54 *Port Philip Gazette* 25 April 1846.
55 *Port Philip Patriot* 8 and 9 June 1846.
56 *Port Philip Patriot* 15 June 1846.
57 *Port Philip Patriot* 14 June 1841.
58 *Port Philip Gazette* 23 May 1846; *South Australian* 30 June 1846.
59 *Argus* 2 June 1846.
60 *The Australian* 1 February 1843; *Peoples Advocate* 22 June 1850.
61 *Sydney Gazette* 19 November 1828.
62 *Sydney Monitor* 16 October 1840.
63 *Bell's Life of Sydney* 18 August 1848.

64 Brody, D. (1989) Time and Work During Early American industrialism, *Labor History*, 30(1):5–46.
65 *Port Philip Gazette* 7, 14 and 21 June 1847.
66 *Commercial Journal* 14 December 1844.
67 *Port Philip Patriot* 8 March 1847; *Port Philip Gazette* 10 March 1847.
68 *Argus* 30 September 1851.
69 *Sydney Morning Herald* 5 February 1849.
70 *Port Phillip Gazette* 21, 25 March, 11 April, 23 May and 8 July 1840, Barry's notes at p. 76; VPRS 51 Unit 2, 19–20; Croke's notes-VPRS 21 Unit 1 Bundle 1; Garryowen, 90 cited in Mullaly, P. (2008) *Crime and Punishment in the Port Phillip District 1835–51*, 716–717.
71 *Argus* 14 May 1847.
72 *South Australian Register* 18 September 1850.
73 See Fraser, W. (1970) Trade Unionism, in Ward, J. ed. *Popular Movements c.1830–1850*, MacMillan, London, 94. Important exceptions include Turner, H. A. (1962) *Trade Union Growth, Structure and Policy*, Allen & Unwin, London.
74 Simon, C. (1994) Labour Relations at Manufactures in the Eighteenth Century: The Calico Printers in Europe, *International Review of Social History*, 39(Supplement):132.
75 TAHO CSO 1/708/15494 4 April 1834; 1/895/19022 8 December 1836 and 5/4/70 16 and 31 January 1837; *Tasmanian* 16 February 1838; *Colonial Times* 14 May 1839; *Hobart Town Advertiser* 17 October 1843 and 21 October 1848.
76 *Sydney Monitor* 24 January 1840; *Commercial Journal* 15 February 1840; *Port Philip Patriot* 6 February 1840; *Sydney Monitor* 3 December 1840; *Sydney Herald* 16 December 1840.
77 *Australasian Chronicle* 22 May 1841.
78 *Colonial Times* 15 June 1847 and 16 July 1847.
79 *Sydney Morning Herald* 5 October 1842; *Australasian Chronicle* 6 October 1842.
80 *South Australian Register* 1 July 1846.
81 *South Australian* 6 March 1849 and *South Australian Register* 7 March 1849 and 23 March 1850.
82 *Sydney Morning Herald* 27 April 1846; *Hobart Town Courier* 3 June 1846.
83 *Sydney Herald* 3 December 1840.
84 *Sydney Herald* 3 February 1840; *The Australian* 20 February 1840; *Port Philip Herald* 1 June 1841.
85 Quinlan, M. (2004) Australia 1788–1902: A "Working Man's Paradise?", 219–250.
86 *Trumpeter* 3 June 1842.
87 Materne, J. (1994) Chapel Members in the Workplace, 53–82.
88 Minute book of the Herald Office Chapel 4 December 1848 to 31 January 1866, Document 2825b Deposit Series T39/84 Mitchell Library.

9 Organisation in Government and Community Services

Introduction

Government played a substantial role in the colonies, providing essential physical, economic and administrative infrastructure, including a legal regime privileging private property and subordinating workers, land-distribution policies and the provision/allocation of labour. In the convict period government directly engaged in construction, manufacturing and other activities. For several reasons, including geographic remoteness and a small population dispersed across a vast continent, the state continued to be more prominent in economic activity than countries like the UK and United States over succeeding decades. This impacted on worker organisation.

Patterns of Organisation and Collective Action

Table 9.1 indicates considerable organisation amongst government and community-service workers, the vast majority convicts employed in construction/labouring gangs, Female Factories, farms, government-manufacturing and administration. Free-labour taking collective action included labourers, council workers, police, soldiers, watchmen, clerks and postal workers. There is evidence of 353 strikes by convicts and 23 by free workers, but unlike some other industries strikes were far outweighed by NSCA for both. Collective absconding represented 92.5% of NSCA by convicts, but only 35.4% of NSCA amongst free workers (mainly soldiers and navy sailors). Petitioning was used by both convicts and free government workers, but especially the latter. There are only five instances of worker-initiated court actions—probably an understatement. Four were by convicts over OHS (won one, lost one and two unknown), while the other was a successful suit for unpaid wages. There were also several instances of collective sabotage, including incidents in June and August 1842 when women at the Launceston Female Factory broke tables, stools and other articles during a series of disturbances.[1]

For government-convicts, the ranking of issues in dispute is similar for both strikes and NSCA apart from the issue of hours, largely due to workers being prosecuted for collective absences (Table 9.2). For free workers as

Table 9.1 Summary of Organisation and Activity in Government Services 1788–1850

Nature of activity	1788–1800	1801–10	1811–20	1821–30	1831–40	1841–50	Total	Percentages
Convict Workers								
All Organisation	9	32	130	1381	1336	410	3299	
Involvement	59	128	458	5390	5699	1598	13332	
Adjusted Involvement*	64	131	485	5471	5771	1655	13577	
Strikes	1	4	14	104	133	97	353	9.9
NSCA	9	26	118	1315	1375	356	3199	90.1
Total	10	30	122	1419	1418	453	3552	
Absconding	2	21	118	1239	1258	288	2962	
Court actions		1		1	2		4	
Petitions				3			4	
Sabotage				1	3	7	11	
Bans			1	2	2		4	
Free Workers								
All Organisation		3	5	13	23	88	132	
Formal Organisation			1	1		2	3	
Involvement		9	35	35	74	475	628	
Adjusted Involvement*		14	35	51	80	535	715	
Strikes			1	1	7	15	23	16.9
NSCA		3	6	11	17	76	113	83.1
Total		3	6	12	24	91	136	
Absconding		2	2	3	1	32	40	
Court actions						1	1	
Petitions		2	1		2	18	21	

* Estimate based on median membership to zero count organisations.

Table 9.2 Strikes and Non-Strike Disputes by Issue in Government 1788–1850

Nature of activity	1788–1800	1801–10	1811–20	1821–30	1831–40	1841–50	Total*	Percentage*
Convicts								
Strikes								
Wages/remuneration			1		3	3	7	2
Working conditions		1	9	37	70	48	165	46.7
Management behaviour				5	23	22	50	14.2
Hours of work	1	1	3	58	53	44	160	45.3
Jobs/employment						2	2	0.6
Health & safety			1	13	27	12	53	15
Work methods					1	1	2	0.6
Unknown		2	2	7	1	1	13	3.7
NSCA								
Wages/remuneration			2		3	4	9	0.3
Working conditions	6	21	112	1289	1350	310	3088	96.5
Management behaviour	2	2		11	58	62	135	4.2
Hours of work					10	4	14	0.4
Health & safety		2	3	13	18	19	55	1.7
Work methods					10	4	14	0.4
Unknown		5	2	18	14	31	70	
Free-Labour								
Strikes								
Wages/remuneration					1	6	7	30.4
Working conditions				1	4	4	9	39.1
Hours of work					4	6	10	43.5
Health & safety					1	5	6	26.1
Unknown					1	1	1	4.3

(Continued)

Table 9.2 (Continued)

Nature of activity	1788–1800	1801–10	1811–20	1821–30	1831–40	1841–50	Total*	Percentage*
NSCA								
Wages/remuneration			1	2	3	18	24	20.2
Working conditions		1	4	8	13	59	85	75.2
Management behaviour						4	4	3.5
Hours of work			2		3	4	9	8
Jobs/employment				1		2	3	2.7
Health & safety		1			1	3	5	4.4
Work methods						1	1	0.9
Legislation						1	1	0.9
Unknown		2	1	1	1		5	4.4

* Exceeds totals strikes/NSCA and 100% because of multiple issue strikes/NSCA

with convicts, working conditions headed the rankings for strikes/NSCA, but wages were a more significant issue. Like convicts, hours and OHS were important issues in strikes but caution is needed given the small numbers.

Informal Workplace Conflict

Collective Action by Convicts

Much construction prior to 1840 was undertaken by government-convicts (Illustration 9.1). Their ill-treatment, including harsh discipline and inadequate rations—exacerbated by corrupt overseers—on road/chain-gangs, caused considerable insubordination and some public debate (see Chapter 4).[2] Management of convict gangs varied between different locations, stages of construction projects, the character/practices of those in charge as well evolving over time in terms of military oversight, accommodation and other factors too numerous to list here.[3] Within the confines of this book, it is only possible to provide a few illustrations of the types of collective action and the issues that drove it.

While absconding was pervasive, other types of action were common. In March 1825 convicts at the Launceston Barracks were charged with absenting themselves and two months later 20 convicts at the Macquarie Harbour

Illustration 9.1 Convict Chain Gang

'A Chain Gang, Convicts going to work at Sydney N.S.Wales', this work is a plate from within the publication 'A Narrative of a visit to the Australian colonies', (ca.1842) by James Backhouse. The original illustration is thought to have been by Edward Backhouse. Source: State Library of New South Wales.

penal settlement struck. Assaults on overseers were less common but not rare, illustrated by a case in December 1843 when 32 Pankhurst boy convicts at New Town VDL attacked their overseer.[4] Every major settlement or site of convict gangs experienced regular instances of dissent. Between 1825 and 1827, instances of strikes, go-slows and collective absconding by public works gangs in Launceston were being brought before the courts on average every 7 to 10 days (sometimes more frequently). There is a gap in court records after this, but the same pattern resumes when records do (1833). Only a fraction of convict gang dissent was reported in the press, possibly because it was so frequent as to be hardly newsworthy, but also because publicising the degree of convict insubordination would have unnerved local settlers and discouraged potential immigrants who read colonial papers to get information on what to expect.

Collective absconding was most prevalent amongst parties building roads and the like, although attended by difficulties obtaining food and on occasion attacks from Aboriginals like a group who absconded from George Town in 1819.[5] Between early March and 12 May 1834, records indicate at least four instances of collective absconding and a strike by convicts in the Sorell Rivulet road party along with individual dissent, including an assault on Superintendent Kelsh. One striking worker complaining he had no shoes, another stating he had received no breakfast and others complaining of illness or ill-treatment.[6] Some like William Underwood, John Barlow, James Pitman and Joseph Shuttleworth absconded repeatedly, notwithstanding ever harsher penalties including extended sentences, lengthy periods of hard-labour in chains and doses of the lash. In July there was another round of protests over food and harsh treatment. John Boyce threatened to kill Kelsh 'if ever I can get an opportunity' and John Roberts, labelled Kelsh a 'slave driver.'[7] Boyce was not alone in threatening Kelsh. Collective protests continued throughout 1834, including a strike in December where those involved claimed they had refused work because they had no rations. Several others who complained about Kelsh received 12 months in chains for their troubles.[8] Kelsh moved to another gang (Sandy Bay) and in October 1835 several convicts prosecuted for absconding pleaded 'bad usage and privations of rations, by the overseer Mr Kelsh' including being given sheep's tongue instead of meat. Presiding magistrates (Spode and Clark) interviewed other gang-members who corroborated the claims.[9] This atypical response was possibly influenced by Kelsh's prior 'form', but even then it had little effect.

Some gangs resorted to petitions. In June 1820 the Windsor road-gang pleaded for restoration of their old level of rations. Two years later Bathurst District convicts also petitioned over their sugar and tea rations.[10] Most petitions failed. On occasion gang-members went absent to steal food. Even assigned-servants supplying food ran a risk. Henry Vaughan gave some of his food to a road party member in New Norfolk, was prosecuted and given 25 lashes for insolence during the court proceedings which clearly grated on his sense of justice/charity.[11] The ineffectiveness and risks of lodging a formal complaint of mistreatment encouraged absconding even amongst those in chains who commonly broke their irons beforehand. Some were caught in the act, as occurred with six belonging to the Bridgewater gang constructing a causeway across the Derwent River in 1834. They were charged with 'defacing' their irons. Three other gang-members convicted for refusing work the same day were flogged or had their sentences extended.[12]

Rations and harsh treatment sparked strikes and sabotage. In April 1821, nine members of the South Head road-gang near Sydney were flogged and lost their 'usual indulgences' (extra rations) for striking.[13] In October 1826 members of the Lapstone iron-gang mutinied, knocking the handles out of their axes and hoes.[14] In May 1827 Laragay's road-gang at Longbottom (now Concord) struck over deficient rations and two months later complained to the Sydney Bench of corruption involving the contractor supplying meat.[15] Protests also took a violent form. On 23 August 1833 members of the Port Macquarie iron-gang assaulted their overseer Thomas Milbourne. Eleven were tried in the NSW Supreme Court for assault with intent to kill, seven being convicted and executed. Young female convict Mary Cartwright testified the assault had been provoked when the overseer attacked one man with a cutlass. Tried for perjury, she was sentenced to two hours in the pillory and seven years in a penal settlement.[16]

Other issues sparked collective action including management intrusion into their every waking hour like domestic servants. Demeaning rituals of supplication to authority were the norm. Any failure could earn a court appearance as it did for two members of the Campbell Town chain-gang, one for failing to remove his hat and another for failing to add 'sir' when stating 'here' at roll-call.[17] Other irritants were attempts to prevent gang-members smoking while working, recreational activities like playing cards or having a tipple in the local pub.[18] Refusal to work in front of other gang-members was deemed insubordination because it could spark strikes spreading or giving credence to issues in dispute.[19]

The system encouraged overseers (often ex-convicts) to act like petty tyrants keen to stamp their authority and view the slightest non-compliance as intolerable. Several members of the Campbell Town (VDL) chain-gang were charged with insubordination for refusing to put down their pipes 'in the presence of the gang' in April 1841. At the suggestion of an invariably 'helpful' Bench, the charge was downgraded to 'misconduct—smoking contrary to orders' and their time in the gang extended by a month. Overseer Richard Hughes did over-reach himself however on the same day, when he charged William Seaward with refusing work. Seaward was not attached to the gang and indeed free.[20] Three weeks later Thomas Todd—convicted of assaulting another overseer on the same gang (Spencer) with a stick—told magistrates he would rather be hanged than serve another 12 months under Spencer. Such extreme sentiments were not especially rare. Todd received 80 lashes and was removed to another part of VDL to safeguard Spencer from a second and more murderous assault.[21] Five months later (October 1841) four gang-members assaulted overseer Hughes. Two were removed to Port Arthur, while another (George Kean) received 100 lashes.[22] When another gang-member John Leonard sent a complaint directly to the Governor—a breach of regulations—the Campbell Town Bench gave him an extra six months in chains for spreading 'falsehoods.'[23] These incidents—by no means exceptional—highlight how readily an oppressive and lopsided regime spiralled into escalating rounds of reciprocal violence, a historical lesson still to be learned.

Disputes over workloads were especially common. In February 1834 Joseph Jackson and three other members of the Sutton Forest No. 4 road-gang were tried for refusing work, telling their overseer 'they had done quite enough' that day.[24] In a classic example of effort-bargaining, convict gangs restricted their output not simply by working slowly but with a range of less discernible devices like 'lifting a pick and merely letting it fall.'[25] Superintendents and overseers used a range of devices to extract more effort, including task-work and setting minimum output quotas like amounts of stone broken or cartloads of material shifted. Nevertheless, frequent mismatches between actual output and what was deemed acceptable continued. In 1837 the Deep Gully (VDL) gang superintendent charged several groups with neglect, arguing they refused to break more than a yard of stone each day at most.[26] In August 1844 four members of the Cleveland Depot (VDL) convict party were sentenced to periods of solitary confinement for completing insufficient work.[27] Hundreds of similar cases were brought before the courts, themselves only indicative of a more pervasive struggle. The significance of 'go-slow' tactics reinforces the need to incorporate all forms of collective action into any assessment of worker mobilisation.

Overseers were promoted from the ranks to push for a faster pace of work, but their efforts were subject to ongoing contestation. On 30 March 1835 six members of Ross Bridge construction gang were prosecuted for neglect/idleness, one telling overseer Thomas Edwards 'it is very little work I'll do.' Barely a month later overseer Edwards was himself charged with insolence for responding saucily to Superintendent Charles Atkinson's chastisement that his men were still working too slowly and threatening to return Edwards 'to the barrows'.[28]

Workload disputes overlapped with hours of work and other issues. On Saturday 4 March 1848 members of the Campbell Town Probation Party refused to go to Ross (12 km away) because it would infringe on the half-day to which they were entitled. Several days later another group going to the mines refused to travel on a Sunday.[29] There is clear evidence gangs compared their hours to others although these were mandated for all gangs. On 30 August 1848 the Avoca Probation Station (VDL) gang stopped work, saying they all wanted to leave for Campbell Town where hours were 8 am to 3:30 pm. Three ringleaders received 30 days' hard-labour in chains.[30] Those with high-demand skills like stonemasons also had an incentive to reduce their workload/hours so they could work for themselves. In May 1835 three members of the Ross Bridge gang were ordered to be flogged for working for themselves 'in government hours' and ten days later another three stonemasons in Ross were punished for the same offence.[31] Weather conditions also sparked disputes. In July 1834 three members of the Deep Gully gang received 20 lashes for leading a strike over working in the rain. One, George Cooper, told the superintendent 'no chain-gang was worked in such weather.'[32] Again, these are but a few examples of collective action by convict gangs.

Government-convicts engaged in other activities also took collective action. In April 1805, several Sydney flour millers were flogged for neglecting work/repeated disobedience and the following day two smiths received similar punishment.[33] In 1817 sawyers at Pennant Hills struck over rations and increased workloads that affected their capacity to work on their own time. Two ringleaders were sentenced to 100 lashes.[34] Similar tensions were evident 30 years later when probationers at Spring Hill (VDL) refused to cut 700 feet of timber weekly, telling their overseer they wouldn't cut 500 feet for wages of £10 per-annum.[35] Effort-bargaining over workloads was widespread if not pervasive. Many convicts seem to have done as little as they could get away with, helping to explain the shift in sentiment as free-labour became more available. Free workers also engaged in effort-bargaining, but the terms of exchange were somewhat different, especially regarding wage rates and the punishments available.

Other government-convicts taking collective action included those at the Emu Plains Government farm, who petitioned over their rations in 1822—they had previously complained about conditions in 1819. Several clearing gangs took similar action in 1822.[36] In 1825, 87 convicts on the hulk *Phoenix* in Sydney harbour mutinied over poor food and clothing.[37] In February 1846, 800 convicts at Norfolk Island locked themselves in the Lumberyard, refusing work until a detachment of troops threatened to fire upon them.[38] This followed a strike over rations in December 1845—the two incidents may have been connected.[39] In July 1835 convicts working as lamplighters in Sydney struck work with two being flogged. The other, who claimed illness in mitigation, received 30 vigorous days on the treadmill.[40] Convicts-clerks also took industrial action. In December 1837 a Hobart Chief Police Magistrate's office clerk was convicted of 'inciting his fellow servants to strike for wages.'[41] Convict-clerks employed by the Launceston gaoler and magistrate also struck in 1845 when refused additional rations.[42]

Some convicts like those (usually ex-seamen) serving as crew on pilot and government harbour boats bargained over conditions. This included those on pilot boats taking ships from Low Head, entrance of the Tamar River, 50 km up river to Launceston—a long and difficult voyage even before the river became heavily silted from land clearing/agriculture. In October 1843 pilot John Babington prosecuted boatman John L Reid for insolence, telling the George Town Bench Reid had complained that unlike other pilots he didn't give his crew money for staying over in Launceston.[43] Other pilots, like Joseph Cordell, probably didn't thank Babington for this observation which breached convict regulations. Nonetheless, the admission was indicative of widespread 'under-the-counter' bargaining.

Convicts in Female Factories regularly engaged in collective dissent, especially group absconding (the earliest recorded case in 1813), including smaller factories like those at Bathurst, Ross and George Town.[44] Absconding groups were typically small but other types of protest often involved larger numbers. In 1826, 22 women at the Hobart Female Factory rioted and a year later around 100 women at the Parramatta Female Factory rioted and absconded when their bread and sugar ration was stopped, some still at large a month later.[45] In 1832, 40 women from the same Factory were sent to Newcastle following a strike.[46] This didn't work either. In 1836 the *Sydney Monitor* reported that women in the third class at the Factory had entered a compact, naming the ringleaders as Polly Maloney and Sally McGee and speculating whether Maloney was the same person tried for murdering Captain Waldron in 1834 (see Chapter 4).[47] Three years later, women at the Launceston Factory rioted over rations.[48] Some disputes were classic examples of effort-bargaining. In October 1823, 16 women engaged in weaving at the Hobart Female Factory were prosecuted for wetting the yarn to cut their workload (output was measured by weight). Ringleaders Elizabeth Boucher, Mary Ann Kelly, Ellen Stewart and Margaret Morgan were sentenced to the Crime Class for 3 months plus seven days on bread and water.[49]

Collective action was not confined to transported convicts. In May 1848 native convicts in Fremantle protested at the poor quality of their accommodation, and two years later convicts absconded from Hillman's road-gang and headed for Bunbury (WA) but were apprehended suffering from thirst and hunger.[50]

Collective Action by Free Workers

A wide array of free government workers took collective action, illustrated by the following examples. Collective absconding was common amongst military forces stationed in the colonies. For example, in 1808 five sailors deserted the HMS *Porpoise* and four decades later the Melbourne *Argus* lamented.

> The repugnance of the soldiers belonging to the detachment of the 68th Regiment in Melbourne to exchange their comparatively easy life in this Province for a renewal of the hardships they so recently underwent in New Zealand, is sufficiently exemplified in the number of desertions which have taken place, not fewer than sixteen of the men having absented themselves from the barracks since it was known the Regiment was under orders for New Zealand.[51]

Soldiers also resorted to strikes or strike-threats. In April 1804 a detachment guarding the Risdon Cove VDL settlement 'came close to mutiny, after complaining of too many duties to perform.'[52] In February 1840, 10 soldiers in Sydney gaol escaped to lodge a complaint about rations and corruption before the Governor. Sentenced to the treadmill, they refused work until rations were served and were placed in irons.[53] Five years later members of the Sydney garrison struck over removal of their grog allowance.[54] Bans were also used. In 1839 the Norfolk Island military detachment blocked an attempt by the penal settlement's commandant to demolish their houses.[55]

On rare occasions soldiers took extreme measures more typical of wartime. In November 1826 seven members of the 57th Regiment based in Sydney committed robberies or maimed themselves to obtain a discharge with one, Joseph Sudds, being motivated by the distress being experienced by his wife and family in the UK. Sudds and another Patrick Thompson were stripped of the uniforms in front of the troops and sentenced to seven years' transportation to Moreton Bay. Sudds self-harmed and died the next day, arousing a furore in the press and causing Governor Darling to send a series of despatches to London justifying the actions.[56]

Groups of police constables (overwhelmingly ex-convicts) in NSW and VDL were charged with neglect of duty, including absence from their posts. Others misused their powers for personal gain, something encouraged by rewards for apprehending absconders and bushrangers. Three George Town petty constables (all ex-convicts) were convicted of laying a false charge against Thomas Pickett to prevent him receiving a reward for apprehending two absconders and thereby receive the reward themselves.[57] All three were dismissed from the police, but only one received a gaol sentence. Although it didn't help these three, police often used their knowledge of law with more calculated pleas and defences to escape conviction or mitigate penalties than was generally the case with other workers. Courts also played a part and it was not unusual for police convicted of neglect to be fined rather than suffering more severe penalties.

Petitioning was a preferred device for government workers to protest their conditions. In 1840 clerks in the Sydney General Post Office Letter Department petitioned for additional remuneration (overtime) for working beyond their regulated hours.[58] There were attempts to reverse salary cuts made during the early 1840s downturn, including petitions by clerks employed at the Sydney Police Office in 1845 and 1847.[59] Windsor District Council local officers also petitioned the NSW Legislative Council over unpaid salaries.[60] Lower level government officers took action on other issues. In 1844 Launceston Post Office clerks protested their heavy workloads but didn't get a sympathetic response.[61] On occasion, action went beyond petitioning. In 1848 five labourers employed in the Pyrenees (now Victoria) sued a government surveyor (Delittle) for unpaid wages. Counsel for Delittle argued the men were Crown employees not covered by the *Master and Servants Act* and the matter was referred to the Governor.[62] Others taking action included the crew of the VDL government schooner *Waterloo* that protested cuts to their wages and grog allowance in 1826, as well as the NSW government schooner *Isabella's* crew who struck work in 1837.[63]

Unemployed workers engaged on relief-work during economic downturns also took collective action. In January 1834 relief labourers near Guilford west of Perth refused to work for rations-only, demanding 2s per-day.[64] In May 1841, 184 Adelaide relief workers struck over the same issue.[65] Similarly, in April 1842, 200 immigrants employed on Liadrets Beach road near Melbourne struck over a wage cut. Eight months later unemployed labourers in the same town combined, refusing wage offers below a certain rate.[66]

Multi-Workplace Informal Collective Action and Formal Organisation

Centralised determination of employment conditions by government predisposed workers to multi-workplace agitation. Aside from mutual insurance, formal organisation was not an option. Again, a few examples illustrate this point. In January 1842 VDL government clerks petitioned for a wage increase, arguing they couldn't maintain respectability and NSW government salaries should be a benchmark.[67] This early appeal to comparative wage justice was eventually acceded to, but the increase still hadn't been paid a year later. Their salary was labelled a miserable pittance unlikely to attract trustworthy civil servants.[68] In December 1849 the VDL Subordinate Government Officers Benefit Society was established with the Governor's encouragement but was short-lived.[69] The only comparable body was the Australian Clerks Provident Society, covering government and private sector clerks in Sydney (Chapter 10). After 1850, efforts at formal organisation gained momentum.

Largely ignored by historians, there is a long history of collective action by police. In July 1816 police constables memorialised Governor Macquarie, arguing a decision to no longer pay them in spirits (common currency at the time) halved their wages.[70] Nine years later they established a benefit society.[71] In 1834 mounted police complained their duties were too heavy due to under-staffing.[72] Between August and October 1846, police protested their wages, including a petition to the NSW Legislative Council from Sydney police inspectors, sergeants and constables.[73] Similar protests had occurred in Melbourne since 1840. In 1846 the Constabulary Benevolent Society of Melbourne and County of Bourke was established to provide funeral, sickness and widow benefits, with a subscription of one day's pay per month.[74]

There is scattered evidence of multiple-workplace action amongst others working for government, sometimes contractors such as a strike over wages and rations by Gundagai District mail contractors in 1844.[75] In 1850 watch-house keepers in the Port Philip District petitioned for increased wages and holidays, arguing for the rates comparable to Sydney and VDL.[76] Apart from illustrating notions of comparative wage justice (comparable pay for the same job/work), this claim suggests information networks involving occupational groups in different colonies. Roman Catholic school masters petitioned the NSW Legislative Council twice in 1843 after being left unpaid because government funds intended for their salaries had been assigned to erect a new school at Campbelltown instead.[77] Collective action by teachers became increasingly common after 1850.

Conclusion

In NSW and VDL government-convicts were responsible for numerous instances of informal organisation, particularly those in gangs where predominant issues were rations and harsh discipline—paralleling protests by others dependent on institutional food and under strong disciplinary regimes like the military—as well as workloads. For those in road/chain-gangs and secondary-punishment settlements, conditions were especially grim. This, together with the brutal legal regime, goes some way to explaining the incidence of strikes, absconding, incendiarism, assaults and outright revolts born of anger and frustration. The congregation of women in Female Factories was conducive to collective action over rations and discipline. Indulgences, workload and not unrelated remuneration issues were common other convicts like sawyers. The sheer scale of collective action by male and female convicts is significant. Not simply passive recipients of oppression, they absconded in droves and engaged in other forms of resistance that forms an important aspect of early worker mobilisation.

Collective action also occurred amongst free government workers; much of it was multi-workplace because employment conditions were usually determined centrally. The predominant issue was wages/salaries along with workloads. Pay claims included appeals to comparative wage justice—later to become a significant wage-fixing concept in Australia. A series of complaints followed salary cuts during the 1840s depression, budgetary pressures on successive governments (especially VDL) and failure to match shifts in the cost of living. The latter led to even more disputes during the 1850s gold rushes. Petitioning was a favoured form of action, especially amongst clerks and government officers, though other forms of protest were used. There were several attempts at formal organisation, all focusing on mutual insurance.

This chapter reinforces the point that worker organisation was widely spread in terms of occupations and industries, and considering different forms of collective action is essential to examining mobilisation amongst specific subsets of workers and more generally. Preference for specific modes of action and organisation were influenced by several factors including workers' circumstances, workplaces and employer characteristics, the aims being pursued and the regulatory framework.

Notes

1 LC346–12 Launceston 21 June and 15 August 1842.
2 AONSW CSO and 2 October 1821 Complaint re: supervision and behaviour of overseers of road parties in Liverpool Reel 6051 4/1749, 46–48 and conduct of men in road parties in neighbourhood of Liverpool Reel pp63–5; 28 March 1822 Re rations of road parties Reel 6009 4/3505, 89–91.
3 For some studies dealing with the management and conditions in convict gangs, see Karskens, G. (1986) Defiance, Deference and Diligence; MacFie, P. (1988) Dobbers and Cobbers: Informers and Mateship After Convicts, Officials and Settlers on the Grass Tree Hill Road-gang, 112–127; Rosen, S. (2006) That Den of Infamy, the No. 2 Stockade Cox's River.
4 *Tasmanian and Port Dalrymple Advertiser* 30 March 1825, TAHO CSO 1/8/124 cited in Maxwell-Stewart (2008) *Closing Hell's Gate*, 141; *Hobart Town Courier* 5 January 1844.
5 *Hobart Town Gazette* 10 April 1819.
6 LC375–1–1 New Norfolk 12 May 1834.
7 LC375–1–1 New Norfolk 29 and 30 July 1834.
8 LC375–1–1 New Norfolk 17, 24 and 29 December 1834.
9 *Colonial Times* 20 and 27 October 1835.
10 AONSW CSO Reel 6050 4/1747, 62–4, 10 June 1820 and Reel 6065 4/1798, 165.
11 LC375–1–1 New Norfolk 11 September 1838.
12 *Colonial Times* 11 March 1834.
13 *Sydney Gazette* 7 April 1821.
14 *The Australian* 7 October 1826.
15 *Sydney Gazette* 1 June 1827; *Australian* 11 July 1827.
16 *Sydney Gazette* 14 and 30 November 1833; *Sydney Herald* 21 November 1833.
17 LC-1–3 Campbell Town 22 October 1838.
18 See for example LC143–1–2 Fingal 2 December 1848.
19 See for example LC-1–6 Campbell Town 4 December 1841 and 15 February 1842.
20 LC83–1–5 Campbell Town 28 April 1841.
21 LC83–1–5 Campbell Town 18 May 1841.
22 LC83–1–6 Campbell Town 29 October 1841.
23 LC83–1–6 Campbell Town 11 November 1841.
24 Sutton Forest Bench Book 3 February 1834.
25 Govett cited in Rosen, S. (2006) That Den of Infamy, the No. 2 Stockade Cox's River, 240.
26 LC375–1–2 New Norfolk 31 August and 6 September 1837.
27 LC83–1–6 Campbell Town 16 August 1844.
28 LC83–1–1 Campbell Town 27 April 1835.
29 LC83–1–8 Campbell Town 6 and 8 March 1848.
30 LC143–1–2 Fingal 30 August 1848.
31 LC83–1–1 Campbell Town 20 May 1835.
32 LC375–1–2 New Norfolk 25 July 1837.
33 *Sydney Gazette* 21 April 1805.
34 Robbins, W. (2001) The Management of Convict Labour Employed by the New South Wales Government 1788–1830, 34–37.
35 LC390–1–2 Oatlands 4 October 1847.
36 AONSW CSO 3 November 1819 re condition of convicts at the Agricultural Establishment at Emu Plains and Fiche 3044 4/1829 No.100, 30 June 1822; 28 May 1822 re lack of salt in provisions for clearing parties Reel 6054 4/1758 p36a; 29 August 1822 Re bad management and conduct of clearing parties Reel 6054 4/1758, 39–39c; 27 November 1822 Re rations for clearing parties during harvest time Reel 6009 4/3506, 483.

37 *The Australian* 17 November 1825.
38 *Cornwall Chronicle* 1 July 1846.
39 *Sydney Morning Herald* 28 October 1846.
40 *Sydney Monitor* 22 July 1835.
41 *Cornwall Chronicle* 23 December 1837.
42 *Cornwall Chronicle* 22 January 1845.
43 LC156–1–2 George Town 13 October 1843.
44 *Sydney Gazette* 21 August 1813.
45 Hendriksen, G., Liston, C. and Cowley, T. (2008) *Women Transported: Life in Australia's Convict Female Factories*, 56; *Sydney Gazette* 31 October 1827.
46 *Sydney Gazette* 6 October 1832.
47 *Sydney Monitor* 19 December 1836.
48 *Cornwall Chronicle* 11 May 1839; *Bents News and NSW Advertiser* 1 June 1839.
49 Hendriksen, G., Liston, C. and Cowley, T. (2008) *Women Transported: Life in Australia's Convict Female Factories*, 55.
50 *Perth Gazette* 13 May 1848; *Inquirer* 18 December 1850.
51 *Sydney Gazette* 6 November 1808; *Melbourne Argus* 18 June 1847.
52 Walker, J. (1989) *Early Tasmania*, M C Reed Government Printer Hobart, 49 cited in Johnson, M. and McFarlane, I. (2015) *Van Diemen's Land: An Aboriginal History*, 87.
53 *Sydney Monitor* 28 February 1840 and 2 March 1840.
54 *Morning Chronicle* 3 December 1845.
55 *Sydney Gazette* 19 September 1839.
56 *Sydney Monitor* 19 January 1829.
57 LC156–1–2 George Town 4 June 1845.
58 *The Australian* 23 July 1840.
59 *Bell's Life of Sydney* 30 August 1845; *The Australian* 15 July 1847.
60 *Argus* 9 October 1846.
61 *Cornwall Chronicle* 17 January 1844.
62 *Argus* 4 and 18 August 1848.
63 TAHO CSO 2676; *Sydney Gazette* 2 May 1837.
64 AOWA CSO 47; 6/215, 6/230 and 204.
65 AOSA CSO 1841/2 and 1841/2A.
66 *Hobart Town Courier* 29 April 1840 and *Port Philip Patriot* 12 December 1842.
67 *Hobart Town Advertiser* 21 January 1842.
68 *Launceston Examiner* 18 January 1843.
69 *Hobart Town Courier* 26 December 1849 and 20 March 1850.
70 Byrne, P. (1993) *Criminal Law and the Colonial Subject*, 157 and 201.
71 I thank Barrie Dyster for drawing my attention to this. *The Australian* 25 August 1825.
72 *The Australian* 17 February 1834.
73 *Will o' the Wisp* 15 August 1846; *Argus* 9 October 1846; and *Bell's Life of Sydney* 17 October 1846.
74 *Port Philip Patriot* 13 March 1846 and *Port Philip Gazette* 23 April 1846.
75 *Sydney Morning Herald* 10 October 1844.
76 *Melbourne Daily News* 14 May 1850.
77 *Australasian Chronicle* 4 November 1843.

10 Organisation in Commercial, Personal Services and Retailing

Introduction

Workers also organised in domestic service, hospitality, retailing, commercial and professional services. Aside from domestic service, these activities were overwhelmingly found in towns, where increasing numbers of shop-assistants, clerks and hotel-staff provided goods, recreation, financial/mercantile and legal services to the growing population, including a wealthy middle-class.[1] Organisation amongst these workers in the 19th century has received comparatively little notice. While organisation was largely informal and single workplace-based, there is evidence of wider organisation, including unions formed by clerks and shop-assistants.

Patterns of Organisation

Table 10.1 identifies 169 instances of organisation in commercial and personal services, overwhelmingly informal and confined to a single workplace. Most prior to 1841 involved convict domestics, predominantly female, who absconded or were prosecuted for refusing work/absence, insolence and insubordination. Convicts, including women, also dominated early instance of collective action by retail workers. Three court actions in retailing were convict complaints about rations (two won and one outcome unknown), while one involving service workers involved unsuccessful wage claims by free female domestics in Melbourne. After 1841, organisation of free workers including domestics, clerks and shop-assistants assumed significance—the latter connected to the early-closing movement with its reliance on consumer boycotts/retailer pledges. This explains the relatively large number of bans.

Working conditions and management behaviour were dominant issues for strikes/NSCA amongst service workers, with recreational absences by domestics—especially convicts—accounting for hour-related strikes (Table 10.2). In contrast hours was the dominant issue for retail workers, reflecting disenchantment with long hours, something experienced by both convicts and free-labour. As with bakers and butchers hours overlapped with OHS.

Table 10.1 Summary of Organisation and Activity in Services and Retailing 1788–1850

Nature of activity	1788–1800	1801–10	1811–20	1821–30	1831–40	1841–50	Total	Percentages
Commercial and Personal Services								
All Organisation	1		2	14	117	36	169	
Formal Organisation						1	1	
Involvement	6		6	28	240	1090	1370	
Adjusted Involvement*	6		6	32	260	1098	1402	
Strikes	1			5	19	17	42	
NSCA			2	10	99	18	129	
Total	1		2	15	118	35	171	
Absconding			2	9	75	6	92	
Court actions						1	1	
Petitions						2	2	
Deputations						1	1	
Press letters						1	1	
Retailing								
All Organisation			1	1	12	18	32	
Formal Organisation					1	16	17	
Involvement			2	2	21	421	446	
Adjusted Involvement*					25	1381	1406	
Strikes			1	1	5	2	9	
NSCA					6	19	27	
Total			1	1	11	18	34	
Absconding					2		2	
Court actions					3		3	
Petitions						1	1	
Deputations						1	1	
Mass meetings					2	2	4	
Press letters						3	3	
Bans					1	24	25	

* Estimate based on assigning median membership to zero count organisations.

Table 10.2 Strikes and NSCA by Issue in Services and Retailing 1788–1850

Nature of activity	1788–1800	1801–10	1811–20	1821–30	1831–40	1841–50	Total*	Percentage*
Commercial and Personal Services								
Strikes								
Wages/remuneration						1	1	2.4
Working conditions				4	7	7	18	42.9
Management behaviour				2	4	4	10	23.8
Hours of work	1			2	12	11	16	38.1
Jobs/employment					1		1	2.4
Health & safety					1		1	2.4
Work methods				1			1	2.4
NSCA								
Wages/remuneration					3	3	6	4.7
Working conditions			2	9	95	14	120	93
Management behaviour					5	8	13	10.1
Hours of work					6		6	4.7
Jobs/employment						3	3	2.3
Health & Safety				1	4		5	3.9
Retailing								
Strikes								
Wages/remuneration				1			1	11.1
Working conditions						1	1	11.1
Hours of work					5	1	6	66.7
Unknown						1	1	11.1

(Continued)

Table 10.2 (Continued)

Nature of activity	1788–1800	1801–10	1811–20	1821–30	1831–40	1841–50	Total*	Percentage*
NSCA								
Wages/remuneration					1	1	2	9.1
Working conditions					3	1	4	18.2
Hours of work					1	14	15	68.2
Health & safety					1	1	2	9.1

* Exceeds totals strikes/NSCA and 100% because of multiple issue strikes/NSCA

Informal Workplace-Based Collective Action

Much collective action by service workers was confined to a single work-place as the following examples illustrate.

Cooks, Waiters and Domestic Servants

Living under the thumb of masters on a 24-hour basis proved too much for many convict domestics, who sought temporary release by visiting friends or a pub and then risked being prosecuted for absence, insolence or drunk-enness. In April 1828 Dr Halloran's (Birchgrove) servants were charged with all three offences under an 18th-century English master and servant law (colonial legislation was enacted later that year).[2] In May 1832 Super-intendent of Public Works Joshua Thorpe charged James Bryan, William Baker, Patrick Lyhee and Alice Green with being absent for four hours on Sunday. Alice received a month in the Female Factory. Her male colleagues got three days on the treadmill.[3] In July 1833 Jane Mitchell and Eliza-beth Lowe received 14 days in the Female Factory after leaving Thomas Icely's Point Piper residence for the 'dense atmosphere of Sydney.'[4] When five of Thomas Archer's assigned-servants took time-off on Saturday, the two women received solitary with Mary Law getting an additional three days for 'talking while in solitary confinement.'[5] Taking 'recreation' on the employer's premises was at least as risky. In February 1840 three female domestics assigned to Dr Paton received 14 days solitary for imbibing spirits and neglect.[6]

Typically workers didn't mount a defence, probably because it was seen as pointless and might induce 'pay-back' when returned to their master/mistress. In February 1831 Charles Moore's (Surry Hills) assigned-servants complained bitterly of being ill-treated only to be told this 'was no justifi-cation for running away' (28 days on the treadmill).[7] Some female domes-tics mocked the court, their masters or both. In 1836 the *Sydney Gazette* reported

> Kate Hoy, Maria Hely, and Ellen Gorman, were charged with bolting and becoming remarkably funny, which caused them to dance a three-handed reel in George-Street, to the amazement of folks returning from Church, after a little trouble and a short chase they were secured. In defence they all commenced, chattering at once with the greatest vol-ubility, expatiating upon their respective merits; better servants never lived—they were quite the thing—always did as ordered, couldn't think how it occurred, This harangue was cut short by each of them being sent to the Factory for a month. They left the Court jabbering like so many talkative magpies.[8]

Some charged with insolence escaped with a reprimand like Mrs Whit-ton's assigned-servants in March 1834.[9] More commonly, those who couldn't hold their tongue paid a price. H T Glass charged William Leighton, James Moss and Benjamin Jones with insolence and insubordination. Glass told the Sydney Bench Leighton and Moss behaved 'tolerably well' until led astray by an 'incorrigible' Jones. Jones got 50 lashes, Leighton and Moss 10 days on the treadmill.[10] Ringleaders were often singled out for exemplary treatment, like Francis Crowe prosecuted for insolence, disobedience of orders and 'creating a riot in his master's house' in October 1835.

Outright refusals to work were common. Ann Fogarty, Mary Thompson and Anne Weylon refused work when their master (Campbell) forced entry into the laundry where they were meeting a man. Weylon asked to be returned to the Female Factory, complaining Campbell had 'spite' against her because she refused to give evidence for him in a court case some time before. Like her compatriots, who made no defence, Weylon got 28 days then to be returned to Campbell's service.[11] Few workers would have been unaware of the risks of mounting a defence, encouraging their disrespect for the judicial apparatus. On occasion solidarity amongst household servants following a disciplinary action by the employer escalated into a succession of refusals to work. This occurred at the Keach estate northern VDL in June 1849 when Samuel Martin, Mathew Connolly and Mary Walsh were prosecuted for insubordination—Martin receiving 18 days' solitary confinement while Connolly and Walsh got six months' hard-labour.[12]

Poor rations also caused dissent. Three assigned-servants took revenge on their York St Sydney mistress Elizabeth Pattison for cutting their rations by reporting she possessed stolen coffee.[13] Management behaviour was a significant grievance even if few workers dared to complain except in extreme cases. In December 1838 draper David Jones, founder of a retailing empire, was charged by two female servants with striking them. Jones told the court he became exasperated with their quarrelling and neglect of work. Jones was told to take them before a magistrate and fined 40 shillings.[14] This lenient treatment hardly sent a reassuring message to aggrieved workers. As with rural workers, calculated non-cooperation wore some employers down like one Norfolk Plains landholder (Walker) who returned two female servants deeming them 'useless'.[15]

Free workers, including indentured immigrants, also took collective action. Some indentures covered couples. In April 1830 the Australian Agricultural Company at Port Stephens complained to authorities that the wives of indented servants had refused wash for the hospital and asked what legal measures could be used to 'subordinate' them.[16]

Temporary absence and absconding was common amongst free cooks, waiters and domestic servants. In February 1837 Sydney publican Samuel Bullock warned others from engaging three hired-servants.[17] In July 1844 two hired-servants of Launceston publican Nicholas Clarke received seven days in the cells for being absent.[18] In January 1850 several waiters at Mack's hotel Geelong struck when a fellow waiter refused to share tips as was customary. They had their wages mulcted and agreements cancelled.[19]

In the country married-couples were often employed as domestic servants. In January 1845 a couple hired as cook and laundress respectively refused work and then absconded from their Bathurst employer (Raines). The Bench mulcted their wages.[20] Employers also contended with serial dissent. In May 1837 Mr Barton Macquarie Place, Sydney raised John Keating's wages when another hired-servant left but then charged Keating with neglecting work.[21] Determined to restore order, Barton issued warrants against two other servants for absconding. He agreed to drop charges against James Gilligan, now a cook at Knight's Hotel George Street, following a plea from his new employer.[22] Barton brought a second charge of neglect against Keating who was gaoled for a month.[23] All to no effect, as Barton's wife was soon advertising for a cook and three other servants, all wanted immediately.[24]

Retail and Warehouse Workers

Like domestics, convicts working in shops and warehouses and living under their employer's nose often sought free-time and recreation. In September 1820 Simeon Lord had several assigned-servants flogged and imprisoned for 14 days for 'neglect of work and frequent absence'.[25] In February 1831 James Wiltshire, who supplied beef and other goods to whaling ships, charged several men with absence. Wiltshire complained that notwithstanding repeated punishment one (Cheeseman) returned 'as bad as ever' and wanted him sent to an iron-gang but the magistrates decided 20 days in the cells was enough.[26] A Launceston retailer's (Palmer) servants escaped with a caution after being found in a public-house.[27]

Food quantity/quality also caused disputes. In April 1832 Sydney general-dealer Pearson Simpson's assigned-servants complained about their food. Lodging the complaint, Thomas Flanagan claimed that despite 'having a good set of teeth in his head, and most powerful digestive organs, he was literally starved by his master.' The servants had received a five-day allowance of eight pounds of beef (chiefly bone) consisting of shank-based soup on day one, a diluted version of this on day two, five potatoes each on the following two days, and bone-hash, potatoes and crusts of bread on the final day (Good Friday). As this was the third or fourth complaint against Simpson the Bench referred the case to the Governor.[28] This case highlights the problematic nature of 'approved channels' even in the face of compelling evidence.

Despite being proscribed, convicts also demanded wages (Chapter 2). In June 1827 Patrick McMann and Henry Muggleton assigned to a Sydney tobacconist (James) refused work when he couldn't pay their weekly 'gratuity' in suitable currency. McMann received a week's solitary confinement while Muggleton was discharged due to his 'general good character.'[29] The Bench castigated James but took no further action, implicit recognition that paying convicts was widespread. Free workers too took action over wages, although this was problematic if they could be readily replaced. In

June 1850 Fremantle timber and general merchant, J W Davey's labourers threatened to strike unless their pay was increased to five shillings per-day plus rations. They lost when Captain Henderson offered a group of 'pensioners' for 2/6 per-day.[30]

Multi-Workplace Collective Action and Formal Organisation

Cooks, Waiters and Domestic Servants

On occasion domestics from several workplaces absconded together like Margaret Hollands and Ann Jenkins caught in Longford in December 1844.[31] Multi-workplace dissent domestics was also organised by women in Female Factories. In May 1839 the *Cornwall Chronicle* reported a combination at the Launceston Female Factory. Those assigned into service worked until they had acquired clothing and other items then engaged in misconduct (insolence, absence or drunkenness) until returned to the Factory. Goods were then shared amongst their associates. In one exchange, a servant returning drunk challenged her mistress if 'it don't suit you turn me in I would rather be in the factory.'[32] The *Chronicle* advocated making the Factory more unpleasant by engaging women to unpick oakham or similar tasks.[33]

   In 1845 amidst claims of a domestic servant shortage in Melbourne, a number combined to demand higher wages and shorter engagements. The *Port Philip Patriot* claimed young women broke their engagements under the *Master and Servant Act* 'for trivial reasons' to negotiate better conditions. Several prosecuted their employer for unpaid wages. Fourteen-year-old Mary McCulloch was accused of breaking her agreement, with her mother advising her to only engage on a weekly basis—far shorter than the norm of 6 months to a year. Mary's claim was dismissed, the presiding magistrate remarking that the arrival of VDL domestic servants would soon break the combination. Mary's mother vigorously dissented the decision and was briefly gaoled in the watch-house for 'unruly conduct.'[34] Newspapers demanded others involved should forfeit their wages.[35] There was no further reference to the combination.

Clerks

Like police, Sydney clerks formed a benefit society in November 1844. The Australian Clerks Benevolent Fund Society registered as a friendly society in 1846. Stated objectives were providing clerks employed by government, banks and merchants with sickness and unemployment benefits and death benefits including an annuity of £6/10 to £13 paid quarterly to widows and children for three years based on member subscriptions and public donations.[36] A move to extend coverage to attorney's clerks failed.[37] Weekly meetings were initially held at the ex-Council chambers George St then the School of Arts, *Royal Hotel* George St and finally the committee's rooms at 160 Liverpool St. The governing structure resembled trade societies with a president, two vice presidents, secretary and committee of management elected annually. Activists included A G Dumas, William Perry, J Vannett, R Garrett, B P Griffin and J (Stephen) Greenhill. Dumas worked for Treasury, another official (Hutchinson) worked in the Supreme Court, while others worked for private merchants, banks and the offices of the *Sydney Herald*.[38]

Despite support from notable citizens, like the Chief Justice, Colonial Secretary and the Governor, the society struggled to secure a viable membership. In October 1845 amidst complaints of 'general apathy' the society was retitled the Australian Clerks Provident Society and its membership extended beyond clerks.[39] It continued to experience problems, including internal splits and resignations.[40] In 1846 the Committee of Management recommended cost-cutting measures, including abandoning unemployment relief (but continuing sickness relief) and suspending relief to widows until the number of contributing members reached 100. These measures, predicted to give the society funds of £207 9s 9d to invest, were adopted but had limited effect.[41] In January 1849 the Committee's fourth annual report conceded:

> The business of the institution has, for the last year, been almost in abeyance, and its numbers during that period have slightly decreased, by the removal of some of its members. Its funds have also decreased, by the subscriptions of some of the members who retired having been returned to them, with interest at three per cent and the payments due by the members during the past year not having been as yet collected . . . they feel surprised that an institution, having such patrons, with a code of rules and regulations founded on those of the most flourishing institutions of a similar nature in the mother country, holding out advantages which no other society in the colony can do, with a small funded property, and without debts, does not advance with greater rapidity.[42]

Hopes for improvement weren't realised. Even with public donations claims threatened to outweigh its funds. In October 1850 the society was dissolved, donating its remaining funds to the Benevolent Society.[43] As with trade societies, the society's demise highlighted the vulnerability of small bodies operating mutual insurance. Nonetheless, early attempts at organisation like this provide a context for later developments.

Hours of Work and the Early-Closing Movement

By far the most substantial mobilisation of service workers was the early-closing movement. Modelled on UK initiatives and predating the eight-hour movement amongst tradesmen, it was concerned with the nexus between working hours and trading-times that typically ran 10–12 hours, sometimes more, per-day, six days a week. Shop-assistants used moral suasion to secure agreement amongst retailers, or subgroups like drapers or grocers, to close their shops earlier. This could only be addressed on a multi-workplace/town-wide basis and required a degree of formal organisation. Some retailers were sympathetic, supporting or even helping campaigns for ethical, religious and practical reasons. Long hours weighed heavily on smaller self-employed retailers. Others resisted or soon broke ranks to gain a competitive edge over rivals.

In NSW organisation first occurred in 1840, a year after a series of letters had advocated the measure.[44] In December 1840 the Sydney Assistant-Drapers Association was formed, agitating for shops to close at 6 pm for half the year and 7 pm for the remainder. Supporting arguments mirrored those in Britain, namely the health, moral and self-improvement benefits of shorter hours. The Association held public meetings and memorialised employers. One disgruntled *Sydney Gazette* correspondent labelled the association a combination 'forcing employers to yield to their wishes' but supporting letters were more typical.[45]Despite some employer support, the effort fizzled after a month. The only tangible outcome was a library and reading room, in 1842 converted into a public library retitled the Commercial Reading Rooms.[46] In March 1841 the *Sydney Gazette* argued emulating the Melbourne early-closing agreement would encourage assistants to 'enter more warmly into the interests of their employers.'[47] Nothing eventuated. In May 1842 the principal Sydney drapers entered an arrangement to close at 6 pm in winter and 7 pm in summer, but this was short-lived.[48]

Agitation revived in September 1844 with the formation of the Sydney Committee of Assistant-Drapers at *Toogood's Hotel* Market St (subsequently meeting at the School of Arts). Garnering support from church leaders amongst others, it organised letters to the press and sent a memorial to master-drapers signed by 87 assistants.[49] Initially, 25 of 35 master-drapers signed the pledge to close at 6 pm, another four promised to adhere without signing, one acquiesced conditionally and several refused. More signed but it still wasn't unanimous.[50] The *Morning Chronicle* tried to persuade hold-out Joseph Farmer (later founder of a major department store) by publishing British evidence on the adverse health effect of late hours.[51] Others labelled opponents disreputable, narrow-minded and unchristian.[52] In December a public meeting chaired by the Mayor, and attended by prominent citizens, added its support.[53] Nonetheless, resistance continued and in January 12 assistant-drapers left a recalcitrant employer. Like a trade society, W H Brett (chairman pro tem) announced they would financially support members refusing to accept 'unreasonable hours.'[54] This strike was exceptional, the usual tactic being to encourage a consumer boycott of offending firms. The campaign was sufficiently successful to annoy the Gas Company whose earnings from lighting were damaged by early-closing.[55]

As in 1842 success didn't last. Agitation revived in March 1848, a meeting at the *Royal Hotel* establishing the Sydney Assistant-Drapers Association with activists, like E B Johns, prominent in earlier campaigns. Unlike earlier bodies, the association also aimed to operate as a benefit society but there is no evidence this was realised.[56] Like other unions, office-holders consisted of a president, two vice presidents, two auditors, a secretary, a treasurer and a 12-member committee of management elected on a six-month basis. To publicise its cause, the association organised monthly concerts at Mr Clarke's Rooms, Elizabeth St.[57] Again success was short-lived. By February 1850 aggrieved assistants, like 'Voice from the Counter' were complaining about the late-hour system.[58]

Organisation followed a similar pattern in Melbourne but encapsulated a wider spectrum of retail workers. In February 1841 assistant-drapers secured an early-closing agreement but within two months some masters were breaking ranks.[59] In March 1846 drapers and clothier's assistants campaigned for shop shutting by 7 pm. By early April, 17 (of 18) master's names were appended to an advertised agreement.[60] However, several broke ranks in June with further complaints of non-observance in October.[61] The movement revived in April 1847 with another agreement.[62] Success was short-lived. By August the *Port Philip Gazette* was urging assistants to follow the lead of the Hobart Mercantile Assistants Association.[63] In April 1848 renewed efforts secured majority agreement to close shops at 7 pm (Saturday excepted) but quickly lapsed. Another effort the following year failed.[64] In May 1850, 30 master-drapers signed an agreement like that of 1848, but it too rapidly lapsed.[65] Other retail workers to take action included Melbourne grocer's-assistants who secured a short-lived agreement in 1841 and renewed their efforts in July 1846.[66] In 1847 shop-assistants in Geelong secured an agreement with 15 retail establishments, including drapers, grocers, ironmongers and saddlers.[67]

In VDL, shop-assistants in Launceston, Campbell Town and Hobart campaigned for early-closing in January 1847, with agreements reached in Campbell Town (February) and Launceston (June).[68] In Hobart 65 principle retailers signed on in February 1847. Despite periodic reports of firms reneging, the agreement seems to have held for at least six years.[69] One reason for success was the formation of a robust organisation, the Hobart Mercantile Assistants Association that survived until the mid-1850s. The Association met weekly (plus electing officers every six months) at Langley's Academy Melville St and subsequently its own Collins St rooms. Supported by leading retailers and citizens—several holding honorary positions—the association charged a six-month subscription of 5 shillings to operate a library and published its rules (Illustration 10.1) and annual reports (some survive). Membership grew from 80 in 1847 to reach 146 in 1851.

Early-closing was initiated in Adelaide in 1846 along similar lines to other colonies.[70] Assistants working for drapers, ironmongers, grocers and other

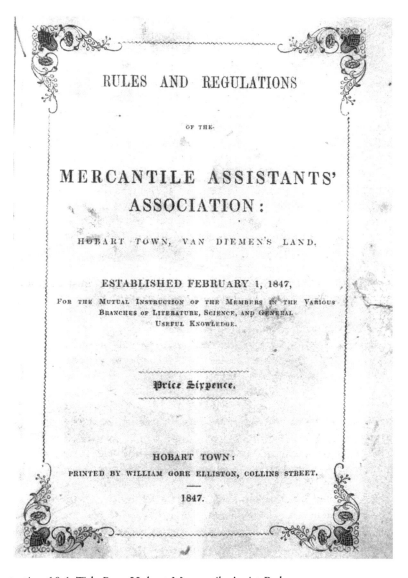

Illustration 10.1 Title Page Hobart Mercantile Assist Rules

'Rules and Regulations of the Mercantile Assistant's Association' William Gore Elliston 1847', call number DSM/374.2/H; State Library of New South Wales.

shopkeepers met at *Conlon's Hotel*, along with some small storekeepers supporting the cause. Deputations to retailers secured an agreement commencing on 25 April 1846 closing shops at 7 pm between March and September and 8 pm between October and February (except Saturday).[71] As elsewhere, the agreement didn't hold. In February 1850, 50 retail workers met at *Ottaway's Hotel* Rundle St to form the Adelaide Early-Closing Association, a more broadly-based organisation mirroring recent developments in the UK.[72] On 1 March 1850 the association's secretary announced 'all the respectable merchants of the city' had agreed to close their shops at 7 pm Saturday excepted.'[73]

While assistant-drapers associations were still being formed in the 1850s, the early-closing association model adopted in Adelaide came to dominate before slowly giving way to shop-assistant unions in the 1880s. The Hobart Mercantile Assistant Association was an exception to the pattern of short-lived mobilisations that continued long after 1850. Repeated failure ultimately led to a switch of tactics to pursuing laws mandating trading hours that first bore fruit in Victoria in 1885 ultimately yielded pioneering social protection laws in Australia and New Zealand.[74]

Conclusion

This chapter identified three distinctive streams of collective action amongst service workers. First, there was small-scale action by domestic servants (mostly female) and those employed in hotels (convict and free) that rarely extended to multiple workplaces let alone formal organisation. Second, a similar pattern amongst retail workers prior to 1840 was followed by significant efforts at formal organisation, modelled on the UK, to pursue shorter working hours through the early-closing of shops. Largely ignored, this involved almost as many workers in formal organisations as unions of tradesmen in manufacturing (Chapter 8) and grew in significance after 1850. Third, there was a single attempt to establish a benefit society of private sector and government clerks in Sydney also drawing on UK models.

Notes

1 Butlin, N. (1994) *Forming a Colonial Economy: Australia 1810–1850*, 155–165.
2 *Sydney Gazette* 28 April 1828.
3 *Sydney Gazette* 12 May 1832.
4 *Sydney Gazette* 25 July 1833.
5 LC362–1–4 Longford 22 and 29 June 1840.
6 LC362–1–4 Longford 12 February 1840.
7 *Sydney Gazette* 24 February 1831.
8 *Sydney Gazette* 8 November 1836.
9 *Colonial Times* 11 March 1834.
10 *Sydney Gazette* 23 May 1833.
11 *Sydney Monitor* 23 July 1834.
12 LC83–1–9 Campbell Town 11 June 1849.
13 *Sydney Gazette* 8 June 1839.
14 *Sydney Monitor* 13 December 1838.
15 LC362–1–3 Longford 1 September 1836.
16 *In the Service of the Company: Letters of Sir Edward Parry, Commissioner to the Australian Agricultural Company*, 48–49.
17 *Sydney Herald* 6 February 1837.

18 *Cornwall Chronicle* 31 July 1844.
19 *Geelong Advertiser* 11 January 1850.
20 *Sydney Morning Herald* 31 January 1845.
21 *Sydney Gazette* 20 May 1837.
22 *Sydney Gazette* 23 May 1837.
23 *Sydney Monitor* 22 May 1837.
24 *Sydney Herald* 11 May 1837.
25 *Sydney Gazette* 30 September 1820.
26 *Sydney Gazette* 24 February 1831.
27 *Cornwall Chronicle* 25 November 1837.
28 *Sydney Monitor* 2 May 1832.
29 *Sydney Gazette* 13 June 1827.
30 *Inquirer* 19 June 1850.
31 Longford LC362–1–6 21 December 1844.
32 *Cornwall Chronicle* 11 May 1839.
33 *Launceston Examiner* 11 May 1839.
34 *Port Philip Patriot* 14 and 15 May 1845.
35 *Port Philip Gazette* 26 February 1845 and 14 May 1845, *Star and Working Man's Guardian* 31 May 1845.
36 *Morning Chronicle* 13, 20 and 23 November 1844. Index to Register of Documents Lodged with the NSW Register of Friendly Society.
37 *Australian Daily Journal* 27 November 1844.
38 *Sydney Morning Herald* 30 May 1846.
39 *Sydney Morning Herald* 1 November 1845.
40 *Sydney Morning Herald* 14 January 1846.
41 *Sydney Morning Herald* 25 July 1846.
42 *Sydney Morning Herald* 27 January 1849.
43 *Sydney Morning Herald* 19 October 1850.
44 *Sydney Herald* 17 July 1839; *Commercial Journal* 16 November 1839; *Sydney Monitor* 13 December 1839.
45 *Sydney Gazette* 17 December 1840.
46 *Sydney Herald* 9 January 1841.
47 *Sydney Gazette* 13 March 1841 and *The Australian* 21 June 1844.
48 *South Australian* 6 May 1842 citing *The Australian*.
49 *The Australian* 1 and 12 November 1844.
50 *The Australian* 1 November 1844.
51 *Morning Chronicle* 9 November 1844.
52 *The Australian* 18 November 1844.
53 *Morning Chronicle* 11 December 1844.
54 *Sydney Herald* 7 January 1845.
55 *The Australian* 22 May 1845.
56 *Sydney Morning Herald* 24 March 1848.
57 *Bell's Life of Sydney* 10 March 1869; *Sydney Morning Herald* 13 June 1849.
58 *Sydney Morning Herald* 1 and 11 February 1850.
59 *Port Philip Herald* 19 February 1841; *Port Philip Patriot* 22 February 1841 and 5 April 1841.
60 *Port Philip Patriot* 3 and 4 April 1846.
61 *Argus* 9 June 1846 and 10 October 1846.
62 *Port Philip Patriot* 7 and 13 April 1847.
63 *Port Philip Gazette* 25 August 1847.
64 *Port Philip Patriot* 20 April 1848; *Argus* 5 June 1849.
65 *Argus* 10, 20 and 28 May 1850; *Melbourne Daily News* 31 May 1850.
66 *Sydney Gazette* 13 March 1841; *Port Philip Patriot* 7 July 1846.
67 *Port Philip Gazette* 14 August 1847; *Geelong Advertiser* 20 August 1847.

68 *Cornwall Chronicle* 30 January 1847, 3 and 6 February 1847 and 19 June 1847.
69 *Hobart Town Courier* 6 February 1847, 3 April 1847, 5 June 1847, 15 December 1847; *Colonial Times* 2 February 1849.
70 *South Australian* 11 April 1846.
71 *Adelaide Observer* 18 April 1846.
72 *South Australian Register* 23 January, 6 and 7 February 1850.
73 *South Australian* 1 March 1850.
74 Quinlan, M., Gardner, M. and Akers, P. A. (2005) Failure of Voluntarism, 161–178; Quinlan, M. and Goodwin, M. (2005) Combating the Tyranny of Flexibility: The Struggle to Regulate Shop Closing Hours in Victoria 1880–1900, *Social History*, 30(3):342–365.

11 Peak and Political Organisation

Introduction

This chapter examines two additional forms of worker organisation, namely inter-union collaboration and political mobilisations by workers. Many craft unions engaged in political activities. This chapter examines political mobilisations that were not unionate but point to interconnections with union leaders playing a pivotal role in wider alliances of workers. Rallying points included convict competition, unemployment, pernicious labour laws and democratic representation. There is evidence of over 20 political organisations of workers prior to 1851. Many were short-lived, but some large and influential organisations were established, including a wide spectrum of workers.

Peak Organisation

Peak union organisation in Australia is commonly seen to originate in the 1850s with the eight-hour day movements and Melbourne Trades Hall Council. There is evidence of organisation 15 years prior to this. In Sydney a group of trade society delegates including J Bib, J McEachern and W Edwards played a leading role organising protests against a new master and servant bill in 1840. In December 1840, a Committee of Trades representing 10 trade societies presented W A Duncan, editor of the *Australasian Chronicle*, with a watch and a testimonial recognising his support in this campaign and for trade unionism more generally.[1] The Committee of Trades seems to have fulfilled the role of a union peak council pursuing both industrial and political objectives. Certainly, Sydney trade societies collaborated (Chapter 8). A journeyman tailor told the *Sydney Monitor* that even if the union's financial resources were exhausted, 'they have the funds of other trade societies at their command'.[2] The Committee may have continued or revived in 1846 when newspapers reported a combination of societies covering virtually every trade provided financial support to striking carpenters.[3] Indeed, it is only from this that a Nailers' Society is known. If the Committee of Trades didn't survive the early-1840s depression, cooperation continued informally. There is fragmentary evidence of informal collaboration amongst the trades prior to 1840 in Sydney and Hobart. The models for this were clearly drawn from the UK where meetings of trades delegates in particular towns was long established, and by the early 19th century a number had formed committees of trades to pursue mutual causes like opposing the *Combination Acts*.[4]

Bodies calling themselves trades unions were established in Sydney and Hobart in the mid-1830s. It is unclear whether they were nascent peak bodies or associations formed for political purposes, more probably the latter although these roles were never entirely separate.

Struggles Over the Labour Market Competition: Convicts and Immigration

Capitalism's enduring strategies for extracting a surplus entails an search for unorganised labour and efforts to 'flood' labour markets at workplace/industry/trade, region or national level. Unions and political organisation of workers sought to resist these strategies by controlling the labour market—as true of the early 19th century as it is today. Colonial free workers saw convicts as a threat. Similarly, a union movement built by emigrants often opposed immigration, particularly indentured workers, but also state-assisted emigrants from the countries they once called home (Chapters 7 and 8). From the early 1830s workers mobilised against these perceived threats to their living standards in small and economically-volatile colonies.

Convict Competition

As in VDL, changing assignment policies in NSW that were viewed as manipulating the labour market became enmeshed in disputes within particular trades, as occurred between masters and journeymen printers in early 1840.[5] More generally, workers organised protest meetings calling for an end to convict transportation to reinforce the Molesworth Committee's recommendations (1839).[6] Ending transportation didn't stop competition from convicts still under sentence in the colony. In 1843, amidst widespread unemployment, washerwomen—some reports suggest over 1000—petitioned the Legislative Council protesting the Parramatta Female Factory's laundry was denying them work.[7] In VDL polite society isolated itself from convicts but unlike shipbuilders and free-shipwrights protesting vessels built in penal settlements, most employers had no qualms about using convict labour.[8] Angered by the impertinence of a petition opposing convict assignment, the *Launceston Advertiser* asserted:

> Appropriations of prison-labour is the indefeasible right of every respectable inhabitant of this colony. It is the inherent system of the island, and produces that low average value of hired labour under which, it is the

direct fair presumption, every emigrant has selected this in preference to any other colony.[9]

In 1834 a number of Hobart trades petitioned the Governor against both state-sponsored immigration and convict competition. They got no sympathy from Governor Arthur's administration which was committed to using convicts to suppress workers' combinations and keep wages down.[10] A meeting of Immigration Committee five months earlier was also explicit about the role of convicts in checking combinations of free workers.[11] This sparked more generalised agitation. On 16 December 1834 free emigrants met at Ramsay's *Edinburgh Wine Vault* to protest government notices aimed at collecting loans made for passage assistance. Claiming they had been induced to emigrate by 'false representations', the mechanics resolved to send an authentic statement of conditions back to Britain. They complained of doing grubbing work (tree and stump removal) to support their families because assigned-convicts did half the colony's mechanical work, and there was a more than adequate labour supply from apprentices and convicts receiving their ticket-of-leave.[12] In January 1835 a further meeting at the *Cabinetmakers' Arms* Liverpool St established a Trades Union. Secretary A. Reid urged mechanics to attend another meeting to consider its rules a month later.[13] The organisation was short-lived but the wider agitation had effects, with masters protesting a Government resolution not to assign further convicts.[14]

On 8 December 1836, 12 free coopers petitioned Lt Governor Snodgrass protesting competition from assigned-convicts. A week later mechanics called a general meeting at the *Man of Ross* Liverpool St, probably in response to an employer push to reinstate the previous assignment policy.[15] In January 1837 a petition from Hobart master-tailors claimed most free journeymen were ex-convicts of 'dissipated habits' while another from master-bootmakers claimed journeymen couldn't be obtained at any wages.[16] Two days later, Governor Franklin found this patchwork of inconsistent and unsupported assertions (free journeymen unavailable at any price?) to be 'reasonable' and directed the Colonial Secretary to consult with magistrates and the Assignment Board.[17] By March 1837 the Governor acceded to the masters' petitions to prevent 'exorbitant' wage demands in printing, bootmaking, tailoring, painting and other trades. The Governor's response emphasised assigned-convicts should not receive wages or do paid outwork—requirements widely flouted in practice.[18]

Worker concerns the labour market was being manipulated against their interests were not imaginary. The struggle was real and seen as such by employers and government. Political protests captured widely held sentiments, exemplified by a Launceston mechanic who signed his letter to the *Cornwall Chronicle* 'A Kidnapped Emigrant.'[19] Others wrote home. Giving evidence to the VDL Executive Council in 1837, a merchant (Kemp) lamented that 'mechanics have written to their friends at home, advising them not come out' before going on to complain about a blacksmith's combination.[20]

Labour conditions in VDL deteriorated in the 1840s. In October 1843 the Hobart Joiners, Cabinetmakers, Carpenters, Coachmakers and Turners United Trades Benefit Society was established with C T Haskell as its secretary.[21] Meeting initially at the *Jolly Hatters Inn* and then the *Mogul Tavern*, the body wasn't so much a multi-trade benefit society, itself indicative of weakness amongst mechanics, as a vehicle for petitioning the Governor to abolish the probation passholder regime in these trades. Its formation as the Legislative Council was considering regulations on the hiring of convicts holding probation passes seems more than coincidental.[22]

In 1844 Hobart mechanics organised again—initiating an ongoing campaign against transportation.[23] In August 1844 Thomas Hayward, John Morrison, George Reynolds, Thomas Carroll, William Simpson and A M Nicol amongst others organised a numerously attended meeting at the Temperance Hall Bathurst St that heard evidence 396 mechanics were jobless, including 50 carpenters, 58 stonemasons, 70 tailors and 100 shoemakers. A committee was elected, including William Jeffrey, to memorialise the Governor demanding the probation system be suspended.[24] Governor Wilmot referred the memorial to the British Secretary of State for the Colonies who subsequently rejected it.[25] A second meeting condemned the Governor's referral, declaring he was misinformed by employers and publishing a detailed list of employment by trade, wage rates and living costs for a family with two children—shades of the Harvester basic wage judgement 63 years later.[26] A Committee of 14 mechanics was appointed to obtain information on distress and raise public subscriptions for relief. The Committee of Free Operatives established an office (14 Brisbane St) serving as a free employment register and dispensing relief to unemployed workers and their families. The latter was made more urgent by the Government's decision to stop dispensing charity to the poor from the Commissariat. The Committee's other objective was to end transportation.

The employment register provided mechanics to employers at official government rates. Funded by donations (£135 by January 1845) from religious leaders, merchants and some government officials including the Comptroller General and Treasurer, employment and relief activities were reported at monthly public meetings by the secretary—WCD Smith then P. Parkinson. A non-operative, Henry Chapman, acted as treasurer.[27] Faced with increased demands from the distressed, Committee funds were rapidly depleted; it sought additional support from sources including W P Kay, the Public Works Architect. Kay referred the request onto the Colonial Secretary with the acerbic comment 'the mechanics in Hobart Town all invariably refuse to work for 4 shillings a day and that their master tradesmen now give 5 shillings and in some cases more.' The Governor rejected the request through his secretary James Bicheno, an Anti-Chartist whose comments on these and other documents reveal an abiding condescension towards working people.

In June 1845 the Committee suspended register and relief activities, conceding funding problems had been exacerbated by unfounded concerns donations 'might be perverted to the purposes of a trades union' or used only to assist skilled workers.[28] It expressed hope a body like the Launceston Benevolent Society (still extant) would assist the poor.

Middle-class support for the Committee was also eroded by its political activities. In March 1845 it protested overmanning of ships coming to colony from Britain with seamen being discharged on arrival and thrown into destitution—seamen having made an identical complaint two years earlier.[29] The Committee also organised a petition from 118 mechanics and 121 operatives (including gardeners, labourers, shopmen, domestics, grooms and miners) requesting free passage to another colony. The Governor Sir John Eardley-Wilmot replied he had no finances for such a venture.[30] In May 1845 the Committee organised a contingent of 200 working men marshalled by delegates to march from the *Jolly Hatters Inn* to a public meeting demanding an end to transportation.[31] In July the Committee organised a protest against Lord Stanley's (Secretary of State for the Colonies) rejection of anti-transportation petitions from Hobart and Launceston.[32]

This activism attracted criticism, with allegations Committee members like emancipist joiner Thomas Murphy preferred to live off 'the public bounty' than the Governor's offer of employment at reduced wages.[33] Responding, the Committee stated it drew 'no invidious distinction between free emigrants and emancipists' foreseeing its inherent evil and recognising that union is strength'.[34] This principal was also followed in NSW. Opposition to convict competition didn't mean ex-convicts were excluded from worker organisation be they unionate or political. This prevented a divisive split weakening free-labour, given large numbers of ex-convicts. It was indicative of a wider stance. Hostility to state-sponsored immigration didn't translate into hostility to immigrants. The critical concern was about jobs and wages, which also drove efforts to inform non-European indentured workers of colonial wage rates (Chapters 2 and 6).

Thereafter, the Committee maintained an informal existence before its members led renewed agitation. Governor Eardley-Wilmot appended disparaging comments to a public anti-transportation petition (with 1750 signatures), alleging most workers leaving VDL were thieves or miners heading for South Australia even as newspapers conceded there was an oversupply of labour.[35] Inspired by moves in Launceston in April 1847 seven trade representatives, including William Watson, William Jeffrey, Samuel Buller and A M Nicol organised a meeting of over 200 at the *Jolly Hatters Inn* to renew agitation.[36] In a debate over whether the petition should be confined to operatives, Journeymen Tailors delegate, John Williams, urged collaboration with sympathetic employers, arguing his society had driven probationers from tailoring establishments by demonstrating they were inefficient and expensive. Jeffrey and Nicol saw advantages coordinating opposition while maintaining independence. The meeting opted for a separate operatives' petition that acknowledged working-class involvement in the 1845 public petition. William Jeffrey was appointed to the Committee of 'influential gentlemen' planning the great public protest against transportation. The number of worker delegates was later increased to four—Smith, Dickenson, Jeffrey and Williams.[37] By May the Free-labour Committee coordinating the operatives' campaign consisted of 12 representatives of different occupations, all but one mechanics. Along with John Morgan's *Britannia and Trades Advocate*, the *Hobart Town Advertiser* supported the 'working classes' campaign, labelling the cheap labour argument for transportation as fallacious because low wages also meant lower demand and consumption.[38]

In addition to collecting petition signatures and organising worker attendance at public meetings, the Committee pressured government tendering practices, informing the Comptroller General probationers corruptly tendered for public contracts under assumed names.[39] In August 1847 Jeffrey wrote to the new Governor Sir William Denison asking whether new building work contracts would specify using free-labour to prevent contractors using probationers at 9d per-day as occurred presently.[40] The Governor's secretary (Bicheno) replied contractors could use any labour they chose. The union also pressured the government's acceptance of new convict arrivals, including 3000 from Sydney, by organising protests. Williams and Jeffrey reiterated they held no harsh feelings towards prisoners but were simply demanding 'fair play.'[41]

The Committee also targeted employers, establishing the Hobart Town Trades Union (HTTU) with a House-of-Call for free-labour at William Champion's *Jolly Hatters Inn*. Joiner A M Nicol was elected HTTU secretary. All callings were to have delegates acting co-jointly at particular establishments with masters as honorary members on payment of two shillings per-quarter. Workers' subscriptions were 1d per week.[42] The HTTU called on shipbuilder and brewer Peter Degraves (Chapter 8) to explain his continued employment of probationers.[43] Employer responses were mixed, at best. In December 1847 the *Britannia and Trades Advocate* reported gains were being offset by 'mushroom employers' springing up under the probation system.[44] Recalcitrant employers like James Ward continued the practice of 'gulling', advertising for '40 good bootmakers at the highest wages.'[45]

In mid-1848 the HTTU opposed employer demands for additional labour with a petition signed by over 1200 detailing unemployment in specific trades and amongst labourers and urging Governor Denison to contradict reports more ticket-of-leave holders were required. Bicheno replied most convicts would be sent to Launceston and unemployment amongst building workers was normal in winter.[46] Jeffrey responded the unemployment was unrelated to seasonal conditions and irrespective of where convicts were 'set adrift', competition for work would cause free-labour to desert the colony. Denison remained unmoved telling the British Secretary of State wages in VDL were 'amply sufficient' then inconsistently adding the exodus of free-labour was due to higher mainland wages. Patrician by birth,

Denison remained wedded to transportation as a plank of British policy and because he believed it served business interests in VDL.[47] The Secretary of State rebuffed the Hobart operatives' petition, telling Jeffrey there was no prospect transportation would cease.[48]

The rebuff sparked another round of protest meetings calling on employers to sign a pledge not to engage future convict arrivals unless they possessed a conditional pardon. Jeffrey and Williams cautioned against further petitions, pointing to a succession of governors and officials like Bicheno who believed wages were too high.[49] A strongly-worded remonstrance was sent to the Governor, asserting the operatives' rights as British subjects had been sacrificed to penal science. It accused Denison of misrepresenting the state of the colony, ignoring the wishes of the great majority, and ended anxiously anticipating his recall as 'your continuance cannot be attended with good but only greater evils.'[50] *Britannia and Trades Advocate* editor John Morgan almost certainly wrote the remonstrance—the highpoint of his involvement in the Union. Notifying Morgan it would be forwarded to London, Bicheno dropped the 'pro forma' nature of such replies by saying the statements were 'unfounded.' Denison defended his stance in a despatch accompanying the remonstrance. Denison wasn't recalled, serving on ardently defending transportation even as wider public sentiment shifted until 1852 when he was promoted to Governor of NSW.[51]

The HTTU entered a dormant phase in 1849, suspending its subscriptions and meetings. However, as wider community opposition to transportation mounted, its leaders, especially Williams, Jeffrey and Smith, pushed a requirement that those signing anti-transportation petitions pledge not to employ prisoners arriving after 1 January 1850. This call for consistency and commitment caused some eminent anti-convictism speakers to baulk, with a public meeting opting for a less demanding motion that the pledge was 'highly desirable.'[52] Jeffrey and Williams were elected onto an Anti-Transportation League Committee to cooperate with its Launceston counterpart, and to draft a pledge on not employing convicts.[53] It was indicative of the importance of workers to the campaign. They had been at it longer, were more united, and could muster large numbers for meetings and petitions.

The HTTU collected signatures for the pledge and promised to publish the names of those who signed but later reneged. It established a registry office for free-labour and amended its rules to include ticket-of-leave holders. It rejected John Morgan's self-serving proposal to exempt some categories of convicts like engravers and printers.[54] In October 1850 the Union wrote to the Governor seeking information on the disposal of convicts recently-arrived on the *Nile*, reiterating that 'the free working class . . . continue to be distressed and oppressed by a system which places them in competition with probationers and other prisoners in the labour market.'[55]

Over the next two years the HTTU continued agitation, condemning those undermining its efforts and praising others like Hobart merchants who opposed probationer engagement on the wharves.[56] It also tried to influence those elected as the colony inched towards representative government. The Union remained active as the gold rushes increased demand for labour. In July 1852 then secretary John Williams publicly rejected Director of Public Works W P Kay's claim that carpenters were demanding 16 shillings per-day, stating mechanics would refuse to leave the colony if offered half that.[57] A month later new secretary William Stafford attacked a despatch from Governor Denison arguing the only remedy to high wages was a steady supply of prisoner labour.[58]

Other VDL workers mobilised against convict competition, most notably in Launceston. In 1842 building mechanics in Longford petitioned against convict competition.[59] In 1844 Launceston operatives held a protest meeting. Asked by the *Cornwall Chronicle's* reporter whether he would guarantee to not demand exorbitant wages, secretary (pro tem) William Wilson quoted Adam Smith that working men were entitled to more than subsistence wages. Wilson added that, like others, the reporter clearly felt working men had no business having a family.[60] The meeting appointed a Committee— representing seven trades and two labourers including a gardener appropriately named Flowers—to prepare a petition for the Governor and British government.[61] Agitation quickly lapsed but revived in April 1847, with over 400 mechanics and working men attending a meeting. As in 1844 labourers were more conspicuous participants than in Hobart, although the final petition (with 640 signatures) was simply addressed as from residents of Launceston.[62] The Secretary of State's response that VDL would continue as a penal settlement sparked further protests in October 1848. The committee including almost all those involved in 1847, like plumber John Denney, and some who led the 1844 protest (Flowers, Young and Rattray).[63] Another petition was dispatched. Almost a year later (28 August 1849) the operatives' chief representative (John Crookes) was told by Bicheno it had been 'graciously received'—in other words ignored.[64]

While awaiting this rebuff, operatives formed an Anti-Probationer League, receiving support from some employers like a cabinetmaker named Bell—awarded a prize for his sympathetic stance.[65] Meetings on combatting transportation led to the formation of the Launceston Working Men's Association (LWMA) in February 1849 with members pledging to have no dealings with employers of probationers.[66] The LWMA survived throughout 1849—a period of inactivity in Hobart. In 1850 John Denney and several others were prominent in public anti-transportation meetings. Denney decried the victimisation of workers who had taken a stand and chastised employers, who 'ought to have been the leaders in every action against transportation; but instead of this the mechanics—the labouring classes— were the first to oppose the hiring of prisoners (hear, hear).'[67] As in Hobart, worker agitation increasingly emphasised a pledge so employers using probationers would be ostracised socially and experience economic costs.

In sum, workers initiated the VDL anti-transportation campaign and remained its most consistent critics. They helped shift public sentiment and provided crucial support for the final campaign's success. It was a significant mobilisation that avoided potentially divisive splits between emigrants and ex-convicts. It was largely overlooked when Dr John West, anti-transportation theologian and newspaper editor in Launceston (and later Sydney), wrote his influential *The History of Tasmania*.[68]

The ending of transportation in NSW (1840) and VDL (1853) seems decisive in retrospect. The actuality was more nuanced, marked by periodic efforts to renew transportation in NSW until the early 1850s or extend it to new regions from British and colonial interests which only succeeded in Western Australia. Workers rallied against proposals to renew transportation to NSW in 1844 and 1846.[69] In December 1846 delegates from different trades signed a requisition for the Mayor to convene a public meeting at the Sydney Racecourse (now Hyde Park) to petition the Queen and both houses of British parliament against renewed transportation.[70] In April 1847 the Sydney Operatives Anti-Transportation Committee published accounts detailing donations from trade societies, a wide range of individuals (mechanics to government officials) and support from employers (like scaffolding for the racecourse meeting) and a publican (meeting room) as well as a breakdown of expenditures. The remaining surplus was donated to the Benevolent Asylum.[71] The British government continued to export convicts who had completed part of their sentence and held a conditional pardon, known as Exiles, to NSW. Shiploads of Exiles arrived in Geelong and Portland in 1845 and Port Philip in 1846.[72] When another group arrived on the *Hashemy* in Sydney in June 1849, workers were active in massive community-wide protest rallies and a petition calling on the Queen to dismiss Earl Grey.[73] In South Australia the prospect of partially-pardoned convicts arriving from VDL in 1845 sparked protests. WWG Nicholls, the only working-class speaker at the meeting, challenged prominent citizens to sign a pledge not to engage ex-convicts at lower wages.[74]

Assisted Free and Indentured Immigrants

Concerns emigration from the UK would saturate the labour market emerged early. In May 1833, 21 mechanics met to consider petitioning the Secretary of State for the Colonies and Commissioners of Emigration and convened a meeting of Sydney 'working mechanics' on 7 June at the *Edinburgh Castle* Hotel Pitt St.[75] The Committee of 21 told this meeting (chaired by Richard Hipkiss) it had transmitted 'a correct account of the wages given to mechanics and labourers in Sydney' to the Emigrant Friend's Society to forward to UK government ministers. The Committee reported that notwithstanding unemployment amongst free mechanics, the Board of Assignment currently had 2000 applications for prison labour from employers. Subsequent meetings involved ticket-of-leave holders and several employers sought to disrupt proceedings.[76] A third meeting resolved to memorialise the Governor to stop assignment to government officers, while another meeting in August 1833 was presented with details on wages for different trades and categories of labourers, reproduced in the *Sydney Herald*.[77] Lasting around four months, agitation sought to discourage UK emigration and pressure the NSW government on convict competition.[78]

The early-1840s depression sparked renewed agitation. In December 1841 placards called a public meeting to petition against 'the proposed loan for immigration purposes.' The meeting included impassioned speeches against employers pushing for extra labour, one speaker stating 'the Lords Macarthur (James and Hannibal) . . . wanted to make slaves of the labouring classes.'[79] The *Sydney Herald* opposed the movement, refusing to report a subsequent meeting.[80] The campaign had some effect with the Governor withdrawing the immigration funding bill. All but one of the trades involved (watchmakers) had organised societies.[81]

Efforts to introduce indentured non-European labour also aroused working-class protests.[82] In January 1843 the Mayor was persuaded to convene a public meeting at the Sydney racecourse to rally opposition to 'coolie' immigration and a protest petition was sent to the Queen.[83] In November 1849 fellmongers and woolsorters at Barker's mills in Waterloo South Sydney were discharged after refusing to train 18–20 indentured Chinese workers in their trades. At a numerously attended meeting at *Shipman's Hotel*, Brickfield Hill, an association of the working classes against 'coolie' emigration from China was proposed but rejected by the fellmongers and woolsorters who wanted to focus on their own dispute.[84]

Jobs and Unemployment Relief

The 1840s depression led groups of NSW workers, including trade societies, to petition the Governor or Legislative Council for relief. When journeymen and master cabinetmakers petitioned for a duty on imported furniture, some like journeyman Benjamin Sutherland, wanted imports prohibited given prevailing unemployment.[85] In June 1844 journeymen and master printers urged the government to close its printing office.[86] Importantly, in 1843 trades representatives established a broadly-based political body, the Mutual Protection Association (MPA), to represent distressed mechanics and others. Irving and Cahill argue their agitation frightened government sufficiently to initiate a major public works project (building a Customs House) to 'mop up unemployment and defuse political anger.'[87] Similar protests occurred in Melbourne where over 200 unemployed labourers 'wanting a means of subsistence' memorialised the Melbourne Town Council for temporary work.[88]

South Australian workers had also mobilised over unemployment relief in 1841. To reduce costs, the government had cut relief payments and withdrawn relief for those refusing work in the country. Almost 200 relief workers petitioned the Governor, claiming lower payments wouldn't provide bare necessities for their families.[89] The Governor's response was to reduce relief to rations only. Most of the men (137) signed a memorial stating they were striking until their claims were reconsidered.[90] Feeling betrayed, workers organised protest meetings in Adelaide in August 1841, one at the *Turf Hotel* so large hundreds couldn't gain admittance.[91] The South Australian Working Men's Association (SAWMA) was established to provide relief to the destitute and enhance the 'intellectual enjoyment' of workers. Office-holders/activists included John Norman (chair), William Holmes (secretary), George Wells, Cornish and Wakeham. The Governor refused to accept a petition which 1200 signed calling him to reverse his policies because it was a copy without signatures. The government was primarily concerned with curbing dissent, introducing new master and servant and labour enticement laws—the latter to prevent 'deceptive' efforts encouraging workers to leave for other colonies. Additional police were appointed to spy on the SAWMA and relief workers dispersed throughout the countryside.[92] Country jobs offered weren't always appropriate or accepted, with one farmer (J Reed) claiming 45 sent to his district had refused jobs driving bullocks and fencing.[93]

The SAWMA forwarded descriptions of labour market conditions to Britain and other colonies. It condemned the Government's policies for inducing employers to offer wages that made them little more than slaves. The Governor argued the SAMWA's demands interfered with relations between employers and employed, ignoring that recently enacted laws did precisely this.[94] SAWMA chairman John Norman led deputations to the Governor on behalf of the working classes, one (31 August) with a petition requesting land grants for unemployed labourers—antithetical to the Wakefield model.[95] Like other requests, it was rejected.

The disaffection caused concern. In September 1841 the Commissioner of Police (O'Halloran) asked Colonial Secretary Robert Gouger for more police to report on SAMWA meetings.[96] These police reports were regularly forwarded to government authorities.[97] Some newspapers labelled the SAWMA an illegal combination. Throughout October the SAWMA continued to organise meetings, deputations and memorials to the Governor but to little effect and it lapsed soon after.[98] Opposition was renewed in early 1842 with one speaker being loudly applauded for calling on the Governor to resign and be replaced with someone who had read Tom Paine's *Rights of Man*.[99] The meeting ended with three groans for the Emigration Board but little more. Notwithstanding its rapid demise, the SAWMA was an important step in political mobilisation, alarming government sufficiently to spy on it and causing some uneasy employers to petition the governor to send destitute emigrants to Sydney in August 1842.[100] The combination of public agitation, depressed conditions and government finances slowed emigration to the colony. Some SAWMA activists were prominent in agitation against master and servant laws (1847) and campaigns to enfranchise workers (1850). WWG Nichols proposed an unemployed refuge and jobless emigrants continued sporadically complaining about being misled.[101]

In VDL unemployment and distress amongst free-labour was inseparable from the question of convict competition. Like the SAWMA, the HTTU tried to administer relief while agitating, and did so successfully for a time, before foundering on the rocks of prejudice and condescension that working people could administer their own support—prejudices still dominant when the *Titanic* sank.[102]

In Western Australia the tiny labour market oscillated between bouts of labour shortage and job scarcity. In July 1832, 26 unemployed and starving mechanics and labourers in Fremantle petitioned the Governor for food. The Governor authorised relief-work at 2/6 per-day with a higher rate for those with large families.[103] Eighteen months later there were further applications for relief. Relief labourers complained about their rations, some refusing to work for rations alone.[104] Workers unable to get regular work looked to opportunities in neighbouring colonies. In November 1835 an advertisement offered mechanics with passage to Sydney on the *Currency Lass* with the fare payable in weekly instalments.[105] Like other colonies (and UK workhouses) relief was minimal so recipients would seek paid work. In July 1838 the daily family allowance was cut by 1lb after a magistrate claimed 'some women are so well satisfied with the allowance that they are not disposed to seek work.'[106] For their part, employers looked to labour that could be tied to the colony for some years, beginning the push for convict transportation that succeeded in 1852.[107] Like South Australia and New Zealand, the WA Legislative Council considered a labour enticement law to stop workers signing contracts with employers in other colonies. There were further complaints about work scarcity in 1845—something eagerly reported in South Australian newspapers.[108] The *Inquirer* conceded some employers made exorbitant charges for rations and misled servants on wages.[109] Workers kept leaving for other colonies notwithstanding dire warnings of illusory greener pastures.[110]

The Struggle Against Pernicious Labour Laws and the Suppression of Collective Action

Another political rallying point was opposition to pernicious labour legislation, especially master and servant laws. Employer interests repeatedly sought stronger laws to subordinate workers (Chapter 2), leading to often large worker protests in most colonies, including Western Australia where the Shepherds Club and Mutual Protection Society (1843) opposed 'the dangerous powers conferred on Magistrates'.[111] In VDL convict competition was a more pressing challenge but after transportation ended (1853), employers pushed for tougher master and servant laws and workers, including women, engaged in large protests.[112]

In September 1840 Committee of Trades delegates responded to proposed changes to NSW master and servant legislation by organising protest meetings and a petition with 3300 signatures.[113] One meeting of 1000 working men ended with three groans for Hannibal Macarthur.[114] The agitation succeeded in mitigating some provisions.[115] At a dinner celebrating this, trades delegates acknowledged *Australasian Chronicle* editor W A Duncan's contribution, presenting him with a gold-medal inscribed with the names of the 10 trades involved.[116] The Carpenters and Joiners Society anniversary dinner also toasted Duncan's 'defence of the Rights of the Working Man.'[117]

In 1845 renewed protests, including shepherds and other workers in Melbourne were sparked by further legislative revisions, most notably a compulsory discharge certificate to prevent workers engaging without a certificate from their previous employer.[118] Discharge certificate systems had been used in the merchant-marine and echoed earlier controls on convicts and passholder provisions used in slave colonies—demonstrating the often blurred boundaries between regulating free and unfree-labour.[119] The protests failed and other colonies followed suit with South Australia introducing a bill featuring written-discharge requirement and other provisions impeding worker-rights in 1847. The *South Australian Register* labelled it a blatant piece of class legislation, serving employer interests.[120] Protest meetings in the Adelaide working-class suburbs of Hindmarsh and Bowden were followed by others in the rural/mining districts of Glen Osmond and the Barossa.[121] Hindmarsh meeting chairman (John Godlee) told the audience their efforts would 'mitigate the threatened evil which was hanging over the head of the *real producers*.'[122] Memorials sent to the Governor labelled the bill an 'invasion of our rights and privileges as British subjects,' pledged workers wouldn't engage under it, and warned the law would frighten off prospective emigrants.[123] The Legislative Council refused to accept a memorial from German emigrants because they were foreigners—something condemned by a German (Beel) at the Glen Osmond meeting.[124] The agitation pushed an already divided Legislative Council into amending several provisions.[125]

The protests against master and servant laws used common arguments, namely they were more oppressive than UK laws; infringed on workers' rights as British subjects; lacked reciprocity regarding offences, procedures and penalties; extended the convict regime to free workers; and would discourage emigration.[126] Protesters knew these points would be reproduced in the British press, magnifying their impact.

Workers also mobilised to defend their collective rights. During the Burra copper mine strike (1848), the Board of Directors prosecuted the editor of the *South Australian Register* for his reporting of the incident. A public meeting condemned this action, Robert Mahon stating:

> So long as Mr John Stephen employed his powerful pen in persuading people to come hither, they (the capitalists) were satisfied with him; but now . . . were willing to crush him . . . Because he would not consent to see men reduced to the necessity of sending their children to be yoked as beasts of burden underground, in order to eke, with their wages an

insufficient support . . . They wished to reduce the men to the condition of their fellows in England.'[127]

One resolution adopted opened with the line 'a fair day's wages for a fair day's work for us and our children should be the working man's watchword in South Australia.' That employment conditions and life prospects of workers and their children should exceed those in the UK was a sentiment enunciated at numerous gatherings throughout the colonies.[128] For emigrants, improving their prospects was pivotal to their decision to leave family and friends for a distant land. The colonially born and convicts also believed they were owed a better life given the wealth of the colonies.

Asserting the right to organise and receive a fair wage was inherently political because it struck at the core of laissez-faire capitalism—as it still does under neoliberalism, no more than a re-badging of laissez-faire. In 1834 Hobart master tailor Thomas Lightfoot lamented the journeymen's society had urged his workers 'to stick up for their rights, privileges and higher wages, and no longer allow masters to make a property out of the sweat of their brow.'[129] In December 1846 Adelaide Cordwainers secretary John Portwine proclaimed no-one should question our labour as 'belonging collectively and individually to us, and if we wish to demand a reasonable price for it, we have the same right in common with any other class of tradesmen.'[130] Another Adelaide trade society official declared master and journeymen interests were inimical and combination was 'socialism itself and therefore radically good.'[131] Class sentiment was never far away. George Wells—a bootmaker and prominent spokesman for Adelaide working people—told one newspaper editor:

> You speak of working men as degraded beings and willingly enter the list on behalf of employers. The reason why, I suppose, is because you belong to their class.[132]

Political Mobilisation and the Struggle for Democracy

Although Australian historians conventionally located organised labour's contribution to the rise of social democracy to the second half of the 19th century, in *The Southern Tree of Liberty* Irving demonstrated worker mobilisations in the 1830s and 1840s were a driving force in the push for democratic government and a wider (if still gendered) franchise in New South Wales.[133] There is evidence of similar developments in other colonies. Social dislocation/unrest in the 1850s was important in bringing change but it built on earlier developments. This chapter summarises these developments in the barest detail.

Emigrant workers brought radical political ideas with them. In 1840 a group of Owenite socialists formed the Colonial Society for the Advancement of the Social System.[134] The society struggled and in early June Secretary

James Cochrane indicated more members were needed before embarking on 'definitive measures'.[135] A month later the owner of their meeting place refused them admittance on religious grounds with the *Sydney Herald* urging the government to crack down on blasphemous, obscene and disorderly speeches given at the Sydney racecourse on Sunday.[136] Aside from attempts at organisation, there were public debates like a prolonged one over socialism and capital/labour relations in the *South Australian Register* in the first half of 1850.[137]

In NSW workers were involved in the push for a representative assembly from the early 1830s, initially led by a radical element within the Australian Patriotic Association (APA) including self-employed tradesman Richard Hipkiss who had been involved in the 1832 reform bill agitation in Britain. Hipkiss unsuccessfully opposed a proposal of W C Wentworth and others to tie influence within the APA's committee to the level of funds subscribed.[138] Over the next two years the so-called 'trade union party' (including Hipkiss, Rudder, McDermott, Keith, Hardy and Poole) campaigned that all APA members should participate in policy making, calling public meetings 'until the trades union man obtained his public right.'[139] They opposed land distribution favouring the wealthy and were probably behind a petition to the Secretary of State calling for small land grants in 1836.

In December 1835 the trade union party took a strong stance on the colony's proposed constitution, arguing for elections by ballot and a franchise including all free males over 21 years with a minimal property qualification 'as there were "40 shilling" voters at home.'[140] This was opposed by wealthier APA members like Wentworth who drafted the despatch in January 1836 setting a qualification of £10 per-annum for city freeholders and £5 in the country. In 1838 the trade union party split over the APA's stance on transportation, but by 1840 trades' delegates had formed the Committee of Trades to pursue a wide political brief.[141] In 1842 popular government and an extended franchise was the subject of renewed agitation complicated by concerns a landholder-dominated legislative assembly would reintroduce transportation.[142] Workers, small shopkeepers and others like Irish ex-soldier Henry McDermott pushed for a wider franchise.[143] They failed but had more success with the franchise for the Sydney City Council elections.[144]

In 1843 trades representatives championed the candidacy of ex-convict Chippendale distiller Robert Cooper, affectionately known as Robert the Large, to the first partially-elected Legislative Council. Given the £2,000 property qualification for candidates, Cooper was their best option. Cooper hadn't forgotten his humble origins and championed the cause of distressed victims of the 1840s depression. Despite a vigorous campaign including public meetings, marches and attacks on the booths of opposing candidates, Cooper wasn't elected. The property qualification for voting (rent equivalent to £20 per-annum) excluded all but the best-paid workers. However, in the aftermath trades delegates formed the Mutual Protection Association (MPA) which soon boasted 500 members and nominated its own candidates (including McDermott) for the 1843 and 1844 City Council elections. They were duly elected. It also established its own newspaper, the *Guardian*, run by a committee of four—bootmaker Daniel Coughlan, carpenter William Crosbie (Crosby), cabinetmaker Robert Stewart and upholsterer Benjamin Sutherland.[145]

In South Australia working people began agitating for a wider franchise in 1850. In July/August, meetings in Hindmarsh formed an Elective Franchise Association (EFA) with a Chartist platform of universal suffrage, vote by ballot, annual elections, no property qualifications, no nominee members and no state religious endowment. An important colony-specific addition to the platform was abolition of British control of the land-fund—colonial land sales used to fund emigration.[146] Bootmaker George Wells was pro tem secretary with John Norman, another ex-SAWMA activist as chairman. Norman told a meeting that in Britain the weight of history and interest groups stymied reform but in a new country like theirs a near perfect constitution should be framed.[147] In the same month a meeting at the *Black Horse* hotel Adelaide formed the Complete Suffrage League also with Chartist objectives of 'full and fair representation of the people.'[148] One speaker (Bryan) argued working men should be freer than England. Another (Bevan) stated:

> The rich and learned had no need to exert themselves—there was no fear but that property would be represented; but it was incumbent on the masses to demand the right of sharing in the making of laws which they were called upon to obey. What had driven them from their mother country? Why the evils induced by class legislation, which had peopled the workhouses and prisons. Let them avert such a fate for themselves and their children (*cheers*).[149]

The Complete Suffrage League and EFA soon merged to form the South Australian Political Association (SAPA). Establishing several branches, SAPA became prominent in its role in public debate over the new constitution. It eschewed middle-class involvement. Conservative newspapers criticised its 'immodest demands' and 'violent language' that portrayed class interests as inimical and advocated socialism.[150] George Wells responded that they were demanding recognition of the contribution working people made to colony. Bryan stated that when newspapers 'spoke of a purse-proud aristocracy they meant those who looked down upon labour with contempt.'[151] SAPA's campaign failed to prevent a property qualification and workers subsequently formed a new body to pursue reform.[152]

In VDL, campaigning for a wider franchise had to await the ending of transportation. Nonetheless, sufficient workers secured the vote to influence who got elected. From 1851 the Hobart Town Trades Union used its electoral clout to try and ensure working people had a legislative voice. In February 1851 a Jeffrey/Watson motion argued it was the Union's duty to assist electing those individuals who 'exerted themselves to stop transportation.'[153]

The chosen candidate was T D Chapman, a merchant and later Premier. Scrupulously avoiding damaging divisions between emancipated convicts and other free workers, the HTTU rushed to Chapman's defence when he was accused of rejecting emancipist support.[154] In April 1851 pro-transportationists tried to disrupt a HTTU meeting, labelling many members emancipists.[155] Chapman topped the poll to the part-elected Legislative Council in 1851 and also relied on working-class support when running for the newly established Legislative Assembly in 1856. Chapman's platform included reforming the hated *Master and Servant Act*, although he later reneged on this under pressure from rural employers.[156] Nonetheless, the HTTU had been effective in mobilising workers.

Political mobilisations by workers must be viewed in the light of resistance from influential elements including wealthy landholders like Alexander Berry and those with a propertied middle-class view of democracy like W C Wentworth. Some, like Sir William Denison, hankered for a more finely gradated society with a local aristocracy so all would know their place.[157] Landholder James Macarthur and Wentworth went so far as to advocate a titled peerage in NSW in the early 1850s. They got no traction, being tellingly lampooned by solicitor and Irish convict's son Daniel Deniehy. Drawing on Aboriginal dream-time mythology of a fierce Diprodoton-like beast inhabiting billabongs, Deniehy labelled them a Bunyip aristocracy. The satire included suggestions Macarthur's coat of arms should include a rum-keg in honour of his father's involvement in the infamous Rum Corps. Deniehy captured community hostility to the highly stratified society that operated in Britain.[158] Elements of old fealty did hang on for generations, with the local elite aping their English 'betters' in schooling, manners, accent and titular gongs along with obsequious and vicarious adoration for the English nobility (now thankfully confined to media-pumped exuberant train-spotting of the Royal Family's procreation, marriages and odd visits).

Political agitation and working-class mobilisation

Political mobilisation by workers was a prominent feature of NSW, VDL and South Australia by the 1840s. Increasingly it took on an institutional form like the SAWMA, MPA, the HTTU and SAPA. There is evidence of ready cross-over of trade societies into wider political alliances, community networks, organisational hubs and recognised activists/leaders. The *Southern Tree of Liberty* contains a map of meeting places in 'democratic Sydney' including large outdoor venues like Hyde Park/Racecourse; larger indoor venues like the Mechanics School of Arts in Pitt St and City Theatre in Market St; and smaller meeting venues like the *Edinburgh Castle Hotel* corner of Pitt and Bathurst St, the *Crown and Anchor* on the corner of George and Market Streets and Vercoe's Temperance Coffee House in Pitt St.[159] These meeting places were all in close proximity as were the Mutual Protection Association's rooms (116 King St) and offices of newspapers sympathetic to working people—the *Australasian Chronicle* (67 Pitt St) and *The Citizen* (104 King St and later 76 York St). Meeting places are clustered between King and Druitt streets with smaller groups near Circular Quay/the Rocks to the north and in Brickfield Hill (now George St) and Pitt Streets from the corner with Liverpool Street three blocks south on the less feted western side.

The database used for this book provides similar evidence for other urban centres like Hobart, Adelaide, Melbourne and Launceston. For example, meeting places like the *Lamb Inn* and *Jolly Hatters* in Hobart clustered around working-class districts like Wapping near Sullivan's Cove and up towards North Hobart including lower Melville and Brisbane Streets. Meeting places in central Adelaide included the *Royal Oak* in Hindley St with another cluster in Hindmarsh north of the city. In Launceston the Infants School in Frederick St and several other venues were well situated for meetings of working people, being close to the modest cottages (many still to be found) south of the city-centre near the old brickfields (now Brickfields Park).

Adding to the geographic footprint of worker mobilisation is an identifiable group of spokespersons for working people, articulating their concerns. Irving compiled a list of trade society activists, sympathetic publicans and others involved in political mobilisations between 1846 and 1854. At least 35 were active prior to 1850, including some like painter John Carruthers and upholsterer Benjamin Sutherland involved in the Mutual Protection Association (MPA).[160] Benjamin Sutherland was MPA secretary (1843–44), one of the publishers of its newspaper the *Guardian*, gave evidence to the Select Committee on Distressed Labourers (1844), led agitation against convict competition (1843 and 1844) and in endorsing candidates in the municipal elections (1844). Activists from a wide range of trades were involved in successive political mobilisations (master and servant, anti-transportation/convict competition, anti-immigration, jobs and constitutional reform), including stonemasons named Carlisle (1846–54), William Maxwell (1843–51) and J Lynch (1841–54); painters J Carruthers (1840–50), Edward Mullens (1841–52) and Edward Knight (1844–51), cabinetmaker Robert Stewart (1844–51), carpenters William Crosby (1840–44) and J Coleman (1843–44) and bootmaker Daniel Coughlan (1844–50). A number like Coleman held official positions in trade societies before, during or after their involvement in political agitation.[161] Some MPA activists later became members of four radical organisations involved in the 1850s constitutional reform/franchise debates, including bootmaker Daniel Coughlan, painter/glazier Edward Knight, stonemason William Maxwell and painter Edward Mullens.[162]

In South Australia T Y Wakeham involved in the first builders union (1838) was prominent in the South Australian Working Men's Association (1841). George Dent was involved in the 1840 bakers' society, agitation over master and servant legislation (1847) and defending newspaper editor John Stephenson during the Burra miners' strike (1848). Bootmakers' union official George Wells was even more prominent in political agitation, help-ing instigate the Hindmarsh Elective Franchise Association (1850).[163] Wells was an influential and recognised spokesperson for working people, more so than avowed socialist WWG Nichols who also spoke regularly at public gatherings.

In VDL Hobart trade society activists like Samuel Buller (sawyer), J G Kitchen (printer) and John Williams (tailor) were involved in the political agitation against transportation. Cabinetmaker William Jeffrey was promi-nent in virtually every instance of political agitation between 1844 and 1851, chairing meetings and as the principal spokesman for the 'working classes'. Other prominent activists included tailor John Williams (involved in every protest between 1844 and 1852), carpenter W.C.D. Smith, and gardener J Dickenson. Jeffrey and Chartist transportee William Cuffay's agitation car-ried over to the 1850s. There is evidence of 30 others prominent in protests, the vast majority skilled tradesmen including sawyers, butchers, carpenters, joiners, bricklayers, plasterers, stonecutters, stonemasons, wheelwrights and printers.[164] Craft workers had the advantage of education/literacy and organisational experience. Some at least spoke on behalf of working people generally. In Launceston too there were recognised spokesmen like plumber John Denney who told an anti-transportation meeting the higher classes might hear of the evils but 'the working population felt them.'[165] Other Launceston activists included William Johnstone, a gardener named Flow-ers, a plasterer named Rattray, a painter named Young, and labourers J Silcock and John Crooke.

Aside from Sydney laundresses in 1843, women played a limited role in political mobilisations but their involvement began to increase in the 1850s, including dissent on the Victorian goldfields and agitation against master and servant laws in Tasmania.

Worker Mobilisation and Class Formation

Though no longer so fashionable, class remains an elemental characteris-tic of capitalist society. Thompson argued the English working class had emerged by the 1830s although it was different from the working class com-posed predominantly of mass semi-skilled industrial workers half a century later.[166] In short, the working class does not just emerge but continues to change. In *Class Structure in Australian History*, Connell and Irving took a dynamic approach to class relations, pointing to the emergence of a rul-ing class and working class and subsequent changes to both. Using differ-ent methods and new information, this book examined a similar terrain between 1788 and 1850, focussing on worker organisation while also trying to explain it.[167] In *Working Class Formation: Patterns in Western Europe and United States* Katznelson and Zolberg pointed to inter-country differ-ences in working-class formation and contingent factors explaining this, including differences in periodisation and as Thompson emphasised—the working class made itself and the organisational contours of this varies between societies.

The majority of convicts and free settlers came from England where class formation was well advanced. The combination of transportation, almost entirely composed of working people, with a rapid transition to relatively capital-intensive economy with few opportunities for economic independence contributed to a society where class formation occurred rapidly. Class is a relational concept. Although this book only touched on it, this included the emergence of a powerful group of capitalists like landholder James Macarthur, merchants Robert Campbell and Edward Lord, and a professional middle-class.[168] While shaped by global influences, the emerging class structure also reflected particularities of colonial capitalism, including the conspicuous role played by the state in facilitating accumulation process, and the industry-mix giving rise to specific interests. It was also marked by tensions as colonial workers sought to throw off the shackles in a new society, rejecting the forelock-tugging obsequiousness and finely-defined status gradations to which their employers and rulers often aspired.[169]

Another important aspect of Thompson's argument concerns agency related to organisational manifestations of class. A characteristic of class formation shared by almost all countries were attempts to establish unions even if outcomes varied considerably. Unions are a pivotal response to inequality at work under the capitalist mode of production. With all their limitations, unions were and remain the clearest and most undiluted expression of worker organisation that enhances class identity. This helps explain why after 700 years the role and influence of unions remains deeply contested even in countries where they have legal recognition. While collective action by workers is common and central to working-class formation, Katznelson argues

> There are always impediments to collective action, to those occasions when "sets of people commit pooled resources, including their own efforts, to common ends." . . . Both the content and form of collective action are high variable and this variation demands explanation.[170]

Examining the conditions of early Australian society, including the political economy of particular industries and political/regulatory structures, and the ways different groups of workers took collective action this book attempts to contribute to that project. Earlier chapters charted the scope and patterns of organisation and the language of dissent, arguing it was critical to include informal, while recognising the importance of formal organisation. Within the context of often volatile formal organisation, workers also mobilised politically—the focus of this chapter. As Irving has argued for NSW, industrial activism seamlessly transitioned into political activism, involving many of the same activists and therefore both manifestations of organisation need to be considered as a whole. Political activities provided continuity and broadened the sense of working-class identity. That this entailed shared views or a language of class is evident in the public meetings, petitions and other activities associated with this agitation.

In *The Southern Tree of Liberty* Terry Irving argued that by the 1840s there was an identifiable working class in NSW. This book concurs and extends it to the Australian colonies more generally. Indeed, by the mid-1850s the Australian working class had secured most Chartist demands, well ahead of its counterpart in Britain, and this more rapid trajectory of political/social progress continued over the next half-century.

Conclusion

From the early 1830s workers began to mobilise politically, sometimes in alliance with middle-class radicals/progressives or local manufacturers, but far more often independently. Those from trade societies or with experiences of political struggles in Britain played a conspicuous role initiating, coordinating and leading this agitation. Though on a smaller scale, there are parallels in the types of organisation and activity to what was occurring during the 1820s and 1830s in the United States.[171] By the 1840s these struggles increasingly involved a wider spectrum of the working community and public statements, advertisements, petitions and letters indicate their leaders recognised this. Contrary to received wisdom, there is evidence of class identification in the language, modes of organisation, objectives and action.

Notes

1 *Australasian Chronicle* 26 December 1840. This was confirmed by Duncan's daughter when interviewed by Leila Thomas.
2 *Sydney Monitor* 17 September 1840.
3 *Hobart Town Courier* 23 September 1846 and Dyster, B. (1989) *Servant and Master*, 126–127.
4 Fraser, W. (1970) *Trade Unionism*, 99.
5 *Commercial Journal* 15 February 1840.
6 *Sydney Herald* 6 and 17 October 1840 and 12 November 1840.
7 *Australasian Chronicle* 23 December 1843, and *Star and Workingman's Guardian* 4 January 1844.
8 TAHO CSO 1/649/15077 19 March 1833.
9 The editor of the Hobart Town Couriers was supported the petition. *Launceston Advertiser* 8 May 1834; *Colonial Times* 1 April 1834.
10 See for example TAHO CSO 1/774/16539.
11 TAHO CSO 1/528/11502 Immigration Committee evidence and correspondence 4 and 5 July 1834.
12 *Trumpeter* 26 December 1834.
13 *Colonial Times* 10 February 1835.
14 *Colonial Times* 13 January 1835.
15 TAHO CSO 1/895/19022; *Tasmanian* 16 December 1836.
16 TAHO CSO 5/4/70.
17 TAHO CSO 5/4/40.

18 *Hobart Town Courier* 17 March 1837.
19 *Cornwall Chronicle* 1 April 1837.
20 TAHO GO 33/27, 1106.
21 *Trumpeter* 3 November 1843 and 8 December 1843.
22 *Hobart Town Advertiser* 17 November 1843.
23 Quinlan, M. (1986) *Hope Amidst Hard Times: Working Class Organisation in Tasmania 1830–1850*, Industrial Relations Research Centre Monograph, University of New South Wales, 58–80.
24 *Hobart Town Advertiser* 20 August 1844.
25 TAHO GO 1/70/32.
26 *Hobart Town Advertiser* 6 September 1844.
27 *Hobart Town Advertiser* 28 January 1845.
28 *Hobart Town Advertiser* 13 June 1845.
29 TAHO CSO 8/101/2131.
30 TAHO CSO 8/139/2815.
31 *Colonial Times* 7 May 1845.
32 TAHO CSO 8/187/3175.
33 *Hobart Town Herald* 11 July 1845.
34 *Hobart Town Advertiser* 25 July 1845.
35 TAHO GO 33/52/209; *Van Diemen's Land Observer* 12 June 1846.
36 *Britannia and Trades Advocate* 29 April 1847.
37 *Hobart Town Courier* 28 April 1847.
38 *Hobart Town Advertiser* 4 May 1847. Morgan's support didn't extend to unions, severely criticising a strike by journeymen tailors in the same year.
39 *Britannia and Trades Advocate* 13 May 1847.
40 TAHO CSO 24/24/581 9 August 1847.
41 *Hobart Town Courier* 16 October 1847; *Britannia and Trades Advocate* 21 October 1847.
42 *Britannia and Trades Advocate* 3 June 1847.
43 *Britannia and Trades Advocate* 17 June 1847.
44 *Britannia and Trades Advocate* 16 December 1847.
45 *Hobarton Guardian* 21 January 1848,
46 TAHO CSO 24/55/1921.
47 Bennet, J. (2011) *Reluctant Democrat: Sir William Denison in Australia, 1847–1861*, Federation Press, Annandale.
48 TAHO CSO 24/55/1921.
49 *Hobart Town Courier* 20 December 1848.
50 TAHO CSO 24/88/2643.
51 TAHO GO 33/65.
52 *Hobart Town Courier* 8 December 1850.
53 *Hobart Town Courier* 25 September 1850.
54 *Hobart Town Courier* 19 October 1850.
55 Like others, the request was refused TAHO CSO 24/270/5363.
56 *Launceston Examiner* 5 January 1851; *Britannia and Trades Advocate* 3 March 1851.
57 *Colonial Times* 6 July 1852.
58 *Colonial Times* 10 August 1852.
59 TAHO CSO 22/19/779.
60 *Cornwall Chronicle* 4 September 1844.
61 *Launceston Examiner* 5 September 1844.
62 TAHO CSO 24/13/291; *Launceston Examiner* 21 April 1847.
63 *Launceston Examiner* 28 October 1848.
64 TAHO CSO 24/89/2673.
65 *Launceston Examiner* 17 January 1849.

66 *Launceston Examiner* 20 and 27 January 1849; *Colonial Times* 20 February 1849.
67 *Launceston Examiner* 14 August 1850. See also *Cornwall Chronicle* 7 September 1850.
68 A protest flag now held in the Launceston Queen Victoria Museum and Art Gallery is the earliest one to bear a striking resemblance to the current Australian flag. West, J. (1852–1971 reprint) *The History of Tasmania*, Angus and Robertson, Sydney.
69 *Australian* 17, 20 and 21 May 1844.
70 *The Citizen* 12 December 1846.
71 *Sydney Morning Herald* 7 April 1847.
72 Bennet, J. (2011) *Reluctant Democrat*, 60.
73 Ferguson, L. (2013) *FitzRoy: Beyond the Rumours*, Pilar Publishing, Killara, 148–152.
74 *South Australian Register* 10 September 1845.
75 *Sydney Herald* 3 June 1833.
76 *Sydney Herald* 15 and 22 July 1833.
77 *Sydney Herald* 19 August 1833.
78 *Sydney Herald* 26 August 1833.
79 *Sydney Herald* 23 December 1841.
80 *Sydney Herald* 21 and 23 December 1841.
81 Terry, D. (1951) The Development of the Labour Movement in New South Wales 1833–1846, 110.
82 *The Sun and NSW Independent Press* 28 January 1843 and 4 February 1843; and *Sydney Record* 27 January 1844.
83 *Sydney Morning Herald* 18 January 1843 and for response see NSWGG 26 January 1844.
84 *Bathurst Free Press* 17 November 1849 citing report in *The People's Advocate*.
85 *Sydney Morning Herald* 18, 26 and 30 January 1843 and *The Temperance Advocate* 8 February 1843.
86 *Morning Chronicle* 8 June 1844.
87 Irving, T. and Cahill, R. (2010) *Radical Sydney: Places, Portraits and Unruly Episodes*, UNSW Press, Sydney, 48.
88 *Melbourne Times* 4 March 1843.
89 AOSA CSO 1841/2.
90 AOSA CSO 1841/2a.
91 *Adelaide Independent* 12, 19 and 26 August 1841.
92 *South Australian* 3 September 1841; AOSA CSO 1841/617; and AOSA CSO 1841/621. For press reports on 'enticement', see *South Australian Register* 21 and 28 November 1840.
93 AOSA CSO 1841/569 20 August 1841.
94 *South Australian Register* 16 October 1841.
95 AOSA CSO 1841/588.
96 AOSA CSO 1841/617 7 September 1841.
97 See for instance AOSA CSO 1841//679A4 29 September 1841.
98 *Adelaide Independent* 14 October 1841; AOSA CSO 1841/735 27 October 1841.
99 *South Australian Register* 5 February 1842; *South Australian* 17 February 1842.
100 AOSA CSO 1842/251 15 August 1842 memorial of Edward Stephen and others.
101 *Adelaide Observer* 12 April 1845; *South Australian* 8 August 1849.
102 Gregson, S. (2012) Women and Children First? The Administration of Titanic Relief in Southampton, 1912–59, *English Historical Review*, 127(524):83–109.
103 AOWA CSO/53 10 July 1832.

104 *Perth Gazette* 7 January 1834; AOWA CSO 47 16 January 1834; CSO 6/215 27 January 1834 and 6/230 10 February 1834.
105 *Perth Gazette* 28 November 1835.
106 AOWA CSO Rough Register of Inward Correspondence April-November 1838, memo 7 July 1838.
107 See for example *Perth Gazette* 13 October 1838. In 1847 York and Toodyay district landholders met to petition for convict labour. *Perth Gazette* 30 June 1847.
108 *South Australian Register* 29 November 1845; *Perth Gazette* 13 December 1845.
109 *Inquirer* 23 July 1845.
110 *Inquirer* 8 October 1845 and 12 August 1846.
111 *Perth Gazette* 21 January 1843.
112 TAHO CSO 1/42/714 and 1/59/1254; *Hobart Mercury* 4 May 1855.
113 *Sydney Monitor* 29 September 1840.
114 *Sydney Herald* 30 September 1840.
115 *Sydney Monitor* 29 September 1840.
116 *Australasian Chronicle* 26 December 1840.
117 Terry, D. (1951) The Development of the Labour Movement in New South Wales 1833–1846, 109.
118 *Port Phillip Gazette* 24 December 1845.
119 Hay, D. and Craven, P. eds. (2004) *Masters, Servants, and Magistrates in Britain and the Empire*.
120 *South Australian Register* 4 April 1847.
121 *South Australian Register* 8 May 1847.
122 *South Australian Register* 21 April 1847 and 9 July 1847.
123 AOSA CSO A(1847) 467, 475 and 1563; *South Australian Register* 24 April 1847, 28 April 1847 and 5 May 1847.
124 South Australia was a favoured destination for those escaping religious persecution in Prussia. *South Australian Register* 8 May 1847.
125 AOSA CSO A(1847) 467.
126 Quinlan, M. (2004) Australia 1788–1902: A "Working Man's Paradise?"
127 *South Australian Register* 16 December 1848.
128 See for example Irving, T. (2006) *The Southern Tree of Liberty*, 41.
129 *Tasmanian* 14 March 1834.
130 *South Australian Register* 9 December 1846.
131 *South Australian Register* 1 July 1846.
132 *South Australian Register* 9 December 1846.
133 Irving, T. (2006) *The Southern Tree of Liberty*.
134 *The Australian* 25 April 1840.
135 *The Australian* 11 June 1840.
136 *Sydney Herald* 15 July 1840.
137 *South Australian Register* 12, 15, 20, 21, 23 and 25 March 1850; 1, 2, 4, 6, 12, 15, 16, 17 and 27 April 1850; 6 and 7 May 1850.
138 *Sydney Gazette* 26 November 1835.
139 Terry, D. (1951) The Development of the Labour Movement in New South Wales 1833–1846, 103.
140 Terry, D.H.M. (1951) The Development of the Labour Movement in New South Wales 1833–1846, 106.
141 Terry, D.H.M. (1951) The Development of the Labour Movement in New South Wales 1833–1846, 107–109.
142 Terry, D.H.M. (1951) The Development of the Labour Movement in New South Wales 1833–1846, 110.
143 Irving, T. (2006) *The Southern Tree of Liberty*, 40.
144 *Australasian Chronicle* 7 and 12 July 1842.

145 Irving, T. and Cahill, R. (2010) *Radical Sydney*, 46–53.
146 *South Australian Register* 26 July 1850; 8 August 1850 and 2 October 1850.
147 *South Australian Register* 27 September and 2 October 1850.
148 *South Australian Register* 7 October 1850.
149 *South Australian Register* 8 October 1850. See too *South Australian Register* 14, 15, 16 and 24 October 1850; *Adelaide Observer* 26 October 1850.
150 *South Australian* 4 November 1850.
151 *Adelaide Times* 2 and 13 November 1850; *South Australian* 7 November 1850.
152 *South Australian Register* 28 November 1850 and 5, 6 and 12 December 1850; Moss, J. (1985) *Sound of Trumpets*, 69.
153 *Britannia and Trades Advocate* 3 March 1851.
154 *Britannia and Trades Advocate* 15, 18 and 21 September 1851.
155 *Hobart Town Advertiser* 4 April 1851.
156 Roe, M. (1965) *Quest for Authority in Eastern Australia 1835–1851*, Melbourne University Press, Melbourne, 11; *Tasmanian Daily News* 8 February 1858.
157 Bennet, J. (2011) *Reluctant Democrat*, 25.
158 McKay, A. (1850) Analysis of the Australian Colonies' Government Bill, London cited in Bennet, J. (2011) *Reluctant Democrat*, 381.
159 Irving, T. (2006) *The Southern Tree of Liberty*.
160 Irving, T. (2006) *The Southern Tree of Liberty*, 265–267.
161 Irving, T. (2006) *The Southern Tree of Liberty*, 256–260.
162 Irving, T. (2006) *The Southern Tree of Liberty*, 268–270.
163 *South Australian Register* 8 August 1850 and 2 October 1850.
164 Quinlan, M. (1986) *Hope Amidst Hard Times: Working Class Organisation in Tasmania 1830–1850*, Industrial Relations Research Centre Monograph, University of New South Wales, 63.
165 *Launceston Examiner* 21 April 1847 and 14 August 1850.
166 Katznelson, I. (1986) Working Class Formation: Constructing Cases and Comparisons, in Katznelson, I. and Zolberg, A. eds. *Working Class Formation: Nineteenth Century Patterns in Western Europe and the United States*, Princeton University Press, New Jersey, 3–4.
167 Connell, R. and Irving, T. (1980) *Class Structure in Australian History: Documents, Narrative and Argument*, Longman Cheshire, Melbourne.
168 For a study of this in one colonial town see Fry, K. (1993) *Beyond the Barrier: Class Formation in a Pastoral Society, Bathurst 1818–1848*, Crawford House Press, Bathurst.
169 Smith, B. (2008) A Cargo of Women, 77.
170 Katznelson, I. (1986) Working Class Formation: Constructing Cases and Comparisons, 20.
171 Pessen, E. (1956) The Workingmen's Movement of the Jacksonian Era, *The Mississippi Valley Historical Review*, 43(3):428–443.

12 Re-Evaluating Worker Mobilisation

This book examined how and why workers came together, drawing on evidence from the Australian colonies and relating this back to earlier forms of organisation in Europe as well as the political economy of the colonies. Founded as a small and remote penal settlement, the colonies rapidly transitioned to a vibrant capitalist society, an increasingly important part of not just imperial but global trade and movements of capital and people. The state, both imperial and colonial, played a conspicuous role in this transition through policies on land distribution, labour supply and the subordination of workers that advantaged capital. While Australia may be an exemplar of state-facilitated capitalism, there are clear parallels with slave societies in the Americas and elsewhere from the 17th century. Further, as argued in Chapter 1, the pivotal role of the state which stretches back over 600 years in Europe has received insufficient recognition in accounts of worker mobilisation. This point remains as true today. Governments facilitated the rise of neoliberalism from the 1980s by changing their fiscal, taxation, welfare, migration and employment policies; tendering, public ownership and privatisation practices and business and labour market regulation, which have had substantial effects on unions.

To overcome the often fractured accounts identified in Chapter 1 and using a large database (representing about 60–70% of organisations for which evidence survives), the book considered a wide array of worker organisation, formal and informal, involving unfree and free workers, men and women, European and non-European, all industries and occupations, industrial and political. It also considered a wide array of forms of collective action. Considering all forms of organisation and collective action provided a more complete picture of the scope and nature of worker mobilisation and how regulation and the political economy of particular industries shaped patterns of dissent. Confining analysis to formal organisation, or failing to examine the relationship between formal and informal organisation, arguably provides a misleadingly narrow picture of worker mobilisation. The trajectory of mobilisation is more complex and previously neglected groups or industries assume more significance. For example, beyond their conspicuous involvement in Female Factory riots, the book revealed a wider pattern of collective dissent by women, including absconding and combinations by free domestics and tailoresses. The latter entailed an attempt to unionise almost 30 years before a strike/union in the same town (Melbourne) widely viewed as marking the beginnings of female unions. The same point can be made with failing to incorporate often ephemeral political mobilisations.

Workers used a wide array of different types of collective action, including go-slows, insolence/threats, strikes, riots, absconding, sabotage, petitioning and public demonstrations. The book identified clear patterns that differed by servitude-status, gender, occupation, industry and over time. Regulatory constraints not only made group absconding a more favoured option than strikes for convicts, the same applied to seamen, soldiers and free domestics and rural workers. The higher incidence of sabotage amongst rural workers or petitioning by government workers is also more comprehensible. Distinctive patterns in the use of specific forms of collective action were marked for some groups of workers (see for example rural workers, shop-assistants and tradesmen) and this also applied to a lesser degree with regard to key objectives and issues. One issue identified as being understated or corralled to a few groups in previous accounts of worker mobilisation was OHS. It was repeatedly shown that focusing only on strikes painted a misleading picture and that the type of action taken was shaped by the issue being pursued, the capacity of workers, the employers they dealt with and other factors.

Evidence of organisation and collective action was identified in all industries and many occupations although predominantly informal and small-scale—typically a handful of workers. That doesn't make it insignificant. Considering all types of organisation uncovers the contribution of groups that include convicts, government workers, shop-assistants, whalers and merchant seamen, either neglected or only seen to mobilise much later. While organisation by craft workers was important, collective dissent appeared most intense in those industries that were pivotal to the colonial economies, namely those building infrastructure (mainly government), key export industries (especially wool and whaling) and maritime transport. However, this aspect shouldn't be overstated. Widespread shipboard collective action by seamen has been identified elsewhere and at earlier times. The incidence of small-scale informal collective action by farm/rural workers using long-established methods of dissent also raises questions about whether a level of pre-existing collective dissent in the UK formed an important backdrop to eruptions like Captain Swing.

In examining worker organisation four layers or transition points were identified. At the base was pervasive battle over substantive conditions (like wages, hours and safety) and subordination/inequality/indignity at work best evidenced (but see too absconding notices, logbooks, diaries) by hundreds of thousands of prosecutions of individual workers. These cases provide a window, fragmented but still informative, of the lived experience of workers. Notwithstanding differences within and between convict and free-labour in terms of regulation (especially punishments) and the scale of prosecutions, Chapter 2 pointed to significant commonalities. These commonalities included the issues in dispute, forms of dissent, and the determination of the state apparatus and employers to subordinate labour into compliant servitude counter-posed by workers' networking and assertion of customary rights, some drawn from Britain and others 'invented' in the colonies. The next layer were numerous instances of small-scale collective action at particular workplaces as small groups of workers acted in concert over the same issues as those described in Chapter 2, again asserting customary rights. The third layer/level consisted of multi-workplace/regional collective action as workers turned to wider alliances and the fourth layer was formal organisation.

A transition from single-workplace dissent to multi-workplace/regional alliances and formal organisation was identified in all industries and most occupations. The speed of the transition varied greatly, being fairly rapid in the case of the trades with their long history of prior organisation and stronger bargaining position. It was much slower for others like service and pastoral workers and indeed it would be decades after 1850 or even longer before unions would begin to establish a strong presence. Nonetheless, however rapid the transition from informal to formal organisation, most unions formed prior to 1851 were short-lived. While craft unions were at the vanguard of it, organisational volatility only slowly diminished over the course of the 19th and early 20th centuries. The substitution of informal organisation for formal organisation was more rapid but didn't really accelerate until the 1880s and even then instances of informal organisation continued.

Notable exceptions to the transition from single to multi-workplace organisation and then to unions were self-employed watermen, cab-drivers and some carters whose conditions were largely determined by government. The large Burra copper mine was the only instance of single informal workplace organisation transitioning to a union. Being a large and relatively remote mine, there were probably contemporary parallels in North America if not elsewhere, but the multi-mine organisation of Newcastle coalminers presaged a more common pattern in Australia. Another exception were shop-assistants pursuing early-closing, illustrating a wider point that some issues, like shorter hours and to a lesser degree wage increases, could only be practically pursued on a multi-firm/regional basis. Related to the last point, comparing informal and formal organisation also demonstrated how unions were able to pursue objectives and deploy methods not available to informal organisation like mutual insurance and craft controls on labour supply as well as supporting longer strikes and helping members brought before the courts. With the exception of shop-assistants, most early unions pursued mutual insurance. However, beyond this there were different patterns of organisation and collective action in the industries examined.

While other studies have to varying degrees pointed to a transition from informal to formal organisation, this book has emphasised the importance of viewing this in the context of a more pervasive/endemic struggle over labour subordination. Through its methods and by attempting to assess different types of organisation and an array of action by different categories of workers, the book can form a reference point for comparisons with worker mobilisation in earlier/later periods and other countries/locations. Such exercises will almost certainly require research-teams and large/long-term funding (more commonly found in the sciences) as well as international collaboration.

One critical comparison point is the extent of and relationship between collective action by free and unfree-labour. Unlike the Caribbean or North America which also received transported convicts, in Australia convicts were the principal source of unfree-labour. The finding of this book is that there were far more instances of organisation of convict workers than free workers—well over three times overall and even higher for women—with an estimated total involvement of almost 19,000 compared to just over 15,000 for free workers. While convicts were far more likely to abscond collectively than most free workers, they were also involved in more strikes even if those involving free workers were on average larger. Collective action by convicts peaked in 1833 for reasons requiring further investigation before falling and being overtaken by a rising level of organisation by free workers, including unions in the 1840s. The ranks of free workers taking informal collective action, joining unions and political mobilisations included many ticket-of leave-holders and emancipated convicts. The seamless transition was not surprising given that both convicts and free emigrants were working people from the same parts of the UK and had witnessed if not been involved in the social dislocation associated with the industrial revolution as well as sharing a legacy of earlier dissent. While critical to building the infrastructure and economy of the east-coast colonies, the weight of convict resistance, both individual and collective, probably encouraged the shift to free-labour at least in some industries as it became more available.

Nonetheless, these points only capture part of the relationship between free and unfree-labour. Unlike free workers, convicts couldn't form or join unions until they obtained a ticket-of-leave and as this book also demonstrated, assigned-convicts were used as strike-breakers and more generally convicts were used to suppress free-labour combinations which had wider effects. Unions emerged more rapidly in the free colony of South Australia and the soon to be colony of Victoria with relatively few convicts. In NSW unions spread and consolidated after transportation ended in 1840. However, in VDL where transportation continued until 1853, union formation slipped backwards—notwithstanding promising beginnings in the 1830s and changed economic conditions (which in any case included the effect of transportation)—and offers at best a partial explanation. The initially free colony of Western Australia remained too small to experience a 'take off' in union organisation and even when convicts were introduced (1853–68), growth was slow until gold discoveries in the 1880s.

The foregoing observations about convict collectivism and simultaneous inhibition of free-labour organisation are not contradictory, but rather the outcome of constructing/exploiting more subordinated and therefore vulnerable categories of workers. Some predominantly rural employers looked for new categories of workers they perceived and treated as more exploitable, especially Asians and Pacific Islanders under indenture. However, this remained small scale. Both imperial and colonial governments designated Australia as European-settler colonies (decades before White Australia) and did nothing to facilitate their efforts and the outcomes were mixed. Assisted and unassisted migration (encouraged by the gold rushes and growing prosperity) were sufficient to meet the need of an increasingly urbanised society relying on capital-intensive rural/agricultural and mining exports. Only the wet and warm north-east cost was suited for plantation labour and about 62,000 indentured Pacific Islanders were imported to work in the sugar industry between 1863 and 1904, being treated appallingly and also taking a considerable level of informal collective action. While there are commonalities, the relationship between unfree and free-labour is contingent on a number of factors, including periodization, the category of unfree-labour and others just mentioned. More systematic and comparative research of free and unfree-labour in different countries/regions and over longer-time spans is likely to yield new and important insights into the history of worker mobilisation.

At the same time, another key finding was that rather than a simple dichotomy between free and unfree, the subordination of workers involved a series of regulatory-constructed gradations (including indenturing) and even free workers were heavily subordinated by the legal regime of the time. Subordination and inequality at work were (and remain) inseparable components of the capitalist mode of production. The rising influence of organised labour over 120 years after 1850 mitigated to varying degrees the primacy of individual contracts and bestowed workers with a series of collective rights as well as a floor of regulatory minimum labour standards and social protection laws (like OHS and workers' compensation). Unions were a primary but not the only response to the consequences of inequality on the lived experiences of working communities. They allied to other progressive social movements (like elements of first wave feminism) and Anti-Sweating Leagues, and created or supported political parties. In combination these mechanisms partially redressed inequality, spreading some wealth across the community, and limiting the most barbaric social consequences of laissez-faire capitalism. Growing political mobilisation and fears within the ruling elite wrought by catastrophes, especially the Great Depression and not-unrelated World War Two, secured further concessions including extending the welfare state (healthcare, aged and disability pensions), more progressive tax-regimes and full-employment geared to economic policies. In the three decades after 1945 labour's share of income relative to capital increased significantly.[1] This was the result not only of direct union influence on collective regulative of working conditions (then at its height) but also the redistribution affected by Keynesian economic policies which organised labour had also played a significant role in bring about. In so doing organised labour made no small contribution to the building of a more encompassing and robust social democracy.[2]

But these gains were partial both in degree and the countries affected (mainly North America, Western Europe, Japan and Australasia), not entrenched, and since the 1980s have come under sustained attack from the rise of neoliberalism which overthrew Keynesian economic-redistributive and full-employment policies. Neoliberalism implemented tax cuts for the rich (almost optional tax for large corporations), cut social-welfare, pursued policies like 'free' trade agreements (with weak or non-existent labour standards safeguards), competitive tendering and privatisation, as well as restructuring the regulatory architecture affecting labour markets and facilitating employer practices like contingent jobs, private-equity takeovers, downsizing and offshoring/supply chains.[3] Together with the rising influence of finance capital, these developments weakened unions and increased inequality.[4]At the very time offshoring/global supply chains and technological change were destroying jobs and hollowing out whole communities in the United States and elsewhere (no connection to depression and increased drug-use there?), global movements of labour reached unprecedented levels, including many highly vulnerable workers on short-term visas or no visa/undocumented workers in harvest, construction, the growing informal sector and elsewhere.[5] In Australia in 2013 over 25% of 15–24-year-olds were unemployed or under-employed, many of the latter locked into a cycle of part-time temporary jobs.[6] Others not registered as unemployed were excluded from the labour market altogether (no job and not in full-time education). This generational social tragedy of epic proportions is found to greater or lesser degree in Europe and North America (if not elsewhere). With notable exceptions, like Bernie Sanders, it has been ignored by politicians of all persuasions.[7]

In Australia union density has fallen by well over half on the most optimistic estimate since 1975 and substantial falls have occurred in virtually all the 'old-rich' countries (including Japan), even those like Sweden where unionisation was once around 80% of the workforce.[8] Evidence that more equal societies were more efficient[9] as well as fairer was ignored amidst an ongoing mantra of tax cuts for the rich/trickle-down economics and removing burdensome regulatory red-tape on business. In Sweden, Australia, the UK and other countries supposedly progressive political parties—some created by unions at the turn of the 20th century—played a pivotal role in this shift, claiming to do neoliberalism 'light'—an impossibility becoming increasingly evident. The shocking Grenfell inferno in 2017 was not an accident but highlighted the consequences of neoliberal policies on social protection epitomised by the infamous One-in/Two-out and One-in/Three-out rule on new legislation—new regulation requires the removal of existing regulations—implemented by successive UK governments and copied by the Trump-administration in the United States.

Subordination and inequality at work were and remain central to capitalism, whether that be clothed in the language of master and slave, master and servant or master and seamen from the 16th to 19th centuries or in the neoliberal discourse of flexible labour markets/market choice, multitiered subcontracted supply chains, franchisee self-employment or portfolio employment. The movement of work to countries in Asia and elsewhere was overwhelmingly driven by a search for cheaper, more vulnerable/compliant and mostly non-unionised labour. In other words, more readily subordinated labour. This shift has not as yet resulted in much by way of the unions in these countries getting greater traction let alone securing a substantial redistribution of the growing wealth generated. The reasons are not hard to find. In a race to the bottom, governments fall over themselves to make their countries attractive to foreign business. In totalitarian regimes like China—currently the world's manufacturing hub—nominally free workers (many internal migrants with inferior rights) have no right to join let alone establish independent unions. Official unions are Communist Party functionaries and collective action largely occurs as informal workplace strikes, much like those that occurred in Australia 170 years ago even if the scale differs. In other crony-capitalist regimes like South Korea and more especially Thailand, Vietnam and Myanmar, unions are suppressed, strikes broken with state assistance, leaders gaoled and as in China much collective dissent remains informal. In short, a crucial mechanism for redistributing income that made countries wealthy by raising total consumption levels and spreading social risk is missing and even corroding in those countries where it did occur last century.

History repeats but the same progression cannot be presumed. The growing inequality in the West is not helping to reduce wealth inequalities in those countries where work has shifted. Rather, the ruling elite in both, the fragment of the one-percent, is accumulating massive wealth while all but the upper middle-class in the old-rich countries have begun to feel the residual pain.[10] In key respects the new world of work in the 'Gig Economy' bears a striking resemblance to that of laissez-faire capitalism in the 19th century.[11] Meetings of the ruling elite like the World Economic Forum have begun to refer to inequality as a risk but just one in a list. There is little sense of concern let alone any determination to change policy settings that might alter things—at their expense—because neoliberalism is unsustainable. The ruling few—be they global corporate CEOs or Beijing princelings—and the neoliberal economists, financiers, corporate/tax lawyers, global agencies like the OECD, media outlets, politicians and others who serve them, aren't uneasy.

Notes

1 Bengtsson, E. and Waldenstrom, D. (2015), Capital Shares and Income Inequality: Evidence from the Long Run, IZA Discussion Paper No.9581, Bonn
2 Grayling, A. (2007) *Towards the Light: The Story of the Struggles for Liberty and Rights That Made the Modern West*, Bloomsbury, London.

3 Bennett, L. (1999) Swings and Shifts in Australian Industrial Relations: Employer Dominance in the 1990s, *New Zealand Journal of Industrial Relations*, 24(3):231–256.

4 Vachon, T., Wallace, M. and Hyde, A. (2015) Union Decline in a Neoliberal Age: Globalization, Financialization, European Integration, and Union Density in 18 Affluent Democracies, *Socius*, 2:1–22; Stockhammer, E. (2015) Rising Inequality as a Cause of the Present Crisis, *Cambridge Journal of Economics*, 35(30):935–958; Dabla-Norris, E., Kochhar, K., Ricka, F., Suphaphiphat, N. and Tsounta, E. (2015) *Causes and Consequences of Income Inequality: A Global Perspective*, International Monetary Fund, Paris.

5 Castles, S., De Haas, H. and Miller, M. (2014) *The Age of Migration*, Palgrave Macmillan, Basingstoke.

6 Australian Workforce and Productivity Agency (2014) *Labour Force Participation: Youth at Risk and Lower Skilled Mature-Age People: A Data Profile*, Commonwealth of Australia, Canberra.

7 Hudson, J. (2017) *Youth Labor Market Conditions and the NEET Population in the EU: Do Poor Labor Market Opportunities Discourage Youth?* M.A. Thesis, University of Central Florida.

8 Vachon, T., Wallace, M. and Hyde, A. (2015) Union Decline in a Neoliberal Age: Globalization, Financialization, European Integration, and Union Density in 18 Affluent Democracies, *Socius*, 2:1–22.

9 Wilkinson, R. and Pickett, K. (2009) *The Spirit Level: Why More Equal Societies Almost Always Do Better*, Allen & Unwin, London.

10 Pusey, M. (2003) *The Experience of Middle Australia: The Dark Side of Economic Reform*, Cambridge University Press, Cambridge; Graves, F. (2016) *Understanding the New Public Outlook on the Economy and Middle-Class Decline: How FDI Attitudes Are Caught in a Closing of the Canadian Mind*, SPP Research Papers, University of Calgary.

11 Quinlan, M. (2012) The "Pre-invention" of Precarious Employment: The Changing World of Work in Context, *The Economic and Labour Relations Review*, 23(4):3–24.

Index

aboriginals 17, 149, 154, 155, 167, 185, 240, 283

absconding 3, 5–9, 14, 18, 23–4, 36–8, 40–4, 50–3, 55, 58, 66–7, 75–6; by different groups 100, 105–6, 111, 114, 117, 122, 125, 130, 133, 136–40, 142, 144–5, 149–51, 153, 168–71, 173, 177–8, 180, 182, 184, 189–90, 192, 195, 202–3, 206, 212, 218–19, 224, 226–7, 235–6, 239–41, 244, 247, 252, 256–7, 294; form of collective protest 93–8

Adelaide 23, 46, 66, 76, 99–102, 148, 153–4, 160–2, 184, 187, 201, 206–8, 223–6, 228–9, 232, 246, 261, 263, 277, 280, 282, 284

Africa 8–10

African Americans 4; *see also* slaves

agricultural and rural workers 2–4, 8, 99, 168–87; *see also* reapers; shearers

agriculture and rural activities 167–8

apprenticeship and craft controls 3, 8, 38–9; regulation of 91–5, 98–9, 226–7, 232

Archer family (VDL landholders) 100–1, 169, 171, 173–5, 184, 255

archival and other sources used 22–4

Arthur, George (VDL Lt Governor) 15, 19, 106, 173, 213, 269

Asia and Asian workers 7–10, 13, 56, 297, 299; *see also* Chinese workers; India

assaults 44, 52, 57–8; by workers 58–9; on workers 62, 66, 93–5, 98, 111, 139, 143–4, 149, 156, 175, 212, 240–2, 247

Assignment of convicts: system and regulation 16–19, 35–9; *see also* convicts

Atkinson, Alan 7, 29, 67

Australian Agricultural Company 14, 189, 192, 256

bakers 77–81, 89, 128, 131, 140, 210, 221–4, 227–9, 251, 274

bans 25, 94–5, 98, 114, 135, 150, 170, 203, 219, 236, 245, 251–2

Banton, Mary 6, 28

Bathurst 17, 23, 37, 49–50, 52, 103, 111, 179, 183, 186, 194, 240, 244, 257

Berry, Alexander 95, 178–9, 212, 283

Bicheno, James 270, 272–4

Big data 24–5

Bigge Report 15–16, 19, 40, 178

Blacksmiths 77–80, 85, 218, 222–3, 270

Bligh, William (NSW Governor) 15

boot and shoemakers 61, 77–80, 128, 131, 222–4, 227, 229, 269, 272, 280, 282, 284

Bourke, Sir Richard (NSW Governor) 15–16, 64, 179–80

Boyd, Benjamin 182–3

Brazil 7

bricklayers 78–80, 85, 89, 122, 128, 206–7, 209, 285

brickmakers 49, 78–9, 89, 102, 128, 131, 201, 211–14

Brisbane 23, 50, 76, 147, 153, 181, 212, 217

Brody, David 4, 27

building and construction activity 7, 12–18, 61, 168, 193, 201, 211, 213, 240, 272, 276, 294, 296

Bunyip aristocracy 283

bushranging and bushrangers 8, 42, 58; and worker organisation 98, 111, 125, 139, 245

butchers 79, 89, 128, 131, 222–3, 227–8, 251, 285
Butlin, N. 32

cab drivers 160–2
cabinetmakers 77, 79, 89, 99, 128, 131, 201, 206, 210–14, 222, 270, 276, 282, 284, 285
Cahill, Rohan 276
Campbell Robert 14, 22, 181, 286
Campbelltown (NSW) 212, 247
Campbell Town (VDL) 60, 65, 80, 96, 138, 171, 218, 241, 242, 261
Canada (including references to North America) 1, 26, 75
Canal builders and navvies 5, 17
capital formation and economy 7, 11, 13–18, 20, 22, 26, 35, 42, 45, 56, 112, 168, 195–6, 268, 286, 293, 297–9
Captain Swing 4, 27, 100–1, 195, 294
Caribbean 6–7, 16, 58, 64, 111, 135, 145
Carpenters and Joiners 77–81, 85, 89, 102, 117, 128, 131, 153–4, 206–11, 214, 231, 267, 270, 274, 279, 284–5
carters, carriers and dray drivers 42, 48, 87, 89, 102, 128, 131, 151, 160–2, 295
Chartism 4, 100–1, 270, 282, 285, 287
Chinese workers: rural 8, 20, 51, 56, 181–3; manufacturing 276
Christopher, E. 9, 31
Civil servants or government officers 246–7
Clements, N. 24
clerks 16, 66, 79, 85, 87, 89, 98, 122, 128, 131, 230, 235, 243, 245–7, 251, 258–9, 263
closed shop 3, 94, 98
clothing 7, 18, 36–7, 47–50, 62, 106, 153–4, 169, 174, 178–9, 182, 186, 221, 225, 243
coachmakers 77, 79, 85, 87, 89, 128, 131, 207, 217, 222–3, 270
Cole, GDH 2, 27
collective bargaining 2, 94, 98, 223
Combination Acts and use of 2, 10, 35, 85, 213, 221, 228, 268
common rule 2, 210, 223–4
Commons, John 1–2, 26
compositors *see* printers
compulsory unionism *see* closed shop
Connell, R. 285

conspiracy 6, 44, 64, 100, 138–9, 188, 221, 228
construction *see* building and construction
construction and general labourers 3, 37, 77, 79, 85, 87, 90–1, 98–9, 102, 125, 128–32, 142, 151, 201, 207, 214, 230, 235, 245–6, 258, 271–2, 274–8, 285
convicts 1–2, 6–10, 11–12; absconding 83–4, 95; agitation against 275, 279–80, 283, 286, 294, 296; courts and collective action 140, 142–5, 147, 151, 159–60, 168–9, 171, 173–86; extent of prosecution of 51–3, 95–7; government gangs 251, 257, 267–73; regulation of 43–4; rural 188–9, 192, 195, 201, 203, 206–8, 211–12, 214, 217–18, 229, 231, 235, 237, 239–47 ; shipboard bonds and revolts 114; strikes 135–8; taking collective action 104–5; transportation and american revolution 17–19; types of and gangs described 36–40; *see also* female factories
convicts use to suppress combinations 159–60, 213, 269, 296
cooks and domestic servants 14, 17–19, 41, 44, 58–60; close supervision of 77, 87, 89, 90–1, 125, 128, 130–1, 255–6, 258, 263, 271, 294
Cooper-Busch, B. 5, 28, 156
coopers 77, 89, 128, 131, 154, 156–7, 218, 221–3, 225, 229, 269
cordwainers *see* boot and shoemakers
corruption: of officials 48, 192, 239, 241, 245, 272
courts 43–5; court action by workers 136–44; extent of prosecutions over work 45–63; logistics of litigation 63–6; magistracy and bias 93–5, 173–4; use against collective action 168; as venue for struggle 62–3; *see also* regulation
Cox Oliver, C. 6, 28
craft unions (journeymen's societies): compared to other unions 98, 206–11, 213–14, 218–24, 229–31; origins of 2–4, 10, 12, 85; rules and governing structures 214, 231; *see also* specific trades and unions
Craven, Paul 10, 30, 31
crimping 36, 39, 52, 97, 102, 153, 158; *see also* absconding; seamen; whalers

Crowley, F. 24, 27, 32
Cuffay, William 100–1, 285
curriers 77, 79–80, 85, 222, 229
customs, networks and solidarity 1,
    4, 49, 63, 67, 75, 85, 98–107, 147,
    157, 174–5, 179, 184–6, 188–9,
    195–6, 208, 256, 295

Darling, Ralph (NSW Governor)
    14–16, 179, 245
death penalty and execution 58, 111,
    141, 143–4, 180–1, 193, 241
Degraves, Peter 14, 56, 102, 221, 272
Denison, Sir William (VDL Governor)
    272–4, 283
Denney, John 275, 285
deputations 93–5, 98–9, 114, 203, 211,
    213, 219, 228–9, 252, 262, 277
desertion *see* absconding
Dobson, CR 2, 27, 153
domestics *see* cooks and domestic
    servants
drapers' assistants 78–81, 99, 260–3;
    see also shop assistants and
    warehouse workers
dressmakers/tailoresses 91, 226;
    union 294
Dublin, Thomas 5, 28
Duffield, Ian 7, 29, 32, 33
Duncan, WA 267, 279
Dyster, B. 19, 32, 208

early closing 85, 89, 102, 122, 145,
    251, 259–63, 295
effort bargaining 7, 49, 62–3, 67,
    176, 189; *see also* go-slows; wage
    bargaining
engineers, millwrights and founders 78,
    86, 100, 222–3
England 1, 9–10, 60, 65, 104–5, 144,
    158, 180, 211, 280, 282, 286; *see
    also* United Kingdom
Entwistle, Anne 100
Europe 1–4, 9–12, 20, 75–6, 95, 153,
    157–8, 162, 195, 210, 222, 276,
    285, 293, 297–8
exports 14–15, 19, 21–2, 26, 148–9,
    167–8, 188–9, 194–5, 232, 294, 297

feigning illness 6
fellmongers and woolsorters 80,
    222–3, 276
female factories 8, 13, 17; nature of
    37, 39, 46, 53–5, 59, 87, 91, 97, 99,

100, 103–5, 111, 130, 142–3, 235,
    244, 247, 255, 256, 258, 268, 293
female workers *see* domestic servants;
    dressmakers; women
Fingard, Judith 5
flags of convenience and crewing
    agencies 8
flash language *see* insolence
flogging: for collective action 144, 155,
    174, 177, 192–3, 212, 218, 240–3,
    256; lashes and corporal punishment
    6, 41, 46–50; use of 56–60, 63–6,
    138–42
food/rations 18–19, 21, 23, 36–8,
    40–1, 47–51, 62, 65, 75, 93, 95,
    99, 111, 140, 145, 149, 153–6,
    159, 169, 173–8, 180–4, 187, 189,
    192–5, 207, 212–13, 239–41,
    243–7, 251, 256, 258, 277–8
Fox, Alan 2, 27
France 5, 7; interest in Australia 12
free labour 6, 8–11; extent of
    prosecution of 51, 66–7, 83–7, 93,
    114–15, 120–1, 123–5, 133, 136–8,
    140–1, 159, 168–9, 171, 176,
    183–4, 195, 207, 213, 229, 235,
    237, 243, 271–3, 278, 294, 296–7;
    regulation 44–5; transition to 20–2,
    25–6, 40–2
fremantle 14–15, 62, 148, 153–4, 159,
    244, 258, 278
friendly benefits *see* mutual insurance

gaol sentences 8, 42, 44–7, 50–1,
    54, 56–7, 61–3, 104, 138–42; and
    collective action 144, 157, 160, 174,
    178, 181–2, 184–5, 192, 194, 213,
    228, 245, 257–8, 299
Geelong 23, 56, 61, 65, 76, 80, 148,
    153, 159, 161, 182, 184, 187–8,
    256, 261, 275
George Town (VDL) 47, 59, 240,
    244–5
Gig Economy 11; and Uber 299
Gollan, R. 4
Goodrich, Carter, L. 2, 27
go-slows: as method 125, 130, 144,
    173, 192, 240, 242, 294; neglect/
    work restriction 6–9, 67, 91–5
Goulburn 53, 173
government 3, 13–14, 16–21; convict
    administration and role in labour
    market 26, 36–40, 42–3, 46–9, 57,
    62, 64–5, 87–8, 91, 95–6, 98–101,
    105, 117, 125–6, 130, 137–8, 140,

142, 144, 148–9, 151, 153, 158–62, 168–9, 171, 174, 178–9, 183, 186–7, 189, 192–3, 201, 203, 207, 211–13, 218, 229, 235–47, 258, 263, 269–87
government boat-crews 42, 91, 147, 151, 243–4
Gregory, M. 104
grocers' assistants 78, 260–1; *see also* drapers' assistants; shop assistants
guestworkers and temporary foreign workers: historical parallels 183
Gupta, R. 9, 30

Harbour, Macquarie (VDL) 18, 53, 58, 96, 104, 147, 239
Hay, Doug 10, 27, 29–31, 42, 143
Head-shaving of female convicts 142
health *see* mutual insurance; OHS
Hill, Christopher 4, 27
Hindle, Mary 100
Hindmarsh, B. 96, 104, 169, 175
Hobart 14, 17, 23, 43, 48, 49, 50, 51, 53, 56, 59, 60, 63, 65, 75, 76, 85, 93, 99, 101, 102, 103, 106, 111, 117, 122, 140, 142, 147–9, 153–6, 158–62, 173–4, 192–3, 206–8, 212–14, 221–5, 228–9, 243–4, 261–3, 268–74, 280, 282, 284–5
Hobart Town Trades Union 272–3, 278, 283
Hobsbawm, Eric 4, 27
hotels 101–2; as union venues 208
Hours of work 18, 36–41; regulation of 54, 59–62, 65–7, 91–3, 101, 130, 133–5, 145, 149, 152, 156, 159, 169, 171–2, 174–5, 184, 189, 191, 204–5, 211, 218, 220, 227–8, 235, 237–9, 241–3, 245, 251, 253–5, 259–63, 294–5; *see also* early closing
House of Call 2–3; and hotels 159, 201–2, 206, 208, 210, 213–14, 219, 221–3, 272; and tramping system 85, 91, 94, 95, 101–2
Humphries, Jane 5, 28
Hunter Valley 14, 179–80, 188, 192, 194, 212

immigration and immigrants 5, 12–13; Europeans 211, 269; exploitation of non-Europeans 183–4; numbers of 106; to suppress combinations 213; urging selection to avoid industrial agitation 182–3
imports 19, 217, 227, 276

incendiarism 56–7, 111, 169–71, 178; *see also* sabotage
indentured workers 7–9, 51, 55–6; as category of labour 181–5, 221
India and Indian workers: manufacturing 221; rural 7–8, 15, 21, 181–3
indulgences 19, 39–40, 47–9, 63, 168, 212, 241, 247
industry and trade 11–22
insolence and abuse 6–8, 23, 46–8, 54–7, 59, 62–4, 93–4, 103–4; flash language 91–3; method of collective action 98, 104, 114–25, 139, 155, 169, 173, 177–8, 185–6, 218, 240, 242–3, 251, 255–6, 258
Ireland 10, 12, 13, 20, 99, 104, 105, 183, 210
Irving, Terry 24, 276, 284–7

Jeffrey, William 99–100, 270–2, 285
jobs/employment 91–3, 99; gulling 221–3
journeymen's associations *see* craft unions

Katznelson, I. 285–6

labourers *see* construction and general labourers
labour market 3, 9, 11–22, 26, 35, 67, 75, 85–7, 106, 162, 183, 195, 221, 225, 232, 268–9, 273, 275, 277–8, 293, 298
land: distribution policies, size, topography and climate 12, 15–17, 21–2, 26, 95–6, 145, 147–8, 160, 167–8, 235, 277, 281–2, 293
larceny and collective action 91–4, 139
Launceston 15, 17, 23, 46, 49, 51, 54, 57–8, 61, 75–6, 78, 80, 103, 147, 153, 157–60, 168, 173, 212, 217, 222–3, 226, 228, 230–1, 235, 239–40, 244–5, 256–8, 261, 268–9, 271–5, 284–5
Launceston Working Men's Association 275
laundresses 17, 60, 91, 130, 256–7, 268, 285
Leeson, RA 2, 27
letters to the press 23, 66, 99, 150, 168–70, 189–90, 201–3, 211, 218–19, 224, 229, 252, 260, 287
Linebaugh, Peter 9, 27, 29, 31
Lis, Catherine 3, 27, 209–10

Liverpool (NSW) 176, 178
Lord, Jnr Simeon 173, 178
Lord, Simeon 14, 218, 257
Lucassen, Jan 3, 27

Macarthur, Hannibal 105, 176–8,
    276, 279
Macarthur, James 65, 105, 176,
    276, 283
Macarthur, John 15
Macquarie, Lachlan (Governor) 13,
    15, 105
made demands 93–5, 224
Maitland 16, 23, 75–6, 85, 102, 105,
    122, 144, 147, 179, 181, 183, 187,
    194, 207, 221
Maloney, Mary 181, 244
management behaviour 59–61; close
    supervision 91–3, 135
manufacturing 13–15, 217
maritime activity 147–9, 162; *see also*
    sealing; whaling
maritime labour law 21, 35–9, 41–3,
    52, 59, 59
Marx, K. 17, 33
mass meetings 150, 189–90, 195,
    201–3, 211, 218–19, 252
master and servant law 10, 21, 24,
    35–9, 41–3, 46, 60–1, 67, 101, 185,
    213, 245, 255, 258, 267, 277–9,
    283, 264–85, 298
Mauritius 7, 106, 145, 156
Maxwell-Stewart, Hamish 7–8, 29, 30,
    32, 34, 44, 104
McCoy, M. 9, 31
McGregor, Sarah 181
medieval worker organisation 1–3,
    7–8, 10
Melbourne 17, 23, 75–6, 91, 122, 147,
    153, 161, 182, 206–7, 209–11, 213,
    222–9, 232, 244, 246, 251, 258,
    260–1, 267, 276, 279, 284, 294
mercantile and shipping interests 52–3,
    153, 157, 251
Merritt, A. 24, 43–4
Middle-Ages 3, 7–10, 175
middle class 15, 251, 271, 282–3,
    285–7, 299
mining and miners 3, 24, 80, 85, 87,
    89, 99, 125, 128, 130–1, 162,
    188–96, 271, 284, 295
misconduct 18, 46, 50=51, 54–5, 66,
    93–5, 139–40, 184, 241, 258
Montgomery, David 4, 27

Moreton Bay (Qld) 18, 21, 37, 39, 41,
    67, 96, 181, 245
Morgan, K. 7, 29
Mudie, James 98, 144, 179–81
mutiny 8, 15, 41, 44, 46, 100, 105,
    138, 142, 144, 153–5, 177–8, 180,
    241, 243, 245
mutual insurance 3, 91–3, 158–60,
    185, 194–5, 207–9, 221–3
Mutual Protection Association 276,
    281, 283–4

nailers 79, 210, 218, 224, 267
Newcastle (NSW) 18, 36–7, 43, 147–8,
    189, 192, 217, 244, 295
New South Wales 12–14, 15–22, 24,
    26, 36–43, 49, 53, 64–6, 76, 95–7,
    102, 112, 114, 130, 140, 142–3,
    147–9, 153, 168, 171, 178–84, 186,
    188–9, 192, 194, 206, 209, 214,
    217, 227, 231, 241, 245–7, 260,
    268, 271, 273, 275–81, 283, 286
New Zealand 26, 140, 155, 244,
    263, 289
Nichol, W. 7, 30
Nicholls, WWG 100, 275
non-strike collective action 112–14;
    building and building materials
    218–20; compared to strikes,
    by location and if informal or
    not 114–25; by issue 135–44;
    manufacturing 201; maritime
    168–70; by occupation, industry and
    gender 133–5; outcomes 149–52;
    rural 201–3; size and duration
    125–32; *see also* absconding;
    assaults; bans; Court, court action;
    insolence; made demands; sabotage
Norfolk Island 18, 36, 40, 58, 111,
    180, 243, 245
Norman, John 277, 282

Oatlands (VDL) 20, 103, 176, 217
occupational health and safety (OHS)
    61–2, 91–3, 133–4, 152, 156–7,
    169, 172–4, 189, 191, 194–5,
    204–5, 209–10, 218, 220, 227–8,
    237–8, 253–4, 260, 297; *see also*
    food; hours of work
Oxley, Deborah 7–8, 24, 29, 30

Pacific islands labour 6, 8–9, 13, 21,
    36, 182, 297
painters and glaziers 77–8, 80, 89, 128,
    131, 206–7, 210, 284

Parramatta (NSW) 17, 23, 46, 54,
56–7, 93, 99, 105, 111, 142–3, 182,
212, 214, 244, 268
paviors 78, 206
Perth (WA) 23, 76, 148, 168, 185, 187,
207, 213, 246
petitions 93–5, 98–9, 101–2, 122,
130, 149–50, 153, 159, 160–1, 170,
183, 189–90, 194, 201–3, 207,
211, 213–14, 218–19, 227, 228–9,
235–6, 240, 243, 245–7, 252,
268–83, 287
Phillip, Arthur (Governor) 15
piracy 5, 37, 58, 96, 143–4, 158
plantations and plantation labour 8–9,
17, 20, 104, 106, 167, 297
plasterers 78, 89, 138, 131,
206–10, 285
plumbers 78, 80, 128, 131, 206–7
police 40, 42, 51–2, 66, 77, 79, 85, 87,
98, 130, 236, 245–6, 258
political economy 11–22; of the
colonies 26, 145, 147–8, 286, 293
political mobilization: anti-immigration
275–6; class formation and identity
285–7; convict competition and
transportation 95, 228–9, 268–75;
jobs and unemployment relief
276–8; institutions, networks and
leadership 283–5; pernicious labour
laws 278–80; struggle for the vote
and democracy 280–3; *see also*
deputations; petitions
population of colonies: convict, free
and gender 12–13
Port Arthur 18, 122, 142, 175, 189,
192, 242
Portland 23, 51, 148, 187, 207, 275
Port Macquarie 18, 177, 241
Portugal 7
postal workers and letter carriers 89,
128, 131, 235, 245
printers 3, 24, 77, 79–80, 85, 87, 101,
128, 131, 221–4, 226, 229–31, 268,
273, 276, 285
printers chapel 3, 231
property offences and crime 7, 42,
144, 101, 111; *see also* bushranging;
larceny; sabotage

Queensland (Moreton Bay) 9, 15,
16, 24, 26, 41, 61, 76, 114, 147,
166, 206

reapers 19, 36, 97, 102, 168, 176,
186–8
Rediker, Marcus 5, 9, 28, 31, 46,
153, 162
regulation: Middle Ages 7–8, 9–10; of
work in the colonies 34–42
Reid, Kirsty 7, 43
revolts 247; Castle Forbes Estate
179–81; peasant 6, 8, 10–11, 12, 58,
64, 104–5; shipboard 111, 140, 143,
149, 155
riots 4–5, 8–9, 93–5, 99, 100–1, 103,
111, 130, 142, 171, 244, 256, 293–4
Road transport 148, 160, 162; *see also*
cab drivers; carters
Robbins, W. 24, 32
Rudé, George 4, 8, 27, 100
rural labourers *see* agricultural and
rural workers

sabotage 4, 6–7, 19, 40, 56–7, 93–5,
98, 125, 138–40, 169–71, 178, 190,
193, 219, 235–6, 241, 294; *see also*
incendiarism
saddlers 80, 223–5, 227
Sanders, Bernie 298
Saunders, K. 9, 30
sawyers 17, 36, 41, 77–8, 80, 87, 90,
102–3, 125, 129, 132, 140, 193,
210–14, 243, 247, 285
Scotland 104
sealing and sealers 14–15, 148, 153–4
seamen 2–3, 5, 10, 21–4, 38–9;
absconding 59, 62–3, 65, 77, 79,
85, 87, 90–1, 93, 95–9, 102, 104–5,
114, 125, 129–30, 132–3, 137–8,
142–5, 149, 153–8, 162, 174, 189,
230, 243, 271, 294, 298; regulation
of 41–4, 46–7, 50, 52–3; *see also*
whalers
self-employed workers: brickmakers
211; cabdrivers and carters 11,
160–2; organisational trajectory 295
shearers and sheep-washers 90, 97,
102, 117, 129, 132, 168, 184, 186–8
shepherds 19–20, 48, 56, 77, 79, 85,
144, 167, 181–5, 187–8, 278–9
shipwrights 77, 80, 86, 90, 102, 129,
132, 157, 218, 222–4, 229, 268
shop assistants and warehouse workers
66, 81, 85, 122, 135, 251, 257–8,
260–3, 294–5
Shorter, E. 5, 28, 122

slaters and shinglers 78, 206–7, 213
slaves and slavery 6–9, 12, 51, 95, 111, 179, 182
Smith, Babette 104
soldiers 3, 23, 235, 244–5, 294
Soly, Hugo 3, 27, 209–10
South Australia 12, 15, 17, 24, 26, 38–9, 40, 46, 53, 66, 76, 114, 147, 148, 153, 157, 187, 189, 193–5, 207, 214, 224, 225, 271, 275–84
South Australian Political Association 282–3
South Australian Working Men's Association 277–8, 282–3
The State 1–2, 5, 9–11; role in colonial economy 25–6, 35, 45, 87, 93, 95, 137, 144, 149, 155, 228, 235, 273, 286, 293–5; role in shaping work 11–22; *see also* government; regulation
stonemasons 206–10
strike fund 95, 122, 209–10, 224–5
strikes: building and building materials 201–3; compared to other collective action 5, 6, 93–5, 112–14; by issue 133–5; by location and whether formal or not 113–14; manufacturing 218–20; maritime 149–52; by occupation, industry and gender 125–32; outcomes 135–44; rural 168–70; size and duration 114–25
subcontracting and sweating 11, 227–8, 232
Sutherland, Benjamin 276, 282, 284
Sydney 12–14, 16, 23, 26, 39, 43, 46–59, 61–3, 66, 76, 84–6, 93, 96–7, 99–102, 105, 122, 130, 138, 140, 147–9, 153–5, 157–60, 162, 176–86, 201, 206–14, 217–18, 221–7, 229, 231–2, 239, 241, 243–6, 255–61, 263, 267–8, 272, 275–8, 281, 283, 285
Sydney Committee of Trades 267–8

tailors 2, 10, 44, 57, 77–81, 85, 93, 122, 140, 210, 222–9, 232, 269–71
task work and work methods 18–19; convicts 61–2
tattoos 8
teachers 247
Terry, Samuel 14, 105

Thompson, Edward 4, 27, 29, 42–4, 62, 67, 143, 285, 286
threats and threatening letters 4, 48, 57, 75, 93–5, 98, 139, 154, 161, 180, 182, 188, 194, 228, 240, 294
Tilly, Charles 5, 28, 122
tobacco twisters 221
Tolpuddle martyrs 100
transportation 7, 11–12, 16–17, 19–20, 26, 38–40, 83, 99–101; political/industrial dissidents 104, 135, 141–2, 168, 181, 211, 245, 268, 270–5, 278, 281–6, 296; *see also* convicts
Tyler, Peter 101, 108

Uber *see* gig economy
Unemployed relief workers 203, 246, 276–8
unemployment 2, 91, 222, 246, 258–9, 267–8, 270, 272, 275–8, 298
unfree labour 6–9, 14, 25, 45, 84, 195, 279, 296–7; *see also* convicts; indentured workers; slaves
unilateral regulation 2–3, 94–5, 98, 208, 210–11, 223–4
unions: building 206–10; building materials 213–14; commerce and retailing 258–63; compared to informal organisation 84–5; and court action 137; details of those formed 76–81; effect on strike and NSCA size and duration 121–2; government 246–7; hostility to European immigrants 211; and inequality at work 293–8; manufacturing 218–32; maritime and transport 157–61; methods 98–9; mining 194–5; peak bodies 267–8; and political mobilisation 275–85; rural 185; size and duration 85–7; *see also* craft unions; Medieval worker organisation
United Kingdom (Britain) 1–2, 7–8, 11–12, 15, 20–1, 26, 35, 40–1, 50, 99, 101, 104, 148, 168, 175, 180, 183, 210–11, 217, 227, 229, 232, 260, 269, 271, 277, 281, 282–3, 287, 295
United States of America (including references to North America) 1, 4–8, 11, 17, 26, 36, 51, 75–6, 111, 145, 147–8, 153, 160, 162, 167, 194, 293, 295–8

Van Diemen's Land (Tasmania) 12–14, 15–24, 26, 36–8, 40, 42–5, 47–8, 53, 57, 60–1, 63–4, 76, 84, 96, 100–1, 104, 112, 135, 138, 142, 147–9, 153, 158, 169, 174–5, 178, 183, 185–9, 192, 206, 209, 213–14, 217–18, 223, 226, 229, 231, 240–3, 245–7, 256, 258, 261, 268–75, 278, 282–3, 285, 296
Van Diemen's Land Co. 14, 175
Victoria (aka Port Phillip District) 15–16, 22, 23, 24, 26, 76, 101, 111, 114, 147, 148, 159, 184, 188, 213, 214, 245, 263, 285

wages and wage bargaining 3, 8, 11, 17, 19, 20, 36–41; regulation of 44, 46–52, 55, 62–3, 65–6, 91–3, 98, 102, 105–6, 122, 133–5, 138–40, 145, 149, 152–4, 156–7, 159–61, 168–9, 171–2, 176–7, 181–9, 191–2, 194–5, 204–7, 210–14, 218, 220–1, 225–9, 232, 235, 237–9, 243, 245–7, 253–4, 256–8, 269, 271–80, 294
wages unpaid/theft 8, 41, 44, 50–1, 98, 138–40, 149, 169, 184, 192, 218, 221, 235, 245, 258
watermen and boatmen 2, 42, 52, 79, 85, 101, 151, 158–60, 162, 295
Way, Peter 5, 28
weavers 11, 79, 100, 227
Webb, Sidney & Beatrice 1–3, 26–7
Wells, George 99, 101, 227, 277, 280, 282, 285
Wentworth, William Charles 56, 97, 181, 281, 283
Western Australia 12, 17, 22, 24, 26, 38–9, 40–1, 46, 55–6, 76, 85, 114, 148, 153, 183, 185, 187, 206, 275, 278, 296
whaling and whalers 5, 14–15, 38–9; regulation of 43, 87, 90, 102, 148–9, 154–8, 162
wharf labourers 90, 129–30, 132, 151, 158–60, 162
wheelwrights 77, 79–80, 85, 223–4, 285
Wilberforce, William 12
Williams, John 271, 274, 284, 285
women 4–5, 43; assaults on 91, 103, 111; before the courts 58–9; organisation amongst 181, 278, 285, 294; prosecution of convict women 53–5; see also domestics; female factories; laundresses
wool: importance of 15, 167–8; see also agricultural and rural workers
wool staplers 79, 85, 223, 226
worker involvement: by industry, occupation and gender 87–91; by location and whether convict or free 83; numbers by period 82; objectives and methods 91–1
working class: class formation 272–3, 275, 276, 279, 283–4, 285–7; songs, doggerel, satirical mimicry 4, 16, 24, 44, 101–4
working conditions 14, 44, 53, 91–3, 133–4, 149, 152–4, 160, 171–2, 174, 177, 182, 188–9, 191, 204–5, 218, 220, 237–8, 251, 253–4
work methods 61–2, 93, 133–4, 149, 152, 172, 191, 194, 204–5, 207–8, 211, 220, 237–8, 253; see also subcontracting; task work

Zolberg, A. 285

For Product Safety Concerns and Information please contact our EU
representative GPSR@taylorandfrancis.com
Taylor & Francis Verlag GmbH, Kaufingerstraße 24, 80331 München, Germany

www.ingramcontent.com/pod-product-compliance
Ingram Content Group UK Ltd.
Pitfield, Milton Keynes, MK11 3LW, UK
UKHW020937180425
457613UK00019B/439